American Politics and the African American Quest for Universal Freedom

HANES WALTON, JR.
UNIVERSITY OF MICHIGAN

ROBERT C. SMITH
SAN FRANCISCO STATE UNIVERSITY

LONGMAN

An Imprint of Addison Wesley Longman, Inc.

New York • Reading, Massachusetts • Menlo Park, California • Harlow, England
Don Mills, Ontario • Sydney • Mexico City • Madrid • Amsterdam

Photo Credits

Page 10: White House Historical Association; page 21; copyright © Elliott Erwitt/Magnum Photos, Inc.; page 33: AP/Wide World Photos; page 55: Corbis/Bettmann; page 58: White House; page 94(L): copyright © Hulton Getty/Liaison Agency; page 94(R): Douglass, Frederick, 1818-1895. Unidentified photographer, after © 1847. Daguerrotype, 8 X 6.9 cm. NPG.80.21. National Portrait Gallery, Smithsonian Institution; page 101: Schomburg Center for Research in Black Culture. Photo by John Lei/OPC. page 111: AP Photo/S. F. Examiner; page 121: AP Photo/Khue Bui; page 127: photograph © Eve Arnold/Magnum Photos, Inc.; page 130: Osvaldo Jimenez/Sipa Press; page 146: Crobis/Bettmann-UPI; page 149: Corbis/Bettmann-UPI; page 181: Corbis/Reuters; page 199: First Reading of the Emancipation Proclamation before the Cabinet (Lincoln and his Cabinet), steel engraving by Carpenter, F. B., ca. 1861. Missouri Historical Collection; page 206: Cecil Stoughton, LBJ Library Collection; page 215: Ackad, Collection of the Supreme Court of the United States; page 220: UPI/Corbis-Bettmann; page 245: © Hulton Getty/Liaison Agency; page 246: Yokchi R. Okamoto, LBJ Library Collection; page 247: The White House; page 268: © Stephen Ferry/The Gamma Liaison Network; page 281: The White House/Gamma Liaison; page 293: Corbis/Jacques M. Chenet.

Text Credits

Page 325: Reprinted by arrangement with The Heirs to the Estate of Martin Luther King, Jr., c/o Writer's House, Inc. as agent for the proprietor. Copyright © 1963 by Martin Luther King, Jr. Copyright renewed 1991 by Coretta Scott King.

Editor in Chief: Priscilla McGeehon
Acquisitions Editor: Eric Stano
Marketing Manager: Megan Galvin
Supplements Editor: Mark Towes
Project Manager: Ellen MacElree
Design Manager: John Callahan
Cover Designer: Kay Petronio
Art Studio: ElectraGraphics, Inc.
Technical Desktop Manager: Heather A. Peres
Electronic Page Makeup: Sarah Johnson
Printer and Binder: Von Hoffman Graphics
Cover Printer:Von Hoffmann Graphics

Please visit our website at http://www.awlonline.com

ISBN 0-321-07038-0

12345678910—VHG-0302010099

To our great grandparents (whose names we do not know)
and their struggles in the African American quest for freedom

The Negro people have fought like tigers for freedom, and in doing so have enhanced the freedom struggles of all other people.

CONTENTS

PART V Public Policy   261

CHAPTER 15 Domestic Policy and the African American Quest for Social and Economic Justice   263

CHAPTER 16 The African American Quest for Universal Freedom and U.S. Foreign Policy   279

Appendix   303

TABLES

FIGURES

BOXES

PREFACE

This book examines the institutions and processes of American government and politics from the perspective of the African American presence and influence. We want to show how the presence of Africans in the United States affected the founding of the Republic and its political institutions and processes from the colonial era to the present. Blacks, for example, took no part in the drafting of the Declaration of Independence or the design of the Constitution; however, their presence exerted a profound influence on the shaping of both these seminal documents. And so it has been throughout American history.

The book in structure follows that of standard works in political science on American government and politics. It is unique, however, in three respects.

First, it is organized around two interrelated themes: the idea of universal freedom and the concept of minority-majority coalitions. In their quest for their own freedom in the United States, blacks have sought to universalize the idea of freedom. In their attack on slavery and racial subordination, black Americans and their leaders have embraced doctrines of universal freedom and equality. In doing so they have had an important influence on the shaping of democratic, constitutional government and on expanding or universalizing the idea of freedom not only for themselves but for all Americans.

But blacks have not acted alone. Indeed, given their status as a subordinate racial minority they could not act alone. Rather, in their quest for freedom blacks have sought to forge coalitions with whites—minority-inspired majority coalitions. Historically, however, because of the nation's ambivalence about race, these coalitions tend to be unstable and temporary, requiring that they be constantly rebuilt in what is an ongoing quest. These two themes, the quest for universal freedom and minority-majority coalitions, are pursued throughout much of the book.

The second distinctive aspect of this study is that it is historically informed. In each chapter we trace developments historically. Relevant historical background is critical to understanding the evolution of race and the American democracy. Such material also brings contemporary events into a sharper focus.

Third, in the political behavior chapters (3–6, 9–10), we try to provide students not only with the most current knowledge on the topics but also with information on how the discipline of political science has approached the study of the topics in general and with respect to blacks specifically. In several of these chapters we focus on Gunnar Myrdal and the powerful influence his *American Dilemma* has had on the study of black political behavior.

We first talked about writing this book nearly a decade ago. Our principal rationale for writing it is that we saw a void in the available literature. We believe that race is the most important cleavage in American life, with enormous impact on the nation's society, culture, and politics. Indeed, as we show throughout this book, race has always been the enduring fault line in American society and politics—thus, the need for a volume that treats this important topic with the seriousness it deserves. This is what we seek to accomplish in a study that has historical sweep and depth and is comprehensive in its coverage of the subject. Although this book is written so as to be readable and interesting to undergraduate students, we have sought to maintain the highest intellectual standards. We believe the study of the rich, varied, and critical presence of African Americans in *all* areas of the political system demands nothing less.

Before closing, we would like to say a word about the intellectual tradition on which this book is based. The scholars who are the founders and innovators in the study of African American politics literally created this scholarly subfield out of nothing. Working in small African American colleges, without major financial support or grants and with large numbers of classes and students, these scholars launched in small steps and limited ways a new area of academic study. They published in obscure and poorly diffused journals and little known presses, which resulted, in many instances, in their work being overlooked and undervalued. Racism's manifestations in the academy allowed much valuable work to remain unseen. Not only was the result of their research made invisible, but these scholars themselves became invisible in their profession. Of this unseen tradition it has been written:

> The second research tradition in America's life is the unheralded, the unsung, unrecorded but not unnoticed one. Scholars belonging to this tradition literally make something out of nothing and typically produce scholarship at the less recognized institutions of higher learning. These are the places, to use Professor Aaron Wildavsky's apt phrase, where the schools "habitually run out of stamps" and where other sources of support are nonexistent. . . . [Yet] here . . . scholars . . . nevertheless scaled the heights, and produced stellar scholarship.[1]

They persisted and persevered. And while their work is scattered and sometimes difficult to locate, it formed the basis for a new vision and perspective in political science. Beginning in 1885, the discipline of political science emerged during an era of concern about race relations and developed its study of race politics from this perspective. In essence, this race relations perspective on the study of African American politics focused on the concern of whites about stability and social peace rather than the concerns of blacks about freedom and social justice.[2]

This perspective by the 1960s had become the major consensus in the discipline on the study of race. It offered a different perspective on political reality from that of blacks who during this period were trying to empower themselves in American politics. Thus African American political scientists offered a different perspective, a challenge to the consensus. Instead of focusing on how the African American quest for freedom might distress whites and disrupt stability and social peace, this new perspective focused on how an oppressed group might achieve power so as to provide solutions to long-standing social and economic problems. This perspective deals with freedom and power rather than stability and social peace.

Our book is a part of this intellectual tradition. The purveyors of this tradition include Professors Robert Brisbane and Tobe Johnson of Morehouse College, the ever-erudite Samuel DuBois Cook at Atlanta University and Professors Emmett Dorsey, Bernard Fall, Harold Gosnell, Robert Martin, Vincent Browne, Nathaniel Tillman, Brian Wienstein, Morris Levitt, and Charles Harris at Howard University. Their insightful ideas, cogent theories, and brilliant teaching made this book possible. When we sat down at the Holiday Inn in Jackson, Mississippi, in March 1991 (at the annual meeting of the National Conference of Black Political Scientists), to develop the theme for this book and lay out its goals and structure, we were standing on the shoulders of these pioneering political scientists. They built the intellectual foundation. We hope this work makes them proud. We hope it will do the same for our children.

Finally, a note on style. We use the terms _black_ and _African American_ interchangeably, having no preference for either and viewing each as a legitimate and accurate name for persons of African descent in the United States.[3]

ACKNOWLEDGMENTS

In addition to our colleagues selected by Addison Wesley Longman to read and comment on the manuscript, we are also grateful to Mack Jones of Clark-Atlanta University's political science department, Wilbur Rich of Wellesley's political science department, and Charles Henry of the African American Studies Department at the University of California, Berkeley, for their reading of the manuscript and their suggestions that led to its improvement. We are especially grateful to Professor Jones for his detailed chapter-by-chapter critique. Sekou Franklin provided research assistance for Professor Smith.

Margaret Mitchell Ilugbo typed several of the draft chapters for Walton and Greta Blake designed the tables and figures for the book. We appreciate their fine work. Finally we are grateful to our families—Alice, Brandon and Brent and Scottie, Blanch, Jessica and Scottus-Charles—for their endurance and support during our nine years of work on this project.

Scottie Smith's help was indispensable in the preparation of the manuscript. Her discerning and untiring work is deeply appreciated.

HANES WALTON, JR.
ROBERT C. SMITH

NOTES

1. Hanes Walton, Jr., "The Preeminent African American Legal Scholar: J. Clay Smith," _National Political Science Review_ 6 (1997): 289.
2. Hanes Walton, Jr., Cheryl Miller, and Joseph P. McCormick, "Race and Political Science: The Dual Traditions of Race Relations Politics and African American Politics," in John Dryzek et al., eds, _Political Science and Its History: Research Programs and Political Traditions_ (New York: Cambridge University Press, 1994): 145–74; Hanes Walton, Jr., and Joseph P. McCormick, "The Study of African American Politics as Social Danger: Clues from the Disciplinary Journals," _National Political Science Review_ 6 (1997): 229–44.
3. For discussion of the various controversies about names in African American history—that is, what should persons of African origins in the United States call themselves—see W. E. B. Du Bois "The Name Negro," _The Crisis_ 35 (March, 1928): 96–101; Lerone Bennett, "What's in a Name?" _Ebony,_ November, 1967; Ben L. Martin, "From Negro to Black to African-American: The Power of Names and Naming," _Political Science Quarterly_ 106 (1991): 83–107; Robert C. Smith, "Remaining Old Realities," _San Francisco Review of Books_ 25 (Summer 1990): 16–19; Ruth Grant and Marion Orr, "Language, Race and Politics: From 'Black' to 'African American,'" _Politics & Society_ 24 (1996): 137–52; and Sterling Stuckey, _Slave Culture: Foundations of Nationalist Theory_ (New York: Oxford University Press, 1987): chap. 4, "Identity and Ideology: The Names Controversy."

ABOUT THE AUTHORS

Hanes Walton, Jr., professor of political science at the University of Michigan, is a graduate of Morehouse College. He holds a master's degree in political science from Atlanta University and a Ph.D. from Howard. He is the author of twelve books (all except one dealing with African American politics) and more than sixty articles, essays, and reviews. His most recent book is *African American Power and Politics: The Political Context Variable*. He is a member of the editorial boards of numerous academic journals and has served as a consultant to the National Academy of Sciences, the Educational Testing Service, and the National Endowment for the Humanities. He has been a Ford, Rockefeller, and Guggenheim Fellow and holds membership in several honor societies, including Pi Sigma Alpha, Alpha Kappa Mu, and Phi Beta Kappa. For two years, he worked on Capitol Hill in the office of African American congressman Mervyn Dymally of California. Professor Walton has taught African American politics and American government at the graduate and undergraduate levels for more than twenty-five years. In 1993 he was the recipient of Howard University's Distinguished Ph.D. Alumni Award.

Robert C. Smith is professor of political science at San Francisco State University. An honors graduate of the University of California, Berkeley, he holds a master's degree from UCLA and the Ph.D. from Howard. He is author or co-author of more than forty articles and essays and nine books including *Race, Class and Culture: A Study in Afro-American Mass Opinion; Racism in the Post–Civil Rights Era: Now You See It, Now You Don't; We Have No Leaders: African Americans in the Post–Civil Rights Era; African American Leadership;* and the forthcoming *Gaps, Gulfs and Chasms across the Color Line: Controversies in American Culture*. He is associate editor of the *National Political Science Review* and general editor of the State University of New York Press African American Studies series. He has taught African American politics and American government for more than twenty years. In 1998 he was recipient of Howard University's Distinguished Ph.D. Alumni Award.

PART I

Foundations

1

Universal Freedom Declared, Universal Freedom Denied: Racism, Slavery, and the Ideology of White Supremacy in the Founding of the Republic

So, what is this thing called freedom? In 1865 General Oliver O. Howard, commissioner of the Freedmen's Bureau, asked an audience of newly freed slaves, "But what did freedom mean? It is necessary to define it for it is apt to be misunderstood."[1] William Riker writes, "The word 'freedom' must be defined. And volumes have been written on this subject without conspicuous success in reaching agreement."[2] Orlando Patterson begins his book *Freedom in the Making of Western Culture* with the observation that "freedom, like love and beauty, is one of those values better experienced than defined."[3] Finally, John Hope Franklin, in *From Slavery to Freedom: A History of Negro Americans* writes,

> It must never be overlooked that the concept of freedom that emerged in the modern world bordered on licentiousness and created a situation that approached anarchy. As W. E. B. Du Bois has pointed out, it was the freedom to destroy freedom, the freedom of some to exploit the rights of others. It was, indeed, a concept of freedom with little or no social responsibility. If, then, a man was determined to be free, who was there to tell him that he was not entitled to enslave others.[4]

The idea of freedom is therefore a contested idea, with many often conflicting and contradictory meanings. Since the idea of freedom—universal freedom—is central to this book, in this first chapter we must attempt to define it because, as General Howard said, it is apt to be misunderstood.

In the last two decades an important body of scholarship has emerged on how the idea and practice of freedom began in Europe and the United States. These historical and philosophical studies suggest that the idea of freedom—paradoxically—is inextricably linked to the idea and institution of slavery.[5] With respect to Europe, "it now can be said with some confidence," according to Patterson, "that the idea and value of freedom was the direct product of the institution of slavery. Where there has been no slavery there has never been any trace of freedom even as a minor value."[6] And in the United States, "without the institution of slavery America in all likelihood would have had no democratic tradition and would not have come to enshrine freedom at the very top of the pantheon of values."[7] In other words, the very idea of freedom in the Western world has its origins in the struggles of the slave to become free.[8]

FREEDOM: A TYPOLOGICAL ANALYSIS

The word *freedom* is difficult to define. Indeed, a number of writers on the subject have concluded that the effort to construct an objective or universal definition may be futile. Increasingly, therefore, students of the subject have sought not to define the term in one all-encompassing definition but rather, given the rich, varied, and conflicting meanings of the word, have sought instead to develop typologies of freedom that are broad and varied enough to cover the diverse shades of meaning held by scholars as well as ordinary women and men.

In Table 1.1, three typologies of freedom are displayed. These typologies are drawn from the most recent scholarship on the subject. Again, these writers do not attempt to develop one universal definition of the term but see freedom as having multiple shades of meaning. Patterson identifies three types of freedom. *Personal freedom* is defined as giving a person the sense that, on the one hand, he or she is not coerced or restrained by another person in doing something desired, and on the other hand, that one can do as one pleases within the limits of that other person's desire to do the same. *Sovereignal* or *organic* freedom is simply the power to act as one pleases, without regard for others, or

TABLE I.I
Typologies of Freedom

Patterson	Foner	King
Personal	Natural[b]	Liberal
Sovereignal[a]	Civil	Autonomy
Civic	Political	Participatory
	Social	Collective Deliverance

[a]In his article Patterson uses the term *organic* instead of sovereignal to refer to this type of freedom.
[b]Foner uses the term *rights* rather than freedoms.

Sources: Orlando Patterson, *Freedom in the Making of Western Culture* (New York: Basic Books, 1991): 3–5, and Patterson, "The Unholy Trinity: Freedom, Slavery and the American Constitution," *Social Research* 54 (Autumn 1987): 556–59; Eric Foner, *Reconstruction: America's Unfinished Revolution, 1863–1877* (New York: Harper & Row, 1988): 231; Richard King, *Civil Rights and the Idea of Freedom* (New York: Oxford University Press, 1992): 26–28.

simply the ability to impose one's will on another. *Civic freedom* is defined as the capacity of adult members of a community to participate in its life and governance.[9]

Eric Foner discusses four notions of freedom—he prefers the term *rights*—that were part of the political vocabulary of the nation's leaders on the eve of the civil war. *Natural rights,* those rights or freedoms inherent in one's humanity, are what Jefferson in the Declaration referred to as life, liberty, and the pursuit of happiness. *Civil rights* can be defined as equality of treatment under law, which is seen as essential to the protection of natural rights. *Political rights* involve the right to vote and participate fully in governing the community. *Social rights* involve the right to freely choose personal and business associates.[10]

King identifies "four [principal] meanings of freedom within American/western thought that link up with the language of freedom and the goals of the civil rights movement."[11] *Liberal freedom* is the absence of arbitrary legal or institutional restrictions on the individual, including the idea that all citizens are to be treated equally. *Freedom as autonomy* involves an internalized individual state of autonomy, self-determination, pride, and self-respect. *Participatory freedom* involves the right of the individual to participate fully in the political process. *Collective deliverance* is understood as the liberation of a group from external control—from captivity, slavery, or oppression.[12]

Clearly, there is considerable overlap among the types of freedom addressed by Patterson, Foner, and King, especially in the realm of politics or the right of citizens to equal treatment under law and the right to vote and participate in the governance of the community. However, two of the types identified have special relevance to the African American experience and to this book's theme of universal freedom. First, throughout their history in the United States African Americans have consistently rejected the idea of organic or sovereignal freedom, the notion that one person or group should have the freedom to impose their will on another without regard to the rights of others. This is the freedom of might makes right, of the strong to oppress the weak, of the powerful to dominate the powerless, the freedom of the slavemaster to enslave. From its beginning, African American political thought and behavior has been centrally concerned with the abolition of this type of freedom and in doing so African Americans developed the idea of universal freedom, a freedom that encompasses natural rights, civil rights, and social rights. In rejecting the Patterson notion of sovereignal freedom, blacks in the United States fully embraced King's idea of freedom as collective deliverance. As part of a captive, oppressed, enslaved people, one could expect nothing less. However, in fighting for their own liberation, for their freedom, blacks have had to fight for universal freedom, for the freedom of all people. As Aptheker puts it, "The Negro people have fought like tigers for their freedom, and in doing so have enhanced the freedom struggles of all people."[13]

FREEDOM, POWER, AND POLITICS

All the typologies of freedom listed in Table 1.1 are related in one way or another to power or the lack of power, and power is central to politics and political science. As Lasswell and Kaplan write in their classic study *Power and Society*, "The concept of power is perhaps the most fundamental in the whole of political science: The political process is the shaping, distribution and exercise of power."[14] The definition of power,

Minimalist
Definition

like freedom, however, also has an ambiguous, elusive quality.[15] At a minimum, scholars agree that A has power over B to the extent that A can affect B's behavior or get B to do something B otherwise would not do. Max Weber, one of the founders of modern sociology and political science, writes, "In general, we understand by 'power' the chance of a man or a number of men to realize their own will in a communal action against the resistance of others who are participating in the action."[16] Political scientists generally analyze power in terms of (1) its bases, (2) its exercise, and (3) the skill of its exercise in particular circumstances, situations, or contexts. With respect to African American politics Jones writes that it is "essentially a power struggle between blacks and whites, with the latter trying to maintain their superordinate position vis a vis the former."[17] In analyzing African American politics as a quest for universal freedom we need to think in terms of blacks seeking to alter their subordinate status vis-à-vis whites in American society, and the bases of power they have and may choose to use, skillfully or not, in the power struggle, during any given time, place, and context.

Thomas Jefferson and the Writing of the Declaration

After voting to declare independence, the Continental Congress appointed a committee to draft a document setting forth the reasons for the revolution. The committee was composed of Robert Livingston, Roger Sherman, Benjamin Franklin, John Adams, and Thomas Jefferson. The other members turned the task of drafting to Adams and Jefferson, and according to Adams, Jefferson was asked to actually write the document because his writings were characterized by a "peculiar felicitousness of expression."[18] The Declaration, however, is not the creation of one man. Rather "eighty-six substantive revisions were made in Jefferson's draft, most of them by members of the Continental Congress who also excised about one fourth of the original text."[19] Jefferson was said to be extremely displeased by the changes in his draft and for the remaining fifty years of his life was angry, arguing that the Congress had "mangled" his manuscript.[20]

The majority of the substantive changes or deletions in Jefferson's draft—including the most famous—focused on the long list of charges against King George III. Most historians think that the charges against the King in the Declaration as finally approved are exaggerated, and in any event they are misplaced since many of the actions complained of were decisions of the Parliament rather than the King. The King, however, made a more convenient target than the anonymous, amorphous Parliament.

The most famous of the changes deleted from Jefferson's draft was the condemnation of the King for engaging in the African slave trade. Jefferson had written:

> He has waged cruel war against human nature itself, violating the most sacred rights of life and liberty in the persons of a distant people who never offended him, captivating and carrying them into slavery in another hemisphere, or to incur miserable death in their transportation thither. This piratical warfare, the opprobrium of infidel powers, is the warfare of the Christian King of Great Britain. Determined to keep open a market when MEN should be bought and sold, he has prostituted his negative for suppressing every legislative attempt to prohibit or restrain this execrable commerce; and this assemblage of horrors might want no fact of distinguished die, he is now exciting these very people to rise among us, and to purchase that liberty of which he deprived them, by murdering the people upon whom he also obtruded them, thus paying off former

crimes committed against the liberties of one people, with crimes which he urges them to commit against the lives of others.[21]

This passage, which was to be the climax of the charges against the King, was obviously an exaggeration and an especially disingenuous one; the colonists themselves (including Jefferson) had enthusiastically engaged in slave trading and, as was made clear to Jefferson, had no intention of abandoning it after independence. Jefferson recalls that "the clause too, reprobating the enslaving of the inhabitants of Africa, was struck out in compliance to South Carolina and Georgia, who had never attempted to restrain the importation of slaves and who still wished to continue it."[22] Not only was there opposition to the passage from the southern slave owners but more tellingly, as Jefferson went on to say, "our northern brethren also I believe felt a little tender under these cencures; for tho' their people have few slaves themselves yet they have been pretty considerable carriers of them."[23] In other words, virtually all the leading white men in America, Northerner and Southerner, slave owner and non–slave owner, had economic interests in the perpetuation of slavery. Indeed a good part of the new nation's wealth and prosperity was based on the plantation economy. To be consistent, one might have thought that the Continental Congress would also have deleted the phrase on the equality of men and their inherent right to liberty. They did not, apparently seeing no inconsistency since the words did not mean what they said (see Box 1.1).

The magnificent words of the Declaration of Independence declaring freedom and equality as universal rights of all "men" was, however, fatally flawed, compromised in that the men who wrote them denied freedom to almost one-fourth of the men of America. To understand how the idea of universal freedom was fatally compromised in America, one needs to see Thomas Jefferson as the paradigmatic figure: author of the Declaration, preeminent intellectual, acquaintance through correspondence of eminent African American intellectual Benjamin Banneker, and a man with perhaps a genuine love relationship with a black woman—and also a racist, a white supremacist, and a slave owner.[24]

BOX 1.1

Like Humpty Dumpty Told Alice,
"When I Use a Word It Means What I Say It Means"

Before the ink was dry on Jefferson's Declaration there was controversy about what was meant by the words "all men are created equal." Rufus Choate, speaking in 1776 for Southerners embarrassed by Jefferson's words, said Jefferson did not mean what he said. Rather, the word *men* referred only to nobles and Englishmen who were no better than ordinary American freemen. "If he meant more," Choate said, it was because Jefferson was "unduly influenced by the French school of thought."[a] (Jefferson was frequently accused of being influenced by Jean Jacques Rousseau's writings, a charge that he denied.) On the eve of the civil war, Chief Justice Roger B. Taney, in his opinion in the *Dred Scott* (1857) case, said that on the surface the words "all men are created equal" applied to blacks. Yet he concluded, "It is too clear for dispute that

(Continued)

BOX 1.1 Continued

the enslaved African race were <u>not</u> intended to be included, and formed no part of the people who framed and adopted the Declaration." Similarly, during his famous debates with Abraham Lincoln, Stephen Douglas argued that the phrase simply meant that Americans were not inferior to Englishmen as citizens. It was Lincoln's genius at Gettysburg in his famous address to fundamentally repudiate Choate, Taney, and Douglas in what Garry Wills calls an "audacious" and "clever assault." Lincoln accomplished this by claiming that the Civil War had given rise to a "new birth of freedom" that had been conceived by Jefferson "four score and seven years ago" when he wrote the Declaration.[b] Conservative scholars have long attacked Lincoln's "radical" redefinition of the meaning of the Declaration. Wilmore Kendal, writing a century after Gettysburg, argued that the word *men* in the Declaration referred to property holders or to the nations of the world but not men as such, writing blatantly that "the Declaration of Independence does not commit us to equality as a national goal."[c] And as Daniel Boorstin, the former Librarian of Congress and author of the celebrated *The Americans: The Democratic Experience* (New York: Vintage Books, 1974), writes, "We have repeated that 'all men are created equal' without daring to discover what it meant and without realizing that probably to none of the men who spoke it did it mean what we would like it to mean."[d]

[a]Quoted in Carl Becker, *The Declaration of Independence: A Study in the History of an Idea* (New York: Vintage Books, 1922, 1970), 27.

[b]Garry Wills, *Lincoln at Gettysburg: The Words That Remade America* (New York: Touchstone, 1992).

[c]Wilmore Kendal, *Basic Symbols of the American Political Tradition* (Baton Rouge: Louisiana State University Press, 1970), as cited in M. E. Bradford, "How to Read the Declaration of Independence: Reconsidering the Kendal Thesis," *The Intercollegiate Review* Fall 1992: 47.

[d]Ibid., p. 46.

Racism and White Supremacy Defined

We have described Jefferson—one of the great men of American history and one of the most enlightened men of his day—as a racist and white supremacist; therefore, we should define these terms since they are key distinguishing features of the African American experience in the United States.[25] They are also central to the analysis presented throughout this book. Racism and the ideology of white supremacy are fundamental to an understanding of certain crucial features in the development of the American democracy as well as the different treatment of black and white Americans.

Racism as a scientific concept is not an easy one for the social scientist. It is difficult to define with precision and objectivity; also, the word is often used indiscriminantly and in an inflammatory way. We start by distinguishing between racism and the set of ideas used in the United States to justify it. The latter we refer to as the ideology of white supremacy or black inferiority. In the United States, racism was and to some extent still is justified on the basis of the institutionalized belief that Africans are inherently inferior people. We refer to an individual who holds such beliefs as a *white supremacist*.

By racism we mean, following the definition of Carmichael and Hamilton in *Black Power,* "the predication of decisions and policies on considerations of race for the purpose of subordinating a racial group and maintaining control over it.)[26] The definition says nothing about why this is done, about racism's purposes or rationales; thus it does not imply anything about superiority or inferiority of the groups involved. It does not say, as many definitions and concepts of racism do, that racism involves the belief in the superiority, inherent or otherwise, of a particular group and that on this basis policies are implemented to subordinate and control it. Rather, the definition simply indicates that whenever one observes policies that have the intent or effect of subordinating a racial group, the phenomenon is properly identified as *racism,* whatever, if any, the justificatory ideology may be.

Carmichael and Hamilton's definition is particularly useful to political scientists because it focuses on power as an integral aspect of the phenomenon. For racism to exist, one racial group (or individual) must have the relative power—the capacity to impose its will in terms of policies—on another relatively less powerful group or individual. Without this relative power relationship, racism is a mere sentiment: Although group A may wish to subordinate group B, if it lacks the effective power to do so, then the desire remains simply a wish.

Carmichael and Hamilton also write that racism may take two forms: individual and institutional.[27] Individual racism occurs when one person takes into consideration the race of another to subordinate, control, or otherwise discriminate against an individual; institutional racism exists when the normal and accepted patterns and practices of a society's institutions have the *effect* or *consequence* of subordinating or discriminating against an individual or group on the basis of race.[28]

It is in this sense that we refer to Thomas Jefferson as a white supremacist and a racist. He believed that blacks were inherently inferior to whites, stating in his *Notes on Virginia* that they were "inferior by nature, not condition" (see Box 1.2). He also was a racist, individually and institutionally, in that he took the race of individual blacks into consideration so as to discriminate against them, and he supported, although ambivalently, the institution of slavery that subordinated blacks as a group.

━━━ BOX 1.2 ━━━

Thomas Jefferson's *Notes on Virginia* and the Idea of the Inferiority of the African People

In the Declaration of Independence, Jefferson engaged in a kind of moral reasoning to reach his conclusions as to the self-evident equality of men. In his *Notes on Virginia* written several years later, he engaged in a more scientific approach to the analysis of the problem of racial inequality.[a] In doing so, Jefferson the slaveholder made an eloquent condemnation of slavery, proposing his view of a just and equitable way to end slavery in the United States while simultaneously offering what he took to be scientific proof of the inferiority of the African people. Understanding Jefferson's views on race is therefore critical to an appreciation of how racism fundamentally compromised the idea of universal freedom at the very creation of the American Republic.[b]

(Continued)

BOX 1.2 Continued

Thomas Jefferson is the embodiment of the contradiction in the American democracy between its declaration of universal freedom and equality and its practice of slavery.

In 1780 Francois Barbe-Marbois, the secretary of the French legation in Philadelphia, sent a letter to each of the state governors requesting that they answer questions on the particular customs and conditions in their states. Jefferson delayed his response until after he left the governor's office. Although Jefferson offered a general assessment of conditions in the state, his *Notes* are best known for what he said about slavery, the African people, and Virginia society.

While defending the institution of slavery Jefferson nevertheless saw it as evil and unjust, writing, "There must doubtless be an unhappy influence on the manners of our people produced by the existence of slavery among us. The whole commerce between master and slave is perpetual exercise of the most boisterous passions, the most unremitting despotism on the one part, and degrading submission on the other."[c] And in a famous passage that would be echoed by Abraham Lincoln during the civil war, Jefferson suggested that God would surely punish America: "Indeed, I tremble for my country when I reflect that God is just; that his justice cannot sleep forever. . . . The almighty has no attribute which can take side with us in such a contest."[d]

Since slavery was an evil, but a necessary one given the need for labor in the plantation economy, Jefferson proposed a revision in Virginia law that would gradually free the slaves; train them; provide tools, seeds, and animals; and then transport them to a new land as a "free and independent people" while simultaneously sending ships "to other parts of the world for an equal number of white inhabitants" to replace them.[e]

Jefferson anticipated that the inevitable question would be why not simply free the slaves and integrate them into Virginia society, thereby saving the money involved in colonialization of the slaves and the transportation of the whites. His response was first that "deep rooted prejudices entertained by whites, ten thousand recollections by the blacks of injuries they have sustained, the real distinctions which nature has made and many other circumstances" made impossible the integration of the black and white populations on the basis of freedom and equality.[f] Indeed, Jefferson believed that if the races were not separated, "convulsions" would occur, probably ending in the "extermination of one or the other race."[g]

Jefferson was not satisfied to base his argument for racial separation on these essentially practical arguments. Rather, he wanted to be "scientific," to base his conclusions on the "facts," on his "empirical observations." Thus, in the *Notes* he advocated what was one of the first of many "scientific proofs" of black inferiority as justification for black subordination. First, he argued that blacks compared to whites were less beautiful, had a "strong and disagreeable odor," and were more "ardent after their female." Ultimately, however, for Jefferson the basis of black inferiority was his "suspicion" that blacks were "inferior in faculties of reason and imagination."[h] Noting that the differences he observed between blacks and whites might be explained by the different conditions under which they lived, Jefferson rejected this explanation, concluding it was not their "condition" but their "nature" that produced the difference.[i]

---

[a]This distinction between Jefferson's moral reasoning in the Declaration and his scientific approach in the *Notes* is the central theme of Jean Yarbrough, "Race and the Moral Foundation of the American Republic: Another Look at the Declaration and the Notes on Virginia," *Journal of Politics* 53(February 1991): 90–105. Yarbrough argues that "the self-evident truths of the Declaration rest on a kind of moral reasoning which is morally superior to and incompatible with the so called scientific approach Jefferson adopts in the *Notes*" (p. 90).

[b]A comprehensive treatment of Jefferson's views on race is in Winthrop Jordan, *White over Black: American Attitudes toward the Negro, 1550–1812* (Baltimore, MD: Penguin Books, 1969): chap. 12, "Thomas Jefferson: Self and Society."

[c]Thomas Jefferson, *Notes on the State of Virginia*, edited by William Peden (Chapel Hill: University of North Carolina Press, 1954): 162–63.

[d]Ibid.

[e]Ibid., pp. 138–39.

[f]Ibid., p. 138. This was also the view of Abraham Lincoln (see chapter 14). In *Democracy in America* (New York: Knopf, 1945)—probably the single most important and influential book ever written on the subject—Alexis de Tocqueville also reached the same pessimistic conclusion that blacks and whites could not live together on the basis of freedom and equality. Tocqueville thought that whites would either subjugate the blacks or exterminate them. See *Democracy in America*, vol. 1, edited by Phillips Bradley (New York: Vintage Books, 1945), chap. 18.

[g]*Notes on the State of Virginia*, pp. 138–39.

[h]Ibid.

[i]Ibid.

PHILOSOPHY, POLITICS, AND INTEREST IN CONSTITUTION FORMATION

The framers of the Constitution were influenced in their work by their readings in philosophy and history. But the framers were also practical politicians and men of affairs, and as in all politics, they were men with distinct interests. In what is generally a sympathetic portrayal of the framers, the historian William Freehling writes, "If the Founding Fathers unquestionably dreamed of universal freedom, their ideological posture was weighed down equally with conceptions of priorities, profits, and prejudices that would long make the dream utopian."[29] The first or principal priority of the framers was the formation and preservation of the union of the United States. This priority was thought indispensable to the priority of profit—that is, to the economic and commercial success of the nation. And as Freehling notes, their concern with profits grew out of their preoccupation with property, and slaves as property were crucial; thus, "it made the slaves' right to freedom no more 'natural' than the master's right to property."[30] It was this crucial nexus between profits, property, and slavery that led the men at Philadelphia to turn the idea of universal freedom into a utopian dream.

African Americans in the Constitution

As far as we can tell from the records of the federal convention, slavery was not the subject of much debate at that gathering. Certainly its morality was never at issue, although there were several passionate opponents of slavery present including the venerable Benjamin Franklin, president of the Pennsylvania Society for Promoting the Abolition of Slavery. But neither Franklin nor any other delegate proposed abolition at Philadelphia, knowing that to do so would destroy any possibility of union. Hence, slavery was simply just another of the issues (such as how the small and large states were to be represented in the Congress) that had to be compromised to accomplish the objective of forming the union.

Slavery is dealt with explicitly in four places in the Constitution, although the words *slave* and *slavery* are never used. It was James Madison, generally considered the "Father of the Constitution," who insisted that all explicit references to slavery be excluded.[31] Madison is also the author of the most important and infamous of the clauses dealing with slavery—the so-called three-fifths compromise.

Before the Sixteenth Amendment was adopted (permitting Congress to tax income directly), Congress could impose and collect taxes only on the basis of a state's population. The larger a state's population, the greater was its tax burden. For this reason the southern states insisted that the slaves not be counted, as, like horses and cows, they were property. However, for purposes of representation in the House (where each state is allocated seats on the basis of the size of its population), the South wished to count the slaves as persons, although they of course could not vote. This would enhance the power of the South not only in the House but also in choosing the president, since the number of votes a state may cast for president in the electoral college is equal to the total of its representation in the House and Senate. The northern states, on the other hand, wished to count the slaves for purposes of taxation but not representation. Hence, the great compromise. In Article I, Section 2, paragraph 3:

> Representatives and direct taxes shall be apportioned among the several states that may be included within this union, according to their respective numbers which shall be determined by adding to the whole number of free persons, including those bound to service for a Term of years and excluding Indians not taxed, three fifths of all other persons.

The effect of this decision was to increase the South's share of House seats from 41 percent to 46 percent. In attempting to justify or explain this compromise, Madison (in *The Federalist Papers* #54) disingenuously puts his words in the mouth of a fictional Southerner:

The Federal Constitution, therefore, decides with great propriety on the case of our slaves, when it views them in the mixed character of persons and property. . . . Let the slaves be considered, as it is in truth a peculiar one. Let the compromising expedient of the Constitution be mutually adopted which regards them as inhabitants, but as debased by servitude below the equal level of free inhabitants; which regards the slave as divested as of two fifths of the man.[32]

But as Professor Donald Robinson so astutely observes,

It bears repeating . . . that Madison's formula did not make blacks three-fifths of a human being. It was much worse than that. It gave slave owners a bonus in representation for their human property, while doing nothing for the status of blacks as nonpersons under the law.[33]

Robinson also notes that Madison, among others, favored the direct election of the president by the people but rejected the idea because he said it "would gravely disadvantage the south since slaves of course could not vote."[34] Thus, slavery is in part responsible for the existence of the undemocratic electoral college in which, as has happened twice before in 1876 and 1888, a person can lose the presidency while winning a majority of the votes of the people.

The other clauses dealing explicitly with slavery include Article I, Section 9, paragraph 1, prohibiting the Congress from stopping the slave trade before 1808 and limiting any tax on imported slaves to ten dollars; Article V prohibiting any amendment to the Constitution that would alter the 1808 date or rate of taxation on imported slaves; and Article IV, Section 2, paragraph 2, requiring the northern states to return slaves who escaped to freedom back to their bondage in the South. As far as we know, none of these provisions caused much controversy at the convention, although the fugitive slave clause in Article IV initially would have required that escaped slaves be "delivered up as criminals"; this, however, was modified to relieve the states of the obligation.[35]

The framers, while committed to freedom, had a limited, nonuniversal vision of it. Freedom was for some—the some who were white men with property, including property in other men, women, and children. Professor Robinson cautions us, "One wants to be fair to the framers, and above all to avoid blaming them as individuals for the sins of the culture, in which we all share. We must be careful not to imply that they should have done better unless we are prepared to show how better provisions might have been achieved politically." Fair enough. But Robinson continues, "At the same time, we must be lucid in recognizing the terrible mistakes made at the founding. In the end the framers failed on their own terms."[36] This too is fair enough.

Constitutional Principles and Design

In designing the Constitution the framers were guided by two overarching and interrelated principles. First, the primary object of government was the protection of private property, and second, the power of government had to be limited to avoid tyranny. These two principles are interrelated because a government of unlimited powers could itself become a threat to private property, thereby undermining one of its core purposes. These two principles gave rise to what are the two most important contributions of the framers to the art and practice of government: the idea of the separation of powers of the government into distinct parts or branches, and federalism.

In *The Federalist Papers #10*, James Madison, a man of little property himself, wrote, "The diversities in the faculties of men from which the rights of property originates is not less an insuperable obstacle to uniformity of interests. *The protection of these faculties is the first object of government*" (emphasis added).[37] How does government carry out its first object in a democratic society? The problem confronting the framers, stated simply, was this: In a democratic, capitalist society where only a minority has property but a majority has the right to vote, it is likely the majority will use its voting rights to threaten the property rights of the minority. To avoid this danger while preserving what Madison called the "spirit and form" of democracy was the principal objective of the framers in designing the Constitution.

How is this objective attained? The principal means is through the separation of powers. Again, we quote Madison. Writing in *The Federalist Papers #47* he argued, "No political truth is certainly of greater intrinsic value or stamped with the authority of more enlightened patrons of liberty than that . . . the accumulation of all powers, legislative, executive and judiciary, in the same hands . . . may justly be pronounced the very definition of tyranny."[38] It was not, however, the mere separation of powers of the government into four distinct parts (including the two parts of the Congress); in addition, the Constitution allowed the people—the voters—to elect directly only one of the four parts: the House of Representatives, arguably the least powerful of the four.

The second major principle of constitutional design was federalism, a system of government in which powers are shared between a national (federal) government and the governments of the several states. The last of the Bill of Rights, the Tenth Amendment, establishes this federal system by *delegating* some powers to the federal government, *prohibiting* both the states and federal government from exercising certain powers, and *reserving* all others to the states. The major powers of the federal government were limited to regulating commerce and the currency, conducting diplomacy, and waging war. Everything else done by the government was to be done by the states.

As Robinson writes, when this system of government was being devised, "tensions about slavery were prominent among the forces that maintained the resolve to develop the country without strong direction from Washington."[39] In limiting the power of the federal government in Washington, the framers simultaneously limited the possibility of universal freedom. Again, to quote from Robinson's *Slavery in the Structure of American Politics:*

> Therefore, in the United States a political system "exquisitely" sensitive to elements of which it was composed and whose structure, both formal and informal, was geared to frustrate and facilitate public action at the national level could not be expected to produce action to end slavery, particularly when the group with the most immediate interest in overthrowing slavery was itself completely unrepresented.[40]

African Americans, however, given their status first as slaves and subsequently as a poor, oppressed minority, have always found the status quo unacceptable. They favored—and favor today—rapid, indeed radical, change in the status quo. And they have also favored action by the federal government rather than the states. Historically, African Americans and their allies have made an important contribution to universalizing freedom through their support for a powerful federal government. The power of the federal government has increased markedly during three periods in American history: the Reconstruction era in the 1860s, the New Deal era in the 1930s, and the civil rights–Great Society era of the 1960s. In two of these periods the black quest for freedom was central to the expansion of federal power (see chapter 2 for more detailed discussion of these three periods of expanding federal power). And as we show in the chapter on public opinion, African Americans remain the most distinctively and persistently liberal of all the various groups of the American population, strongly supporting an activist, interventionist federal government.

SELECTED BIBLIOGRAPHY

Becker, Carl. *The Declaration of Independence: A Study in the History of an Idea.* New York: Vintage Books, 1922, 1970. The classic study of the writing of the Declaration.

Beard, Charles. *An Economic Interpretation of the Constitution.* New York: Free Press, 1913, 1965. The classic, controversial book suggesting that the framers of the Constitution wrote an undemocratic document in order to protect their economic interests.

Brown, Robert. *Charles Beard and the Constitution: A Critical Analysis of an Economic Interpretation of the Constitution.* New York: Norton, 1965. A comprehensive critique of Beard's controversial book.

Davis, David Brion. *The Problem of Slavery in Western Culture.* Ithaca, NY: Cornell University Press, 1966. An early, groundbreaking study of the interrelationship between slavery and the emergence of freedom as a value in the Western world.

Farrand, Max. *The Framing of the Constitution of the United States.* New Haven, CT: Yale University Press, 1913. A short, readable account of the writing of the Constitution by the scholar who prepared the four-volume documentary record of the proceedings of the Philadelphia convention.

Freehling, William. "The Founding Fathers and Slavery." *American Historical Review* 77 (1972): 81–93. A generally sympathetic account of how slavery influenced the framers' work on the Constitution.

Harding, Vincent. *There is a River: The Black Struggle for Freedom in America.* New York: Harcourt Brace Jovanovich, 1981. A lyrical, poetic, inspiring narrative.

Jordan, Winthrop. *White over Black: American Attitudes toward the Negro, 1550–1812.* Baltimore: Penguin, 1968. A monumental study tracing the origin and development of white attitudes toward Africans and African Americans from the sixteenth century through the early years of the United States.

Patterson, Orlando. *Freedom in the Making of Western Culture.* New York: Basic Books, 1991. The most recent study of how freedom in the West emerges out of the experience of slavery.

Robinson, Donald. *Slavery in the Structure of American Politics.* New York: Harcourt Brace Jovanovich, 1971. The best book on the role slavery played in the debates and compromises that shaped the writing of the Constitution.

The Federalist Papers. Introduction by Clinton Rossiter. New York: New American Library, 1961. The authoritative interpretation of the Constitution written during the debate on ratification by James Madison, Alexander Hamilton, and John Jay. It is also a classic in American political thought.

NOTES

1. Eric Foner, *Reconstruction: America's Unfinished Revolution, 1863–1877* (New York: Harper & Row, 1988): 77.
2. William Riker, *Federalism: Origins, Operation and Significance* (Boston: Little, Brown, 1964): 140.
3. Orlando Patterson, *Freedom in the Making of Western Culture* (New York: Basic Books, 1991): 1.
4. John Hope Franklin, *From Slavery to Freedom: A History of Negro Americans* (New York: Knopf, 1980): 31.
5. See Patterson, *Freedom in the Making of Western Culture* and his "The Unholy Trinity: Freedom, Slavery and the American Constitution," *Social Problems* 54 (Autumn 1987): 543–77. See also Edmund Morgan, *American Slavery, American Freedom: The Ordeal of Colonial Virginia* (New York: Norton, 1975); David Brion Davis, *The Problem of Slavery in Western Culture* (Ithaca, NY: Cornell University Press, 1966), and his *The Problem of Slavery in the Age of Revolution* (Ithaca, NY: Cornell University Press, 1975).
6. Patterson, "The Unholy Trinity," pp. 559–60. Patterson, in *Freedom in the Making of Western Culture,* contends that freedom is a uniquely Western value and that "almost never outside the context of western culture and its influence, has it [non-Western culture] included freedom. Indeed, non-western peoples have thought so little about freedom that most human languages did not even possess a word for the concept until contact with the West" (p. x). While there is much of value in Patterson's studies, we are not persuaded by the argument that freedom in its origins is a uniquely Western value. On the contrary, we believe freedom is a fundamental, driving force of the human condition.
7. Patterson, "The Unholy Trinity," p. 545.
8. We believe this generalization is an overstatement. While slavery was undoubtedly important in the genesis of the idea of freedom, one could also argue that the idea of freedom in the Western world could in part stem from the desire of people to be free from harsh rule, treatment, or prohibitions that fall short of slavery (freedom of religion, for example). This seems especially so in the history of the United States.
9. Patterson, *Freedom in the Making of Western Culture,* pp. 3–5.
10. Foner, *Reconstruction*, p. 231.
11. Richard King, *Civil Rights and the Idea of Freedom* (New York: Oxford University Press, 1992): 26.
12. Ibid., pp. 26–28.
13. Herbert Aptheker, *A Documentary History of the Negro People in the United States*, vol. 1 (New York: Citadel Press, 1967): 1.
14. Harold Lasswell and Abraham Kaplan, *Power and Society: A Framework for Political Inquiry* (New Haven, CT: Yale University Press, 1950): 26.

15. Robert Dahl, "The Concept of Power," *Behavioral Science* 2 (July 1957): 201–15.
16. Max Weber, "Class, Status and Party," in Gerth and Mills, *From Max Weber*, (New York: Oxford, 1958): 180.
17. Mack Jones, "A Frame of Reference for Black Politics," in Lenneal Henderson, ed., *Black Political Life in the United States* (New York: Chandler Publishing, 1972): 9.
18. Carl Becker, *The Declaration of Independence: A Study in the History of an Idea* (New York: Vintage Books, 1922, 1970): 320.
19. Joseph Ellis, "Editing the Declaration," *Civilization* (July/August 1995): 60. See Becker's *The Declaration of Independence* for a detailed analysis of the various changes made in Jefferson's original draft.
20. Ellis, "Editing the Declaration."
21. Becker, *The Declaration of Independence*, pp. 212–13.
22. From *The Writings of Thomas Jefferson*, p. 324, as cited in Becker, *The Declaration of Independence*, p. 25.
23. Ibid.
24. A comprehensive treatment of Jefferson's views on race is in Winthrop Jordan, *White over Black: American Attitudes toward the Negro, 1550–1812* (Baltimore, MD: Penguin Books, 1969): chap. 12, "Thomas Jefferson: Self and Society."
25. Mack Jones, "A Frame of Reference for Black Politics," in Lenneal Henderson, ed., *Black Political Life in the United States* (New York: Chandler Publishing, 1972): 7–20.
26. Stokely Carmichael and Charles Hamilton, *Black Power: The Politics of Black Liberation* (New York: Vintage Books, 1967): 3–4.
27. Ibid.
28. Jenny Williams, "Redefining Institutional Racism," *Ethnic and Racial Studies* 8 (1985):323–75; Louis Knowles and Kenneth Prewitt, *Institutional Racism in America* (New York: Prentice Hall, 1969); Robert C. Smith, *Racism in the Post–Civil Rights Era: Now You See It, Now You Don't* (Albany: SUNY Press, 1995): 54–75.
29. William Freehling, "The Founding Fathers and Slavery," *American Historical Review* 77 (1972): 83.
30. Ibid.
31. Lance Banning, *The Sacred Fire of Liberty: James Madison and the Founding of the Federal Republic* (Ithaca, NY: Cornell University Press, 1995).
32. *The Federalist Papers*. Introduction by Clinton Rossiter (New York: New American Library, 1961): 337.
33. Donald Robinson, "The Constitutional Legacy of Slavery," *National Political Science Review* 4(1994): 11.
34. Ibid., p. 12.
35. Ibid.
36. Ibid.
37. *The Federalist Papers*, p. 78. In a way, whether Madison or any of the other framers were themselves men of property is irrelevant since, as Donald Robinson writes, "Everyone of them had made a pile of money, married a wealthy woman or committed his professional life to the service of wealthy clients." Donald

Robinson, *To the Best of My Ability: The Presidency and the Constitution* (New York: Norton, 1987): 65.

38. Ibid., p. 301.
39. Robinson, *Slavery in the Structure of American Politics,* p. 435.
40. Ibid. In his more recent book on the American political system, Robinson calls for major modifications in the separation of powers so that the federal government may act more coherently and rapidly. See his *To the Best of My Ability: The Presidency and the Constitution,* chapter 12.

CHAPTER 2

Federalism and the Limits of Universal Freedom

Robert Bork, nominated in 1987 by President Reagan for a seat on the Supreme Court, argues that federalism is an important means to protect individual liberty and freedom. Bork argues that indeed federalism is the Constitution's most important protector of an individual's freedom and that it has been of special value to African Americans in their quest for freedom. With respect to African Americans, Bork writes,

> People who found state regulations oppressive could vote with their feet and in massive numbers they did. Blacks engaged in the great migration at a time when southern states blatantly discriminated. . . . of course this freedom to escape came at a price. But if another state allows you the liberty you value, you can move there and the choice is yours alone, not dependent on those who made the Constitution.[1]

In his classic study *Federalism: Origins, Operation and Significance*, William Riker rejects Bork's arguments about the relationship between federalism and freedom, stating flatly that "federalism may have more to do with destroying freedom than encouraging it."[2] With respect to federalism and the African American quest for freedom, Riker is equally harsh in his condemnation: "The main beneficiaries throughout American history have been southern whites, who have been given the freedom to oppress Negroes, first as slaves and later as a depressed caste."[3] Thus, for Riker, "if in the United States one disapproves of racism, one should disapprove of federalism."[4]

For African Americans, at least until the 1960s civil rights revolution, federalism has had an ambivalent, contradictory effect on their quest for universal freedom. The Civil Rights Act of 1964 universalized freedom throughout the United States with respect to race discrimination. Prior to the 1960s, however, federalism operated in an ambivalent way with respect to race, since each state was free to make any laws it wished regarding the oppression of blacks. So, for example, in 1640 Virginia was the first state to pass laws legally enslaving blacks, but in the 1780s Massachusetts was the first state to legally abolish slavery. And in the antebellum era, antislavery abolitionists used the power of northern state governments to undermine slavery in the South by refusing to return escaped slaves as required by the Constitution and the Fugitive Slave Act—thus, the idea of north to freedom, of following the north star, of north to freedom's promised land. In this sense, until the abolition of slavery in the 1860s, federalism allowed some space, although limited, for African American freedom in the United States.

Similarly, once a system of rigid segregation was imposed in the South beginning in the 1870s, blacks, as the Bork quote points out, begin once again to look to the North for freedom, to vote with their feet in the great migration from the South. In Figure 2.1, data are displayed on the percentage of African Americans living in the "rigidly segregated" southern states (see Box 2.1, "The 'Absurd' Career of Jim Crow"), compared to the more "flexibly segregated" northern states. In 1870, 81 percent of the African American population lived in the rigidly segregated South. Then, starting in the 1920s, a slow, steady migration of African Americans began to the more flexibly segregated North so that by 1970 only 55 percent of African Americans still lived in the South.[5] The Civil Rights Act of 1964, the Voting Rights Act of 1965, and the Fair Housing Act of 1968 universalized freedom insofar as they made racial discrimination illegal throughout the United States, north and south. Therefore, one should probably qualify Riker's blanket condemnation of federalism because during the eras of slavery and segregation, it did provide some opportunity in the North for the exercise of limited forms of freedom.

Figure 2.1 The Percentage of the African American Population in the Rigid (South) and Flexible (Non-South) Segregated States: 1870–1970

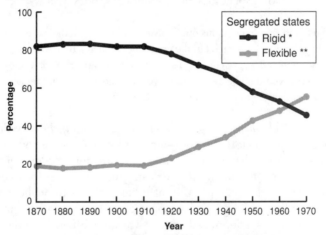

Sources: Adapted from U.S. Bureau of Census, *Negro Population in the United States: 1790–1915* (Washington, D.C.: Government Printing Office, 1918), pp. 43–44 for the data from 1870 to 1910. U.S. Bureau of Census, *Negro Population in the United States: 1920–1932* (Washington, D.C.: Government Printing Office, 1935), pp. 9–11 for the data from 1920 to 1930. U.S. Bureau of Census, *Census for Population: 1050 Vol. II: Characteristics of the Population: Part I United States Summary* (Washington, D.C.: Government Printing Office, 1951), Table 59, pp. 1–106, for the 1950 data. And the U.S. Bureau of Census, *Historical Statistics of the United States: Colonial Times to 1970* (Washington, D.C.: Government Printing Office, 1975), pp. 24–37 for data for 1940, 1960, and 1970. All calculations were prepared by the authors.

*Rigid segregated states are the eleven states of the old Confederacy.

**Flexible segregated states are the other states of the Union.

━━━━━━━━━━━━━━━ **BOX 2.1** ━━━━━━━━━━━━━━━
The "Absurd" Career of Jim Crow[a]

As most Americans are aware, with the end of Reconstruction and the adoption of the doctrine of "separate but equal" by the Supreme Court in *Plessy v. Ferguson,* the southern states required or permitted the separation of blacks and whites in virtually all areas of life, public and private. Schools, playgrounds, swimming pools, beaches, parks, hotels, hospitals, libraries, restaurants, cemeteries, water fountains, toilets, and buses and street cars were all segregated. Interracial sex, marriage, and love were also outlawed. Jim Crow's strange career, however, in some places bordered on the absurd. Alabama prohibited blacks and whites from playing checkers together; in some states schoolchildren of different races could not use the same books; Louisiana established separate districts for black and white prostitutes; in Oklahoma blacks and whites could not use the same public telephone. In North Carolina young children could be arrested for interracial kissing. Finally, in Georgia and several other states blacks were required to use separate polling places, separate courthouse doors, separate record rooms, separate record books, separate pens and ink, and separate color-coded tax receipts—white for white taxpayers and pink for blacks.

[a]C. Vann Woodward, *The Strange Career of Jim Crow* (New York: Oxford University Press, 1966). Woodward writes that the origin of the term *Jim Crow* to refer to racial segregation is "lost in obscurity"; however, it is probably related to minstrel songs done by whites in blackface.

FEDERALISM: ORIGINS AND OPERATIONS IN THE UNITED STATES

Federalism—the sharing of the powers of government between the national (federal) government and the governments of the states—along with the separation of powers, is one of the major contributions of the framers of the Constitution to the art and practice of government. In Western political thought, the *sovereign power* of the government (its supreme, absolute, unrestrained authority over its citizens) could not be divided. Jean Bodin, the leading Western philosopher on the idea of sovereignty, argued that sovereignty could not be divided, that it was indivisible and must reside in a single person (a monarch) or institution (parliament).[6] The framers of the American Constitution rejected Bodin's idea of the indivisibility of the sovereign power of government on the theory that since the people of the United States were sovereign, they, if they wished, could divide sovereignty in order to create a well-ordered government that would secure their liberties.

The idea that ultimate sovereignty or power of the government rests with the people is the underlying philosophical principle of the American government that shapes both federalism and the separation of powers. However, there is a practical reason that the framers felt compelled to adopt the federal system: Without federalism it is unlikely that there could have been a union of all the thirteen states. Some of the framers favored a unitary rather than a federal government. The Virginia delegation at Philadelphia proposed in its "Virginia Plan" essentially a unitary government; in this the people as a whole would elect the House and the House in turn would elect the Senate, the president and the judiciary. Under the plan, the Congress would have unlimited powers to "legislate in all cases to which the separate states are incompetent . . . [and] to negative all laws passed by the several states, contravening in the opinion of the national legislature under the Articles of the union."[7] In other words, the Congress was to have unlimited powers, including the power to "negative" or veto acts of the state legislatures.

The Virginia Plan was rejected by the convention on several grounds. A major reason, however, was that the southern slaveholding states feared that a unitary government with the power to "negative all laws passed by the states" might interfere with their wish to maintain slavery. Thus, philosophical principles aside, federalism was necessary in the United States for wholly practical reasons: to establish the Union.[8]

Who Is Sovereign: The People or the States? An Old Debate Renewed

It is generally accepted today that the whole people of the United States are sovereign and that acting collectively created the United States government. This, however, was not always the accepted view. Thomas Jefferson, for example, apparently believed that the United States was created by the states rather than the people and consequently each state had the right to act independently of the federal government by nullifying (vetoing) federal laws with which it disagreed.[9] This view was firmly rejected by Lincoln and in a sense was settled by the civil war. However, in a recent case, Supreme Court Justice Clarence Thomas in a dissenting opinion (joined by the Chief Justice and Justices O'Connor and Scalia) renewed this two-hundred-year-old debate.

The Case is *U.S. Term Limits Inc. et al. v. Thornton et al.*, a case dealing with whether a state (in this case Arkansas) could on its own authority impose term limits on its members of Congress.[10] The Court, in a five to four decision, said no, holding that only all the people of the United States by amending the Constitution could limit the terms of members of Congress. (On term limits and their probable impact on African Americans in the Congress, see chapter 11.) In a long dissenting opinion, Justice

Thomas, again writing for himself and three of his colleagues, argued that each state could limit congressional terms because *"the ultimate source of the Constitution's authority is the consent of the people of each state, not the consent of the undifferentiated people of the nation as a whole"*[11] (emphasis added). Noting that the "United States" is consistently a plural noun and that the original preamble to the Constitution read "We the People of the States of New Hampshire, Massachusetts, etc.," Justice Thomas concluded, "The Constitution simply does not recognize any mechanism for action by the undifferentiated people of the nation."[12]

In his opinion for the majority, Justice John Paul Stevens rejected Thomas's analysis. He argued that the states under the Articles of Confederation retained their sovereignty as independent states, but with the adoption of the Constitution, *"the framers envisioned a uniform national system, rejecting the notion that the nation was a collection of states and instead creating a direct link between the national government and the people"*[13] (emphasis added). In a separate concurring opinion, Justice Anthony Kennedy wrote, "In my view, however, it is well settled that the whole people of the United States asserted their political identity and unity of purpose when they created the federal system."[14]

This debate between Justice Thomas and his colleagues on whether the people of the United States or the people of the various states established the Constitution may seem like an arcane, theoretical, academic debate with no practical consequences. It is not. Rather, it is a debate central to the thesis of this book: whether the United States is a nation of uniform, universal rights and freedom, or whether it is one of freedom limited by states' rights. It is also part of an ongoing effort by conservatives on the Court and in the Congress to radically reshape the federal system, by taking power from the federal government and returning it to the states (see the section, "The Rehnquist Court and the Revival of State-Centered Federalism," later in this chapter).

Federalism: Advantages and Disadvantages

Perhaps the most frequently stated advantage of the federal system is that it allows the states to serve as "laboratories" for public policy innovation and experimentation. In other words, each of the fifty states is free to "experiment" with the best ways to deliver education, health, and welfare services, and to provide for the punishment of crime (see Box 2.2). And through the "diffusion of innovation," each state can learn from the successes and failures of the others and change its policies according to what works best.[15] Related to this, federalism grants to citizens "choice," the freedom to move from one state to another in search of a better life.

Another advantage of federalism is that it provides opportunities for minority groups in the country as a whole to be majorities (the Mormons in Utah) or larger, more politically significant minorities (Jews in New York, Latinos in California, or blacks in Louisiana) at the state and local levels. This provision enhances the opportunities for minority groups to participate in politics and to be elected to office, again a situation that would not be possible in a unitary system. This is especially true in the United States because there are not just fifty-one governments (the 50 states and the federal government) but more than 80,000 units of government including county, city, and town governments; school boards, and other special districts. This enormous diversity of

━━━━━━━━━━━━━━━━ **BOX 2.2** ━━━━━━━━━━━━━━━━
Federalism, Felonies, and the Right to Vote[a]

Under federalism, each state is free to set its own qualifications for voting, except the vote may not be denied on account of race, religion, gender, age (18), or the person's failure to pay a poll tax. But under what conditions might citizens lose and then regain the right to vote? As part of the voter registration efforts of the 1996 Million Man March, the National Coalition on Black Voter Participation surveyed each of the states in order to learn whether citizens lost their right to vote as a consequence of conviction for a felony and if so, how they could have the right restored. Thirty-five of the fifty states responded to the survey. Three states (Maine, Utah, and Vermont) with small black populations do not deprive convicted felons of the right to vote. Arkansas and West Virginia have no clearly stated procedures for restoration, three states require action by the governor, and most of the rest require action of the state pardon and parole boards or local election commissions. Mississippi (which at 37% has the largest percentage black population of any state) is different. Its constitution states, "The legislature, *may* by a two thirds vote of both houses, of all members elected, restore the right of suffrage to any person disqualified by reason of crime, but the reason therefore shall be spread upon the journal and the vote shall be by yeas and nays." Thus, in Mississippi it is more difficult for a citizen who has committed a crime to regain the right to vote than it is to impeach the president of the United States. In Mississippi, African Americans are more than three times as likely to be convicted of felonies as whites. Thus, they are three times as likely to lose the right to vote, and once lost, it is very difficult to regain. Perhaps these are mere coincidences, but it is striking that in Mississippi—the state with the worst history of race oppression and the largest black population—citizens find it more difficult than in any other state to regain their voting rights once lost. It is striking because the effect of the Mississippi procedure is to deny the vote to a large number of its black citizens.

[a]Hanes Walton, Jr., and Simone Green, "Voting Rights and the Million Man March: The Problem of Restoration of Voting Rights for Ex-Convicts/Felons" *African American Research Perspectives* Vol 3 (Winter, 1997), pp. 68–74. According to a report by the Sentencing Project, a nonprofit research group, about 1.46 million black men (1 of every 7) have lost their right to vote. See Pierre Thomas, "Felony Convictions Cut Black Vote, Report Says," *Washington Post*, January 30, 1997.

governments is particularly important for African Americans; although they are a national minority, they can become a local majority and control the governments in localities, including many of the nation's larger and more important cities.

There are clear advantages to a federal system, but there are clear disadvantages as well, especially to blacks in their quest for universal rights and freedoms. First, in its essence, federalism is an impediment to universal freedom because it allows the different states to define rights and freedoms for their citizens, even to define who might be a citizen (see Box 2.3). Historically, this power has allowed a minority of southern whites to limit the freedom of African Americans, even against the wishes of a majority of the American people. Second, federalism, as a number of political scientists have shown, tends to lead to irresponsible government.[16] Woodrow Wilson, political scientist and

=== **BOX 2.3** ===

The Fourteenth Amendment and Universal Citizenship

A principal theme of this book is that the presence of the African people in the United States has profoundly affected the nature of its society and politics. So it was with the simple question of who was or who might become a citizen. The political scientist John Roche writes, "The Negro issue cast its disruptive shadows on every aspect of American life, including citizenship. . . . It seems probable that citizenship would early have achieved the content it has today without the Fourteenth Amendment had it not been for the Negro problem."[a] The Fourteenth Amendment universalized citizenship by declaring in its first sentence, "All persons born or naturalized in the United States, and subject to the jurisdiction thereof are citizens of the United States and of the state wherein they reside." Prior to the adoption of the Constitution, each state regulated citizenship (including issuing passports), and five of the thirteen states granted citizenship to "free Negroes." With the adoption of the Constitution, Congress was granted the authority to establish "an uniform rule for naturalization" but not to establish citizenship since this was still a prerogative of the states. Thus, to become a citizen of the United States, one first had to become a citizen of one of the states.

This power of the states to confer limited but not universal citizenship was made emphatic by the Supreme Court in the *Dred Scott* case. In this opinion, Chief Justice Taney wrote that while a state could confer citizenship on Africans, the citizenship was limited to that particular state and did not make the holders citizens of the United States or any other state. The only way blacks could become United States citizens was by an act of Congress, and the Congress, in the fifteen naturalization laws it passed between 1790 to 1854, always specifically limited citizenship to "free white persons." The Fourteenth Amendment for the most part changed all this by conferring citizenship by place of birth—*jus soli*—meaning that even a person born of foreign parents in the United States automatically becomes a citizen. (This contrasts greatly with many other countries where citizenship is *jus sanguinis*—that is, a child's citizenship is determined by that of the parents.)

The Fourteenth Amendment did not completely universalize citizenship. In the United States, unlike many countries, citizenship does not automatically confer the right to vote, hence the need for the Fifteenth and Nineteenth Amendments granting suffrage to blacks and women. In *Elk v. Wilkins (1884)* the Supreme Court held that Indians, although born in the geographical United States, were not citizens since they owed allegiance to their tribes and thus were no more citizens than the children of ambassadors born in the United States. In 1887, Congress granted citizenship to nonreservation Indians; in 1901, citizenship was extended to the five so-called civilized tribes, and finally in 1924, it was extended to all Native Americans in the United States, although several states in the southwest continued to deny Indians the right to vote until the 1960s.

<hr>

[a]John P. Roche, *The Early Development of United States Citizenship* (Ithaca, NY: Cornell University Press, 1949): 2, 17.

twenty-eighth president of the United States, eloquently stated the case for the irresponsibility of divided power in his 1898 book *Congressional Government*. Wilson observed that "the more power is divided the more irresponsible it becomes. A mighty baron who can call half the country to arms is watched with great jealousy, and, therefore restrained with more vigilant care than is ever vouchsafed the feeble master of a single and solitary castle."[17] In other words, citizens are more likely to be aware of and exercise restraint on or greater control of one powerful central government than they are of scores of state and local governments. This situation is even more the case today than when Wilson was writing in 1898, given the development of a national news media (particularly television) that focuses its attention on events in Washington. Average citizens living in Detroit or San Francisco are more likely to be aware of what the president and the Congress are doing in Washington than they are of what the governor and legislature are doing in Lansing and Sacramento.

E. E. Schattsneider has argued that widening or nationalizing the scope of government decision making tends to enhance the power of minority groups.[18] That is, a minority such as African Americans is more likely to be able to influence decision makers in Washington than in any of the fifty state capitals. This is because decisions at the national level tend to be more visible, and minority interest groups tend to be better organized in national than state politics. For this reason, for example, African American leaders opposed the efforts of the Republican congressional majority in 1995 to transfer responsibility for social welfare programs (welfare, Medicaid, food stamps, etc.) to the states. Another reason African Americans oppose the transfer of social programs to the states is that instead of one uniform, universal standard for welfare or Medicaid, there would be fifty-one. Again, this is part of the essence of federalism. As Riker writes, "The grant of autonomy to local majorities to create confused policies has resulted in a cost to the whole society that is probably greater than the cost of uniformity."[19] To relate Riker's point to the theme of this book, uniformity in national policies, as opposed to multiple state policies, is more likely to result in universal rights and freedoms.

RECONSTRUCTION, THE NEW DEAL, AND THE CIVIL RIGHTS MOVEMENT: THE TRIUMPH OF NATIONAL-CENTERED POWER

Throughout American history there has been debate and conflict between those who favor *national-centered power* and those who favor *state-centered power*. Generally, the American political tradition tends to favor state-centered power, and advocates of national-centered power have tended to prevail only in times of national crisis. Even then, the advocates of state-centered power reassert themselves in calls for a return of power to the states. Frederick Douglass during Reconstruction—the first triumph of national-centered power—observed that "no political idea is more deeply rooted in the minds of the country [than] the right of each state to control its own affairs."[20] Thus, it is not surprising that after each period of expanding national power there were subsequent calls for a return of power to the states.

Reconstruction

National-centered power—greater authority and responsibility to the federal government—has triumphed only during periods of crisis. The first such crisis, the gravest in the nation's history, was the Civil War and the effort to reconstruct the South in its aftermath. As Eric Foner, the historian of Reconstruction, shows, an activist federal government as an instrument of reform emerges in the Civil War-Reconstruction era.[21]

During this period the power of the president—particularly his commander-in-chief powers—expanded enormously under Lincoln. Then under President Andrew Johnson, the powers of Congress also expanded as that body passed several civil rights laws requiring the states to accord the newly freed slaves universal freedom and equal rights. For a time during this period, the United States Army was maintained in the southern states to enforce these rights. The federal government also established its first social welfare agency—the Freedmen's Bureau—to provide assistance first to the newly freed slaves and subsequently to poor whites displaced by the war. Finally, three amendments were added to the Constitution: the Thirteenth abolishing slavery, the Fourteenth establishing universal citizenship and equality and fairness under law for all persons, and the Fifteenth guaranteeing voting rights to all men regardless of race. The Fourteenth Amendment eventually was to become one of the most important mechanisms for expanding the power of the federal government in relationship to the states.

The New Deal

National-centered power expanded for a second time during Franklin Roosevelt's New Deal.[22] In the midst of the Great Depression the federal government took on a wide array of responsibilities previously left to the states or market forces, including universal access of the elderly to retirement income, welfare for fatherless children, and government-supported public works jobs for the unemployed. In addition to the beginnings of the modern welfare state, the New Deal also expanded the power of the regulatory state with respect to banking, agriculture, the stock market, and the relationship between workers and their employers. The Supreme Court initially declared many of the New Deal programs unconstitutional because the Court said they exceeded the federal government's Article 1, Section 8 powers. Eventually, however, under pressure from the popular Roosevelt, the Court changed its mind and approved virtually all the New Deal. Thus, for the first time in American history, Congress established a series of universal programs designed to assure the employment and social security of *all* its citizens.

During the New Deal the federal government also established a series of grants in aid to the states and localities—funds to assist them in carrying out their responsibilities in such areas as public works, housing, and health. These grants in aid were vastly expanded in the 1960s as part of Lyndon Johnson's Great Society (by the 1970s there were more than 600 such specific grants covering everything from alcohol and drug abuse to youth training programs). These grants usually come with strings attached; that is, they carry uniform or universal conditions that states and localities must comply with.

The Civil Rights Revolution and the Great Society

The civil rights reforms of the 1960s ushered in the last great expansion of federal power. In a sense these reforms were a second reconstruction or a completion of the first. As in the original Reconstruction, Congress passed three new civil rights laws guaranteeing universal access to the ballot, public education, employment, restaurants, hotels and other public places, and the sale and rental of housing. Two new amendments were added to the Constitution granting the right to vote for president to the largely black city of Washington, D.C., and abolishing the poll tax. The Supreme Court, then the president, and finally the Congress began to enforce the Fourteenth and Fifteenth amendments for the first time in one hundred years. And on two occasions (Little Rock in 1957 and the University of Mississippi in 1962), the United States Army, again for the first time in a century, was deployed in the South to enforce African American civil rights.

Federal social welfare programs also expanded during this period as a part of Lyndon Johnson's Great Society and "war on poverty." Universal access to health care for the elderly and to nursing homes for the poor elderly were guaranteed, as was health care for the poor. The Great Society also provided federal support for elementary and secondary education and loans and grants for college and postgraduate education. Again, these were universal programs, providing support to persons no matter where they lived in the country.

Yet, as always in American history, there was reaction to this expanding power of the federal government from those favoring state-centered power. During Reconstruction, Foner writes, "A more powerful national state and a growing sense that blacks were entitled to some measure of civil equality produced their own countervailing tendencies as localism, laissez-faire and racism, persistent forces in the nineteenth century American life, reasserted themselves."[23] One hundred years later these same persistent, countervailing tendencies emerged in reaction to the Great Society and civil rights reforms of the 1960s. Beginning in 1968 with the election of Richard Nixon, again in 1980 with the election of Ronald Reagan, and again in 1994 with the election of Republican congressional majorities, these forces of localism, laissez-faire, and racism reasserted themselves, continuing the historic tension and conflict between advocates of national-centered and state-centered power.

THE FOURTEENTH AMENDMENT: THE AMERICAN CHARTER OF UNIVERSAL FREEDOM

Of the Fourteenth Amendment, Fred Friendly and Martha Elliot write, "It was as if Congress had held a second constitutional convention and created a federal government of vastly expanded proportions."[24] And of the three Civil War amendments, including the Fourteenth, Justice Samuel Miller in the *Slaughterhouse Cases* wrote,

> No one can fail to be impressed with the one prevailing purpose found in them all, lying at the foundation of each, and without which none of them would have been suggested; we mean the freedom of the slave race, the security and firm establishment of that freedom and the protection of the newly made freeman and citizen from the oppression of those who had formerly exercised dominion over him.[25]

And of the Fourteenth specifically, Justice White wrote, "*It is so clearly a provision for that race . . . that a strong case would be necessary for its application to any other*"[26] (emphasis added).

Although the Fourteenth Amendment did vastly expand the power of the federal government in relation to the states and establish a basis for the protection of the freedom of African Americans, it took one hundred years for this to happen. In the meantime, contrary to Justice Miller's view, the amendment has been applied to persons of other races, including those fictitious persons called corporations. *Indeed, until the 1960s the amendment was more frequently used to protect the freedom of corporations than it was the freedom of blacks*. Thus, to fully appreciate how the amendment became the great charter of universal freedom for all Americans, we need to trace the history of its adoption and implementation from the 1860s to the 1960s.

The Fourteenth Amendment: Origins and Development

The Fourteenth Amendment was approved by the House and Senate in 1866 and ratified by the necessary three-fourths of the states two years later. William Nelson noted that much of the opposition to the amendment, north and south, was "deeply racist" as opponents argued that equality should not be granted to the "inferior races," specifically not just blacks but also Indians and the Chinese on the West Coast.[27] Although racism was the principal basis of opposition, opponents also argued that the amendment violated the principles of federalism as it gave the federal government unprecedented authority to interfere in the affairs of the states.

The Fourteenth Amendment, with five sections, is one of the longest amendments to the Constitution. The most important and controversial part is Section 1, which establishes universal citizenship and declares freedom and equality throughout the United States. As Friendly and Elliot wrote in *The Constitution: That Delicate Balance*, the following seventeen words brought about a "quiet revolution" in American government and politics: *No state shall make or enforce any law which shall abridge the privileges of immunities of citizens of the United States, nor shall any state deprive any person of life, liberty or property without due process of law; nor deny to any person within its jurisdiction the equal protection of the law*.[28] The controversy about this important language is whether its authors intended it to "incorporate" the Bill of Rights—that is, whether the "privileges and immunities" of citizens of the United States are those rights spelled out in the first nine amendments to the Constitution.[29]

Although the principal sponsors of the amendment in both the House and Senate (Representative Jonathan Bingham of New York and Senator Jacob Howard of Michigan) declared during the debates that it would require the states to abide by the Bill of Rights, there is still no agreement even today among scholars who have studied the amendment's history. Some argue that the intent of the Fourteenth Amendment was clearly to incorporate the Bill of Rights.[30] Others are just as certain from their research that this was not the amendment's intent.[31] There is, as Professor William Nelson notes, voluminous research to support both sides of the argument; thus, he concludes there is an "impasse in scholarship."[32] That is, we do not know for sure—and perhaps never will—what was the intent of the framers of the amendment.

The Supreme Court and the Fourteenth Amendment, 1865–1925: Universal Freedom Denied

The Supreme Court historically has also been divided on the intent of the amendment. Immediately after its adoption, the Court took the view that it did not make the Bill of Rights applicable to the states. *The Slaughterhouse Cases* were the first heard by the Court under the Fourteenth Amendment. In his opinion for the Court's majority, Justice Miller rejected the argument that the amendment's privileges and immunities clause incorporated the Bill of Rights, holding that the only rights protected were access to Washington, D.C., and coastal seaports; the right to protection on the high seas; the right to use the navigable waters of the United States; the right of assembly and petition; and the privilege of habeas corpus. Three justices dissented in this case; however, what modern legal scholars call Justice Miller's "pernicious" opinion remained the law of the land until the beginning of the twentieth century.[33]

The Supreme Court took a similar view in its reading of the amendment's equal protection clause when it declared the Civil Rights Act of 1875 unconstitutional. This act prohibited racial discrimination in public accommodations such as hotels, theaters, and streetcars. In the *Civil Rights Cases of 1883,* Justice Joseph Bradley declared that the Fourteenth Amendment's equal protection clause only prohibited discrimination by the states, not private businesses or persons. In language reminiscent of that used today by conservative judges and others who oppose affirmative action, Justice Bradley declared,

> When a man has emerged from slavery, and by the aid of beneficent legislation has shaken off the inseparable concomitants of that state, there must be some stage in the progress of his elevation when he takes the rank of a mere citizen, and ceases to be the special favorite of the laws, and when his rights as a citizen, or a man, are to be protected in the ordinary modes by which other men's rights are protected.[34]

In his dissent, Justice John Marshall Harlan argued that the civil rights law did not make blacks "special favorites of the law" and that the clear purpose of both the Thirteenth and Fourteenth Amendments was to establish and decree "universal freedom throughout the United States." In 1896 in *Plessy v. Ferguson,* the Court continued its narrow reading of the amendment when it declared that racial segregation did not violate the equal protection clause. Again Justice Harlan dissented, declaring that the Fourteenth Amendment made the Constitution "color blind"; but his view was not to prevail until the Supreme Court's 1954 *Brown v. Board of Education* decision.

Ironically, until the 1960s, the Fourteenth Amendment's great charter of universal freedom was used to protect the freedom of corporations rather than that of African Americans or any other real persons. William Blackstone, in his *Commentaries on the Laws of England* published in 1765, defines corporations as "artificial persons who may maintain a perpetual succession and enjoy a kind of legal immortality."[35] In 1905 in *Lochner v. New York* the Supreme Court struck down a New York state law that limited the hours of bakery workers to ten hours a day and sixty hours a week. The Court held that New York's minimum hours law violated "the general rights to make a contract in relation to his business which is part of the liberty of the individual protected by the Fourteenth Amendment of the federal Constitution."[36] New York had passed the law in the exercise of its *police powers*—that is, to protect the health and safety of the workers; however, the Court held that the "liberty of contract" guaranteed by the Fourteenth Amendment's due process of law clause meant that if a business wanted to require its workers to work more than sixty hours a week, the states could not interfere. Using similar reasoning the Court subsequently invalidated other government regulations of business, including child labor laws.[37] The Court's decision in *Lochner* was controversial but it remained the law until the Court changed its mind during the Depression when government regulation of corporations and the economy became more imperative, not to mention popular.

The Supreme Court and the Fourteenth Amendment, 1925–68: The Universalization of Freedom

Today the Fourteenth Amendment is largely used to protect civil liberties and civil rights. *Civil liberties* are generally understood as the rights of individuals that are protected from government abridgement. *Civil rights* are generally understood as the right of minorities (blacks, women, homosexuals) to freedom and equality under the law. The Court first began to interpret the Fourteenth Amendment as protecting civil liberties embodied in the Bill of Rights in 1925, and it began to seriously enforce the amendment's guarantee of equality for blacks and other minorities in the 1950s and 1960s.

In 1925 in *Gitlow v. New York*, the Supreme Court began the gradual process of incorporating or universalizing the Bill of Rights. In this case, the Court for the first time held that "freedom of speech and of the press . . . are among the fundamental personal rights and 'liberties' protected by the due process clause of the Fourteenth Amendment from impairment by the states."[38] In *Gitlow* the Court overturned more than fifty years of prior decisions on the Fourteenth Amendment. Then, as Table 2.1 shows, the Court began a gradual, year by year, amendment by amendment process, sometimes called selective incorporation of the Bill of Rights. In this process, the Court applied the rest of the First Amendment to the states, and then in the 1960s it applied those provisions

---
TABLE 2.1

Dates of U.S. Supreme Court Decisions Ensuring Bill of Rights Protections Nationwide

Freedom	Year of Incorporation/Universalization
Free Speech (1)[a]	1925
Free Press (1)	1931
Freedom of Assembly (1)	1937
Freedom of Religion (1)	1934
Unreasonable Search and Seizure (4)	1949
Cruel and Unusual Punishment (8)	1962
Right to Lawyer in Criminal Cases (6)	1963
No Self-Incrimination (5)	1964
Remain Silent when Questioned by Police (6)	1966

[a]Number in parentheses refers to the amendment to the Constitution addressing that right or freedom. The Court first incorporated the right to privacy in *Griswold v. Connecticut* (381 U.S. 479, 85. S.Ct., 1678), a 1965 case involving the right of married couples to use contraceptives.

Source: Craig Ducat and Harold Chase, *Constitutional Interpretation*, 4th ed. (St. Paul, MI: West, 1988): 845–46.

of the Bill of Rights dealing with the rights of persons accused of crimes (the Fourth, Fifth, Sixth, and Eighth Amendments). And in 1972 in *Roe v. Wade,* the Court interpreted the Fourteenth Amendment as creating a right to privacy (either in the Fourteenth's guarantee of liberty or as a Ninth Amendment unmentioned right) that is broad enough to cover a woman's right to choose an abortion. Thus, by the end of the 1960s virtually all the important provisions of the Bill of Rights had been incorporated or made universal throughout the United States.

With respect to civil rights, in 1954 the Supreme Court declared in *Brown v. Board of Education* that, at least in terms of the public schools, racial segregation was a violation of the Fourteenth Amendment's equal protection clause, reversing the half century precedent set in *Plessy v. Ferguson.* Then in the 1960s, the Congress, responding to the protests and demonstrations led by Dr. Martin Luther King, Jr., passed a series of laws designed to enforce the Fourteenth's guarantee of universal freedom and equality. But in passing the public accommodations section of the 1964 Civil Rights Act (which prohibited discrimination in hotels, motels, and restaurants), the Congress relied not on the Fourteenth Amendment but instead on its power to regulate interstate commerce (because hotels and motels received products or served customers who crossed state lines). Since the Supreme Court in 1883 had invalidated a similar civil rights law based on the Fourteenth's Section 5 enforcement power, the Congress, by using the commerce clause, avoided the problem of having the Court overrule yet another of its precedents. (In general, the Court is reluctant to overturn its prior decisions, relying on the principle of *stare decisis*—let the previous decision stand.)[39] This led Justice William O. Douglas in his concurring opinion in the case, *Heart of Atlanta Motel v. the United States*, upholding the 1964 law to write:

> I am reluctant to . . . rest solely on the commerce clause. My reluctance is not due to any conviction that Congress lacks the power to regulate commerce in the interests of human rights. It is rather my belief that the right of the people to be free of state action that discriminates against them because of race . . . occupies a more protected place in our constitutional system than does the movement of cattle, fruit, steel and coal across state lines. Hence, I would prefer to rest on the assertion of legislative power contained in section 5 of the Fourteenth Amendment which states "The Congress shall have the power to enforce, by appropriate legislation, the provisions of this article"—a power which the Court concedes was exercised at least in part.[40]

One hundred years after the adoption of the Fourteenth Amendment it became the Constitution's great charter of freedom in fact as well as theory, establishing a new vision of universal freedom, equality, and liberty under law for all Americans. It is a vision of freedom that Abraham Lincoln invoked in 1863 at Gettysburg and that Martin Luther King, Jr., invoked a hundred years later at Lincoln's Memorial in Washington (see Box 2.4).

To achieve Lincoln's vision and King's dream required a fundamental transformation in federalism as well as reversal by the Supreme Court of more than fifty years of its decisions on the relationship between federalism and freedom. Unfortunately, for African Americans and others interested in universal freedom, the Supreme Court once more appears to be reversing itself. This time, however, the Court is seeking to limit freedom by reviving old principles of federalism and states' rights.

BOX 2.4

Abraham Lincoln at Gettysburg and Martin Luther King, Jr., at Lincoln's Memorial: Two Speeches in the Quest for Universal Freedom[a]

In 1863 Abraham Lincoln was asked to deliver "a few appropriate remarks" at the dedication of the cemetery at the Gettysburg battlefield. One hundred years later Martin Luther King, Jr., was asked to deliver the closing remarks at the Lincoln Memorial on the occasion of the March on Washington. Lincoln spoke for three minutes before a crowd of 20,000. King spoke for seventeen minutes before a crowd of 250,000. Lincoln spoke on the bloody battlefield at Gettysburg to give meaning to the Civil War. King spoke at the Lincoln Memorial to give meaning to the civil rights movement's bloody battles then taking place in the South. Of all the American presidents, Abraham Lincoln was the most gifted in the rhetoric of freedom, and of all the leaders of the African American people, Martin Luther King, Jr., was the most gifted in the rhetoric of freedom. Each man in his own time and his own way sought to universalize the idea.

Lincoln at Gettysburg invoked the words of Thomas Jefferson written "four score and seven years ago" in order to declare that *all* men are created equal and that the Civil War that would free the slaves had ushered in "a new birth of freedom." King at Lincoln's Memorial invoked the words of Lincoln's Emancipation Proclamation written as King said "five score years ago" to declare that he had a dream of universal freedom, a dream that one day "*all* of God's children, black men and white men, Jews and Gentiles, Protestants and Catholics, will be able to join hands and sing in the words of the old Negro spiritual 'Free at last! Free at last! Thank God Almighty, we are free at last!'"

Abraham Lincoln was murdered on April 15, 1865. Martin Luther King, Jr., was murdered on April 4, 1968. Neither man died in vain because by their words and deeds they helped to remake the idea of freedom for America and the world.

Dr. Martin Luther King, Jr. delivers the "I Have a Dream" speech from the Lincoln Memorial, August 28, 1963.

[a]On Lincoln's address, see Garry Wills, *Lincoln at Gettysburg: The Words That Remade America* (New York: Touchstone, 1992), and on King's "I Have a Dream Speech," see Taylor Branch, *Parting the Waters: America in the King Years, 1954–63* (New York: Simon & Schuster, 1988): 875–83.

The Rehnquist Court and the Revival of State-Centered Federalism

The "states are not mere political subdivisions of the United States." So said Justice Sandra Day O'Connor in *New York v. United States*, a case invalidating a federal law that required the states either to regulate low-level radioactive waste within their boundaries or assume legal liability for it.[41] Justice O'Connor's observation in this case and the decision of the Court seem to represent an attempt by the Court's conservative majority to radically alter the existing relationship between the federal government and the states. In doing so the Court is reopening once again the two-hundred-year-old debate between advocates of national-centered versus state-centered power in American politics.

Ever since his appointment to the Court by President Nixon in 1972, Chief Justice Rehnquist (he was elevated to the Chief Justice position by President Reagan in 1986) has been an advocate of state-centered federalism, arguing that much of the Court's federalism jurisprudence since the New Deal was wrong and not supported by a fair reading of the Constitution. Until the 1980s, Rehnquist was a lonely dissenter, as his views on federalism (and civil liberties and civil rights) were not shared by his colleagues on the nine-member Court. However, with the appointments of Justices O'Connor, Antonin Scalia, and Anthony Kennedy by President Reagan, and Justice Thomas by President Bush, Rehnquist now frequently commands a narrow five-person majority on many federalism and Fourteenth Amendment cases.

Several recent cases decided by the Court suggest that it may be returning to its Reconstruction era jurisprudence. Earlier in this chapter we discussed Justice Thomas's extraordinary dissent in the term limits case in which he argued that the federal government has only those powers expressly granted or necessarily implied in the Constitution. In his opinion for the Court's narrow majority in the term limits case, Justice John Paul Stevens said this of Thomas's dissent: It would seem to suggest

> that if the Constitution is silent about the exercise of a particular power—that is, where the Constitution does not speak either expressly or by necessary implications—the federal government lacks the power and the states enjoy it. . . . Under the dissent's unyielding approach, it would seem *McCulloch* was wrongly decided. Similarly, the dissent's approach would invalidate our dormant commerce clause jurisprudence.[42]

Although Thomas and his colleagues did not prevail in the term limits case (Justice Kennedy, as he occasionally does, voted with the Court's more centrist or liberal justices in this case), in several important cases involving the powers of Congress and federal-state relations, the conservatives have been in the majority. In *United States v. Lopez*, the five-person conservative majority declared unconstitutional a federal law that prohibited the possession of guns near a school.[43] This was the first time since the New Deal that the Court invalidated an act of Congress based on its exercise of its commerce clause powers. Similarly, in *Seminole Tribe v. Florida*, the Court held (again five to four) that individuals could not sue a state to enforce federal laws or rights passed by Congress pursuant to its authority under the commerce clause. Such suits, Chief Justice Rehnquist said, were an "unconstitutional intrusion on state sovereignty." In deciding this case, the Court overturned its own decision of six years earlier in *Pennsylvania v. Union Gas*, in which it explicitly held that Congress could use its commerce clause authority to grant rights to citizens enforceable in the federal courts against the states.[44] In his dissent in *Seminole Tribe,* Justice Stevens used unusually strong language, describing the majority's decision as "a sharp break with the past," "shocking" and "profoundly misguided."[45]

In its 1996–97 and 1998–99 terms, the Court continued its "sharp break with the past" in the area of federalism. In the 1996–97 term, the Court's conservative majority invalidated three federal laws, the Religious Freedom Restoration Act (providing that no state or locality could enforce laws that "substantially burden" religious observances without showing a "compelling need"); a provision of the "Brady" gun control law requiring state law enforcement officials to conduct background checks of prospective gun purchasers; and the Communications Decency Act (prohibiting obscene or indecent material on the Internet). In the 1998–99 term, the Court also decided three cases that increased the power of the states at the expense of Congress and of private citizens. The first made states immune from suits by state employees for violations of federal labor law. The second made states immune from suits by patent owners for infringement of their patents by state universities or other state agencies, and the third prevented persons from bringing unfair competition cases against the states. Summing up these cases, the *New York Times* legal correspondent concluded that they represented "the most powerful indication yet of a narrow majority's determination to reconfigure the balance between state and Federal authority in favor of the states."[46]

SELECTED BIBLIOGRAPHY

Curtis, Michael. *No State Shall Abridge: The Fourteenth Amendment and the Bill of Rights.* Durham, NC: Duke University Press, 1988. A strong argument for the case that the Fourteenth Amendment was intended to incorporate the Bill of Rights.

Foner, Eric. *Reconstruction: America's Unfinished Revolution, 1863–1877.* New York: Harper & Row, 1988. The definitive study of the Reconstruction era and the first major expansion of the power of the federal government.

Dye, Thomas. *American Federalism.* Lexington, MA: Lexington Books, 1990. One of the better recent studies of the operations of the federal system.

Grodzins, Morton. *The American System.* Chicago: Rand McNally, 1966. A standard study of the operations of the federal system.

Nelson, William. *The Fourteenth Amendment: From Political Principle to Judicial Doctrine.* Cambridge, MA: Harvard University Press, 1988. A balanced analysis of the debate on the intent of the framers of the Fourteenth Amendment and the Bill of Rights, and the relationship of their intent to federalism.

Riker, William. *Federalism, Origin, Operation and Significance.* Boston: Little, Brown, 1964. An important study whose thesis is that federalism in the United States operates to limit freedom and benefit southern racists.

NOTES

1. Robert Bork, *The Tempting of America: The Seduction of the Law* (New York: Free Press, 1990): 52–53. Bork's nomination to the Court was defeated 58 to 42.

2. William Riker, *Federalism: Origins, Operation and Significance* (Boston: Little, Brown, 1964): 140.
3. Ibid., pp. 132–33.
4. Ibid., p. 155.
5. On the great black migration from south to north between the 1920s and the 1960s, see Neil Flingstein, *Going North: Migration of Blacks and Whites from the South 1900–1950* (New York: Academic Press, 1981), and James Grossman, *Land of Hope: Chicago, Black Southerners and the Great Migration* (Chicago: University of Chicago Press, 1989).
6. Jean Bodin's political theory and idea of sovereignty are discussed in George Sabine, *A History of Political Theory*, 4th ed. (Hinsdale, IL: Dryden Press, 1973): 377–84.
7. Max Farand, *The Records of the Federal Constitutional Convention* (New Haven, CT: Yale University Press, 1937), vol. 1, cited in Riker, *Federalism*, p. 22.
8. Of the 180 plus governments in the world, about seventeen are federal—mostly large nations like Australia, Canada, India, and Nigeria.
9. The most famous proponent of this view in American history is South Carolina's Senator John C. Calhoun in his doctrine of "concurrent majorities," which argues that on legislation affecting the interests of the states, both congressional and state legislative majorities should be required. In other words, the states should have a veto over federal laws affecting the state's vital interests. See Calhoun's *A Disquisition on Government*, edited by C. G. Post (New York: Liberal Arts Press, 1963).
10. *U.S. Term Limits, Inc. et al. v. Thornton et al.* #93-1456 (slip opinion) 1995. A slip opinion is a preliminary draft of a decision issued prior to formal publication.
11. Ibid., p. 2.
12. Ibid., p. 3. Justice Thomas contends that the framers deleted the reference to the states in the Preamble because they were not certain that all the states would ratify the Constitution.
13. Ibid., p. 1.
14. Ibid., p. 1.
15. See Jack L. Walker's classic article on this topic, "The Diffusion of Innovation among the American States," *American Political Science Review* 63 (September 1969): 880–99.
16. See E. E. Schattsneider, *The Semi-Sovereign People* (New York: Holt, Rinehart and Winston, 1960); Grant McConnell, *Private Power and American Democracy* (New York: Vintage Books, 1966); and Woodrow Wilson, *Congressional Government: A Study in American Politics* (Gloucester, MA: Peter Smith, 1885, 1973).
17. Wilson, *Congressional Government*, p. 77.
18. Schattsneider, *The Semi-Sovereign People*.
19. Riker, *Federalism*, p. 144.
20. Eric Foner, *Reconstruction: America's Unfinished Revolution, 1863–1877* (New York: Harper & Row, 1988): 251.
21. Ibid.; see especially chaps. 6–10.
22. On the New Deal, see William Leuchtenburg, *Franklin D. Roosevelt and the New Deal* (New York: Crowell, 1967), and Otis Graham, *An Encore for Reform: The Old Progressives and the New Deal* (New York: Oxford, 1967).

23. Foner, *Reconstruction*, p. 34.
24. Fred Friendly and Martha Elliot, *The Constitution: That Delicate Balance* (New York: McGraw-Hill, 1984): 18.
25. *The Slaughterhouse Cases*, 16 Wall (83 U.S.) 26 (1873) as reprinted in Kermit Hall, William Wiecek, and Paul Finkelman, eds., *American Legal History: Cases and Materials* (New York: Oxford University Press, 1991): 240.
26. Ibid., p. 240.
27. William Nelson, *The Fourteenth Amendment: From Political Principle to Judicial Doctrine* (Cambridge, MA: Harvard University Press, 1988): 96.
28. Friendly and Elliot, *That Delicate Balance*, p. 18.
29. In 1833 the Supreme Court in *Barron v. Baltimore* held that the Bill of Rights applied only to the federal government.
30. See, for example, Michael Curtis, *No State Shall Abridge: The Fourteenth Amendment and the Bill of Rights* (Durham: Duke University Press, 1988). This is also Foner's view in *Reconstruction*, pp. 251–61.
31. Charles Fairman, "Does the Fourteenth Amendment Incorporate the Bill of Rights: The Original Understanding," *Stanford Law Review* 2 (1949): 5–139.
32. Nelson, *The Fourteenth Amendment*, chap. 1.
33. The term *pernicious* is used by Hall, Wiecek, and Finkelman in *American Legal History* to describe the opinion; p. 241.
34. *The Civil Rights Cases*, 109 U.S. 3(1883) as reprinted in Hall, Wiecek, and Finkelman, p. 241.
35. Ibid., p. 140.
36. *Lochner v. New York* 198 U.S. 45 (1905).
37. Traditionally, the idea of due process of law as it is found in the Fifth and Fourteenth Amendments was *procedural*—that a person would have a fair trial and hearing. *Lochner* and similar decisions introduced the notion of *substantive* due process—the idea that the substance of a legislative act in and of itself could be unfair and thus a violation of due process.
38. *Gitlow v. New York* 268 U.S. 652 (1952). Benjamin Gitlow was a communist who advocated violent revolution. He was convicted under New York's criminal anarchy law. In deciding the case, however, the Court did not overturn his conviction but simply made the theoretical point that the free speech clause applied to the states.
39. Another reason that the commerce clause rather than the Fourteenth Amendment was used is that it permitted the leaders of the Senate to refer the bill to the Commerce Committee (which was chaired by Senator Warren Magnuson, a pro-civil rights liberal from Washington) rather than the Judiciary Committee, which was chaired by James Eastland, a racist, white supremacist from Mississippi. See Robert Loevy, *Hubert Humphrey and the Civil Rights Act of 1964: First Person Accounts of Congressional Enactment of the Law That Ended Racial Segregation* (Albany: State University of New York Press, 1996).
40. *Heart of Atlanta Motel, Inc. v. United States*, 379 U.S. 241 85 S.CT., 348 (1964).
41. *New York v. United States*, 505 U.S. 144 (1995).
42. Justice Stevens's reference to McCulloch is to *McCulloch v. Maryland* (4 Wheaton 316), decided in 1819. This case, along with *Marbury v. Madison* (1 Cranch, 137, 1813), in which the Court first asserted its power of judicial review,

is one of the landmark cases in the development of constitutional jurisprudence in the United States. In *McCulloch* the Court established two fundamental principles that Thomas's dissent appears to challenge. The first is the doctrine of implied powers, which asserts that Congress has powers beyond those expressly listed in Article 1, Section 8; second is the doctrine of the supremacy of federal laws over those enacted by the states.

43. *United States v. Lopez*, #93-1260, 1995 (slip opinion).
44. *Pennsylvania v. Union Gas* 491, U.S. 1, 24 (1989).
45. *Seminole Tribe of Florida v. Florida et al.* #94-12, 1996 (slip opinion).
46. Linda Greenhouse, "States Are Given New Legal Shield by Supreme Court," *New York Times on the Web* (June 24, 1999).

PART II

Political Behaviorism

CHAPTER 3

Political Culture

In political science, *political culture* is generally understood in terms of "psychological or subjective orientations towards politics."[1] Specifically, political culture refers to political orientations—attitudes toward the political system and attitudes toward the role of the individual in the system. Simply put, the concept refers to the individual's attitudes, beliefs, and values about politics and the political system.

The concept of political culture has been divided into three components: (1) a *cognitive* component—knowledge and beliefs about political reality; (2) an *affective* component—feelings with respect to politics, political leaders, and institutions; and (3) an *evaluative* component—one's commitment to political values and ideas.[2]

THE CONCEPT OF POLITICAL CULTURE AND THE INVISIBILITY OF AFRICAN AMERICANS

The concept of political culture in modern political science was invented by Almond and Verba in their classic study, *The Civic Culture*, a book comparing political cultures across five nations.[3] In this original study, blacks were invisible.[4] Almond writes: "Our American sample yielded only under a hundred black respondents, hardly representative of the black population. Hence, we failed to deal with the political attitudes of American blacks."[5]

In evaluating this pioneering empirical work on the concept, one analyst declares, "One major omission from the description of American politics in *The Civic Culture*, which seems rather glaring in retrospect is the absence of any separate treatment of the political culture of America's black minority."[6] He concludes with the observation: "The omission of a control variable as important in the American political context as race was a costly sacrifice for the sake of comparability as the events of the subsequent decade made clear."[7] Thus, in its initial formation and operationalization, the African American political subculture did not appear, and in its second reincarnation or "renaissance," no portrait of the African American political subculture was visible.[8]

But this did not happen simply because political scientists were oblivious to the matter of race. David Easton, between the initial formation of the concept and its subsequent reformulation, offers new insights. His redefinition of the concept

> acknowledges that various subgroups in the political system distinguished by race, ethnicity, language, religion and the like may be regulated by different normative and value systems and conceptions of authority, and these are regarded as political subcultures. Thus, a *subculture or political subculture* refers to patterns that are dominant within the respective subgroups, but which other members of the system may choose to ignore and reject without remorse, guilt, shame, condemnation, or fear of sanctions. In short, there is not a single homogeneous political culture but a composite of several subculture variations.[9]

THE LITERATURE ON THE AFRICAN AMERICAN POLITICAL CULTURE

Not all political scientists have avoided investigating how race and political culture linked and intersected with each other to shape African American political behavior. There is a small but growing body of literature that has (1) defined the concept, (2) explicated some of the essential component parts, and (3) provided a residual empirical testing of some of the component parts of African American political culture. This literature tended to explore the concept by observing conventional African American political behavior. However, a recent study of the 1992 Los Angeles riots postulated and then demonstrated that the African American political culture influences, informs, and impacts unconventional political behavior as well, and that manifestations of these influences can be found in the political attitudes of individual African Americans.[10]

What is African American political culture? Currently, it "is composed of both intrapsychic and external systemic factors that originate from elements both inside and outside of the black community."[11] A recent theoretical work by Professor Charles Henry added to the definitional equation by asserting that this culture places "its emphasis on identity and self-respect and . . . [that it is] coded in a black church tradition that blends a sacred and secular vision."[12]

Earlier, several African American social scientists like W. E. B. Du Bois and Ralph Bunche had suggested as one measurable component of African American political culture, *political consciousness*—that is, the supporting of African American political candidates, organizing African American political parties, holding state and national political conventions, and forming political caucuses and leagues. Speaking of this self-conscious type of political activity, Ralph Bunche said, "The Negro is very much a political animal and . . . his political urges will find expression in other channels whenever he is deprived of participation in the usual political processes."[13]

Two African American political scientists, Charles Hamilton and Matthew Holden, delineated additional component parts of the African American political culture, including the importance of the spoken word.[14] African American political rhetoric, or what David Howard-Pitney calls the African American Jeremiad (political sermon), has been demonstrated to be an essential element in the African American political culture and it has a significant and influential impact on African American political behavior.[15]

To the components of (1) political consciousness and (2) political sermons, Holden added the element of political factionalism. This is the force that works against group unity—contending, contentious, and clashing ideologies such as nationalism versus integration.[16] Furthermore, Holden identified political opposition to racism as a central component of the African American political culture. And culturalist Maulana Karenga has mapped out the specific features of oppositional politics in the community's political culture as they were expressed in the rhetoric of Malcolm X.[17]

Beyond the literature on defining the African American political culture concept and specifying its component parts, there are the efforts to measure the concept empirically. Robert Smith and Richard Seltzer used a residual measurement technique to show that elements of African American political culture existed in African American mass political attitudes.[18]

Smith and Seltzer found three elements of African American political culture that distinguishes it from the culture of whites. First, blacks of all social classes, to a greater degree than white people, were alienated or distrustful of the government and societal institutions as well as suspicious or distrustful of the motives of other individuals. Second, blacks of all social classes were more religious than whites. Third, blacks were distinctively a liberal group, especially on issues of the economy and the welfare state.[19]

Along with the empirical study of Smith and Seltzer, some equally interesting theoretical work is emerging. An exploration of the 1992 Los Angeles riots survey, for example, revealed the possibility of not only a linkage between riot behavior and community values and norms, but also a strong correlation between political attitudes, the resultant behavior, and the African American political culture. This research suggested that the African American political culture shapes both conventional and unconventional community behavior, such as riots, protest demonstrations, strikes, marches, and protest theater.[20] Thus, both theoretical and empirical efforts are under way on the concept. And when this literature is seen in a collective fashion and then synthesized to expose its common denominator, one sees that the African American political culture contains both supportive and opposition values and beliefs in regard to the American political system.

THE AFRICAN AMERICAN POLITICAL CULTURE: AN EMPIRICAL ESTIMATION

In modern political science, most concepts must have some empirical estimation of their viability if they are to be useful in explicating political behavior. This means that manifestations of the concept under study will appear in the mass political attitudes of African Americans. This crucial assumption is built on the existence of culture bearing and transmitting institutions. The African American community has continually created and generated such institutions of different varieties and successes. Karenga states that Malcolm X was such an institution because he taught African Americans oppositional politics.[21] An earlier work on the African American political culture suggested that men like L. H. Stanton and Clarence Holte, founder and editor of *National Scene*, a monthly black newspaper magazine supplement, operated as culture-bearing institutions.[22] Others have included Martin Luther King, Jr., as well as his national holiday. In fact, if cultural values are to circulate within the political community, culture-bearing institutions must be present and operative. In addition, these institutions must absorb and reject certain features out of the social milieu from which they emerge and develop their own version of the mix of cultural values for transmission. Finally, these institutions need not be permanent or strong institutions to have an impact; rather, they can be fragile, transient, and inconsistent.

Therefore, if we begin with a search for the initial component of political culture—that is, the *cognitive aspect*—it should be sought through survey questions that seek to tap into and reveal the racial consciousness of the African American community. Recently, three national surveys of the African American community asked questions that probed the nature of racial consciousness in mass attitudes.

The first of these were two National Black Election Studies (NBES) conducted in 1984 and 1988. In Table 3.1, we see African American political culture directly, with racial consciousness being the component. The table shows at least three aspects of this consciousness: (1) as it relates to the African American community itself, (2) as it relates to the community's political participation, and (3) as it relates to African American polit-

———————— TABLE 3.1 ————————
The Racial Component (in Percentages) of the African American Political Culture: The National Black Election Study—1984 and 1988

| Aspect of | Years | |
Racial Consciousness	1984	1988
Community Consciousness		
Common Fate for Blacks:	Do you think what happens generally to black people in this country will have something to do with what happens in your life?	
Yes	69.3%	69.6%
No	24.7	21.9
Missing Data	6.0	8.5
Political Consciousness		
Black Vote Makes Difference in Presidential Election:	If enough vote, they can make a difference in who gets elected president.	
Agree Strongly	70.8%	64.7%
Agree Somewhat	16.7	15.8
Disagree Somewhat	5.5	7.6
Disagree Strongly	5.2	5.0
Missing Data	1.7	6.8
Electoral Consciousness		
Vote for Black Candidates:	Blacks should always vote for black candidates when they run.	
Strongly Agree	4.6	7.3
Agree	9.4	12.6
Disagree	39.5	38.8
Strongly Disagree	20.2	19.7
Missing Data	26.3	21.6

Source: National Black Election Panel Study, 1984 and 1988. University of Michigan, Institute for Social Research, Ann Arbor.

ical candidates. Using specific questions that tap these elements, the researchers found substantial empirical support at the individual attitudinal level for this aspect of African American political culture.

In both the 1984 and 1988 elections the community and political consciousness aspects of the culture remained very high and positive. Individuals revealed in their attitudes that the community had a common fate and that voting in presidential elections could make a major difference. (By the second term of the Reagan presidency this belief in the impact of presidential voting was somewhat reduced.)

In terms of electoral consciousness, individual attitudes revealed that black candidates come under scrutiny and that voting for them is not considered the only way to express one's voting behavior. The findings here are consistent with the findings about political consciousness. Voting is important to enhance one's community, but the road to empowerment does not rest solely on supporting black candidates.

Overall, the empirical evidence in Table 3.1 strongly suggests empirical support for the cognitive component of the African American political culture. Racial consciousness is a part of the community's political culture through its attitudes, and this consciousness is based more in the community than in the individual.

Another national survey is the 1993 National Black Politics Survey (NBPS). This survey reveals individual attitudes manifesting the cognitive component of the political culture. Table 3.2 reveals that three-fourths (75%) of all African Americans see themselves linked by a common fate. This shows a very strong sense of community consciousness.

Two-thirds of the community sees the need for political involvement, especially if it provides black political control. Finally, there is the element of electoral consciousness: One-fourth of the community (26%) feels there should be a "racial vote," that blacks should always vote for African American candidates irrespective of ideology, character, issues, and/or past service to the community. Three-fourths of the community disagree with the idea of a "racial vote."

Each of these three aspects of racial consciousness demonstrates that at least one component of the political culture concept is working to shape African American political behavior. And both surveys done in the 1980s as well as the 1993 survey provide empirical evidence for this component.

The second component, the affective component of the African American political culture, should appear in individual-level mass attitudes that express feelings, sentiments, and emotions about presidents, Congress, the courts, the bureaucracy, political parties, laws, and public policies. Among questions related to these political entities, items on presidential approval have occurred with the greatest frequency in national polls and surveys. The Gallup organization,which first asked the public in 1933 if they approved of the president's performance, included too few African Americans in early samples for reliable estimates.[23] Analysis of these approval data have shown that

> presidents do not appeal equally to all groups in the public. Each of the presidents . . . has experienced a different pattern of public support. There has been a considerable range in both the levels and the volatility of presidential approval and each president has had sources of special strength and weakness in support among particular segments of the public.[24]

─────────────────────────── **TABLE 3.2** ───────────────────────────

The Racial Consciousness Component (in Percentages) of the African American Political Culture: The National Black Election Study—1993

Aspect of Racial Consciousness	**Year** 1993
Community Consciousness	
Common Fate for Blacks:	Do you think what happens generally to black people in this country will have something to do with what happens in your life?
Yes	75.0%
No	21.2
Don't Know	3.2
Not Applicable	.6
Political Consciousness	
Black Political Involvement:	Blacks should have control over the government in most black communities.
Strongly Agree	23.3%
Agree	42.0
Disagree	25.5
Strongly Disagree	4.8
Don't Know/Don't Care	3.5
Refused/Not Applicable	.8
Electoral Consciousness	
Vote for Black Candidates:	Blacks should always vote for black candidates when they run.
Strongly Agree	8.8%
Agree	17.2
Disagree	54.6
Strongly Disagree	17.5
Don't Care/Don't Know	1.3
Not Applicable	.7

Source: National Black Politics Survey, 1993, University of Chicago.

In terms of partisan realities and support, this is especially true of African Americans. During the Eisenhower years, for example, the "differences between racial groups . . . were much smaller than under Reagan . . . [and] we know that extreme racial polarization is not inherent in a Republican president."[25]

A recent analysis of these data covering the period 1961 to 1990 demonstrated that "the Democratic party and Democratic presidents could count on substantial support from the black community until the early 1990's, [and that large] racial differences in presidential approval" existed in the Carter, Reagan, and Bush administrations.[26]

Turning to the third and final component of the political culture concept, the "evaluative" one, evidence of this should appear in answers to questions about "trust" in government as well as how well government responds to individuals' needs and demands. The National Election Studies (NES) cumulative data (1952–1994), aggregated by decades for presidential and congressional years, provides fairly reliable estimates. In addition, this procedure gives a time dimension to the empirical results. Table 3.3 indi-

TABLE 3.3

The Evaluative (Trust) Component (in Percentages) of the African American Political Culture: The National Black Election Study—1994

	Levels of Trust[a]			
Presidential Years	1964–68	1972–76	1980–84–88	1992–96
Low Trust	19%	71%	61%	58%
Moderate Trust	11	10	12	17
High Trust	70	19	27	24
Congressional Years		1974–78		1994
Low Trust		65%		67%
Moderate Trust		13		13
High Trust		23		21

[a]Trust is measured by how respondents answered the following question: How much do you think you can trust the government in Washington to do what is right: just about always, most of the time, some of the time, or almost never?

Source: National Black Election Studies Cumulative File, Presidential and Congressional Years, University of Michigan, Institute for Social Research, Ann Arbor.

cates that the trust of African Americans in the American political system peaked in the sixties, the period of heightened civil rights legislation; it dropped in the Nixon-Ford years; and it reached something of a plateau in the 1980s. Trust in the system was lowest in the Nixon-Ford years and has stabilized in the 1980s.

Trust during congressional election years reveals a similar but slightly different pattern. As during the presidential years, trust in the system is generally low; however, unlike the presidential years, this low level of trust is consistent in all years observed for congressional elections, both in 1974–78 and in 1994.

In the past, studies of African American trust have been explained only in terms of individual-level variables, particularly political alienation and cynicism. Academic observers have written that

> studies of political cynicism or distrust frequently focus on the attitudes of black Americans. Political distrust by blacks is not particularly surprising when much of the political attitude literature links negativism with social and economic deprivation. . . . [M]ore recently, however, blacks' confidence in the federal government has fallen to the level of whites while blacks' general political trust lags well behind that of whites.[27]

Many in political science stress political alienation as the cause of this declining confidence, claiming that African Americans are the most unstable and volatile group in the polity. As such, claim such writers, they are dangerous to the polity itself. Not only is such reasoning fallacious, but it also rests on psychological determinants and not systemic ones like governmental responsiveness.

As one looks at a systemic determinant like governmental responsiveness to the African American community, data in Table 3.4 show a clear and significant correlation between low and high responsiveness by government and low and high trust among African Americans. The highest system responsiveness, which took place in the sixties, is

———————————————————— **TABLE 3.4** ————————————————————

The Evaluative (Responsiveness) Component (in Percentages) of the African American Political Culture: The National Black Election Study—1964–1980

	Levels of Responsiveness[a]		
Presidential Years	1964–68	1972–76	1980
Low	19%	21%	24%
Moderate	40	60	48
High	52	19	28
Congressional Years			1970–74–78
Low			24%
Moderate			52
High			23

[a]Responsiveness is measured by how respondents answered a question asking whether they thought the government in Washington paid attention to people like themselves.

Source: National Black Election Studies Cumulative File, Presidential and Congressional Years, University of Michigan, Institute for Social Research, Ann Arbor.

also the period of highest trust; the period in which low responsiveness was greatest closely parallels the period of lowest trust. After 1980, the NES dropped the responsiveness question from its survey; consequently, following the two variables over time is impossible. Because of this omission, future researchers will probably revert to looking for the causes and determinants of African American trust in government in individual and intrapsychic causes instead of systemic ones, such as government performance and responsiveness.

We have found empirical evidence for all three component parts of the political culture concept. We know that at the very least manifestations of the African American political culture tend to surface in the mass attitudes of the community. Second, we can infer from the empirical data that the African American political culture influences and impacts African American political behavior.

SELECTED BIBLIOGRAPHY

Almond, Gabriel, and Sidney Verba. *The Civic Culture.* Princeton, NJ: Princeton University Press, 1963. The classic behavioral study, comparing the political cultures of five nations.

Almond, Gabriel, and Sidney Verba, eds. *The Civic Culture Revisited.* Boston: Little, Brown, 1980. A conceptual and methodological reexamination of the concept by an international group of scholars.

Divine, Donald. *The Political Culture of the United States.* Boston: Little, Brown, 1972. A pioneering behavioralist effort to locate the component parts of the nation's political culture.

Henry, Charles. *Culture and African American Politics.* Bloomington: Indiana University Press, 1990. An examination of the roots and nature of African American culture, focusing on religion and music.

Jones, Leroi. *Blues People: The Negro Experience in White America and the Music That Developed from It.* New York: William Morrow, 1963. An influential study of the centrality of music in African American culture.

Smith, Robert C., and Richard Seltzer. *Race, Class and Culture: A Study in Afro-American Mass Opinion.* Albany: State University of New York Press, 1992. An effort to identify empirically certain components of African American political culture.

Walton, Hanes, Jr. "African American Political Culture: The Moral Voice and Perspective in the Recent Urban Riots." In Hanes Walton, Jr., ed., *African American Power and Politics: The Political Context Variable.* New York: Columbia University Press, 1997. Explores and delineates the existence of the African American political culture in nonconventional political behavior.

NOTES

1. Glenda Patrick, "Political Culture," in Giovani Sartori, ed., *Social Science Concepts: A Systematic Analysis* (Beverly Hills: Sage, 1984): 266.
2. Ibid., pp. 273–85.
3. Gabriel Almond and Sidney Verba, *The Civic Culture: Political Attitudes in Five Nations* (Princeton, NJ: Princeton University Press, 1963). The five nations were the United States, the United Kingdom, West Germany, Mexico, and Italy.
4. For some of the more interesting studies of political culture in the United States, see Donald Devine, *The Political Culture of the United States* (Boston: Little, Brown, 1972), and Daniel Elazar, *American Federalism: A View from the States* (New York: Crowell, 1972).
5. Gabriel Almond, "The Intellectual History of the Civic Culture Concept," in Gabriel Almond and Sidney Verba, eds., *The Civic Culture Revisited* (Boston: Little, Brown, 1980): 23.
6. Alan Abramowitz, "The United States: Political Culture under Stress," in Almond and Verba, *The Civic Culture,* pp. 180–81.
7. Ibid.
8. William Reisinger, "The Renaissance of a Rubric: Political Culture as Concept and Theory," *International Journal of Public Opinion Research* 7 (Winter, 1995): 348.
9. Quoted in Patrick, "Political Culture," p. 272.
10. Hanes Walton, Jr., "African American Political Culture: The Moral Voice and Perspective in the Recent Urban Riots," in Hanes Walton, Jr., ed., *African American Power and Politics: The Political Context Variable* (New York: Columbia University Press, 1997): 93–108.
11. Hanes Walton, Jr., *Invisible Politics: Black Political Behavior* (Albany: State University of New York Press, 1985): 26.
12. Charles Henry, *Culture and African American Politics* (Bloomington: Indiana University Press, 1990): 107.

13. Quoted in Walton, *Invisible Politics*, p. 27.
14. Matthew Holden, Jr., *The Politics of the Black "Nation"* (New York: Chandler, 1973); Charles Hamilton, *The Black Political Experience in America* (New York: Putnam, 1973).
15. David Howard-Pitney, *The Afro-American Jeremiad: Appeals for Justice in America* (Philadelphia: Temple University Press, 1990).
16. Holden, *The Politics of the Black "Nation,"* pp. 43–95.
17. Maulana Karenga, "The Oppositional Logic of Malcolm X: Differentialism, Engagement and Resistance," *Western Journal of Black Studies* 17 (Spring, 1993): 6–16.
18. Robert C. Smith and Richard Seltzer, *Race, Class, and Culture: A Study in Afro-American Mass Opinion* (Albany: State University of New York Press, 1992). This study used the National Opinion Research Center's 1987 General Social Survey, which included an oversample of 544 blacks.
19. Ibid.
20. Hanes Walton, Jr., "African American Political Culture: The Moral Voice and Perspective in the Recent Urban Riots," in Walton, ed., *African American Power and Politics: The Political Context Variable*, pp. 93–108.
21. Karenga, "The Oppositional Logic of Malcolm X."
22. See Walton, *Invisible Politics*, pp. 36–39, and Hanes Walton, Jr., "The Literary Works of a Black Bibliophile: Clarence L. Holte," *Western Journal of Black Studies* 1 (December, 1977): 286–297.
23. Frederick Mosteller et al., *The Pre-Election Polls of 1948* (New York: Social Science Research Council, 1949).
24. George Edward, II, and Alec Gallup, *Presidential Approval: A Sourcebook* (Baltimore: Johns Hopkins University Press, 1990): 188.
25. Ibid.
26. Michael Dawson, "African American Political Opinion: Volatility in the Reagan-Bush Era," in Walton, *African American Power and Politics*, chap. 8.
27. Michael Gant and Norman Luttbeg, *American Electoral Behavior: 1952–1988* (Chicago: Peacock, 1991): 131–32.

CHAPTER 4

Political Socialization

Political culture refers to attitudes, values, and beliefs about politics and the political system. *Political socialization* refers to the ongoing process by which individuals acquire these attitudes, values, and beliefs.[1] In simple terms, political socialization refers to the processes of political learning. For purposes of studying this process, political scientists usually center their attention on what are called *agents of socialization*—those mechanisms by which individuals acquire their attitudes, beliefs, and values.[2] The agents include *family, church, school, peer groups,* the *media* and *political events.*

GUNNAR MYRDAL AND THE POLITICAL SOCIALIZATION OF AFRICAN AMERICANS

In his influential study, *An American Dilemma: The Negro Problem and Modern Deocracy,* Gunnar Myrdal suggested that the political socialization process in black America was dysfunctional because it failed to socialize blacks into the white "mainstream" political culture. This is because, Myrdal argued, the agents of socialization were dysfunctional. Of these agents he wrote:

> The instability of the Negro family, the inadequacy of educational facilities for Negroes, the emotionalism in the Negro church, the insufficiency and unwholesomeness of Negro recreational activity, the plethora of Negro sociable organizations, the narrowness of interests of the average Negro, the provincialism of his political speculation, the high Negro crime rate, the cultivation of the arts to the neglect of other fields, superstition, personality difficulties, and other characteristics are mainly forms of social pathology which, for the most part, are created by caste pressure.[3]

Myrdal's contention that the socialization process in black America was dysfunctional or "pathological" was based on his view that "it is to the advantage of American Negroes as individuals and as a group to become assimilated into American culture, to acquire the traits held in esteem by dominant whites."[4] Although Myrdal noted that certain features of the African American culture and certain agents were positive (mainly the black media), he wrote, "It does not gainsay our assumption that *here in America*, American culture is 'highest' in the pragmatic sense and that adherence to it is practical for any individual or group which is not strong enough to change it" (emphasis by Myrdal).[5]

Since it was clear that blacks were not strong enough to change the dominant culture, they should direct their socialization toward white mainstream culture at the expense of the African American subculture.

THE LITERATURE ON AFRICAN AMERICAN POLITICAL SOCIALIZATION

Myrdal's thesis prevailed and became very influential. Very few of the early socialization studies analyzed African Americans. As a group and as individuals, they were simply omitted.[6] And when such studies did appear, the majority of them offered empirical support for the Myrdal thesis. These studies supported Myrdal's assertion by showing that virtually all the socialization agents in the African American community were dysfunctional.[7]

However, a few of these early studies did find some different realities about African American political socialization that denied the Myrdal thesis. Indeed, in some of these few positive studies one could discern that African American political socialization was different from that of whites, and that "the process has at least three steps, including *resocialization* as well as *counter socialization.*"[8] One of the central agents of socialization in the black community was the church and its religion. Researchers theorized that "in the black community, in sharp contrast to the white, the church plays the dominant role in the socialization process. The family, the school and peer groups in that order are the next significant agents."[9] Among the reasons for the prominence of the church are the (oral tradition and moralism of the political culture) and the political activism of the church.[10] A third factor is that the church and its religion may provide a source and foundation for oppositional politics. God can be seen as a higher power than the institutions of slavery and segregation.

Beyond the literature alluding to different socializing agents in the African American community, such as the church and religion, a recent study uncovered "protest resignations" as a socializing device.[11] In both high appointive positions and local electoral ones, African American officeholders have resigned to protest federal and local policies of discrimination, segregation, and unequal treatment for the African American community. Such individual efforts of courage and sacrifice stress to other members of the African American community the need to stand firm and not compromise on their political rights and the rights of the African American community.

Usually in American society, when African American political rights have been secured through rights-based coalitions that built political majorities and attained civil rights bills, objections and opposition have arisen from the white community. As a result of these frequently strenuous and adamant refusals of some whites (particularly in the South) to comply with the law, federal, state, and local governments have often given in and asked African Americans to compromise their rights—at least temporarily. Occasionally, some African American leaders, like the current conservatives ones, have agreed and encouraged such policies.[12] *Protest resignations resocialize the community to resist and oppose such political compromises.*

There are reasons for the existence and use of these different and unique types of socializing agents in the African American community. Myrdal correctly observed that "different" socializing tactics have been and are

> the result of the rising Negro protest that there is in nearly the entire Negro population, a theoretical belief that Negroes are just as highly endowed with inherent capabilities and propensities as are white people. An emphatic assertion of equality of the Negro people's potentialities is a central theory in the propagation of Negro race consciousness and race pride.[13]

With this assertion, Myrdal embraced what he had earlier denied and declared impossible: African Americans socializing themselves toward an oppositional posture to racism, segregation, and discrimination. His embrace continues: "It cannot be doubted that the spirit of American Negroes in all classes . . . [is] the protest motive . . . [and it] is still rising. . . . Its existence, its popular spread, and its content are a testimony of Negro unrest. Its cumulative effect in spurring race consciousness must be tremendous."[14] Thus "defeatism and racial inferiority, cannot be said publicly. The protest motive does not allow it. No Negro leader could ever preach it. No Negro newspaper could print it. It must be denied eagerly and persistently."[15]

Therefore, despite all the alleged weaknesses which Myrdal claimed for each of the "agents" of African American political socialization, the realities are that these "agents" socialized inside the African American community *an oppositional political culture* and new subcultural agents of socialization. And beyond the church, religion, and "protest resignations" as agents of socialization, there are others—for example, those of civil rights protests. Morris, Brown, and Hatchett write, "The Montgomery bus boycott was a ground-breaking political development. First, it endured for an entire year (381) days despite the intense opposition of the local white community. The long duration of the boycott maximized its local, regional and national influences and visibility."[16] In a word, it socialized: "From a political standpoint, the black community was never to be the same after the Montgomery bus boycott. Indeed, nonviolent movements against racial segregation began to emerge in other communities such as Tallahassee, Florida and Birmingham, Alabama even while the Montgomery movement was still in process."[17] Thus, scholars have concluded: "The movement itself was a tool of political socialization. Its mass tactics required people to learn and execute new forms of political behavior."[18]

But if the civil rights movement became a different agent of political socialization, so did the black power movement that followed. Morris, Hatchett, and Brown write,

> The black-power ideology signalled a more radical thrust in the movement. First, its proponents either relaxed or rejected the goal of racial integration. Second, the strategy of nonviolence was rejected in favor of self-defense and the view that change should be achieved by "any means necessary." Finally, black-power advocates either relaxed or rejected the assumption that the civil rights movement should have an interracial character.[19]

These assumptions differentiated this activity from the older civil rights movement, which was to be expected, given some of the failures and shortcomings of that movement.

After the black power movement,

> the riots became the main mechanism for the resocialization of blacks and the crystal-
> lization of the new nationalist ideology. And . . . the riots themselves were catalytic
> agents in the resocialization of both rioters and blacks as a whole. While a very small
> proportion of blacks . . . took part in the riots, a much larger proportion sympathized
> with the rioters and saw the riots as protest.[20]

This was not only true in the mid and late sixties, but it was true also in the Los Angeles riots of 1992.[21]

One can add to the different socializing agents not only the civil rights movement, the black power movement, and the riots but also cultural events and projects. "The visual, literary, and performing arts in black communities also began to focus on new images of blacks and black life that stemmed from the black power ideology."[22] The arts, which in the past had "concentrated on other issues . . . began to concentrate on black political issues and new images of black identity and culture"[23] (see Box 4.1).

When the black power movement peaked, as the civil rights movement had done before it, a new African American socializing agent appeared—African American Democratic presidential candidates. First came the 1972 presidential campaign of African American congresswoman Shirley Chisholm.[24] Her performance in the Democratic presidential primaries was unique and dramatic. Her effort galvanized thousands of women and African American Democrats.[25] Although the electoral dimension of the Chisholm campaign failed, its socializing influence was important.

In 1984 and 1988, civil rights activist the Reverend Jesse Jackson took a page from Chisholm and entered the Democratic presidential primaries. It was a sensation in the African American community,[26] and at the level of political socialization it generated significant grassroots political activities and local candidacies for office.[27] It also enlarged the number of registered voters. Thus, it socialized both masses and elites in the community.

In the aftermath of these presidential candidacies, a different socializing agent came in the form of the dramatic Million Man March in October 1995.[28] Led by the controversial black nationalist religious figure, Louis Farrakhan, the march brought more African Americans to Washington, D.C., than did King's 1963 March on Washington, and it sent numerous individuals back to their local communities committed and reinvigorated toward developing grassroots self-help organizations and programs.

But not all the different socializing agents that appear in the African American community are aimed at socializing the mainstream. In 1996, African Americans watched the "presidential" candidacy of Alan Keyes in the Republican presidential primaries. Keyes, the first African American to run in the Republican presidential primaries, presented himself as a far-right conservative ideologue.[29] And while he ran throughout the entire primary season, his impact on the African American community was negligible. He was not a major socializing agent. Moreover, his campaign is reminiscence of the 1992 failed attempt of former Virginia governor L. Douglas Wilder, who sought to run on the right as a neoconservative ideologue in the Democratic presidential primaries. Governor Wilder's right-of-center positions and proposed policies failed to socialize or mobilize the African American community, and Wilder dropped out of the primaries just before they started.[30]

=============================== **BOX 4.1** ===============================

African American Music as an Agent of Political Socialization

Many observers of African American culture have pointed to the important role played by music in the socialization process. African Americans have often been heard to say, "You can tell where black people are at any given moment by our music." The novelist James Baldwin once said, "It is only in his music that the Negro in America has been able to tell his story." The political scientist Charles Henry argues that music, especially the blues, is an important socialization agent in African American politics; historian Frank Kofsky has demonstrated a relationship between the revolution in jazz symbolized in the work of John Coltrane and the militant nationalism of Malcolm X; poet and musicologist Leroi Jones points historically to a relationship between black music and black politics; and music critic Nelson George argues that in the 1960s and 1970s rhythm and blues was inspired by and gave inspiration to the civil rights and black power movements.[a]

In a comprehensive study of black music as a political agent during the 1960s, Robert Walker carried out a content analysis of all 1,100 songs that appeared on *Billboard's* cumulative annual best-selling black (soul) listings from 1946 to 1972. Walker's hypothesis was that the events of the 1960s produced a distinctive race group consciousness and solidarity that was manifested in an increase in songs with a political message. His data show a steady increase in "message songs" beginning after 1957 and that a sustained increase of "inordinate proportions" occurred between 1966 and 1969, the peak years of the black movement. By comparing black to white music in this same period, Walker was able to show that this increase in message music was peculiar to black music.[b] Among the popular songs with a political message during this period were James Brown's "I'm Black and I'm Proud," the Temptations' "Message to the Black Man," Marvin Gaye's "Inner City Blues," B. B. King's "Why I Sing the Blues," and Curtis Mayfield's "We're a Winner." Mayfield's "We're a Winner" was thought to be so politically inflammatory that some black radio stations were urged not play it for fear it might cause riots in the summer of 1968.

From "Keep on Pushing" in the 1960s to "A New World Order" in the 1990s, Curtis Mayfield's music has consistently involved political messages or "sermons," often dealing with themes of freedom.

Today rap music may be playing a similar socializing role.[c] Several rap groups—Laguan, Movement EX, Paris, and Public Enemy—have been influenced by the Nation of Islam and its philosophy of black nationalism. Although they are not the dominant themes, issues of racism, joblessness, drugs, crime, police brutality, and the irrelevance of inner city education are the focus of some rap groups. There is also a militant spirit of rebellion and discontent, as in

(Continued)

BOX 4.1 Continued

Public Enemy's "Fight the Power," the theme song of Spike Lee's film "Do the Right Thing." Rap music of course also includes nonpolitical themes, and some of it is sexually explicit, sexist, and homophobic, but it also expresses signs of youthful rebellion and discontent, as did the music of the 1960s and 1970s.

[a]Charles Henry, *Culture and African American Politics* (Bloomington: Indiana University Press, 1990); Frank Kofsky, *Black Nationalism and the Revolution in Music* (New York: Pathfinder Press, 1970); Leroi Jones, *Blues People* (New York: Morrow, 1963); Nelson George, *The Death of Rhythm and Blues* (New York: Dutton, 1989).

[b]Robert Walker, "Soul and Society," Ph.D. dissertation, Stanford University, 1976.

[c]Houston Baker, *Black Studies, Rap and the Academy* (Chicago: University of Chicago Press, 1993).

Overall, not all the different socializing agents that emerge inside the African American community generate the same impact and influence; some, those on the right in particular, generate hardly any socializing tendencies at all. Yet these different agents of the political resocialization of African Americans are clearly visible and have an impact. The question is whether manifestations of these realities can be empirically identified from surveying mass African American attitudes. Professor Ronald Brown has attempted to do so in his work on religion, the church, and African American socialization.

AFRICAN AMERICAN POLITICAL SOCIALIZATION: AN EMPIRICAL ESTIMATION OF RELIGION AND THE CHURCH AS AGENTS

Professor Ronald Brown took the theory about the church and religion as African American socializing agents, reduced them to a psychological dimension, and placed them as testable propositions in questionnaire form in the two National Black Election Studies and the National Black Political Survey. Brown undertook these studies with a variety of different colleagues, but he has been the most consistent and persistent analyst of the religious attribute. In his first work, with colleagues Richard Allen and Michael Dawson, Brown stressed that an African American racial belief system existed and that religiosity influenced and socialized that belief system. Writing about this approach, Brown and his colleagues told "how belief systems in general and this belief system in particular help process, constrain, and bias one's interpretations of reality and influence social and political behavior." The article then shows how "religiosity . . . influences the content of individual African American belief systems."[31]

In their conclusion Brown and his colleagues said, "The replication of the belief system over time is reinforced by the socializing effects of such formal and informal institutions as the black church."[32] Hence, they hypothesized that "those who expressed a strong sense of religiosity will have a strong sense of racial identification and consciousness."[33] The empirical findings were unambiguous: "With respect to religiosity and black belief structure the results indicated as predicted; those scoring high on the religiosity construct are more likely to embrace black autonomy, to express a closeness to both mass and elite groups in the black community."[34] In short, the church and religion are agents of political socialization in the African American community (see Box 4.2).

In a second article, Brown and his colleagues sought to specify a measurement model that would reveal at the individual and attitudinal level the theory that the African American church has been the critical institution in the reproduction of African American beliefs and values as well as a prominent social and political institution in the black community.[35] The results indicate both a strong positive relationship between religiosity and voter participation and a strong relationship between religiosity and political participation.[36] And of all the variables measured, "religiosity had the largest effect on ✓ voting participation."[37]

In a third article, Brown and his colleague, Monica Wolford, wrote:

> It is the thesis of this article that the African-American religious culture socializes individuals to participate in activities that will improve the spiritual and national well-being of group members. This sense of personal obligation was nurtured in slavery, grew into adolescence during the reconstruction and pre-civil rights era; and reached maturity in the civil rights and black power era.[38]

BOX 4.2
The African American Church

Faith in God, the belief that "God will deliver us some day," has been described as the single most common theme in African American culture.[a] Given the central role of religion in black life, the church becomes the central political institution in the black community. Freedom is also central in the African American religious tradition. Lincoln and Mamiya write,

> A major aspect of black Christian belief is found in the importance given to the word "freedom." Throughout black history the term "freedom" has found deep religious resonance in the lives and hopes of African Americans. . . . In song, word and deed freedom has always been the superlative value of the black cosmos.[b]

African Americans are more religious than whites (measured by frequency of church attendance and prayer, and subjective identification with God), and religiously inclined blacks are more likely to vote and engage in other forms of political participation, such as lobbying.[c] The church historically has always been the central arena of the political activities of blacks, the place where the "struggle for power and the thirst for power could be satisfied."[d] In the United States today there are approximately 60,000 black churches, 50,000 clergy, and a membership of more than 17 million. These churches are organized into seven denominations that in turn are organized in a coalition called the Congress of National Black Churches.[e] Although in recent years white evangelical Christians have begun to use the church as a political base (forming the Christian Coalition led by the Reverend Pat Robertson, a 1988 Republican

(Continued)

BOX 4.2 Continued

candidate for president), the black church has always been politically conscious and active.[f] During the 1960s the largest black church denomination—the National Baptist Convention—was led by a conservative, anti-civil rights clergyman, the Reverend J. H. Jackson. Jackson's leadership was challenged by Dr. Martin Luther King, Jr., and other progressive ministers, and the black church became the principal base of the civil rights movement. Today, it is a principal base of political organizing and electoral campaigning, serving as an important source of organizing and fund-raising for Jesse Jackson's two presidential campaigns and as a platform for white politicians seeking the support and votes of African Americans.

Bill Clinton speaking at a black church in Baltimore, the Sunday before the 1998 midterm elections. The church is a major agent of political socialization and mobilization in the black community.

[a]Matthew Holden, Jr., *The Politics of the Black Nation* (New York: Chandler, 1973): 17.

[b]C. Eric Lincoln and Lawrence Mamiya, *The Black Church in the African American Experience* (Durham, NC: Duke University Press, 1990): 3–4.

[c]Robert C. Smith and Richard Seltzer, *Race, Class and Culture: A Study in Afro-American Mass Opinion* (Albany: State University of New York Press, 1992): 29–30, 126–28.

[d]E. Franklin Frazier, *The Negro Church in America* (New York: Schocken Books, 1964): 43.

[e]John Hurst Adams, "Stewardship and the Black Church," *Urban League Review* 9 (Summer 1985): 72–77.

[f]Lincoln and Mamiya, *The Black Church in the African American Experience.*

Brown and Wolford empirically demonstrated that the African American church and religion were a major political resource, and it was this resource operating as a socializing mechanism that accounted for "the persistent moderate to high levels of political action within the African American community."[39] It displaced and/or mediated the "low political efficacy" noted in some of the research on African American political behavior.[40] Finally in a fourth article Brown reported that "two different messages are presented at places of worship—one communicating civic awareness and the other promoting political activity. Greater exposure to the former tends to produce higher levels of racial identity, while exposure to the latter leads to greater perceptions of power imbalance among groups."[41]

Overall, the work of Brown and his several colleagues has established the religious attribute as a major independent variable in shaping African American political socialization and political behavior.[42]

SELECTED BIBLIOGRAPHY

Abramson, Paul. *The Political Socialization of Black Americans: A Critical Evaluation of Research on Efficacy and Trust.* New York: Free Press, 1977. A solid review and assessment of the early literature on black socialization.

Brown, Ronald, and Monica Wolford. "Religious Resources and African American Political Action." *National Political Science Review* 4 (1994): 30–48. A pathbreaking article charting the effects of religion and the church as agents of political socialization.

Conover, Pamela. "Political Socialization: Where's the Politics?" In William Crotty, ed., *Political Science: Looking to the Future, Political Behavior,* Vol. 3. Evanston, IL: Northwestern University Press, 1991. An overview of the origins and evolution of the concept.

Fendrich, James Max. *Ideal Citizens: The Legacy of the Civil Rights Movement.* Albany: State University of New York Press, 1993. A study of the long-term socializing effects of the civil rights movement.

George, Nelson. *The Death of Rhythm and Blues.* New York: Dutton, 1989. An analysis of the relationship between black music and the black movements of the 1960s and 1970s.

Lincoln, Eric C., and Lawrence Mamiya. *The Black Church and the African American Experience.* Durham, NC: Duke University Press, 1990. A comprehensive historical study of the role of the black church.

Morris, Aldon, Shirley Hatchett, and Ronald Brown. "The Civil Rights Movement and Black Political Socialization." In R. Siegel, ed., *Political Learning in Adulthood.* Chicago: University of Chicago Press, 1989. An excellent pioneering article demonstrating the impact and influence of ad hoc and transitory socializing agents in the African American community.

Woody, Jerome, and Renee Baker. "African American Political Socialization: The Protest Resignations of Councilpersons." In Hanes Walton, Jr., ed., *African American Power and Politics: The Political Context Variable.* New York: Columbia University Press, 1997. Explores the role of "protest resignations" as an agent of political socialization in the African American community.

NOTES

1. Pamela Johnston Conover, "Political Socialization: Where's the Politics," in William Crotty, ed., *Political Science: Looking to the Future. Political Behavior,* vol. 3 (Evanston: Northwestern University Press, 1991): 126.
2. Ibid.
3. Gunnar Myrdal, *An American Dilemma: The Negro Problem and Modern Democracy* (New York: Harper & Brothers, 1944): 929.

4. Ibid

5. Ibid

6. Walton, *Invisible Politics* (Albany: State University of New York Press, 1985): 45–47.

7. For an edited volume that includes many of these questionable studies, see Charles Bullock and Harrell Rogers, eds., *Black Political Attitudes* (Chicago: Markham, 1972).

8. Walton, *Invisible Politics,* p. 48.

9. Ibid.

10. Ibid.

11. Hanes Walton, Jr., Oliver Jones, Jr., and Pearl Ford, "African American Political Socialization: The Protest Resignations of Councilpersons Jerome Woody and Renee Baker," in Hanes Walton, Jr., ed., *African American Power and Politics: The Political Context Variable* (New York: Columbia University Press, 1997).

12. Ibid.

13. Myrdal, *An American Dilemma*, p. 758.

14. Ibid., p. 744.

15. Ibid., p. 758.

16. Aldon Morris, Shirley Hatchett, and Ronald Brown, "The Civil Rights Movement and Black Political Socialization," in R. S. Siegel, ed., *Political Learning in Adulthood* (Chicago: University of Chicago Press, 1989), p. 282.

17. Ibid.

18. Ibid., p. 284.

19. Ibid., p. 290.

20. Ibid., p. 292.

21. See Lawrence Bobo, Camille Zubrinsky, James Johnson, Jr., and Melvin Oliver, "Public Opinion Before and After a Spring of Discontent," in Mark Baldassare, ed., *The Los Angeles Riots: Lessons for the Urban Future* (Denver, CO: Westview Press, 1994): 103–134.

22. Morris, Hatchett, and Brown, "The Civil Rights Movement," p. 293. See also Michael Schwarz, *Visions of a Liberated Future: Black Arts Movement Writings* (New York: Thunder Mouth Press, 1989).

23. Morris, Hatchett, and Brown, "The Civil Rights Movement," p. 293.

24. Shirley Chisholm, *The Good Fight* (New York: Harper & Row, 1973).

25. Hanes Walton, Jr., "Black Female Presidential Candidates: Bass, Mitchell, Chisholm, Wright, Reid, Vans and Fulani," in Hanes Walton, Jr., ed., *Black Politics and Black Political Behavior: A Linkage Analysis* (Westport, CT: Praeger, 1994): 251–274.

26. On the Jackson campaigns, see Joseph McCormick and Robert C. Smith, "Through the Prism of Afro-American Culture: An Interpretation of the Jackson Campaign Style," in L. Barker and R. Walters, eds., *Jesse Jackson's Presidential Campaign: Challenge and Change in American Politics* (Urbana: University of Illinois Press, 1988): 96–107; Robert C. Smith, "From Insurgency toward Inclusion: The Jackson Campaigns of 1984 and 1988," in Barker and Walters, *Jesse Jackson's Presidential Campaign,* pp. 215–230. Ronald Walters, *Black Presidential Politics in America: A Strategic Approach* (Albany: State University of New

York Press, 1988). Lucius Barber, *Our Time Has Come* (Urbana: University of Illinois Press, 1989), and Charles P. Henry, *Jesse Jackson: The Search for Common Ground* (Oakland, CA: Black Scholar Press, 1991). Thomas Cavanah and Lorin Foster, *Jesse Jackson's Campaign: The Primaries and Caucuses* (Washington, DC: Joint Center for Political Studies, 1984).

27. Leslie McLemore and Mary Coleman, "The Jesse Jackson Campaign and the Institutionalization of Grass-Roots Politics: A Comparative Perspective," in Hanes Walton, Jr., ed., *Black Politics and Black Political Behavior: A Linkage Analysis* (Westport, CT: Praeger, 1994): 49–60.

28. Hanes Walton, Jr., "Public Policy Responses to the Million Man March," *The Black Scholar* 25 (Fall, 1995): 17–23. Hanes Walton, Jr., and Simone Green, "Voting Rights and the Million Man March: The Problem of Restoration of Voting Rights for Ex-Convicts," *African American Perspectives* (Winter, 1997): 68–74.

29. See Alan Keyes, "A Prophet in the Political Desert," in Ralph Hallow and Bradley O'Leary, *Presidential Follies: Those Who Would Be President and Those Who Should Think Again!* (Dallas, TX: Born Publishing, 1995): 102–109.

30. Paula D. McClain and Steven Tauber, "African American Presidential Candidate: The Failed Presidential Campaign of Governor L. Douglas Wilder," in Hanes Walton, Jr., *African American Power and Politics: The Political Context Variable* (New York: Columbia University Press, 1996), chap. 19.

31. Richard Allen, Michael Dawson, and Ronald Brown, "A Schema-Based Approach to Modeling an African American Racial Belief System," *American Political Science Review* 83 (June, 1989): 421. ✓

32. Ibid., p. 422.

33. Ibid., p. 425.

34. Ibid., p. 433.

35. Michael Dawson, Ronald Brown, and Richard Allen, "Racial Belief Systems, Religious Guidance, and African American Political Participation," *National Political Science Review* 2 (1990): 25.

36. Ibid., p. 36.

37. Ibid., p. 37.

38. Ronald Brown and Monica Wolford, "Religious Resources and African-American Political Action," *National Political Sciences Review* 4 (1994): 31.

39. Ibid.

40. Ibid.

41. Laura Reese and Ronald Brown, "The Effects of Religious Messages on Racial Identity and System Blame among African Americans," *Journal of Politics*, 57 (February, 1995): 24.

42. See also Fredrick Harris, "Something Within: Religion as a Mobilizer of African American Political Activism," *Journal of Politics* 56 (February, 1994): 48. /

CHAPTER 5

Public Opinion

Like many of the terms used by social scientists, *public opinion* has no precise, univer-sally agreed-on definition.[1] Lord Bryce said of public opinion, it is the "aggregate of views men hold . . . that affect the community" whereas V. O. Key in *Public Opinion and American Democracy* specifically links the term to government, writing that public opinion is those "opinions held by private persons which governments find it prudent to heed."[2] Hennessy, on the other hand, writes that it is simply "the complex of prefer-ences expressed by a significant number of persons on an issue of general importance."[3] Lane and Sears avoid the problem of definition altogether, assuming (presumably) that its meaning is obvious. So they write that "opinions have to be *about* something,"[4] and the something they say *public* opinion is about is (1) the political system, (2) the choice of group loyalties and identifications (race, religion, region, and social class), (3) choice of leaders, and (4) public policy preferences.[5]

GUNNAR MYRDAL AND AFRICAN AMERICAN PUBLIC OPINION

Myrdal dismissed the African American socialization process as dysfunctional and one of its products—black public opinion—as irrelevant. Myrdal saw America's race prob-lem as a "white problem," a problem rooted fundamentally in the prejudiced attitudes of whites. Thus, to understand race in America, one needed to see white attitudes as hegemonic while black attitudes were secondary or inconsequential. Myrdal wrote,

> In the practical and political struggles of effecting changes, the views of white Ameri-cans are . . . strategic. The Negro's entire life and, consequently, also his opinions on the Negro problem are in the main to be considered as secondary reactions to more primary pressures from the side of the dominant majority.[6]

In other words, there was no distinct or independent black opinion. Rather, Myrdal be-lieved that "these secondary attitudes, being largely defensive responses to white attitudes and actions were relatively superficial responses, not deeply rooted in the individual psyche or in cultural memory and could easily be altered."[7]

Until the 1980s, the ghost of Myrdal's paradigm haunted the study of African American mass opinion, resulting in relatively few studies of the phenomenon. Blacks were included in national polls and surveys in numbers reflecting their proportion of the population, but typically these surveys yielded too few respondents to produce valid and reliable findings or to explore opinion differences internal to the black community in terms of such things as gender, class, age, or region (the typical national sample of 1,500 to 2,000 persons would include about 150 to 200 blacks).

The ghost of Myrdal was exorcised through a combination of factors. First, African American studies began to grow and develop as a discipline. Second, interest increased in African American society and politics in the traditional disciplines of political science and sociology. Third, scholars began to recognize the radically erroneous nature of Myrdal's argument that black opinion is a mere derivative, secondary, transitory response to white opinion. Gradually and even grudgingly, the social science community recognized that black opinion was worthy of study in its own right.[8]

As a result of these changes, survey and polling organizations began to conduct surveys specifically designed to study black opinion. They systematically "oversampled" the black population to obtain samples large enough to yield valid and reliable results and to permit the study of intragroup opinion within the black community. Altogether, these changes have led in the last decade to "burgeoning research on race as an issue in American life."[9]

But Myrdal was not just influential in arguing for the primacy of white public opinion. Once the race problem in America was defined as an attitudinal problem, the study of racial attitudes became a necessary and crucial feature of race relations. Myrdal's second influence then is that he provided a scholarly justification for the study of racial attitudes in America. Such a study from an empirical perspective could lead to and help improve American society. Here was a central purpose, motive, role, and function for the study of racial attitudes. Myrdal had set the research agenda for the study of race and public opinion.

MODERN RACISM

From the inception of the scientific study of American public opinion more than forty years ago, countless surveys have found that the American public is in general indifferent and uninformed about politics, political leaders, ideologies, and issues.[10] Very few Americans structure their opinions on politics in ideological terms, and their views on issues tend to be ad hoc, inconsistent, transitory, and often contradictory. These generalizations hold for virtually all issues—foreign and domestic—except for race.

In one of the classic studies documenting the lack of ideological or issue content in white American mass opinion, Converse wrote, "For the bulk of the mass public the object with the highest centrality is the visible, familiar population grouping (Negroes) rather than abstract relations among parts of government and the like."[11] More than thirty years later, Kinder and Sanders concluded, "Compared with opinion on other matters, opinions on race are coherent, more tenaciously held and more difficult to alter. . . . [White] Americans know what they think on matters of race."[12] Thus, *the first thing to note about the race opinion of whites is that it tends to be one of the few consistent anchors in the thinking of white Americans.*

Second, in the last thirty years, surveys have shown a steady and generally consistent decline in overt expressions of racist and white supremacist attitudes among white Americans.[13] For example, in 1963, 31 percent of whites agreed with the statement that blacks were an inferior people; by 1978, 15 percent agreed.[14] Studies also show that white Americans by large margins now embrace the *principle* of racial equality.[15]

However, while white Americans in general are less openly racist in their attitudes toward blacks, hostility toward the race has by no means disappeared or withered away. Instead, it has become less obvious, more subtle, more difficult to document. This new, more subtle form of racism has been labeled "symbolic racism," "modern racism," "racial resentment," or "laissez-faire racism."[16] What this research purports to show is that white Americans are not racist in the old-fashioned way; instead, they resent or are hostile to blacks because of the whites' commitment to basic or core American values, particularly individualism.[17] White Americans prize self-sufficiency and individualism, and they believe that black Americans lack these values. Sniderman summarizes the research this way: "White Americans resist equality in the name of self-reliance, achievement, individual initiative, and they do so not merely because the value of individualism provides a socially acceptable pretext but because it provides an integral component of the new racism."[18]

In this modern racism, blacks, according to whites, are not inferior and could get ahead in society except that they lack the initiative or drive to succeed. As a function of individualism, modern or symbolic racism is a product of the "finest and proudest of American values."[19] It is as American as the flag, baseball, the Fourth of July, and apple pie.

Blacks, of course, disagree, viewing racism and racial discrimination as the principal explanation for persistent inequalities between the races.[20] As Kinder and Sanders summarize this racial chasm,

> Whites tend to think that racial discrimination is no longer a problem; that prejudiced has withered away, that the real worry these days is reverse discrimination, penalizing innocent whites for the sins of the distant past. Meanwhile, blacks see racial discrimination as ubiquitous; they think of prejudice as a plague; they say that racial discrimination, not affirmative action is still the rule in American society.[21]

Finally, Hochschild notes that "well off, middle class blacks tend to see more discrimination than poor blacks; see less of a decline in racism; expect less improvements in the future and claim to have experienced more discrimination in their own lives"[22] (see Box 5.1).

Recent Literature on African American Opinion

Several recent book-length studies by African American political scientists have used sophisticated statistical techniques and the 1984 and 1988 National Black Election Survey data to probe in depth black public opinion and its relationship to the vote in the two elections in which Jesse Jackson was a candidate for president. These works include

===================== **BOX 5.1** =====================
The Race Gap Is a Chasm[a]

In the days immediately following the acquittal of O. J. Simpson by a largely black jury of charges of murdering his former wife and her companion, many commentators expressed shock at how divided by color Americans were in their reaction to the verdict. (A *Washington Post* poll found that 85 percent of blacks agreed with the verdict compared to 35 percent of whites.) While these racial differences on the Simpson trial and verdict may have come as a surprise to members of the press and the public, they were not at all surprising to students of race opinion in the United States. These observers routinely report survey and election data that show differences between the races as large as or larger than the differences between blacks and whites on the Simpson verdict. Scholars of race opinion routinely write of a "vast gap between the races," that the races seem to "inhabit different perceptual worlds," of "deep and profound differences," and of a "huge and evidently persistent racial divide."[b]

On ideology and partisanship, for example, whites and blacks are deeply divided. On the central difference between modern liberals and conservatives—the role of the federal government—62 percent of whites but only 38 percent of blacks prefer a federal government that taxes less and provides fewer services. With respect to partisanship, about 80 percent of blacks identify with or lean toward the Democratic party compared to about 40 percent of whites. And not since 1964 have blacks and whites voted in majorities for the same presidential candidate; even then there was a racial divide, with 95 percent of blacks voting for Lyndon Johnson, compared to 60 percent of whites. In the eight presidential elections since 1964, not once have black and white majorities voted for the same candidate. Rather, during these three decades, the black vote has averaged 88 percent Democratic, compared to 43 percent among whites.

Also, blacks are far more likely than whites to believe that the "government deliberately makes sure that drugs are easily available in poor black neighborhoods in order to harm black people"; 64 percent of blacks compared to 6 percent of white agreed with this statement. A comparable racial gap also occurs when respondents were asked whether they believed the Central Intelligence Agency (CIA) was involved in importing cocaine into the black community—78 percent of blacks concurred compared to 16 percent of whites. By a margin of 59 percent to 15 percent, blacks are also more likely to agree that "the government does not make a strong effort to combat AIDS in the black community because the government cares less about black people than about whites." And perhaps most striking, blacks were less likely than whites to deny the possibility that HIV and AIDS are being used as a plot to deliberately kill African Americans: 79 percent of blacks compared to 38 percent of whites.

Less important but nevertheless revealing about the divisions between the races are their television viewing habits. One might think that television as a mass medium would be a force for bridging racial divisions and bringing people together. Yet of the top ten television programs in 1995, only one (*Monday Night Football*) was watched by both black and white families. *Seinfeld,* for example, ranked 2 among whites, 89 among blacks. *Friends* ranked 3 among whites, 111 among blacks. By contrast, *New York Undercover* was 1 among blacks, 122 among whites, and *Living Single* was 2 among blacks, 124 among whites. Commentators frequently re-

(Continued)

BOX 5.1 Continued

fer to the "gender gap" in American politics, the tendency of white women to be somewhat more liberal and Democratic in their vote choice than white men. The race gap is less frequently discussed, thus the surprise about the Simpson verdict. Yet compared to the race gap, the gender gap is trivial, with differences between the sexes rarely exceeding 10 percent; on the other hand, differences between the races frequently exceed 40 percent. In other words, if there is a gap between the sexes, then there is a chasm between the races.[c]

[a]The material here is drawn from Robert C. Smith and Richard Seltzer, *Gaps, Gulfs and Chasms across the Color Line: Controversies in American Culture* (Boulder, CO: Rowman, Littlefield, forthcoming).

[b]These quotes are taken from two recent books comparing opinion differences between the races. See Lee Seligman and Susan Welch, *Black Americans' Views of Racial Inequality: The Dream Deferred* (Cambridge, MA: Cambridge University Press, 1991): 65, and Donald Kinder and Lynn Sanders, *Divided by Color: Racial Politics and Democratic Ideas* (Chicago: University of Chicago Press, 1996): 33.

[c]On the gender gap, see Richard Seltzer, J. Newman, and M. Leighton, *Sex as a Political Variable: Women as Candidates and Women as Voters* (Boulder, CO: Lynne Riener, 1997).

Gurin, Hatchett, and Jackson's *Hope and Independence: Blacks' Response to Electoral and Party Politics*; Katherine Tate's *From Protest to Politics: The New Black Voters in American Elections*; and Michael Dawson's *Behind the Mule: Race and Class in American Politics.*[23]

Collectively these three studies demonstrate that African American political attitudes have (1) a Democratic partisanship bias, (2) a racial consciousness and political orientation, (3) a group interest focus, and (4) a contextual foundation. Although these are not all the elements in African American political attitudes, the empirical support for these was quite strong. Thus, other studies beyond the Jesse Jackson presidential campaigns will surely find new and different elements. Such findings arose in the study of the Los Angeles riots of 1992 and the Million Man March of 1996.

Lawrence Bobo, Camille Zubrinsky, James Johnson, and Melvin Oliver surveyed the Los Angeles African American community before and after the Los Angeles riots of 1992. Theirs was the first survey of its kind, and it revealed that as a result of the riots, class-based differences inherent in the community before the riots realigned themselves after the beating of Rodney King, and African Americans of all classes saw themselves as part of the same community.[24] This was one of the first surveys to reveal the nature of change and stability in African American community attitudes.

Findings from the Million Man March participants in 1996 suggested that as white American attitudes had been changed by the Reagan-Bush presidencies, so had the attitudes of African Americans. African American public opinion began to reflect, in the words of Bobo, a dual sovereignty tendency—that is, views toward black autonomy and nationalism as well as views supportive of certain mainstream values and beliefs.[25] In this climate of backlash and dismantling of civil rights protections, African American mass attitudes and beliefs reflect an ambivalence and a duality of focus. (The attitudes of the participants in the Million Man March are discussed in greater detail in chapter 8.)

AFRICAN AMERICAN IDEOLOGY: LIBERALISM

Political scientists have employed three modes of defining and operationalizing ideology. First, respondents in surveys have been asked directly about the ideological content of their issue, candidate, or partisan preferences.[26] Second, a few students have used in-depth, extended face-to-face interviews with a small number of individuals to explore the underlying foundations of their worldviews.[27] Finally, in probably the most influential approach, efforts have been made to conceptualize mass opinion in terms of "attitude constraint, the degree to which persons have a coherent structure of beliefs that reflects an underlying left-right, liberalism-conservatism dimension."[28]

Although there is some evidence of an increase in recent years in attitude constraint or issue consistency, this evidence is ambiguous.[29] Even those researchers who have found an increase in ideological consistency in mass attitudes conclude that in the United States, "citizens are not guided in their political views by an overarching political ideology—conservatism, liberalism, socialism, or any ideology that would provide an interrelated set of answers to various issue stances."[30] Instead, it still appears that mass opinion, among both blacks and whites, is structured on an ad hoc, issue-by-issue basis, reflecting partisanship, candidate preferences, perceptions of group interests, or the moods, biases, prejudices, and symbols that characterize what Converse called the "nature of the times."[31] Thus, when we refer to ideology, we refer not to abstract ideas but to the opinions that individuals express about the role of government in society, government spending and taxation, and attitudes toward certain social and moral issues. In general, liberalism tends to favor an active role for the government, higher rates of taxation, and government spending and more tolerant attitudes toward such issues as abortion and homosexual rights.

In Table 5.1, data from the 1996 General Social Survey (GSS) are displayed comparing black and white attitudes toward government spending on a variety of problems

---

TABLE 5.1

Racial Differences in Attitudes toward Government Spending on Selected Programs (Percentage Saying Spending Is Too Little/Right Amount)

	Black	White
Environment	75%	59%
Health	81	66
Cities	77	58
Crime	82	67
Drugs	78	58
Welfare	42	10
Social Security	71	49
Parks, Highways	35	39
Race	85	26
Space	26	60

Note: 1996 survey included a sample of 3,000 persons, including more than 400 blacks.

Source: General Social Survey, 1996, University of Chicago, National Opinion Research Center.

facing the country. Specifically, the question asks whether the government was spend-ing "too much money on it [the program or problem], too little, or about the right amount." Responses that indicate too little or the right amount we classify as liberal. That is, a liberal here is one who supports government spending either at present levels or with an increase; a conservative is one who thinks the government is spending too much on the problem or program.

With two exceptions, of the ten programs or policy areas designated, blacks indi-cated that the government was either spending too little or the right amount. The two exceptions are highway spending and space exploration. The differences on highway spending are modest; however, spending on space elicits a substantial difference, with 60 percent of whites indicating that the spending amount is too little or about right, compared to 26 percent of blacks. The 1996 GSS did not ask about the defense budget, but in its previous surveys, similar racial differences have been found on defense spend-ing. These findings show that black Americans tend to favor spending on programs that are devoted to improving the living conditions of people rather than infrastructure, the military, or science and technology.

The biggest difference in attitudes toward government spending is, not surpris-ingly, toward spending to "improve the conditions of blacks": 26 percent of whites say the government is spending too little or the right amount compared to 85 percent of blacks.

The GSS measures the government spending issue by linking support for increased government spending to higher taxes to see whether this alters opinion. It does not. As the data in Table 5.2 indicate, blacks continue to show strong support for government spending on domestic programs, even when told a tax increase might be required to pay for it.

Let us examine two other measures that tap the degree of liberalism among blacks and whites. In Table 5.3 we show opinions on the role of government in assuring the health and well-being of the people—that is, the extent to which respondents embrace programs of *universal rights*. Specifically, the questions ask whether it is the govern-

------------------------------ **TABLE 5.2** ------------------------------

**Racial Differences in Attitudes toward Government Spending
on Selected Programs, Even if Tax Increase Is Required
(Percentage Agreeing)**

	Black	White
Health	87%	64%
Schools	54	25
Retirement Benefits	79	46
Unemployment Benefits	69	21
Culture/Arts	68	51

Source: General Social Survey, 1996, University of Chicago, National Opinion Research Center.

---------------------------------- **TABLE 5.3** ----------------------------------

Racial Differences in Attitudes toward
the Social Welfare Responsibilities of Government (Percentage Saying
Welfare Is Government Responsibility)

	Black	White
To Provide Jobs	74%	33%
Health Care	69	33
Assure Decent Standard of Living	70	33
Decent Living for Unemployed	77	43
Financial Aid to College Students	62	30
Decent Housing for All	50	14

Source: General Social Survey, 1996, University of Chicago, National Opinion Research Center.

ment's responsibility to assure the availability of jobs, health care, a college education, or an overall decent standard of living. On each of these ideas, African American opinion is much more liberal than that of whites.

Table 5.4 shows that among blacks there is even substantial support for moving beyond liberalism toward an embrace of socialist ideas favoring government ownership of electric utilities, banks, and hospitals. Finally, blacks are more likely to agree that it is the government's responsibility to promote an egalitarian society by reducing income differences between the rich and poor: 73 percent compared to 44 percent.

Although blacks are more liberal on the role of the government in universalizing rights, they are not so liberal on social and moral issues. As Table 5.5 shows, blacks tend to be somewhat more conservative on issues of homosexuality, abortion, and school prayer. However, conservatism on these issues does not translate into support for conservative candidates. Instead, blacks tend to vote on the basis of material rather than moral issues.

---------------------------------- **TABLE 5.4** ----------------------------------

Racial Differences in Attitudes toward
Government Ownership of Selected Private Enterprises
(Percentage Favoring Government Ownership)

	Black	White
Electric Utilities	39%	17%
Hospitals	59	20
Banks	47	18
Government Should Reduce Income Inequality between Rich and Poor	73	44

Source: General Social Survey, 1996, University of Chicago, National Opinion Research Center.

—————————————————————— **TABLE 5.5** ——————————————————————

Racial Differences in Attitudes toward Selected Social, Moral Issues

	Black	White
Approve Supreme Court Decision Denying School Prayer[a]	29%	43%
Consider Homosexuality Wrong[b]	75	64
Approve of Abortion for Any Reason a Woman Chooses[c]	49	59

[a]The question read: The United States Supreme Court has ruled that no state or local government may *require* the reading of the Lord's Prayer or Bible verses in public schools. What are your views on this—do you approve or disapprove of the Court's ruling?

[b]The question read: What about sexual relations between two adults of the same sex—do you think it is always wrong, almost always wrong, wrong only sometimes, or not wrong at all?

[c]The question read: Please tell me whether or not you think it should be possible for a pregnant woman to obtain a *legal* abortion: if there is a strong chance of a serious defect in the baby; if she is married and does not want any more children; if the woman's health is seriously endangered by the pregnancy; if the family has a very low income and cannot afford any more children; if she became pregnant as a result of rape; if she is not married and does not want to marry the man; if the woman wants it for any reason.

Source: General Social Survey, 1996, University of Chicago, National Opinion Research Center. The abortion response is from the 1989 survey.

AFRICAN AMERICAN IDEOLOGY: BLACK NATIONALISM

While African Americans embrace most tenets of the liberal ideology, the 1993 National Black Political Survey suggests they are also increasingly nationalistic. Table 5.6 clearly demonstrates strong attitudinal support for African American autonomy or nationalism.

Finally, in regard to the matter of change in African American public opinion, in 1992 a poll of 1,211 African Americans was conducted by *The Detroit News* and Gannett News Service (the questionnaire was developed by a team of African American scholars led by James Jackson). It revealed that the traditional civil rights organizations (NAACP, SCLC, Urban League, and CORE) are not meeting the current needs of today's African American communities. Although African Americans still "embrace the

—————————————————————— **TABLE 5.6** ——————————————————————

Percentage of Support for African American Autonomy in Mass Public Opinion—1993: The National Black Political Survey

Statements from Survey	Percentage Agreeing
Blacks should rely on themselves and not others.	68
Blacks should control the government in black communities.	89
Blacks should participate in black-only organizations whenever possible.	67
Blacks should shop in black stores whenever possible.	84
Black children should study an African language.	70

Source: Michael Dawson and Ronald Brown, "Black Discontent: The Preliminary Report of the 1993–94 National Black Politics Study," Report # 1, University of Chicago. The results are based on a representative, randomly selected sample of the national black population. Percentages are of respondents agreeing with the statement.

─────────────── **TABLE 5.7** ───────────────

Levels of Support (in Percentages) for Civil Rights Groups and Organizations Working in Behalf of the African American Community: 1992

Organizations	%
Black Church	87
National Association for the Advancement of Colored People (NAACP)	87
Urban League	72
Democratic Party	71
Local Organizations	65
Business/Professional Organizations	65
Fraternal Organizations	61
Southern Christian Leadership Conference (SCLC)	57
Government	52
Congress on Racial Equality (CORE)	51
Muslims	40
Republican Party	31
Social Groups	22

Source: Adapted from *The Detroit News and Free Press*, February 23, 1992, p. 6A. Respondents could offer multiple answers.

groups that secured their voting rights and ended legal segregation, they know that it's time for the organizations to move beyond civil rights." And the poll results suggest that "the struggle today should be for quality rather than equality, and the groups should shift their focus from Congress and the courts to the streets and neighborhoods of American cities."[32]

Table 5.7 reveals how effective African American civil rights organizations are thought to be. The African American church now is tied in effectiveness with the oldest and most traditional organization, the NAACP. Second, the Southern Christian Leadership Conference (SCLC), Martin Luther King, Jr.'s, organization, is no longer seen as effective as it once was, and the Congress on Racial Equality (CORE) is seen as the most ineffective of all the former civil rights organizations (black political organizations are discussed in detail in chapter 8).

However, this diminished level of perceived effectiveness cannot and should not be read as if the community has now abandoned these organizations; rather, this finding reflects the change that African American public opinion is going through, since such levels of support would not have existed in the 1960s and 1970s.

SELECTED BIBLIOGRAPHY

Converse, Phillip. "The Nature of Belief Systems in Mass Publics." In David Apter, ed., *Ideology and Its Discontent*. New York: Free Press, 1964. A seminal work on the methodology of studying public opinion.

Dawson, Michael. *Behind the Mule: Race and Class in African-American Politics.* Princeton, NJ: Princeton University Press, 1994. A study that analyzes the relationship between racial and class attitudes and their different influences on individual political behavior.

———. "African American Public Opinion: Volatility in the Reagan-Bush Era." In Hanes Walton, Jr., *African American Power and Politics: The Political Context Variable.* New York: Columbia University Press, 1997. Explores presidential approval attitudes within the African American community during Republican control of the White House under Reagan and Bush.

Key, V. O. *Public Opinion and American Democracy.* New York: Alfred Knopf, 1961. The classic study of public opinion and its relationship to government leaders and the policy process.

Kinder, Donald, and Lynn Sanders. *Divided by Color: Racial Politics and Democratic Ideals.* Chicago: University of Chicago Press, 1996. The most recent and comprehensive study of black-white opinion differences in the United States.

Rosenstone, Steven J., and John Mark Hensen. *Mobilization, Participation and Democracy in America.* New York: Macmillan, 1993. Covers African American attitudes about political mobilization and participation in America's democratic system.

Sigelman, Lee, and Susan Welch. *Black Americans' Views of Racial Inequality: The Dream Deferred.* Cambridge, MA: Cambridge University Press, 1994. A pathbreaking analysis of black opinion about the sources of blacks' inequality in American society and the appropriate means for achieving equality.

Tate, Katherine. *From Protest to Politics: The New Black Voters in American Elections.* Enlarged Edition. Cambridge, MA: Harvard University Press, 1994. Analyzes the attitudes of African American voters in the 1984, 1988, and 1992 presidential elections.

NOTES

1. Bernard Hennessy, *Public Opinion*, 5th ed. (Belmont, CA: Brooks/Cole, 1985).
2. V. O. Key, *Public Opinion and American Democracy* (New York: Knopf, 1961): 14.
3. Hennessy, *Public Opinion*, p. 8.
4. Robert Lane and David Sears, *Public Opinion* (Englewood Cliffs, NJ: Prentice Hall, 1964): 2.
5. Ibid., pp. 2–3.
6. Gunnar Myrdal, *An American Dilemma: The Negro Problem and Modern Democracy* (New York: Harper & Row, 1944, 1962): 1143.
7. Ibid.
8. See Hanes Walton, Jr., *Invisible Politics: Black Political Behavior* (Albany: State University of New York Press, 1985), chap. 4.
9. Paul Sniderman, "The New Look in Public Opinion Research," in A. Finifter, ed., *The State of the Discipline, II* (Washington, DC: American Political Science Association, 1993): 231.
10. Donald Kinder, "Diversity and Complexity and Public Opinion," in A. Finifter, ed., *The State of the Discipline, I* (Washington, DC: American Political Science Association, 1983), and Sniderman, "The New Look in Public Opinion."

11. Phillip Converse, "The Nature of Belief Systems in Mass Publics," in D. Apter, ed., *Ideology and Its Discontent* (New York: Free Press, 1964): 238.
12. Donald Kinder and Lynn Sanders, *Divided by Color: Racial Politics and American Democracy* (Chicago: University of Chicago Press, 1996): 14.
13. Howard Schuman, C. Steeth, and L. Bobo, *Racial Attitudes in America: Trends and Interpretations* (Cambridge, MA: Harvard University Press, 1985).
14. Louis Harris, *A Study of Attitudes toward Racial and Religious Minorities and Women* (New York: National Conference of Christians and Jews, 1978): 16.
15. Schuman, Steeth, and Bobo, *Racial Attitudes in America.* See also Paul Sniderman and Michael Hagan, *Race and Inequality: A Study in American Values* (Chatham, NJ: Chatham House, 1985).
16. David Sears, "Symbolic Racism," in P. Katz and D. Taylor, eds., *Eliminating Racism* (New York: Plenum, 1988); Kinder and Sanders, *Divided by Color*, pp. 272–76; and Lawrence Bobo, J. Klugel, and R. Smith, "Laissez-Faire Racism: The Crystallization of a 'Kinder, Gentler' Anti-Black Ideology," in S. Tuch and J. Martin, eds., *Racial Attitudes in the 1990s: Continuity and Change* (Westport, CT: Praeger, 1997).
17. Sniderman and Hagan, *Race and Inequality*.
18. Sniderman, "Diversity and Complexity in Public Opinion," p. 232.
19. Sears, "Symbolic Racism," p. 54.
20. Lee Seligman and Susan Welch, *Black Americans' Views of Inequality* (Cambridge, MA: Cambridge University Press, 1994).
21. Kinder and Sanders, *Divided by Color*, p. 287.
22. Jennifer Hochschild, *Facing Up to the American Dream: Race, Class and the Soul of the Nation* (Princeton, NJ: Princeton University Press, 1995).
23. Patricia Gurin, Shirley Hatchett, and James Jackson, *Hope and Independence: Blacks' Response to Electoral and Party Politics* (New York: Russell Sage, 1989); Katherine Tate, *From Protest to Politics: The New Black Voters* (Cambridge, MA: Harvard University Press, 1993); Michael Dawson, *Behind the Mule: Race and Class in African American Politics* (Princeton, NJ: Princeton University Press, 1994).
24. Lawrence Bobo, Camille Zubrisky, James Johnson, and Melvin Oliver, "Public Opinion before and after a Spring of Discontent," in Mark Baldassare, ed., *The Los Angeles Riots: Lessons for the Urban Future* (Boulder, CO: Westview Press, 1994): 62–81.
25. See Bobo, Kluegel, and Smith, "Laissez-Faire Racism."
26. Angus Campbell et al., *The American Voter* (New York: Wiley, 1960).
27. See Robert Lane, *Political Ideology: Why the American Common Man Believes What He Does* (New York: Free Press, 1962).
28. Converse, "The Nature of Belief Systems in Mass Publics."
29. Norman Nie, Sydney Verba, and J. Petrocik, *The Changing American Voter* (Cambridge, MA: Harvard University Press, 1976).
30. Ibid., p. 27.
31. Converse, "The Nature of Belief Systems in Mass Publics," p. 241.
32. Janice Hayes and Ellyn Ferguson, "Who Speaks for Black America?" *The Detroit News and Free Press*, February 23, 1992, A1, A6.

CHAPTER 6

African Americans
and the Media

"We wish to plead our own cause. Too long have others spoken for us."[1] So said the editorial in the first edition of the first black newspaper, appropriately called *Freedom's Journal,* founded in 1827 by Samuel Cornish and John B. Russwurm. Since 1827, the black press and the black church have been central institutions in the African American freedom struggle.

GUNNAR MYRDAL AND THE AFRICAN AMERICAN MEDIA

Here is how Myrdal described the African American media:

> Most white people in America are entirely unaware of the bitter and relentless criticism of themselves; of their policies in domestic or international affairs; their legal and political practices; their business enterprises; their churches, schools, and other institutions; their social customs, their opinions and prejudices; and almost everything else in white American civilization. Week in and week out these are presented to the Negro people in their own press. It is a fighting press.[2]

Of all the African American institutions, the press was the most positive, useful, important, and functional in Myrdal's eyes. Throughout his study of it, Myrdal heaped praise and accolades upon the black press. In fact, he could not say enough about it. He talked about it not only as an institution but also in terms of media habits and attentiveness. He wrote:

> Practically all Negroes who can read are exposed to the influence of the Negro press at least some of the time. Perhaps a third of the Negro families in cities regularly subscribe to Negro newspapers, but the proportion is much smaller in rural areas. The readers of the Negro press are, however, the most alert and articulate individuals who form Negro opinion. Newspapers are commonly passed from family to family, and they are some-

74

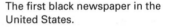

The first black newspaper in the United States.

times read out loud in informal gatherings. They are available in barbershops, passed by word of mouth among those who cannot read. Indirectly, therefore, even aside from circulation figures, this press influences a large proportion of the Negro population.[3]

These insights led him to further assert that "no unifying central agency directs the opinions in the Negro press. . . . By and large the Negro press provides the news and the opinions which its reading public wants."[4] Here one sees very strong media habits and attentiveness among the African American community.

The question arises as to why? And on this point, Myrdal is quite clear:

The more important and open expressions of the Negro protest are to be found in the news coverage of the whole American Negro world and, to an extent, the Negro world outside the United States, and also in the columns and editorials on the status of the Negro people.[5]

For Myrdal, *"The press defines the Negro group to the Negroes themselves* (emphasis by Myrdal). The individual is invited to share in the sufferings, grievances, and pretensions of the millions of Negroes far outside the narrow local community." Hence, "this creates a feeling of strength and solidarity. The press, more than any other institution, has created the Negro group as a social and psychological reality to the individual Negro."[6] For Myrdal, the African American press is a centralizing protest device. It is the driving and motivating force in African American electoral and nonelectoral political behavior. It is the tool that socializes the African American community and carries the message of struggle to the next generation. Finally, it is home to the centerpiece of the African American political culture: *protest.*

In reality, Myrdal assigned the African American newspapers his number one priority. Yet for all the strength, power, and influence that he ascribed to the press, it had no impact on the negative psychic traits and the pathologies he saw as being inherent in the African American community. Such a powerful institution had no power at all in dealing with the social conditions in the community. Myrdal was at best contradictory. He had seen an African American institution, noted its power, but then negated its community reform potential. It was powerful, but not powerful. Listen again as he ascribes to it even more power:

> For this reason the Negro press is far more than a mere expression of the Negro protest. By expressing the protest, the press also magnifies it, acting like a huge sounding board. The press is also the chief agency of group control. It tells the individual how he should think and feel as an American Negro and creates a tremendous power of suggestion by implying that all other Negroes think and feel in this manner. It keeps the Negro spokesman in line. Every public figure knows he will be reported, and he has to weigh his words carefully. Both the leaders and the masses are kept under racial discipline by the press. This promotes unanimity without the aid of central direction.[7]

But with these words and insights, Myrdal leaves it. Other than just keeping the Negro "protest" alive, the African American press was powerless.

However, a closer reading of Myrdal reveals that he did not quite believe his own portrayal. For instance, one of the powerful functions of the press was to attack and remake the stereotypes and negative characterizations that the white press visited on the community. He argued, "The display of Negro 'society news' in the Negro press is partly an answer to the social derogation from the whites."[8] This finding and role Myrdal played down in his analysis.

Although Myrdal's analysis of the African American press left a lot to be desired at the theoretical and interpretive level, a very close reading will reveal brief and vague references to two of its central functions and roles. First, it is a macro-level variable, an institution that promotes group unity and group political behavior. Second, it is a micro-level variable in terms of readers' habits and attentiveness. And the latter finding is clear in its assertion that the African American press is more important for African Americans than the white press is for white Americans.

THE AFRICAN AMERICAN MEDIA AND AFRICAN AMERICANS IN THE MASS MEDIA

Before turning to the literature on African Americans and the media and our empirical estimation, we first examine the contemporary African American media and the presence of blacks in the mainstream or mass media.

The African American Media

Like the media in general, the African American media are quite diverse. They include about two hundred weekly newspapers, approximately 450 black-oriented radio stations, several national circulation news and special interest magazines, and BET, the cable entertainment and information network. (African Americans own nineteen television stations and 181 radio stations.[9]) In general, the black weeklies serve as the voice for the local African American communities, focusing on local rather than national news.[10] Their focus tends to be on the internal black community's civic, cultural, and religious affairs. The mainstream or white media tend to ignore the internal life of the black community, thus the black media serve as a vehicle of intragroup communication and solidarity. Many, although not all, of the black weeklies serve as watch dogs on local government and continue the tradition of a fighting, protest press discussed by Myrdal. For example, while the *Los Angeles Times* tended to present the O. J. Simpson arrest and trial in an unsympathetic way, the black *Los Angeles Sentinel* in effect became Simpson's champion in the media, apparently reflecting the views of the city's black community as the *Los Angeles Times* reflected the views of the city's whites.[11]

At the national level, there are several general circulation news and information magazines including *Ebony, Jet,* and *Emerge.* There are also specialized magazines such as *Essence* (focusing on women) and *Black Enterprises* (focusing on business). Although these magazines occasionally provide critical reportage on race issues and internal black society, culture, and politics, with the exception of *Emerge,* they generally tend to focus on celebrities, consumerism, and showcasing for the black middle class. They tend not to provide much hard news or critical commentary on issues important to the African American community.

African Americans in the Mass Media

Until the 1960s, relatively few blacks were employed in the mass media. In the aftermath of the riots of the 1960s, many newspapers and radio and television stations for the first time began to hire black reporters, editors, and producers.[12] Yet, even today, their numbers in the mainstream, mass media are relatively small. In Table 6.1, data are displayed on African Americans in the nation's radio, television, and daily newspaper workforces. Blacks constitute 5.4 percent of newspaper, 10.2 percent of television, and 6.3 percent of radio workforces. But in the important decision-making positions of news director, blacks make up only 2.9 percent in radio and 2.5 percent in television. Blacks and other minorities in the mass media tend to be concentrated in the larger cities; one-fourth of minority television journalists work in the twenty-five largest cities compared to 10 percent in the nation's smallest cities.[13] The same phenomenon is observed with respect to newspapers. Indeed, 44 percent of the nation's daily newspapers (mostly in smaller cities) have no black reporters.[14]

The mainstream or mass media is just that: "mass" media; this designation means that it gathers and reports news of interest to the mass public—in general, middle-class whites. For this reason, news in the newspapers and on radio and television tends to be essentially the same, whether one watches CBS or ABC or reads the *New York Times* or

--------------------------------- **TABLE 6.1** ---------------------------------

African Americans in the Mass Media: Television, Radio, and Major Newspapers, 1994

Media	% African Americans
Radio	
News Workforce	6.3% (985)[a]
News Directors	2.9% (159)
Television	
News Workforce	10.2% (2250)
News Directors	2.5% (18)
Newspapers	
News Workforce	5.4% (2980)

[a]Numbers in parentheses represent total numbers of African Americans in workforce.

Sources: Data on radio and television personnel are based on a 1994 survey of the nation's approximately 6,640 commercial radio stations and 990 nonsatellite commercial television stations. The surveys were conducted by Vernon Johnson, professor emeritus of journalism at the University of Missouri. Professor Johnson has been conducting surveys of minorities and women in broadcast journalism since 1972. We obtained the 1994 results from Professor Johnson's home page on the World Wide Web. The data on newspapers is drawn from the 1994 survey of the nation's 1,490 daily newspapers, conducted by the American Society of Newspaper Editors. Since 1978, the Society has conducted this survey of the representation of minorities and women in the daily press.

the *Detroit Free Press* or the *Washington Post* or the *San Francisco Chronicle* or *Time* or *Newsweek*, although the *Washington Post* and the *New York Times* do provide more detailed stories on national and international affairs.

In an important study, sociologist Herbert Gans argues that the primary motive guiding the mass media is the preservation of "social order," the prevailing values and power relationships in the society.[15] The African American community, however, tends to be dissatisfied with the prevailing values and power relationships. This dissatisfaction tends to place in a difficult position the African American journalist who wishes to reflect the perspective of his community. She or he must simultaneously seek to balance the "black perspective" on the news with the mass media's social control perspective. A former *Washington Post* reporter describes this as a "creative tension" between "Uncle Tomming and mau mauing."[16]

The Literature on the African American Media

Most of the early literature on the media dealt with the creation of stereotypes. Media scholars Dates and Barlow laid out the theory of this dimension as follows:

> Stereotypes are especially effective in conveying ideological messages because they are so laden with ritual and myth, particularly in the case of African Americans, but, invariably these black representations are totally at odds with the reality of African Americans as individual people. . . . The conflict is indicative of a deep cultural schism, which precipitated the ideological struggle, between white and black image makers in the first place.[17]

These scholars continued their insights with these remarks:

> Black media stereotypes are not the natural, much less harmless, products of an ideal-
> ized popular culture; rather, they are more commonly socially constructual images that
> are selective, partial, one-dimensional, and distorted in their portrayal of African Amer-
> icans. Moreover, stereotyped black images most often are frozen, incapable of growth,
> change, innovation or transformation.[18]

Since the 1950s, content analysis of the mass media has consistently shown that the routine, day-to-day coverage of African Americans is predominantly negative and stereotypical; blacks are portrayed as poor or criminal; or they are shown as entertainers and
athletes. While this kind of coverage declined somewhat in the 1960s during the civil
rights era, it resurfaced in the 1970s and continues to dominate coverage of blacks in the
1990s.[19]

Therefore, with these realities as given,

> the dominant trend in African American portraiture has been created and nurtured by
> succeeding generations of white image makers, beginning as far back as the colonial era.
> Its opposite has been created and maintained by black image makers in response to the
> omissions and distortions of the former.[20]

One of the first works to address this image presentation problem in political terms
was C. Anthony Broh's, *A Horse of a Different Color: Television's Treatment of Jesse
Jackson's 1984 Presidential Campaign.* This monograph found that "black candidates
for the presidency will have to overcome the media's stereotypes. Campaign reporters
explain politics with cliches, and a black presidential candidate will have to learn to con-
front, or to manage, those stereotypes."[21] The media in 1984, Broh argued, refused to
treat the Jackson candidacy seriously.

In the 1988 campaign, the same reality pertained. The Jackson candidacy was essentially dismissed.[22] The same was true of L. Douglas Wilder's 1992 campaign, although he was the former governor of Virginia.[23] In his brief campaign, the media used
the Wilder candidacy to try to undermine and eliminate another possible Jesse Jackson
candidacy.[24] This treatment also occurs at the subpresidential levels.

In their analysis of news coverage of the 1989 New York mayoral contest (David
Dinkins versus Rudolph Guiliani) and the Virginia gubernatorial race (Wilder versus
J. Marshall Coleman), media analysts revealed "that racial references of one kind or
another were a fairly common feature of news about these two campaigns. This daily
supply of ethnic and racial references . . . might conceptually have heightened the
salience of racial attitudes among white voters and contributed indirectly to the election day surprises."[25] The analysts concluded that these "stimuli in the news stream
. . . may activate racial attitudes and stereotypes, crystallizing [white voters'] (perhaps
socially undesirable) opinions, helping to shift their candidate preferences, or encouraging them to turn out on election day."[26] In comparison, the mainstream media
treated the putative 1996 presidential campaign of Colin Powell with great respect
and positive portrayals.

A major study of television coverage of the 1992 Los Angeles riots uncovered a
similar pattern of stereotypical coverage. First, although the Los Angeles riots were the
nation's first "multicultural riots" involving Latinos, blacks, whites, and Asians, the

coverage on both local and network television portrayed it stereotypically as a black riot.[27] For emample, Latinos were a majority of the people arrested for rioting; but when the three local Los Angeles stations reported arrests, almost 60 percent of the people they showed were black. Latinos made up only 24% of the rioters shown on the networks and 33 percent on the local stations.[28] Television news also portrayed the causes of the riots as criminality and lawlessness rather than addressing the underlying problems of racism and poverty or as a protest of the acquittal of the policemen who beat Rodney King. Eighty percent of the local coverage focused on criminality as the primary cause of the riot. And although the three networks did address other causes, 60 percent of their coverage also focused on lawlessness as the principal explanation of the riot.[29]

There is much less literature on the micro-level dimension of the African American media. Using Myrdal's conclusion that the African American press is much more important to blacks than the white press is to whites, Table 6.2 reveals that in the 1970s this observation was still as true as it was in the 1940s when Myrdal produced his study. It applies to newspapers as well as to radio and television. African Americans have clearly factored the African American media into their media habits. And one of the prime reasons is that the African American media, then and now, tend to carry far more positive and healthy images of blacks.[30]

THE AFRICAN AMERICAN MEDIA VARIABLE: AN EMPIRICAL ESTIMATION

Table 6.3 shows the television-viewing habits of African Americans in three presidential election years. In these three years, the majority of African Americans watched television or were exposed to it seven days a week.

However, Table 6.2 shows that only about one-third of the African American community was exposed to newspapers and nearly one-fifth of the community never read the newspapers at all. This finding, however, is highly questionable, particularly in regard to what we learned earlier about African Americans reading the African American press. Both tables do relate that the media at the individual level are important and that the community is constantly exposed to it, both print and electronic.

--------------------------------- **TABLE 6.2** ---------------------------------
Preferred Media Sources of Black Voters and Nonvoters, 1972–1974

Media	Black Voters	Black Nonvoters
Prefer Mostly Black Newspapers	88% (516)	73% (178)
Prefer Mostly White Newspapers	12% (72)	27% (67)
Prefer Mostly Black Radio/TV	79% (521)	88% (198)
Prefer Mostly White Radio/TV	21% (141)	12% (26)

Source: Hanes Walton, Jr., *Invisible Politics* (Albany: State University of New York Press, 1985): 50. The data are drawn from a nationwide survey of 698 black voters and 305 black nonvoters conducted in several stages from 1972 to 1974.

————————————————— **TABLE 6.3** —————————————————

Television Exposure during Presidential Election Years: African Americans, September–November, 1984–1992

Days per Week Respondent Watches Television	1984 %	1988 %	1992 %
None	11	14	7
One	8	2[a]	4
Two	16	10	8
Three	12	7[a]	11
Four	7	6[a]	6
Five	9	7[a]	5
Six	5	2[a]	2[a]
Seven	33	51	56
N	**234**	**98**	**296**

Note: Cell entries represent percentage of all respondents in each category.

[a]Indicates N < 10 in cell.

Source: National Election Studies Cumulative File: 1952–1992.

Now that we have established some idea about African Americans' media habits, we can estimate the amount of attention individual African Americans pay to political news and content. Table 6.4 reveals the percentage of African Americans in each of the last three presidential elections who paid attention to campaign news on television. One-fifth of the community paid "very little" attention. More than three-fourths of the community gave attention to campaign politics. And nearly a third paid "a great deal of attention to political areas."

————————————————— **TABLE 6.4** —————————————————

Television Attention during Presidential Election Years: African Americans, September–November, 1984–1992

Amount of Attention Respondent Pays to Campaign News on Television	1984 %	1988 %	1992 %
None	3[a]	7	4
Very Little	17	16	18
Some	31	31	20
Quite a Bit	19	28	25
A Great Deal	29	18	28
N	**209**	**83**	**274**

Note: Cell entries represent percentage of all respondents in each category.

[a]Indicates N < 10 in cell.

Source: National Election Studies Cumulative File: 1952–1992.

─────────────────────────── **TABLE 6.5** ───────────────────────────

Newspaper Exposure during Presidential Election Years: African Americans, September–November, 1984–1992

Days per Week Respondent Reads Newspapers	1984 %	1988 %	1992 %
None	26	22	29
One	12	13	13
Two	12	8^a	13
Three	9	10	7
Four	5	10	3^a
Five	5	4^a	1^a
Six	2^a	2^a	1^a
Seven	31	30	33
N	**247**	**97**	**296**

Note: Cell entries represent percentage of all respondents in each category.

^{a}Indicates N < 10 in cell.

Source: National Election Studies Cumulative File: 1952–1992.

When we move from attention to television to newspaper coverage of campaigns, the attention is still about the same. Data in Tables 6.5 and 6.6, compared with data in Tables 6.2 and 6.3, suggest a very strong degree of similarity between the print and electronic media habits of African Americans in terms of the attention they pay to political news and information. The empirical information suggests the tentative conclusion that the media are influential in shaping African American political behavior (Box 6.1).

─────────────────────────── **TABLE 6.6** ───────────────────────────

Newspaper Attention during Presidential Election Years: African Americans, September–November, 1984–1992

Amount of Attention Respondent Pays to Campaign News in Newspapers	1984 %	1988 %	1992 %
None	8^a	42	46
Very Little	21	11^a	8
Some	37	24	18
Quite a Bit	19	16	15
A Great Deal	15	7^a	14
N	**180**	**74**	**210**

Note: Cell entries represent percentage of all respondents in each category.

^{a}Indicates N < 10 in cell.

Source: National Election Studies Cumulative File: 1952–1992.

━━━━━━━━━━ **BOX 6.1** ━━━━━━━━━━
I Heard It through the Grapevine:
The Million Man March and the Media

"I heard it through the grapevine" is an expression often heard in the African American community. In the 1960s, Motown artists Marvin Gaye and Gladys Knight and the Pips had best-selling songs of that title, but the phrase is as old as slave society in the United States. It is used to denote the existence in African American culture of an alternative, informal communications network where news, rumors, and information are shared without being filtered through the white mass media.[a]

The mainstream white media ignored Minister Louis Farrakhan's call for a million men to march on Washington. For example, *The New York Times,* whose slogan is "All the News That's Fit to Print," did not report anything about the march until a couple of days before it took place; apparently the paper did not consider a report of what was to become the largest demonstration ever held in Washington to be news that was fit to print. Yet, news of the march became widely known throughout the African American community. How did this come about? How did an event ignored by the mass media become common knowledge on the streets of black America? It appears that most blacks heard it through the grapevine.

According to the Howard University survey of March participants, 65 percent of the men present in Washington said their most important source of information about the march was "word of mouth"; another 44 percent said they heard about it through a black newspaper or radio station, while another 19 percent identified the church or a local march organizing committee as their source.[b] A particularly important source of information on this grapevine was the Nation of Islam's own weekly newspaper, *The Final Call;* it has an estimated circulation of 900,000 and is sold on the street corners in every major American city.[c] The message was also spread by Minister Farrakhan himself in his weekly radio addresses, broadcast on more than fifty stations. Thus, while the mainstream media in effect engaged in a news "blackout" about the march, the alternative black media were able to effectively communicate news of it—almost as effectively as if it had been covered in the daily newspapers and nightly newscasts.

[a]Patricia Turner, *I Heard It through the Grapevine: Rumor in African American Culture* (Berkeley: University of California Press, 1993).

[b]*The Million Man March Poll* (Washington: Howard University, Department of Political Science, 1995): Question 8. The design and results of this poll are discussed in detail in chapter 10.

[c]The estimate of *The Final Call*'s circulation was provided by Professor Erna Smith of San Francisco State University's journalism department.

━━━━━━━━━━━━━━━━━━━━━━━━━

SELECTED BIBLIOGRAPHY

Dates, Jannette, and William Barlow, eds. *Split Images: African Americans in the Mass Media,* 2nd ed. Washington: Howard University Press, 1993. The leading work on the macro-level dimension of the media and African Americans.

Gans, Herbert. *Deciding What's News: A Study of the* CBS Evening News, NBC Nightly News, Newsweek *and* Time. New York: Pantheon, 1979. An important sociological analysis of the relationship between social order and conflict in determining what is the news.

Graber, Doris. *Mass Media and American Politics,* 4th ed. Washington: Congressional Quarterly, 1992. The standard political science analysis of the role of the media in American politics.

Nelson, Jill. *Volunteer Slavery: My Authentic Negro Experience.* Chicago: Nobel Press, 1993. A humorous and passionate account of the travails of the *Washington Post Magazine*'s first black and first woman reporter, a post from which she resigned because she says she was unable to tolerate the *Post*'s "paternalistic culture."

Wolseley, Roland. *The Black Press, U.S.A.,* 2nd ed. Ames: Iowa State University Press, 1990. A general survey of the black press, covering newspapers and magazines.

NOTES

1. See "The First Negro Newspaper's Opening Editorial, 1827" in Herbert Aptheker, ed., *A Documentary History of the Negro People in the United States* (New York: Citadel, 1967): 82.

2. Myrdal, *An American Dilemma*, p. 908.

3. Ibid., p. 909.

4. Ibid.

5. Ibid., p. 910.

6. Ibid.

7. Ibid., p. 911.

8. Ibid., 909.

9. *Black American Information Directory, 1994–95* (Detroit: Gate, 1994).

10. Roland Wolseley, *The Black Press, U.S.A.* (Ames: Iowa State University Press, 1990).

11. Ronald Jacobs, "Civil Society and Crisis: Culture, Discourse and the Rodney King Beating," *American Journal of Sociology* 101 (1996): 1238–72.

12. The National Advisory Commission on Civil Disorders (popularly known as the Kerner Commission) was appointed by President Johnson to investigate the causes of the riots. The Commission's findings pointed to the absence of black reporters and scant coverage of the black community as factors contributing to the discontent that led to the riots. Also, many newspapers and television stations found that without black reporters they could not adequately cover the riots since white reporters were reluctant to go into the black community or did not understand what they saw and heard.

13. See Vernon Johnson, "Minorities and Women in Television News" and "Minorities and Women in Radio News" (University of Missouri, School of Journalism, 1996).

14. American Society of Newspaper Editors, press release on the 1996 Annual Survey on Diversity in the Newsroom, April 16, 1996.

15. See Herbert Gans, *Deciding What's News: A Study of the* CBS Evening News, NBC Nightly News, Newsweek *and* Time (New York: Pantheon, 1979).

16. Jill Nelson, *Volunteer Slavery: My Authentic Negro Experience* (Chicago: Noble Press, 1993).
17. Jannette Dates and William Barlow, "Introduction: A War of Images," in Dates and Barlow, eds., *Split Images: African Americans in the Mass Media*, 2nd ed. (Washington, DC: Howard University Press, 1993): 5.
18. Ibid.
19. See Carolyn Martindale, *The White Press and Black America* (Westport, CT: Greenwood Press, 1986), and Ted Pease and J. Frazier Smith, *The Newsroom Barometer: Job Satisfaction and the Impact of Racial Diversity* (Columbus, OH: E. W. Scripps School of Journalism, Ohio State University, 1991); Martin Gitens, "Race and Poverty in America: Public Perceptions and the American News Media," *Public Opinion Quarterly* 60 (1996): 515–41.
20. Dates and Barlow, "Introduction: A War of Images," p. 3.
21. C. Anthony Broh, *A Horse of a Different Color: Television's Treatment of Jesse Jackson's 1984 Presidential Campaign* (Washington, DC: Joint Center for Political Economic Studies, 1987): 83.
22. Elizabeth Colton, *The Jackson Phenomenon: The Man, the Power, the Message* (New York: Doubleday, 1989).
23. Paula McClain and Steven Tauber, "African American Presidential Candidate: The Failed Campaign of Governor L. Douglas Wilder," in Hanes Walton, Jr., *African American Power and Politics: The Political Context Variable* (New York: Columbia University Press, 1997).
24. See Arnold Gibbons, *Race, Politics and the White Media: The Jesse Jackson Campaigns* (Lanham, MD: University Press of America, 1993).
25. Michael Traogott, Vincent Price, and Edward Czilli, "Polls Apart: Race, Politics and Journalism" (Paper presented at the Annual Conference of the American Association for Public Opinion Research, Pleasant Run Resort, St. Charles, IL, May 20–23, 1993): 12; Michael Traogott and Vincent Price, "The Polls—A Review: Exit Polls in the 1989 Virginia Gubernatorial Race: Where Did They Go Wrong?" *Public Opinion Quarterly* 56 (1992): 245–55.
26. Traogott, Price, and Czilli, "Polls Apart," p. 13.
27. Erna Smith, "Transmitting Race: The Los Angeles Riot in Television News" (Research Paper # R-11, Joan Shorenstein Barone Center, John F. Kennedy School of Government, Harvard University, Cambridge, MA, 1994).
28. Ibid., p. 9.
29. Ibid., p. 11.
30. Walton, *Invisible Politics*, pp. 63–66. See Table 4.3 for the percentages of positive, negative, and neutral images in the African American Press.

PART III

Coalitions, Movements, Interest Groups, Parties, and Elections

CHAPTER 7

Social Movements and a Theory of African American Coalition Politics

For much of their history in the United States, African Americans have been excluded from the normal, routine processes of political participation such as lobbying, voting, elections, and political parties. Indeed, in the Republic's more than two-hundred-year history, African Americans have been included as nearly full participants for less than fifty years, the ten-year Reconstruction period from 1867 to 1877 plus the years since the adoption of the Voting Rights Act in 1965. As for much of their history African Americans have been excluded from the interest group, electoral, and party systems, they have had to resort to social movements challenging the exclusionary system. William Gamson makes this point when he observes that in the United States certain groups have been systematically denied entry into the political process and gain entry only through protest or system crisis—what he calls "the breakdown of the normal operation of the system or through demonstration on the part of challenging groups of a willingness to violate 'rules of the game' by resorting to illegitimate means of carrying on political conflict."[1]

Therefore, before we examine African American interest group, voting, and party behavior, we need to look first at African American participation in social movements. A *social movement* may be understood as a group of persons organized in a sustained, self-conscious challenge to an existing system and its values or power relationships. An *interest group* is typically defined as a group of persons who share a common interest and seek to influence the government to adopt policies favorable to that interest. In other words, movements challenge systems whereas interest groups accept and work within systems. In this chapter we examine the history, development, and contemporary manifestations of African American social movement behavior. Before doing this, however, we develop a theory of African American minority-majority coalition politics.

A THEORY OF AFRICAN AMERICAN COALITION POLITICS

This book has two major themes. The first is that African Americans in their quest for freedom in the United States have sought to universalize the idea of freedom. The second theme is that African Americans—given their status first as slaves and then as an oppressed racial minority—have had to form coalitions with whites to achieve their freedom. Historically, however, these black-white coalitions have been tenuous and unstable, requiring constant rebuilding in an ongoing quest. To understand the dynamic instability of African American coalition politics, we must know some basic concepts and theoretical propositions.

There are various concepts and definitions of coalitions including complicated, technical mathematical ones and social-psychological and economic cost/benefit analyses.[2] But simply, a *coalition* involves two or more persons or groups bringing their resources together to achieve a common objective. When a group can achieve its objectives alone, it is less likely to join a coalition. Historically, as blacks have sought freedom in the United States, this has rarely been the case for them. They have always needed coalition partners to achieve many, if not all, of their objectives. However, blacks frequently have not been able to find coalition partners among whites for their objectives; thus, they have been forced to act alone. Black nationalists in the United States reject in principle the possibility of whites as reliable coalition partners and therefore always embrace the strategy of *intraracial* coalitions among blacks rather than *interracial* coalitions with whites. But even those blacks (the overwhelming majority) who in principle accept the idea of interracial coalitions have also embraced the go-it-alone strategy, when suitable white coalition partners were not available or when independent race group organizations were thought to be preferable or complementary to coalition politics. A final theoretical point is that a coalition, to be viable, must have sufficient resources—money, status, size—to achieve its objectives vis-à-vis opposing groups and coalitions. In summary, a theory of African American coalition politics suggests that blacks will seek to pool their resources with whites, when possible, in order to achieve their objectives; when suitable white partners are not available they will seek to pool their resources among themselves to achieve these objectives.[3]

Historically, as Figure 7.1 shows, African Americans have sought to form or participate in two categories of coalitions. The first type is a *rights-based coalition,* one that seeks to achieve fundamental universal freedom in terms of basic human, constitutional, and legal rights; examples are the abolitionist and civil rights movements. The second is a *material-based coalition,* which seeks access to economic benefits such as land, education, employment, and social security; examples are the populist movement, Franklin Roosevelt's New Deal coalition, or Jesse Jackson's Rainbow Coalition.[4] Historically, also, the rights-based coalitions have had priority over the material-based ones. For example, before the black slaves could fight for land and education, their first objective had to be the abolition of slavery. Similarly, a major objective of black leaders and organizations during the 1970s was to form a material-based coalition to secure passage of legislation guaranteeing full employment (see the discussion of the Humphrey-Hawkins Act in chapter 11). Before this material-based issue could become

Figure 7.1 The Dual Categories for Coalition Formation of African Americans: Rights and Material Based

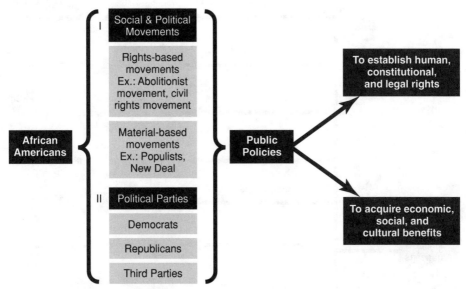

Sources: Adapted from Hanes Walton, Jr., *Black Politics: A Theoretical and Structural Analysis* (Philadelphia: J.B. Lippincott, 1972); and Robert Allen, *The Reluctant Reformers: Reform Movements in the United States* (Washington, D.C.: Howard University Press, 1993).

the priority, however, the rights-based objectives of the civil rights movement had to be achieved.

African American minority-majority coalitions tend to be tenuous and unstable because of racism, white supremacist thinking, and the ambivalence of white Americans toward race and universal freedom and equality. Figure 7.2 displays the white and other coalition partners of blacks from the founding of the Republic in the 1770s to the present. It shows that in both rights-based and material-based coalitions, blacks have over time formed coalitions with all elements of the white population (and since the 1960s, other racial minority groups)—Quakers and Jews, middle-class professionals and poor white farmers, white liberals and white conservatives, rural whites and urban whites, and white men and white women. Yet, as we show in this chapter and in the following ones on electoral and party coalitions, these varied coalitions have frequently been weak and unstable because of the forces of racism and white supremacy.

In summary, here are the basic elements of this theory of African American coalitions, as we use them to analyze black social movements in this chapter, and to examine interest groups, elections, and party behavior in chapters 8, 9, and 10:

- Coalitions with whites are necessary if blacks are to achieve most, if not all, their policy goals, whether rights based or material based.
- Black-white coalitions tend to shift from rights based to material based, depending on historical conditions.

Figure 7.2 African American Coalition Partners, 1700s–1990s

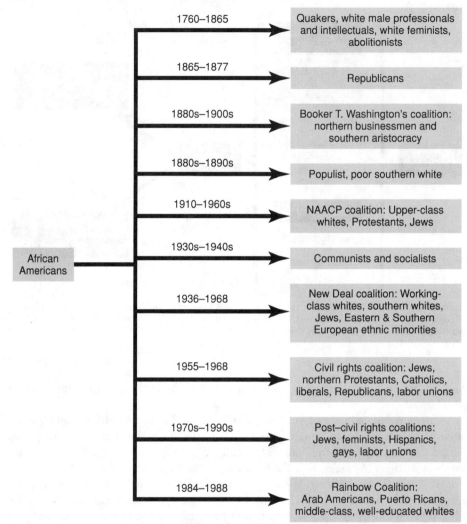

1760–1865	Quakers, white male professionals and intellectuals, white feminists, abolitionists
1865–1877	Republicans
1880s–1900s	Booker T. Washington's coalition: northern businessmen and southern aristocracy
1880s–1890s	Populist, poor southern white
1910–1960s	NAACP coalition: Upper-class whites, Protestants, Jews
1930s–1940s	Communists and socialists
1936–1968	New Deal coalition: Working-class whites, southern whites, Jews, Eastern & Southern European ethnic minorities
1955–1968	Civil rights coalition: Jews, northern Protestants, Catholics, liberals, Republicans, labor unions
1970s–1990s	Post–civil rights coalitions: Jews, feminists, Hispanics, gays, labor unions
1984–1988	Rainbow Coalition: Arab Americans, Puerto Ricans, middle-class, well-educated whites

(African Americans)

Sources: Robert Allen, *The Reluctant Reformers: Reform Movements in the United States* (Washington, D.C.: Howard University Press, 1973); and Robert Smith, *We Have No Leaders: African Americans in the Post–Civil Rights Era* (Albany: State University of New York Press, 1996).

- Viable coalitions with whites are sometimes not possible, forcing blacks to act alone in black nationalist or other forms of intragroup coalitions.
- When coalitions with whites are formed, they tend, because of racism and white supremacist thinking, to be tenuous, unstable, and frequently short-lived, requiring constant rebuilding.

Given these basic theoretical points, we begin by analyzing the first significant African American coalition: the rights-based abolitionist movement.

THE FIRST RIGHTS-BASED MOVEMENT: THE ABOLITIONIST COALITION

The movement that emerged in the 1830s to abolish slavery was the first rights-based coalition in the United States. It, like the early twentieth-century civil rights movement, was organized and led by well-educated, middle- to upper-class black and white males, many of whom (especially among the blacks) were ministers.[5] The abolitionist movement anticipates the conflicts and tensions that have characterized all subsequent reform coalitions involving African Americans and whites, whether rights or material based.

In *The Reluctant Reformers: Racism and Social Reform Movements in the United States,* Robert Allen analyzes six major social reform movements, beginning with the abolitionist movement and including populism, the progressive movement, feminism, the labor movement, and the socialist and communist movements. African Americans were involved in each of these reform movements in coalitions with whites. These alliances span a hundred years, from the 1830s to the 1930s, and as Allen points out, they cover the whole span of social classes from middle- and upper-class whites in the abolitionist movement to poor and working-class whites in the populist and labor movements. Some of these movements were based in the North; some, like the populist movements, were rural; others, like the progressive and labor movements, were predominantly urban. White men led most of these movements, but white women in the 1860s developed a movement of their own. However, as Allen writes, none of these differences among whites—middle class or poor, urban or rural, north or south, male or female—"correlates with anti racist thinking."[6] That is, beginning with the abolitionist movement, racism and the ideology of white supremacy have operated to effectively undermine all reform coalitions in the United States.

The principal white leader of the abolitionist movement was William Lloyd Garrison, who in 1833 founded the American Anti-Slavery Society. The leading black abolitionist was Frederick Douglass. Although both Douglass and Garrison were "militant abolitionists," favoring the immediate abolition of slavery, they differed over strategy and tactics. Eventually these differences led to the breakup of the coalition.

Garrison was an uncompromising critic of slavery and the Constitution that ordained it, as may be seen in the following famous quote from the first issue of his newspaper *The Liberator*:

> Let southern oppressors tremble . . . let northern apologists tremble, let all the enemies
> of the persecuted blacks tremble. . . . Urge me not to use moderation in a cause like the
> present. I am in earnest—I will not equivocate—I will not excuse—and I will be heard![7]

Despite this militancy, Garrison was committed to "moral suasion," nonviolence, and white leadership of the abolitionist movement. Garrison and his followers were also opposed to the formation of the National Negro Congress, discussed later in the chapter. These positions eventually led Douglass and other black abolitionists to break with Garrison and seek their way alone. One hundred years later, similar differences between blacks and whites would lead to a breakup of the civil rights coalition and the emergence of the separatist black power movement.

William Lloyd Garrison and Frederick Douglass, leaders of the abolitionist movement, the first rights-based coalition for universal freedom.

Although the middle-class whites who led the abolitionist movement were not racists, many were white supremacists and based their opposition to slavery not on a belief in the equality of the races but on moral and religious grounds. That is, although blacks might not be the equal of whites, for one man to enslave another was nevertheless a violation of the principles of the Declaration of Independence and Jesus' doctrine of universal brotherhood.[8] This moral and religious basis of the movement led many whites to insist that nonviolent resistance was the only acceptable way to oppose slavery.

Douglass initially embraced Garrison's moralism and nonviolence, but as time went on and these approaches did not prove successful, he and many other black abolitionists abandoned a sole reliance on moral suasion and embraced political action (support for the antislavery Liberty Party) and violent resistance and revolt. The final reason for the collapse of the abolitionist coalition was the issue of who should lead it—in Douglass's words, who should be part of "the generalship of the movement." Douglass argued that whites in the movement ignored blacks, refusing to recognize or respect their leadership. In words that sound like Stokely Carmichael and the 1960 black power advocates, Douglass said:

> The man who has *suffered* the wrong is the man to demand the redress—the man struck is the man to CRY OUT and he who has endured *the cruel pangs of slavery* is the man to *advocate liberty*. It is evident that we must be our own representatives and advocates, but peculiarly—not distinct from—but in connection with our white friends.[9]

This first rights-based coalition did not directly result in slavery's abolition but it did, along with the slave revolts and John Brown's raid at Harpers Ferry, contribute to the climate that resulted in the crisis leading up to the Civil War.[10]

ABOLITIONISM AND FEMINISM

Early feminists—advocates of equality of rights for women—supported the abolition of slavery as part of a general moral stance in favor of universal freedom for all persons. And Frederick Douglass and many black abolitionists were strong supporters of women's rights, again as part of a general moral stance in favor of universal freedom.[11] Thus, these two rights-based movements formed a coalition on the basis of equality and universal freedom for all persons without regard for race or gender. Yet this coalition, like the abolitionist coalition, was tenuous and unstable; in the end, it collapsed.

First, unlike Douglass, many abolitionists, black and white, discriminated against women, refusing, for example, to allow women to sign the Anti-Slavery Society's Declaration of Principles, hold leadership positions in the group, or serve as antislavery lecturers (see Box 7.1). (Women, black and white, later formed their own National Female Anti-Slavery Society.) Although most white feminists were also middle-class profession-

═══════════ BOX 7.1 ═══════════
Maria W. Stewart—Abolitionist and Feminist

O, ye daughters of Africa, Awake! Awake! Arise! No longer sleep or slumber, but distinguish yourselves. Show forth to the world that we are endowed with noble and exalted faculties.

Maria W. Stewart (1832)

Antebellum-era American society was not only racist but sexist and patriarchical. African American women therefore found themselves in two struggles for freedom—for the liberation of their race and for the freedom of their sex. Most men (Frederick Douglass was a noteworthy exception) in the abolitionist movement, whether black or white, shared the sexist and patriarchical views of their times, viewing the woman's role as that of wife and homemaker. They thought it especially inappropriate for women to take part in politics or engage in public speaking. Thus, although black women constituted half the slave population, in general they were discouraged from taking an active part in the abolitionist movement.

A number of African American women rejected the idea that their role should be limited to that of wife and homemaker and became leaders in the freedom struggles of African Americans and women. Students of African American history are familiar with Sojourner Truth and Harriet Tubman, two leading antebellum-era abolitionists and feminists. Maria W. Stewart is less well known although she is probably the first African American woman to take a leadership role in the abolitionist and feminist movements.

(Continued)

BOX 7.1 Continued

Maria W. Stewart was born in Boston in 1803. At age five she was orphaned and became a servant to a white clergyman, where she received her education by attending Sunday School and reading material from the clergyman's library. A deeply religious woman, Stewart was well versed in the Bible, history, and the classics, and she used these materials in her writing and lectures. She was also influenced by David Walker and his *Appeal*.[a] Widowed after only three years of marriage, Stewart began her career as an antislavery and feminist lecturer and writer.

The historian Dorothy Porter describes her as "probably the earliest Negro woman lecturer and writer,"[b] and Marilyn Richardson writes that in September 1832, "Maria Stewart . . . did what no American-born woman, black or white, before her is recorded as having done. She mounted a lecture platform and raised a political argument before a 'promiscuous audience,' that is one composed of both men and women."[c] Stewart's career as a writer and lecturer lasted little more than three years, but during that time, while living in Boston, she published a political treatise and a religious pamphlet, and she gave three public lectures. Her abolitionist views were deeply religious in that she viewed slavery as a violation of Christian principles. She was also a "moral suasionist" in the tradition of William Lloyd Garrison, although like David Walker she also embraced the idea of armed struggle. She strongly opposed the idea of colonialization and emigration to Africa, arguing that universal freedom for African men and women was possible in the United States.

Stewart was an ardent feminist. Not only did she urge black women to join the abolitionist movement, but she also encouraged the formation of black women's rights organizations and literary societies. She supported the then-radical idea that black women should pursue an education and career outside the home, writing, "How long shall the fair daughters of Africa be compelled to bury their minds and talents beneath a load of iron pots and kettles?"[d]

After the Civil War, Stewart became a teacher in the Washington, D.C., schools and later the Matron of Freedmen's Hospital. She died in 1879 at the age of seventy-six. Shortly before her death she received a pension from her husband's service in the War of 1812, which she used to finance the publication of a new edition of her collected essays and speeches, entitled *Meditations from the Pen of Mrs. Maria W. Stewart*.

[a]On David Walker's radical abolitionist manifesto, see Herbert Aptheker, *One Continual Cry: David Walker's Appeal to the Citizens of the Colored World* (New York: Humanities Press, 1965).

[b]Dorothy Porter, "The Organized Educational Activities of Negro Literary Societies, 1828–1846," *Journal of Negro Education* 5 (1936): 569. Porter discusses Stewart's writings in her *Early Negro Writings, 1760–1873* (Boston: Beacon Press, 1771).

[c]Marilyn Richardson, *Maria Stewart: America's First Black Woman Political Writer* (Bloomington: Indiana University Press, 1987): v. This book contains a full compilation of Stewart's writings.

[d]Ibid., p. 38.

---

als, men nevertheless argued that they were inferior to men in status and therefore should not be allowed to exercise freedom on the same basis as men.

On the other hand, many white feminists were white supremacists who embraced the antislavery coalition only as a means to advance the cause of women's rights. As Allen noted, "With the exception of equal rights, feminists and other female reformers shared the same views as the men of their class."[12]

The key issue, however, in the collapse of the black-feminist coalition was black suffrage—whether black men should be granted the right to vote before white women. This issue first emerged with the adoption of the Fourteenth Amendment, which for the first time included the word *male* in the Constitution. Foner contends that feminist leaders felt a "deep sense of betrayal" by this action and "consequently embarked on a course that severed their historic alliance with abolitionism and created an independent feminist movement, seeking a new constituency outside of the reform milieu."[13]

The decisive break came with the adoption of the Fifteenth Amendment, which granted black men the right to vote but denied it to women. Leading feminists opposed the amendment unless women were included because they said it would permit black men, their "inferiors," more rights than white women. Frederick Douglass, a supporter of women's suffrage and vice president of the Women's Equal Rights League, made an eloquent rebuttal to these arguments:

> I must say that I do not see how any one can pretend that there is the same urgency in giving the ballot to the woman as the Negro. With us the matter is a question of life and death, at least in fifteen states of the union. When women are dragged from their houses and hung up on lamp posts; when their children are torn from their arms and their brains dashed on the pavement; when they are the object of insult and outrage at every turn; when they are in danger of having their homes burnt down over their heads; when their children are not allowed to enter schools; then they will have an urgency to the ballot equal to our own.[14]

Douglass's arguments were not persuasive, and by the end of Reconstruction, the white feminist movement had become "predominantly (although not solely) the fight of white women to be included in the rights and privileges of a racist society."[15] This again illustrates our theoretical point about the tenuousness and instability of black-white coalitions. These tensions and conflicts between the women's-based rights movement and the black-based rights movement continue one hundred years later, as reflected in the debate about the inclusion of gender in the Civil Rights Act of 1964 and the debate about affirmative action in the 1990s.

MATERIAL-BASED COALITION: FROM POPULISM TO COMMUNISM

Populism

The populist movement of the 1890s sets the pattern of all future material-based coalitions between whites and African Americans. C. Vann Woodward, the historian of the populist movement, writes, "It is altogether probable that during the brief populist upheaval of the nineties Negroes and Native whites achieved a greater comity of mind and harmony of political purpose [than] ever before or since in the south."[16] A reexamination of Woodward's research on the populist movement shows, as one historian says, that he was "much too generous"; that rather than being a grand coalition of poor whites and blacks, populism from the outset was undermined by the racism and white supremacist thinking of its white leaders who sought to manipulate their black coalition partners for their own interests.[17]

The populist movement emerged out of the economic depression of the 1890s as black sharecroppers and poor white farmers were faced with falling wages and prices, high taxes, and heavy debt. As a result of this crisis there was a material basis for a coalition between these two groups, who by pooling their resources (including their votes) could effectively challenge the power of the dominant economic and political elites. Led by Tom Watson of Georgia, the populists formed the Southern Alliance and later the Populist party, both of which advocated such progressive reforms as debt relief, government ownership or regulation of the railroads, and a graduated income tax. Although some white populists for a time sincerely tried to build a biracial, class-oriented movement, from the outset racism was a major stumbling block. For example, blacks were not allowed to join the Southern Alliance; rather, they were segregated in a separate white-led Colored Farmers Alliance. And while the Populist party appealed for black voter support and allowed blacks to serve as leaders (although in small numbers), it too was eventually undermined as poor whites were convinced by Democratic party leaders that a vote for the interracial Populist party was racial treason.[18] As a result, white populists eventually succumbed to what Richard Hoftstader called the "Negro bogey," and within a decade this first material-based coalition of African Americans and whites had collapsed.[19] Eventually, Tom Watson, the movement's leader, turned from preaching interracial unity and solidarity to an extreme form of racism and white supremacy, supporting lynching and the disenfranchisement of blacks.[20] Thus, within the short span of a decade, populism went from "colored and white in the ditch unite" to "lynch the Negro."[21]

The Progressives

The populist movement was, as Hofstader writes, "the first modern political movement of practical importance in the United States to insist that the federal government has some responsibility for the common weal; indeed it was the first such movement to attack seriously the problems created by industrialism."[22] It was succeeded a generation later by the progressive movement. The progressives, unlike the populists, were largely urban, middle-class professional whites who sought, like the populists, federal regulation of the economy and reforms in the political process, such as the initiative and referendum. It too, however, was affected by the "Negro bogey."[23] The Progressive party, for example, refused to condemn racial discrimination, lynching, or the denial of black voting rights. And one of its principal leaders, President Theodore Roosevelt, was probably the most racist president of the twentieth century (see chapter 12).

The Labor Movement

The African American people are largely a working-class people; therefore, their natural coalition partners should be working-class whites and their trade union organizations. As Carmichael and Hamilton said in their chapter, "The Myth of Coalitions," in the book *Black Power*, "It is hoped eventually that there will be a coalition of poor whites and blacks. This is the only coalition which seems acceptable to us and we see such a coalition as the major instrument of change in American society."[24] For much of American history Carmichael and Hamilton's hope for a coalition with the white working class has been just that, a hope, because "the history of the American labor movement is one long and shameful story of exclusion, discrimination, outright treachery and open violence against Black, Mexican, Chinese and other nonwhite workers."[25] With a few exceptions—the Knights of Labor during Reconstruction and the International Workers of the World early in the twentieth century—American trade unions have either excluded blacks or forced them into segregated unions.[26] Even today, although organized labor has abolished racial segregation and was a major partner in the 1960s civil rights coalition, the white working class continues to exhibit more racist, white supremacist thinking than do middle-class, professional whites. In the early 1980s Robert Bostch conducted a series of interviews with white and black working-class men specifically designed to explore the prospects for coalition politics. Bostch concluded that working-class white men

> exhibit enough racial prejudice so that they could be separated from their black working class peers on a number of issues. . . . Blacks are seen as threatening because they wish to use the powers of the national government to change the rules of meritocracy to gain an unfair advantage. This stereotype embitters white workers toward all governmental power and threatens to alienate whites from blacks, who generally feel they are discriminated against.[27]

As is shown in chapters 9 and 10, blacks and working-class whites were partners, although uneasy ones, in the New Deal coalition (which enacted many of the reform proposals of the populists and progressives), but this was because President Franklin D. Roosevelt scrupulously avoided taking any stand on race issues, even refusing to support antilynching legislation. Once the Democratic party in the 1960s embraced the cause of civil rights, the New Deal coalition of blacks and working-class whites began to collapse. And despite eloquent pleas and constant campaigning on working-class concerns, Jesse Jackson in his two campaigns for president received more support from middle-class white professionals than from poor and working-class whites.

Socialists and Communists

Even socialists and communists have not been able to avoid the "Negro bogey" of racism and white supremacy. The Socialist party was organized in 1901, and although it was ostensibly devoted to a broad-based coalition of workers, it initially embraced racism and white supremacy. Jack London, one of the party's founders, said, "I am first a white man and only then socialist," and the party's newspaper, *Appeal to Reason,* declared, "Socialists believe in justice to the Negro, not social equality. . . . Socialism will separate the races."[28] Only when the socialists began to face competition from the Communist party did they change their racist position, begin to recruit blacks (such as A. Phillip Randolph, the labor leader), and under the leadership of Norman Thomas in the 1930s, take forthright stands against racial segregation and discrimination.[29]

The Communist party, Robert Allen writes,

> has left a lasting imprint on the struggle for racial equality. Despite the generally negative image of the party conveyed in popular media and standard history texts, the

Communist Party in its heyday probably did more than any other predominantly white political group to promote racial equality in American life.[30]

However, as the African American novelist Richard Wright argued in his eloquent essay in *The God That Failed,* although the Communist party supported the cause of racial equality sincerely, it was also a part of a strategy dictated from Russia to manipulate African Americans in order to further the objectives of the Soviet Union.[31]

Historically, blacks have been willing to join as partners in material-based reform coalitions with whites; however, whites have been reluctant, unreliable partners, forcing blacks to act alone or seek white partners in rights-based coalitions.

THE SECOND RIGHTS-BASED COALITION: THE CIVIL RIGHTS MOVEMENT

The NAACP Coalition

The civil rights movement has its origins in the Niagara Conference called by W. E. B. Du Bois in 1905 (see Box 7.2). Four years after the conference, the National Association for the Advancement of Colored People (NAACP) was founded; until the 1960s it was the principal civil rights protest organization. Until the late 1960s, the NAACP was the classic black-white rights-based coalition. It was founded by upper-middle-class white Protestants and Jews on the hundredth anniversary of the birth of Abraham Lincoln. Several of the founders were socialists, including Mary White Ovington and William English Walling. The only black among the founders was Du Bois.

From the beginning, there was tension between blacks and whites in the organization over its leadership and strategy. William Monroe Trotter and a number of other blacks who were involved in the Niagara Conference refused to join the group, arguing that whites could not be trusted to advance the cause of blacks. These tensions over white leadership continued until the 1960s (the association did not get its first black executive director until James Weldon Johnson was appointed in 1920) when blacks took over all the top leadership positions and the overwhelming majority of seats on the executive board.

━━━━━━━━━━━━━━━━━━━ **BOX 7.2** ━━━━━━━━━━━━━━━━━━━

We Face a Condition, Not a Theory: W. E. B. Du Bois and the Changing African American Quest for Universal Freedom

It is often suggested that political philosophy and ideas are the products of the concrete conditions and circumstances of a people. Nowhere is this better demonstrated than in the long life and career of Dr. W. E. B. Du Bois, the greatest scholar and thinker in the history of African American thought. Du Bois was born on February 23, 1868, in Great Barrington, Massachusetts. He died ninety-five years later in the West African country of Ghana on the eve of the 1963 March on Washington. In these ninety-five years, Du Bois's life was one of extraordinary schol-

Dr. W. E. B. Du Bois, preeminent African American intellectual, a founder of the civil rights and Pan-African movements, embraced communism in the last years of his life.

arship and political leadership, a life that at one point or another embraced every tendency in African American thought—integration, black nationalism, and finally socialism and communism.

Du Bois was graduated from Fisk University, a black institution in Nashville, Tennessee, in 1888. In 1895 he became the first African American to receive a Ph.D. from Harvard (he came within a couple of months of earning a second Ph.D. from the University of Berlin). His doctoral dissertation, *The Suppression of the African Slave Trade to the United States, 1638–1870*, was the first volume published in Harvard's Historical Studies series. He later went on to publish fifteen other books on politics and race, three historical novels, two autobiographies, and numerous essays and works of fiction and poetry. While a professor at Atlanta University, Du Bois directed the first large-scale social science research project on the problem of race in the United States. Among his more important books are *Black Reconstruction in America*, a massive study showing that Reconstruction was one of the first efforts in American history to achieve democracy for working people; *The Philadelphia Negro: A Social Study*, the first sociological analysis of an urban community; and *The Souls of Black Folk*, his classic analysis of the psychological, cultural, and sociopolitical underpinnings of the African American experience. Probably no other book has had a greater impact on African American thinking than *The Souls of Black Folk*. In it Du Bois states for the first time the enduring tension in African American thought between integration and nationalism:

> One ever feels his twoness—an American, a Negro, two souls, two thoughts, two unreconciled strivings, two warring ideals in one dark body, whose dogged strength alone keeps it from being torn asunder. . . . He simply wishes to make it possible for a man to be both a Negro and American, without being cursed and spit upon by his fellows, without having the doors of opportunity closed roughly in his face.

In addition to his life of the mind and scholarship, Du Bois was an extraordinary political leader (from the death of Booker T. Washington in 1915 until the mid-1930s, Du Bois was probably the most influential African American leader). Early in his career, Du Bois remarked,

(Continued)

BOX 7.2 Continued

"We face a condition, not a theory." Therefore, any philosophy, ideology, or strategy that gave promise of altering the oppressed conditions of the race should be embraced. And as the conditions of African Americans changed, so did the thought of Du Bois. Early in his career in his famous "Conservation of Races" essay, Du Bois appears to embrace black nationalism and separate development as a means to conserve the distinctive culture of the group. Later, in the face of Booker Washington's accommodation of the segregation and racial oppression that emerged after the end of Reconstruction, Du Bois embraced integration, organizing in 1905 the Niagara Conference as a forum for militant protest for civil rights and universal freedom in the United States. In organizing the Niagara Conference and authoring its manifesto, Du Bois became the "Father of the Civil Rights Movement." Four years later in 1909, Du Bois was the only black among the founders of the NAACP. Until the 1930s he edited *The Crisis*, the NAACP's magazine, using it as a forum to attack white supremacy and racism and to espouse the cause of equality and universal freedom. Watching the deteriorating conditions of blacks during the Depression, Du Bois once again embraced black nationalism, arguing that blacks should develop a separate "group economy" of producers and cooperative consumers. Charging that the NAACP had become too identified with the concerns of middle-class blacks, in 1934 Du Bois resigned from the association and his editorship of *The Crisis*. Du Bois also expressed his interest in nationalism in terms of Pan-Africanism—the idea that the African people everywhere share a common culture and interest. In 1900 he organized the first Pan-African Conference in London, which brought together African leaders and intellectuals from Africa, the United States, and the Caribbean. He was a principal leader of the four other Pan-African Conferences held between 1912 and 1927. And at the end of World War I and again at the end of World War II, Du Bois attended the peace conferences, urging that the European powers develop plans to free their African colonies. Du Bois briefly joined the Socialist party in 1912 and continued to flirt with socialist ideas thereafter; however, during the 1950s he apparently came to the conclusion that universal freedom for blacks and working people could not be achieved under capitalism and so in 1956 he joined the Communist party and shortly thereafter moved to Ghana. The last years of his life were spent editing the *Encyclopedia Africana*, a project funded and supported by the Ghana Academy of Sciences.

In his autobiography, Du Bois wrote,

> I think I may say without boasting that in the period 1910 to 1930 I was a main factor in revolutionizing the attitude of the American Negro toward caste. My stinging hammer blows made Negroes aware of themselves, confident of their possibilities and determined self-assertion. So much so that today common slogans among Negro people are taken bodily from the words of my mouth.

Du Bois was not an immodest man; in fact, he was often referred to as an arrogant elitist, but in regard to the observation above he was not exaggerating.[a]

---

[a]There are several good book-length studies of Du Bois's life and career. See Francis Broderick, *W. E. B. Du Bois: New Leader in Time of Crisis* (Palo Alto, CA: Stanford University Press, 1959); Elliot Rudwick, *W. E. B. Du Bois: Propagandist of the Negro Protest* (New York: Athenaeum, 1968); Gerald Horne, *Black and Red: W. E. B. Du Bois and the Afro-American Response to the Cold War, 1944–63* (Albany: State University of New York Press, 1986); and David L. Lewis, *W. E. B. Du Bois: Autobiography of a Race, 1868–1919* (New York: Henry Holt, 1973).

The Strategy of the NAACP, 1910–1954: Persuasion, Lobbying, and Litigation

The civil rights movement may be divided into three phases, based on the dominant strategy employed to pursue its goals.[32] From roughly 1910 to the 1930s, the dominant forms of activity were persuasion and lobbying. During these years the NAACP developed a campaign of public education and propaganda under the direction of Du Bois, editor of the NAACP magazine, *The Crisis*.[33] This campaign was designed to combat white supremacist propaganda and shape a favorable climate of public opinion on civil rights for African Americans.

The NAACP also engaged in an unsuccessful lobbying effort to convince Congress to pass a law making lynching a federal crime. Under the federal system, lynching—the ritual murder of blacks by southern racists—was a state crime, but southern states refused to arrest and punish the perpetrators. Thus, there was need for a federal law. Although the antilynching legislation twice passed the House, it was defeated in the Senate as a result of southern filibusters.[34] The NAACP was more successful in other lobbying efforts. It succeeded in blocking passage of immigration legislation that would have prohibited the legal entry into the United States of persons of African descent. And in a coalition with organized labor, it was successful in lobbying the Senate to defeat the nomination by President Herbert Hoover of John C. Parker to the Supreme Court because of his alleged antilabor and antiblack views.[35]

From the 1930s to the 1950s, litigation was the dominant strategy of the NAACP. In 1939 the NAACP created a separate organization—the NAACP Legal Defense Fund—and this organization under the leadership of Charles Hamilton Houston and later Thurgood Marshall filed a series of cases in the Supreme Court seeking enforcement of the Fourteenth and Fifteenth Amendments. Several important cases were won during this period, including *Smith v. Allwright,* which invalidated the Texas Democratic party's whites only primary, and the famous *Brown v. Board of Education* decision, which reversed the doctrine of separate but equal established in 1896 in *Plessy v. Ferguson*.[36]

The Southern Christian Leadership Conference and the Strategy of Protest, 1955–1965

The final phase of the civil rights movement involved mass protests and demonstrations.[37] From the 1900s until the 1950s the civil rights movement was dominated by the middle-class, northern-based NAACP coalition. From 1955 to 1965 the movement was dominated by Dr. Martin Luther King, Jr., and the Southern Christian Leadership Conference (SCLC). Unlike the NAACP, SCLC was an intraracial coalition of black ministers and churches based in the South.[38] Beginning with the Montgomery bus boycott, King and SCLC led a series of demonstrations in the South protesting segregation in public places and the denial of black voting rights. King and the SCLC were later joined in the southern protest movement by the Student Nonviolent Coordinating Committee (SNCC), an interracial coalition of black and white college students, and the Congress of Racial Equality (CORE), also an interracial coalition of black and white activists.[39]

Although the strategy of King and his colleagues was to hold peaceful, nonviolent demonstrations, these actions were met with widespread violence by racist southern whites (including the police). This violence, televised around the world, forced a reluctant President Kennedy (and later President Lyndon Johnson) to propose comprehensive civil rights and voting rights legislation. After the violent demonstrations in 1963 at Birmingham, Alabama, President Kennedy proposed the Civil Rights Act, which Congress enacted in 1964. After the violent demonstrations in Selma, Alabama, in 1965, President Johnson proposed and the Congress passed the Voting Rights Act.

Two points should be emphasized about the passage of these laws in 1964 and 1965. First, the president and Congress responded to the demands of the movement only after the violence at Selma and Birmingham was televised. Second, the strategy of protest developed by Dr. King and his associates was deliberately designed to bring pressure on the president and Congress by activating a broad lobbying coalition: liberals, labor, and northern religious groups.[40] It was this broad coalition—not blacks acting alone—that brought about the ultimate passage of the first comprehensive civil rights legislation since Reconstruction.[41] However—as our theory of African American coalition politics predicts—almost immediately after the passage of the Voting Rights Act, this coalition of blacks and whites began to fall apart, as blacks shifted from a rights-based movement politics to a material-based interest group politics.

THE BLACK POWER MOVEMENT AND THE TRANSFORMATION FROM MOVEMENT TO INTEREST GROUP POLITICS

The Origins of the Black Power Movement

The political scientist Sidney Tarrow writes:

> Protest cycles can either end suddenly, through repression, or more slowly, through a combination of features: the institutionalization of the most successful movements, factionalization within them and new groups which rise on the crest of the wave, and the exhaustion of mass political involvement. The combination of institutionalization and factionalization often produce determined minorities, who respond to the decline of popular involvement by turning upon themselves and—in some cases—using organized violence.[42]

This combination of features characterized the end of the civil rights movement.[43]

Two weeks after the signing of the Voting Rights Act, Watts, the black section of Los Angeles, exploded in three days of rioting. The 1965 Watts rebellion was followed by a series of riots in most of the large cities of the North. In 1966, Stokely Carmichael, the newly elected chairman of SNCC, started the black power movement. The urban riots and black power led to a fundamental transformation of the civil rights movement and the emergence of a new structure of black interest organizations.

SNCC—the most radical of the civil rights organizations—sparked this transformation by introducing the rhetoric and symbol of black power during the 1966 Meredith March in Mississippi.[44] For several years, the more nationalistic SNCC workers had attempted to bring a greater number of nationalist themes into the civil rights movement, themes drawn from Malcolm X and the Algerian writer, Frantz Fanon.[45] In 1966 they prepared a position paper that set forth the fundamental themes of black power, including a call for the exclusion of whites from the organization. Although Stokely Carmichael initially joined the majority of the SNCC staff in rejecting these nationalist themes, after he defeated the incumbent SNCC chairman John Lewis (now a congress-man from Georgia) in a bitter and divisive election, he changed his position and em-braced the principles of black power. He then persuaded SNCC to join the Meredith March and use it as a forum to articulate and build support for black power. For a week, television coverage of the March highlighted the divisions within the civil rights move-ment. In his speeches, Dr. King continued to espouse the philosophy of black-white coalitions, integration, and nonviolence, while Carmichael shouted black power and called for racial separatism and violent resistance to attacks by southern racists. Al-though the national media presented black power as a radical, revolutionary movement, it actually had a dual impact on African American politics: one radical, one reform.

THE DUAL IMPACT OF BLACK POWER: RADICALISM AND REFORM

As Figure 7.3 illustrates, the black power movement sparked two separate, distinct, and contradictory developments in black politics. First, it stimulated the development of a

Figure 7.3 The Dual Impact of the Black Power Movement on African American Politics, 1960–1990

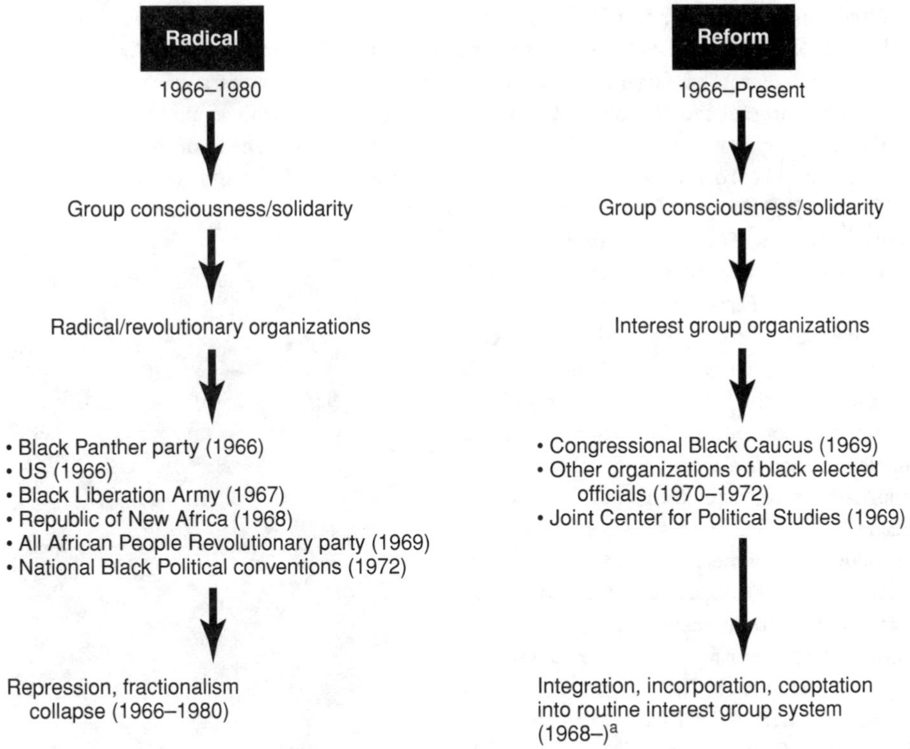

Radical	Reform
1966–1980	1966–Present
↓	↓
Group consciousness/solidarity	Group consciousness/solidarity
↓	↓
Radical/revolutionary organizations	Interest group organizations
↓	↓
• Black Panther party (1966) • US (1966) • Black Liberation Army (1967) • Republic of New Africa (1968) • All African People Revolutionary party (1969) • National Black Political conventions (1972)	• Congressional Black Caucus (1969) • Other organizations of black elected officials (1970–1972) • Joint Center for Political Studies (1969)
↓	↓
Repression, fractionalism collapse (1966–1980)	Integration, incorporation, cooptation into routine interest group system (1968–)[a]

[a]Integration, incorporation, and cooptation are used interchangeably to mean the absorption of previously unrepresented groups into the routine operation of the political system.

Source: Robert C. Smith, *We Have No Leaders: African Americans in the Post–Civil Rights Era* (Albany: State University of New York Press, 1996).

wide variety of radical, nationalistic, and revolutionary organizations and leaders, including Huey Newton and the Black Panther party (see Box 7.3), Ron Karenga and US (a radical cultural nationalist organization), and Imari Obadele and the Republic of New Africa (discussed in chapter 8). For a decade the African American freedom struggle took a sharp turn toward radicalism. However, by 1980, as a result of factionalism and infighting within and among the groups, and political repression by the FBI, the army, and the police, the radical wing of the movement had collapsed.[46]

The second development sparked by black power was the beginning of the integration or incorporation of blacks into routine interest group structure of conventional American politics. Although radicalism and nationalism characterized the early years of black power, ultimately it came to represent, as Figure 7.3 shows, a mild form of reformist black nationalism appealing to race group consciousness, solidarity, and independent, all-black interest group organizations.[47]

BOX 7.3

The Black Panther Party

The Black Panther Party for Self-Defense was founded in 1966, one year after the Watts riot, by Huey P. Newton and Bobby Seale, student activists at Oakland's Merritt College. Two years later, FBI director J. Edgar Hoover declared that the Black Panthers were "the greatest threat to the internal security of the United States" and targeted the group for elimination.[a] By 1970, the party was in disarray and on the verge of collapse as a result of the FBI's systematic campaign of repression and of the group's own factional infighting and corruption.

The Black Panthers adopted the name and symbol, black panther, from the Lowndes County, Alabama, Freedom Democratic Party, which used a black panther as its symbol. (The Lowndes County party was founded in the early 1960s by southern civil rights workers to encourage blacks to register to vote and run for office.) The Panthers, as the full name of the party implies, was originally founded as a "self-defense" organization. Newton and Seale were aware that the police in the nation's big cities frequently harassed and brutalized blacks. To try to stop this kind of police misconduct, the Panthers (dressed in black leather jackets and berets) organized armed patrols and dispatched them to the scene of any police incident involving blacks, Their purpose was to observe the behavior of the officers. Their slogan, to "Observe and protect," was derived from the Los Angeles Police Department's motto, "To serve and protect". Although the Panthers did not intervene in the police incidents, the mere presence of armed black men observing their behavior alarmed the

Huey P. Newton and Bobby Seale, founders of the Black Panther party.

police; soon a series of deadly gun battles occurred between the Panthers and the police in Oakland and San Francisco. Shortly thereafter the California Legislature began consideration of legislation to ban the carrying of loaded weapons in public. To protest this legislation, thirty armed Panthers marched into the state capitol at Sacramento on May 2, 1967. This demonstration received widespread attention and brought the heretofore obscure group to the attention of the nation. The image of armed black men dressed in black captured the imagination of young blacks across the country and Panther party membership and chapters grew rapidly. By late 1968, the group had a membership estimated at three to five thousand and more than thirty chapters throughout the United States. Accompanying this rapid growth in membership, the Panthers adopted the ideology of revolutionary black nationalism and Marxist-Leninism, calling for violent revolution to overthrow the government of the United States. The rapid growth of the Panthers, the ongoing series of urban riots, and the Panthers turn to a revolutionary ideology alarmed government officials and led the FBI to target the group for destruction. Throughout 1968 and 1969, there were violent confrontations between the Panthers and the police. On April 6, 1968, Bobby Hutton, a seventeen-year-old Panther, was killed by the police and the Panther education minister Eldridge Cleaver was wounded. In October 1967, the Panther minister of defense Huey Newton killed an Oakland policeman; a year later Newton was convicted and sent to prison (Newton's trial and imprisonment resulted in "Free Huey" demonstrations throughout the world, bringing further attention to the group). In January 1969, two Panthers were shot to death at a student meeting at UCLA. (This shooting may have resulted from the FBI's efforts to create conflict between the Panthers and the rival organization, US.) In April 1969, twenty-one members of the Panthers were indicted in New York for conspiring to blow up several public buildings; and in December 1969, Fred Hampton, leader of the Chicago chapter, was killed in an early morning raid on his home. An independent citizen's investigation later determined that Hampton was murdered by the police. In 1969 Panther chairman Bobby Seale was bound, shackled, and gagged during his trial in Chicago. With a number of white antiwar protesters, he was on trial for an alleged conspiracy in causing the riots at the 1968 Democratic party convention. Those charges were dropped, but a year later Seale was again on trial; this time in New Haven, Connecticut, charged with thirteen other Panthers with the murder of a former Panther. Although the charges in this case were also later dismissed, partly as a result of Seale's long absence during the trials, the party began to fall into disarray and factional infighting.

In December 1972, the murder charges against Newton were overturned and he returned to his leadership of the group. By all accounts Newton brought a paranoid, corrupt, and violent style of leadership to the Panthers. Addicted to drugs and alcohol, Newton apparently ordered the murder of several factional rivals and eventually was himself accused of murdering a young woman; he fled to exile in Cuba. In the meantime, Eldridge Cleaver, in exile in Algeria, had established a rival, more militant faction of the party, which contributed to further factional infighting.

In its report on the FBI's campaign to destroy the Panthers, the Senate investigating committee found that by 1969 the Panthers were the major target of the FBI's campaign against black groups, accounting for 233 (79%) of 295 authorized actions.[b] The table of contents of the Senate report lists the following actions as part of the FBI's covert action program to destroy the Black Panther party:

1. The effort to promote violence between the Black Panther Party and the United Slaves ("US") Inc.
2. The effort to promote violence between the Blackstone Rangers and the Black Panther Party.

(Continued)

BOX 7.3 Continued

3. The effort to disrupt the Black Panther Party by causing internal dissension.
4. Covert efforts to undermine support of the Black Panther Party and destroy its public image.
5. Efforts to promote criticism of the Black Panthers in the mass media and to prevent the Black Panther Party and its sympathizers from expressing their views.[c]

All these efforts certainly contributed to the party's rapid decline; however, several recent studies show that the Panthers contributed to their own destruction through bloody internal conflicts, thugism, and other forms of corruption, including misappropriation of funds and drug abuse.[d]

In 1973 Bobby Seale ran for mayor of Oakland, losing to the incumbent by 33,000 votes. Subsequently, he moved to Philadelphia, wrote his memoirs (*Seize the Time: The Story of the Black Panther Party,* New York: Vintage Books, 1970), and now markets "Bobby's Barbecue" sauce. In the early 1980s, Eldridge Cleaver returned from his exile in Algeria. After the charges of parole violations against him were dropped, Cleaver moved to Berkeley and became a born-again Christian and ardent advocate of conservative causes. Huey Newton also returned from his exile, was found not guilty of murder, and earned a Ph.D. in philosophy from the University of California at Santa Cruz. In 1989 he was murdered on a dark street in Oakland, apparently in a drug deal gone bad. At the place of his killing someone left a wreath that read "To Huey, for the good years." Hundreds of 1960s radicals and revolutionaries gathered for his funeral and followed the procession through the streets of Oakland shouting, "Long Live Huey P, African people will be free."

Many of the Black Panthers were brave young men and women, willing to sacrifice their lives for freedom. And despite the paranoia and corruption of some of its top leaders, in the early years the party did good works, including forcefully challenging police brutality and providing a variety of community services such as free medical clinics, breakfast programs for poor kids, and food cooperatives. However, once the party turned from a primarily self-defense and self-help group to violent revolution, its destruction was inevitable, since no government that has the power will long tolerate a violent challenge to its authority.[e]

[a]U.S. Congress, Senate, *Select Committee to Study Government Operations with Respect to Intelligence Activities and the Rights of Americans, Book III, Final Report* (Washington, DC: Government Printing Office, 1976): 187.

[b]Ibid., p. 188.

[c]Ibid., p. 187.

[d]Hugh Pearson, *The Shadow of the Panther: Huey Newton and the Price of Black Power in America* (Reading, MA: Addison-Wesley, 1994).

[e]For an overview of the rise and decline of the Panthers, see Charles E. Jones, ed., *The Black Panther Party Reconsidered* (Baltimore, MD: Black Classics Press, 1998).

Black Power and Race Group Solidarity

Black power contributed to an increase in black group identification and solidarity. Political scientist Warren Miller observed, as a result of black power,

> the appropriate dimension for understanding the political behavior of black citizens may have changed. Contemporary black leaders may have helped shape the political meaning of being black in ways black leaders two decades before could not. Certainly, racial identity is now the most useful prescriptive measure of the political choice of many citizens.[48]

────────────────────── **TABLE 7.1** ──────────────────────

Racial Differences in "Group Benefit" Level of Political Conceptualization:
1960–1980

	1960	1964	1968	1972	1976	1980
Whites	31%	25%	20%	24%	23%	28%
Blacks	26%	47%	60%	51%	48%	54%

Source: Paul R. Hagner and John C. Pierce, "Racial Differences in Political Conceptualization," *Western Political Quarterly* 37 (June 1984): 222. Employing data from the Interuniversity Consortium for Political Research at the University of Michigan, Hagner and Pierce identified four major levels of political conceptualization: ideological, group benefit, nature of the times, and no political content. The "group benefit" category measures the extent to which individuals evaluate political issues in terms of their negative or positive impact on the group or group interests.

In Table 7.1, data are displayed showing the extent to which individuals think in "group benefit" terms—that is, the degree to which an individual evaluates political issues and events in terms of their positive or negative impact on the group or group interests.[49] The data show the progression of black political conceptualization in terms of racial group interest during the twenty-year period 1960–80—from 26 percent in 1960 to 54 percent in 1980; comparable figures for whites are 42 percent in 1960 and 28 percent in 1980. Although the highest level of group benefit responses among blacks is observed in 1968 at the high point of the black power movement, even after black power declined in salience, the group benefit percentages did not return to their earlier low levels. And this rise in group-based identification and solidarity is true of all categories of blacks, without respect to gender, education, age, or partisan affiliation.[50]

Black Power, Black Groups, and System Incorporation

Related to this increase in race group consciousness and solidarity, the black power movement also sparked the creation of a large number of new, racially exclusive (all-black) interest group organizations, including for a time an intraracial black coalition—the National Black Political Convention (see Box 7.4). From 1966 to 1969—the peak years of black power activism—more than seventy new black interest organizations were formed.[51] These organizations cover a broad range of interests—business and economic, educational and cultural, and professional and political. Also during this period the growing number of black elected officials began to form racially separate caucuses, including the Congressional Black Caucus and caucuses of black mayors, school board members, and state legislators.[52]

At the beginning of this chapter we discussed the argument of William Gamson that some groups are excluded from the routine system of American interest group politics and gain entry only as a result of a crisis in the system or if the excluded group shows a willingness to violate the "rules of the game" by resorting to illegitimate means for carrying on political conflict. The radical, revolutionary rhetoric of black power, the summers of urban riots from 1965 to 1968, and the revolutionary politics of the Black

<hr>

BOX 7.4

"We Must Unite . . ."—National Negro Congresses, 1830s, 1930s, 1970s

<hr>

In 1838, the Reverend Lewis Woodson, who wrote under the pseudonym Augustine and who with Martin Delaney is sometimes referred to as the "father of black nationalism," wrote these words:

> We should form an institution that will bring the most distant and detached portions of our people together, embrace their varied interests, and unite their whole moral power. Our collected wisdom should be assembled, to consult on measures pertaining to the general welfare, and so direct our energies, as to do the greatest good for the greatest number. Thus, united and thus directed, every weapon that prejudice has formed against us, would be rendered powerless; and our moral elevation would be as rapid, as it would be certain.[a]

The idea of black unity—that black people should form a grand coalition or congress of the race—is one of the oldest and most enduring in the African American political tradition. Three times—in the 1830s, 1930s, and 1970s—blacks have formed such a congress; and although each was successful for a time, in the end each collapsed because of class, institutional, and ideological differences.[b] These three experiments in race congresses spanning a century and a half suggest that African Americans are not and never have been a monolith, and that skin color and a common condition of race oppression are not sufficient to unite all African Americans.

The first effort at a grand coalition of African Americans—the National Negro Congress—was the most successful in terms of duration, meeting on and off from 1830 to 1864. Like the National Negro Congress of the 1930s and the National Black Political Convention of the 1970s, the 1830s congress included all the major political factions in the black community: conservatives and radicals, integrationists and nationalists, nonviolent "moral suasionists" and advocates of violent rebellion. It attracted such leading blacks of the era as Frederick Douglass, Martin Delaney, Henry Highland Garnett, and Lewis Woodson. These diverse personalities and factions were a source of the convention's greatest strength, but they were also the source of its weakness and ultimate collapse because these persons and factions could never reach agreement on common goals and strategies. Martin Delaney and his followers favored emigration. Frederick Douglass and his followers favored abolition and integration. Douglass favored nonviolence while Garnett called for a violent revolt of the slaves. In addition to these differences over ideology and strategy, there were other, continuing disagreements: conflict over what the race should be called—African, Colored American, oppressed American, Negro; debates over the merits of building separate community institutions such as schools, newspapers, and businesses; controversy about whether blacks should engage in what was called "servile" as compared to professional labor; and arguments over whether whites should be allowed to participate in the congress (they were included for a time, but eventually the congress voted to exclude all whites).

There was also class and institutional conflict between the middle-class black establishment of ministers, teachers, and businesspeople who tended to be conservative and integrationist, and the more radical, less well-off persons who tended to favor emigration. In 1854 the emigrationists, declaring that they could no longer work with the integrationists, formed their own congress and began to develop plans for emigration to Haiti and other places outside the United States. Douglass condemned the emigrationist convention as providing "proof to the enemies of the Negro that they were divided in thought and plans," but by 1854 the divisions were plain for all to see and the Negro Congress collapsed, although it reconvened one last time in 1864 to develop plans for postwar reconstruction.

In 1936 a second National Negro Congress was convened under the leadership of A. Phillip Randolph, the socialist trade union leader and a preeminent leader of the 1930s. It too included all the various factions in the black community—liberals and conservatives, Democrats and Republicans, communists and black nationalists—as well as a large contingent of white radicals and communists. According to the official call of the convention, "Let's Build a National Congress," the congress was to be a united front of all blacks without respect to ideology, and it was to develop a "minimum program of action upon which all could agree." But this was not possible. As in the 1830s, middle-class conservative black preachers, businesspeople, and civil rights leaders (including W. E. B. Du Bois) opposed the congress because it included communists. Randolph, to his later regret, responded to this opposition: "Negroes who elect to be communists need make no apology. That is their right. It is guaranteed by the federal constitution. Communists are not criminals." Black nationalists objected to the inclusion of whites. Thus, the basis for unity quickly evaporated.

Historians of this second Negro Congress agree that it had some modest success as a lobbying presence in Washington and was quite effective in organizing blacks at the local level around issues of jobs, housing, and police brutality; however, the ideological, institutional, and racial conflicts were too great for the congress to survive. The 1830s convention met more than a dozen times before it collapsed. The 1930s Congress met only three times before it fell apart. At the 1940 meeting of the Congress, Randolph and most of the blacks who were not communists withdrew, arguing that the congress had been taken over by white communists. Said Randolph, "The large number of white delegates at the Congress make it look like a joke. Why should a Negro Congress have white people in it? Why should communists have a position of control? . . . The American Negro will not long follow any organization which accepts direction and control from any white organization." Randolph, after leaving the congress, went on to form the March on Washington movement, which had some success in pressuring President Franklin Roosevelt to issue an executive order banning racial discrimination in wartime industries (see chapter 12). This movement, unlike the Congress, was not open to whites.

In 1972, blacks once again tried to unite, calling for a National Black Political Convention. According to the Congressional Black Caucus statement calling for the convention, "[It] is to be held for the purpose of developing a national black agenda and the crystallization of a national black strategy for 1972 and beyond." The statement also said, as did the ones issued in 1830 and 1936, that the convention would be "open to all people regardless of party affiliation

(Continued)

BOX 7.4 Continued

or ideology, to reflect the full diversity of interests of 25 million blacks." The co-conveners or leaders of the convention were poet-playwright Amiri Baraka (formerly Leroi Jones and in 1972 a leading spokesman for black nationalists); Congressman Charles Diggs, chair of the Congressional Black Caucus; and Richard Hatcher, mayor of Gary, Indiana.

The three thousand delegates to the convention in March of 1972, like those of the previous congresses, included the full diversity of black thought—nationalists and socialists, conservatives and communists, and Democrats and Republicans. Also, like the prior congresses, the 1972 convention was opposed by the civil rights establishment. Roy Wilkins, executive director of the NAACP, denounced the convention as "separatist" and "radical." Although the convention met five times between 1972 and 1984, the seeds of its dissolution were planted at its first meeting, where there was rancorous conflict between nationalists and integrationists over school busing for purposes of integration, support for the Palestinians in the Middle East conflict, and whether to form a black political party.

The convention adopted a radical, nationalist platform that was quickly disavowed by the Congressional Black Caucus and most black elected officials and civil rights leaders. This led Amiri Baraka to describe members of the Caucus and other elected officials as "Uncle Toms" and "whores" who were bought and paid for by white Democrats. By the time the convention met for a second time in 1974 in Little Rock, most of the black members of Congress (including Congressman Diggs) and elected officials had dropped out of the convention, leaving it largely a conclave of nationalists and radicals with only token representation from integrationists. This made for greater unity until Baraka in 1975 abruptly announced he had changed his ideology from nationalism to communism. Shortly thereafter he was dismissed from his leadership position in the convention, taking with him his core of followers. In 1980 the remaining members of the convention formed the National Black Independent Political Party (NBIPP), but in 1984 it fell apart in a dispute over whether the party should support Jesse Jackson's campaign for president, a position supported by the black nationalists but bitterly opposed by black Marxists in the party who were associated with the white-dominated Socialist Workers Party.

These three efforts at the development of an all-black congress show that the idea of blacks unifying in a single, all-embracing organization to work for the common good is an enduring one, but history indicates that African Americans are too divided—ideologically and organizationally—to allow such an organization to last for any long period of time.

[a]Quoted in Sterling Stuckey, *The Ideological Origins of Black Nationalism* (Boston: Beacon Press, 1972): 135.

[b]On the 1830s congress, see Howard Bell, "National Negro Conventions of the 1840s: Moral Suasion vs. Political Action," *Journal of Negro History* 22 (1957): 247–60, and Bella Gross, "The First National Negro Convention," *Journal of Negro History* 31 (1966): 435–43; on the 1930s convention, see Lawrence Wittner, "The National Negro Congress: A Reassessment," *American Quarterly* 22 (1968): 883–90; and on the 1970s convention, see Robert C. Smith, *We Have No Leaders: African Americans in the Post–Civil Rights Era* (Albany: State University of New York Press, 1996): chap. 2.

Panthers and other groups created a perception of crisis and showed that some blacks were indeed willing to engage in illegitimate forms of political conflict. Thus, the most enduring consequence of black power was reform, not radicalism—the Congressional Black Caucus rather than the Black Panther party.

Yet another consequence of the black power and civil rights movements was their impact on other American citizens, who felt excluded from the system. These black movements of the 1960s served as models for a wave of social movements and interest groups in the late 1960s and 1970s. Among the groups that patterned their activities after the civil rights and black power movements are women, Indians, Mexican Americans, Puerto Ricans, gays, Chinese Americans, the elderly, and to an extent the youth and antiwar protesters.[53]

SELECTED BIBLIOGRAPHY

Allen, Robert. *The Reluctant Reformers: Racism and Social Reform Movements in the United States*. Washington, DC: Howard University Press, 1983. A study of how racism historically has undermined liberal and progressive reform movements in the United States.

Browning, Rufus, D. Marshall, and D. Tabb, *Protest Is Not Enough: The Struggle of Blacks and Hispanics in Urban Politics*. Berkeley: University of California Press, 1984. An influential study of the conditions and policy consequences of multiethnic coalitions in post–civil rights era urban politics.

Carmichael, Stokely, and Charles Hamilton. *Black Power: The Politics of Liberation in America*. New York: Vintage Books, 1967. The influential manifesto of the rationale and strategy for the transformation from civil rights movement politics to black interest group politics.

Freeman, Jo, ed. *Social Movements of the Sixties and Seventies*. New York: Longman, 1983. A collection of papers showing how the African American civil rights and black power movements served as a model for social movement activism of many other groups in American society.

Gomes, Ralph, and Linda Faye Williams. "Coalition Politics: Past, Present and Future." In Ralph Gomes and Linda Williams, eds. *From Exclusion to Inclusion: The Long Struggle for African American Political Power*. Westport, CT: Praeger, 1992. A historical analysis of African American coalition politics and a discussion of future prospects.

Kluger, Richard. *Simple Justice: The History of* Brown v. Board of Education *and Black America's Struggle for Racial Equality*. New York: Vintage Books, 1977. A long but interesting-to-read account of the NAACP's litigation strategy from the 1930s to the 1950s, focusing on a detailed study of the famous *Brown* school desegregation case.

Morris, Aldon. *Origins of the Civil Rights Movement*. New York: Free Press, 1984. A study of the development of the final protest phase of the civil rights movement, focusing on the role of indigenous institutions such as black churches and colleges.

Piven, Frances Fox, and Richard Cloward. *Poor People's Movements: Why They Succeed, Why They Fail.* New York: Vintage Books, 1977. A detailed study of how various reform movements of poor people have been transformed into interest groups and thereby rendered largely ineffective.

Smith, Robert C. "Black Power and the Transformation from Protest to Politics." *Political Science Quarterly* 96 (Fall 1981): 431–444. A theoretical and empirical analysis of the important role of the black power movement in shaping contemporary black politics.

Wilke, H. A. M. *Coalition Politics.* New York: Harcourt, 1985. Although somewhat technical, a useful collection of papers on theory and research on coalition formations in politics.

Zangrando, Robert. *The NAACP Struggle against Lynching, 1909–1965.* Philadelphia: Temple University Press, 1980. A study of the NAACP's lobbying strategy, focusing on the unsuccessful effort to secure passage of federal antilynching legislation.

NOTES

1. William Gamson, "Stable Unrepresentation in American Society," *The American Behavioral Scientist* 12 (November–December 1968): 18.

2. See Aldon Morris and Cedric Herring, "Theory and Research on Social Movements," in Samuel Long, ed., *Annual Review of Political Science*, vol. 2 (Norwood, NJ: Ablex, 1987): 137–98, and H. A. M. Wilkie, ed., *Coalition Formation* (New York: Harcourt, 1985).

3. Ralph Gomes and Linda Williams, "Coalition Politics: Past, Present and Future," in Ralph Gomes and Linda Williams, eds., *From Exclusion to Inclusion: The Long Struggle for African American Political Power* (New York: Greenwood Press, 1992): 129–60.

4. In drawing a distinction between material- and rights-based issues and coalitions, we do not mean to imply that the right to health care or a job might not be appropriately viewed as a civil or citizenship right. Rather, the point is that in the United States a sharp line is usually drawn between economic and political or civil rights, a distinction African Americans and their leaders, willingly or not, have embraced. See Dana Hamilton and Charles Hamilton, *The Dual Agenda: Social Policies of Civil Rights Organizations, New Deal to Present* (New York: Columbia University Press, 1996).

5. On the abolitionist movement, see Leronne Bennett, *Before the Mayflower* (Baltimore: Penguin Books, 1966): chap. 6; John Hope Franklin, *From Slavery to Freedom* (New York: Knopf, 1980): 180–89; and Robert Allen, *The Reluctant Reformers: Racism and Social Reform Movements in the United States* (Washington, DC: Howard University Press, 1983): chap. 2.

6. Allen, *The Reluctant Reformers*, p. 248.

7. Quoted in Allen, *The Reluctant Reformers*, p. 24.

8. Franklin, *From Slavery to Freedom*, p. 182.

9. Quoted in Bennett, *Before the Mayflower*, p. 149.

10. On the slave revolts, see Herbert Aptheker, *American Negro Slave Revolts* (New York: Columbia University Press, 1948), and Eugene Genovese, *From Rebellion to Revolution: Afro-American Slave Revolts in the Making of the New World* (New York: Vintage Books, 1981). On John Brown, see Stephen Oakes, *To Purge This Land with Blood: A Biography of John Brown* (Amherst: University of Massachusetts Press, 1984).

11. Benjamin Quarles, "Frederick Douglass and the Women's Rights Movement," *Journal of Negro History* 25 (1940), and Phillip Foner, *Frederick Douglass on Women's Rights* (Westport, CT: Greenwood Press, 1976).

12. Allen, *The Reluctant Reformers*, p. 128.

13. Eric Foner, *Reconstruction: America's Unfinished Revolution, 1863–1877* (New York: Harper & Row, 1988): 253–54.

14. Quoted in Allen, *The Reluctant Reformers*, p. 143.

15. Ibid., p. 128.

16. C. Vann Woodward, *The Strange Career of Jim Crow* (New York: Oxford University Press, 1966): 64. See also Woodward's detailed study of populism, *Tom Watson: Agrarian Rebel* (New York: Oxford, 1938, 1963).

17. John Herbert Roper, *C. Vann Woodward, Southerner* (Athens: University of Georgia Press, 1987): 114.

18. On blacks and the populist movement, see Charles Crowe, "Tom Watson, Populists and Blacks Reconsidered," *Journal of Negro History* 40 (April 1970): 99–116, and Gerald Gaither, *Blacks and the Populist Revolt: Ballots and Bigotry* (Tuscaloosa: University of Alabama Press, 1977).

19. Richard Hofstadter, *The Age of Reform* (New York: Vintage Books, 1955): 61.

20. Historians disagree as to whether Watson was always a racist or whether his attitudes changed overtime with changing circumstances.

21. This quote is from Roper, *C. Vann Woodward*, p. 121.

22. Hofstadter, *The Age of Reform*, p. 61.

23. On the progressives, see Hofstader, *The Age of Reform*, chaps. 4–7.

24. Stokely Carmichael and Charles Hamilton, *Black Power* (New York: Vintage Books, 1967): 82.

25. Allen, *The Reluctant Reformers*, p. 166.

26. On the racist, exclusionary history of organized labor, see Phillip Foner, *Organized Labor and the Black Worker, 1619–1981* (New York: Praeger, 1974).

27. Robert Bostch, *We Shall Not Overcome* (Chapel Hill: University of North Carolina Press, 1981): 196.

28. Allen, *The Reluctant Reformers*, p. 213.

29. Ibid., p. 215.

30. Ibid. On the important role the communist party played in the African American freedom struggle, see Mark Naison, *Communists in Harlem during the Depression* (Urbana: University of Illinois Press, 1983).

31. Richard Crossman, ed., *The God That Failed* (New York: Harper & Row, 1949). On this point, see also Harold Cruse, *The Crisis of the Negro Intellectual* (New York: William Morrow, 1967): 147–71.

32. See Robert C. Smith, "Politics Is Not Enough: On the Institutionalization of the Afro-American Freedom Struggle," pp. 97–126, in Gomes and Williams, *From Exclusion to Inclusion,* and Robert C. Smith, *We Have No Leaders: African Americans in the Post–Civil Rights Era* (Albany: State University of New York Press, 1996): chap. 1.

33. David Lewis, *W. E. B. Du Bois: Biography of a Race, 1868–1919* (New York: Henry Holt, 1993): chap. 15.

34. Robert Zangrando, *The NAACP Crusade against Lynching, 1909–1950* (Philadelphia: Temple University Press, 1980).

35. Gilbert Ware, "Lobbying as a Means of Protest: The NAACP as an Agent of Equality," *Journal of Negro Education* 33 (Spring 1964): 103–07. On the NAACP's lobbying strategy, see the biography of its long-time chief Washington lobbyist by Denton Watson, *Lion in the Lobby: Clarence Mitchell and the Black Struggle* (New York: William Morrow, 1990).

36. Richard Kluger, *Simple Justice: History of* Brown v. Board of Education *and Black America's Struggle for Racial Equality* (New York: Vintage Books, 1975).

37. Aldon Morris, *The Origins of the Civil Rights Movement* (New York: Free Press, 1984).

38. David Garrow, *Bearing the Cross: Martin Luther King, Jr., and the Southern Christian Leadership Conference* (New York: William Morrow, 1986).

39. Clayborne Carson, *In Struggle: SNCC and the Black Awakening of the 1960s* (Cambridge, MA: Harvard University Press, 1981), and August Meier and Elliot Rudwick, *CORE: A Study in the Civil Rights Movement* (New York: Oxford University Press, 1973). For excellent studies of the heroic role of ordinary people in the civil rights movement, see John Dittmer, *Local People: The Struggle for Civil Rights in Mississippi* (Urbana: University of Illinois Press, 1995), and Charles Payne, *I've Got the Light of Freedom: The Organizing Tradition and the Mississippi Freedom Struggle* (Berkeley: University of California Press, 1995).

40. Michael Lipsky, "Protest as a Political Resource," *American Political Science Review* 62 (1968): 1144–58, and David Garrow, *Protest at Selma* (New Haven, CT: Yale University Press, 1978): chap. 7.

41. The last of the 1960s civil rights acts—the Fair Housing Act of 1968—was enacted shortly after Dr. King's murder, in part as a kind of final memorial tribute to him. Prior to his death the bill appeared to be stalled in the Congress.

42. Sidney Tarrow, "Aiming at a Moving Target: Social Science and the Recent Rebellions in Eastern Europe," *Political Science and Politics* 24 (1991): 15.

43. Smith, *We Have No Leaders,* chaps. 1–2.

44. The Meredith march was initially organized by James Meredith, the first known African American to be graduated from the University of Mississippi, as a "march against fear." It was designed to demonstrate to blacks in the state that they need not fear to exercise their newly gained civil rights. On the second day of the march, Meredith was shot and wounded. The civil rights leadership then decided to continue the march in Meredith's honor and as a means to demonstrate to the nation the continuing climate of fear and violence in the state.

45. Carson, *In Struggle,* chap. 14.

46. By political repression, we mean "a process by which those in power try to keep themselves in power by attempting to destroy or render harmless organizations and ideologies that threaten their power"; see Robert Goldstein, *Political Repression in Modern America* (Cambridge, MA: Schenkman Press, 1979): xvi. The FBI's program of political repression was called COINTELPRO (for counter intelligence program). The black groups targeted by the program included SNCC, SCLC, the Nation of Islam, and the Black Panther party. See Nelson Blackstock, *COINTELPRO: The FBI's Secret War on Political Freedom* (New York: Vintage Books, 1975), and Stephen Tompkins, "Army Feared King, Secretly Watched Him, Spying on Blacks Started 75 Years Ago," *Memphis Commercial Appeal*, March 21, 1993, p. A1.

47. See Robert C. Smith, "Black Power and the Transformation from Protest to Politics," *Political Science Quarterly* 96 (Fall 1981): 431–44, and Smith, *We Have No Leaders,* chap. 1.

48. Quoted in Paul Hagner and John Pierce, "Racial Differences in Political Conceptualization," *Western Political Quarterly* 37 (June 1984): 215.

49. Ibid., p. 214.

50. Ibid., p. 215.

51. Smith, "Black Power and the Transformation from Protest to Politics," pp. 436–37.

52. Ibid.

53. See Jo Freeman, ed., *Social Movements of the Sixties and Seventies* (New York: Longman, 1983).

CHAPTER 8

Interest Groups

As late as the late 1960s, with the exception of the NAACP, the Urban League, and to a lesser extent, SCLC and the National Council of Negro Women, there was little organized black interest group influence on the Washington policy-making process. And even the NAACP and Urban League were engaged mainly in rights-based civil rights lobbying rather than in broader material-based public policy concerns.[1] However, since the 1970s blacks have developed a significant presence in the Washington policy-making process, one which focuses on both rights-based and broader, material-based policy interests.

Table 8.1 displays the contemporary structure of black interest groups, illustrating the range of interest and policy concerns of the organized black community. Many of these groups (such as the National Medical Association, the National Association of Black Manufacturers), like their white counterparts, are special interest organizations, generally pursuing their own narrow professional or economic interests. Others, like Trans Africa, have a single policy focus—in its case, American foreign policy toward Africa and the Caribbean. (On Trans Africa's influence on policy in these regions, see chapter 16). Still others have broad, multiple-policy agendas (the NAACP, the Congressional Black Caucus, the Congress of Black Churches), lobbying on the full range of domestic and foreign policy issues.

BLACK GROUPS, THE "BLACK AGENDA," AND THE PROBLEM OF RESOURCE CONSTRAINT

The broad-based policy agenda encompassing both rights- and material-based issues is one of the major problems confronting the African American lobby in Washington. It is agenda rich but resource poor. Political scientist Dianne Pinderhughes writes,

> The subordinate, dependent status of the black population limits the capacity of black interests to create well funded and supported groups capable of the consistent monitoring required in administration and implementation of law. This same status multiplies the number of potential issue areas of importance to black constituencies, but their re-

---
TABLE 8.1

The Structure of African American Interest Organizations—Selected Groups

CIVIL RIGHTS	ECONOMIC/PROFESSIONAL
NAACP (1909)[a]	National Medical Association (1885)
Urban League (1910)	National Bar Association (1925)
Southern Christian Leadership Conference (1957)	National Business League (1900)
NAACP Legal Defense Fund (1939)	National Conference of Black Lawyers (1969)
National Council of Negro Women (1937)	National Association of Black Manufacturers (1970)
	Coalition of Black Trade Unionists (1972)

PUBLIC POLICY	CAUCUSES OF BLACK ELECTED OFFICIALS
Trans Africa (1977)	Congressional Black Caucus (1969)
Children's Defense Fund (1973)[b]	National Caucus of Black Elected Officials (1970)
National Association of Black Social Workers (1969)	Southern Conference of Black Mayors (1972)
	National Black Caucus of State Legislators (1977)
	National Caucus of Black School Board Members (1971)

RELIGIOUS
National Baptist Convention (1882)
Nation of Islam (1930)
Congress of Black Churches (1978)

[a]Year in parentheses refers to the year the group was organized. For a fairly comprehensive list of black organizations, their purposes and membership, see *A Guide to Black Organizations* (New York: Philip Morris, 1984)—yes, Philip Morris, the cigarette company.

[b]Strictly speaking, the Children's Defense Fund is an interracial advocacy organization; however, it was founded and is led by a black woman—Marion Wright Edelman—and much of its advocacy is for poor and disadvantaged minority children.

source difficulties limit the number of issues they can address, and weaken their likelihood of being taken seriously within any of those areas.[2]

The problem identified by Pinderhughes may be seen by comparing the data in Tables 8.2 and 8.3, which show, respectively, the post–civil rights era black agenda of African Americans and the resources of the three major Washington black interest organizations compared with the resources of selected nonblack Washington-based interest groups.

The Joint Center for Political and Economic Studies is a Washington-based think tank devoted to research on African American affairs (Box 8.1). In 1976 it called a bipartisan (Democrats and Republicans) conference of more than one thousand black elected officials as well as appointed officials then serving in the Carter administration. At the conference's conclusion, the group issued a document, the "Seven Point Mandate," that it said represented a leadership consensus on the post–civil rights era black agenda. The items on that agenda are displayed in Table 8.2.

--- **TABLE 8.2** ---

The Post–Civil Rights Era Black Agenda

Full employment

Welfare reform to include a guaranteed income

Comprehensive national health insurance

Increased federal funding for elementary, secondary, and higher education

Busing for purposes of integrated education

Minority business set-asides

International sanctions on South Africa and repeal of the Byrd Amendment[a]

[a]The Byrd Amendment was an act of Congress permitting the import of chrome from the apartheid regime of Rhodesia in violation of sanctions imposed by the United Nations. It was repealed in 1977 (see chapter 16).

Source: "Seven Point Mandate," Focus 14 (1976): 8. Focus is the monthly newsletter of the Joint Center for Political and Economic Studies.

--- **TABLE 8.3** ---

A Comparison of the Resources of the Three Major African American Interest Organizations with Selected Nonblack Organizations

AFRICAN AMERICAN ORGANIZATION	ESTIMATED MEMBERSHIP	ANNUAL BUDGET
NAACP	450,000; 1,700 local chapters	$ 11.9[a]
Urban League	118 local affiliates	24
Congressional Black Caucus[b]	39 members of Congress	550,000
NON–AFRICAN AMERICAN ORGANIZATIONS		
AFL-CIO	14 million	63
National Association of Manufacturers	2,800 local chapters	17
National Abortion Rights League	400,000	9
Mothers against Drunk Driving	2.9 million	43
Tobacco Institute	13 companies	38
National Rifle Association	2.6 million	89
Sierra Club	600,000	39
American Israeli Public Affairs Committee	50,000	12
Conference of Catholic Bishops	300 bishops	31
National Gay and Lesbian Task Force	15,000	1

[a]Unless otherwise noted, the budget figure is in millions of dollars for the year 1995.

[b]The budget for the Congressional Black Caucus is for the Congressional Black Caucus Foundation, a separate, tax-exempt organization formed in 1982 to raise funds to support the group. The amount is as shown: $550,000. Until 1995, the Caucus itself raised $4,000 from each of its members to support its operations. The Republican congressional majority under Speaker Newt Gingrich discontinued this form of member support.

Sources: Various annual reports supplied to the authors by the different organizations or telephone interviews with spokespersons for the groups.

The agenda includes *rights-based items* (busing for purposes of school desegregation and contract set-asides for minority businesses), but its main items are *material-based, nonracial issues,* such as universal health insurance and full employment. In this sense, the "black" agenda is not really black but is rather a broad-based liberal reform agenda. It is a consensus agenda. With minor changes in emphasis and specifics, the original items remain the principal issues on the black agenda today. (The minor changes involve less concern with busing and more with affirmative action; the Byrd Amendment has been repealed, and abolition of apartheid has removed the need for sanctions on South Africa.)

Blacks therefore have a broad-based material and rights agenda; yet when compared to other lobby groups in Washington—many with narrow, single-issue agendas—black groups have relatively few resources. Table 8.3 displays data on the membership and financial resources of selected Washington interest groups, including the three most important black groups. With the exception of the gay and lesbian lobby, the trial lawyers association, and the lobby group for Israel, all the nonblack associations have greater resources in terms of membership or local chapters than do the three major black groups. And with the exception of the National Abortion Rights League (which has a membership comparable to the NAACP) and the National Gay and Lesbian Task Force, all the nonblack groups have larger budgets than the NAACP, the Urban League, or the Congressional Black Caucus.[3] Also, with the exception of the Conference of Catholic Bishops and the AFL-CIO, most of the nonblack groups are narrow, single-issue groups, focusing their lobbying on one issue such as gun ownership, abortion

Kwesi Mfume, President of the NAACP, arrested outside Supreme Court while protesting the lack of minority clerks at the Court.

========================= **BOX 8.1** =========================

The Joint Center for Political and Economic Studies

Think tanks—organization of scholars and former government officials who do research and planning on domestic and foreign policy issues—are an important part of the policy-making process in the United States.[a] They develop ideas that shape the public policy debate, and unlike university-based scholars, they tend to be directly linked to Washington policy makers, frequently serving in the government for periods of time and then returning to the think tank to do research on policy-related issues. For example, many of the ideas that shaped the Reagan administration's early policy agenda came directly from the Heritage Foundation, a conservative think tank. Other important Washington think tanks include the Brookings Institution, the American Enterprise Institute, and the Urban Institute.

As the civil rights era drew to a close and black politics began its shift from movement-style protests to routine interest group policies, it was early recognized that African Americans needed their own think tank. The Joint Center for Political and Economic Studies was founded to meet this need for policy research and analysis.

The Joint Center's early projects included the collection and dissemination of data on the rapidly growing number of black elected officials (eventually this became its annual *Roster of Black Elected Officials*); the publication of a monthly newsletter; and the provision of technical training, workshops, and publications to black elected officials. The center also from the outset encouraged black elected officials to form caucuses and was instrumental in creating the National Coalition on Black Voter Participation.

In 1972 Eddie Williams became president of the Joint Center. Williams set about to broaden the center's work beyond educational and technical assistance and research support for black elected officials. The result was an announcement that the center would become a "national research organization in the tradition of Brookings and the American Enterprise Institute," rather than simply a "technical and institutional support resource for black elected officials."[b]

Although its budget is modest compared to the budgets of other Washington think tanks, the center has done a remarkable job in facilitating the institutionalization of black politics. Its studies of the growth and development of black elected officials, its work on the implementation of the Voting Rights Act, its work on the development of a consensus black agenda, and its monthly newsletter *Focus* have made the Joint Center the recognized, authoritative source on black politics in the post–civil rights era.[c]

[a]For an analysis of the increasingly important roles played by think tanks in policy making, see James Smith, *Think Tanks and the Rise of the New Policy Elites* (New York: Free Press, 1991).

[b]Joint Center for Political Studies, *Annual Report*, 1991, p. 3.

[c]For a more detailed analysis of the history and development of the Joint Center, see Robert C. Smith, *We Have No Leaders: African Americans in the Post–Civil Rights Era* (Albany: State University of New York Press, 1996): 113–120.

rights, drunk driving, or United States foreign policy toward Israel. And most of these single-issue lobbies, unlike the multiple-issue black groups, have larger budgets. The budget, for example, of Mothers against Drunk Driving (MADD) is larger than the budgets of the three black groups combined, and the budget of the National Rifle Association (NRA) is three times as great as the budgets of the three black groups combined.

The size of an interest group's membership and budget are important resources. A large membership permits grassroots mobilization by letters and phone calls to the media and members of Congress as well as voter mobilization on election day. Money is, as former California House Speaker Jesse Unruh once said, "the mother's milk of politics." It can be employed in a wide range of activities, such as grassroots organizing, voter mobilization, polling, radio and television ads, and litigation. Critically important, a large financial base permits interest groups to form PACs—political action committees—to raise and give campaign contributions to candidates for office. Since the passage of campaign finance reform laws in the 1970s, PACs have become very important in the lobbying-election process, contributing nearly half the money raised by incumbent congressional candidates (federal law limits PAC contributions to $5,000 per candidate; individuals to $1,000). Several of the nonblack groups (the NRA, the trial lawyers, the AFL-CIO) have large PACs that contribute millions of dollars to congressional candidates. None of the black interest groups have PACs, although several unsuccessful efforts were made in the 1970s by a number of black groups to form one.[4]

Given their multiple rights- and material-issue agendas and their relative lack of resources compared to other interest groups, black groups are at a considerable disadvantage unless they can form coalitions with other groups. On most rights-based issues, civil rights lobbying is done through a broad, multiethnic coalition: the Leadership Conference on Civil Rights. (There are, however, tensions within this group; see Box 8.2.) On welfare and poverty issues, the Center for Budget Priorities (a white group) is an effective lobby and advocacy group, and on national health insurance and full employment, the AFL-CIO and the Conference of Catholic Bishops are, with blacks, part of a broad labor-liberal reform coalition. But as shown by the failure to secure effective full employment legislation in the 1970s and the defeat of President Clinton's universal health care plan in the 1990s, this reform coalition has not been able to effectively counterbalance the power of those interests opposed to universal health and employment.

■ BOX 8.2 ■
The Leadership Conference on Civil Rights

The theory of African American coalitions we have developed in this book suggests that such coalitions, whether rights or material based, tend to be unstable and frequently short-lived. While this is generally true, there is one coalition—the Leadership Conference on Civil Rights—that has now lasted almost a half century, although in recent years it too has experienced tensions and conflicts.

(Continued)

BOX 8.2 Continued

The Leadership Conference on Civil Rights (LCCR) is a rights-based coalition. It was founded in 1949 by A. Phillip Randolph, the African American labor leader; Roy Wilkins, assistant director of the NAACP; and Arnold Aronson, a Jewish labor activist. Initially it was a coalition of about forty black, labor, and Jewish and other religious groups whose principal objective was to secure legislation ensuring the civil rights of African Americans, especially those in the South. This coalition, along with the NAACP, was the principal lobby group for the 1964 Civil Rights Act (at that time, Clarence Mitchell, head of the NAACP's Washington office, also was head of LCCR).

The African American civil rights movement of the 1960s and its successes served as a model for other groups facing various forms of discrimination. These groups (women, gays, and other minorities) joined LCCR, expanding its memberships from about forty groups in 1949 to more than 150 today. In 1949, most of the organizations in LCCR were black and it was widely viewed as an African American coalition. Today, this is no longer the case, as black organizations constitute little more than a third of LCCR's membership.[a] The expansion of the coalition has inevitably led to tensions and conflicts along racial, ethnic, and gender lines.

From the beginning there were gender conflicts within the civil rights coalition. African Americans, labor leaders, and spokespersons for working-class women opposed the inclusion of a ban on sex discrimination in employment in the 1964 Civil Rights Act. Labor opposed gender equality in favor of preferential treatment for women: laws limiting working hours and the physical burden of work for women and providing such special benefits as rest and maternity leave. African American leaders (mainly men) opposed the inclusion of gender because they argued that it would take jobs from black men—the putative family bread winner—and give them to white women. By contrast, support for the inclusion of gender came from conservatives (the amendment on sex was introduced by Howard Smith of Virginia, an opponent of civil rights, who thought the inclusion of sex would kill the entire bill) and white upper-class women's groups such as the National Federation of Business and Professional Women. Although African Americans and labor leaders now support gender equality in employment, sex-race tensions continue over affirmative action, with some African Americans arguing that white women are the principal beneficiaries of a program originally set up for blacks. Affirmative action has also caused conflict with some Jewish groups in LCCR; these groups tend to object to racial quotas and preferences (especially in higher education) because quotas historically were used to exclude Jews and because some Jewish leaders see them as a violation of merit and the principle of equality for all persons. Jewish-black tensions in the coalition have also been exacerbated in recent years by conflicts over black support for the Palestinians in the Middle East conflict, Israeli support for the apartheid regime in South Africa, and the anti-semitic remarks of the Nation of Islam's Louis Farrakhan.

Another source of tension in LCCR is between African Americans and Mexican Americans. When the 1965 Voting Rights Act was renewed in 1975, the NAACP opposed the inclusion of an amendment to prohibit discrimination against language minorities. Decisions of LCCR require a unanimous vote of its executive committee, thus the NAACP's opposition effectively killed coalition support, forcing Latino groups in the coalition to act alone in a successful effort to get language groups covered by the Voting Rights Act.[b] Although this issue is now settled, it has left a residue of bad feeling between blacks and Latinos. In addition, some African Americans have expressed concerns about the impact of illegal immigration on the employment opportunities of low-income urban blacks, a position that upsets the Asian American and Hispanic American groups in the coalition.

The LCCR is a rights-based coalition that has endured for fifty years, but its successes in the 1960s, the development of new rights groups in the 1970s and 1980s, and the expansion of the coalition have inevitably created some instability. However, as a broad-based coalition that embraces universal rights for all Americans, it is likely to endure, although not without continuing conflicts and tensions.[c]

[a]Dianne Pinderhughes, "Black Interest Groups and the 1982 Extension of the Voting Rights Act," in Huey Perry and Wayne Parent, eds., *Blacks and the American Political System* (Gainesville: University Press of Florida, 1995): 206.

[b]Ibid., p. 211.

[c]Dianne Pinderhughes, "Divisions in the Civil Rights Community," *Political Science and Politics* 25 (1992): 485–87.

BLACK NATIONALIST MOVEMENTS

Black nationalist organizations are movement rather than interest group organizations. Interest groups accept the legitimacy of the system and seek to have it accept their demands for rights and freedoms; movements challenge system legitimacy and seek fundamental system transformation. Historically, black nationalists have certainly challenged the legitimacy of the American system; in their view, it is incapable of delivering universal freedom and equality. This is shown clearly in the system-challenging rhetoric of nationalist leaders. In 1901 Bishop Henry M. Turner caused a national furor when he said "to the Negro in this country the American flag is a dirty and contemptuous rag. Not a star in it can the colored man claim, for it is no longer a symbol of our manhood rights and freedom."[5] Similar controversial remarks about the flag were made by Louis Farrakhan ninety-five years later in a speech to his followers in Chicago.

Bishop Henry M. Turner and the
First Mass-Based Black Nationalist Movement

The ideology of black nationalism is as old as the African American experience in the United States; until the post-Reconstruction era, however, it was simply the thought of a few intellectuals or the poorly organized efforts of a few remarkable men.[6] The first effort at a nationalist movement on a mass basis was launched by Bishop Henry M. Turner in the 1890s. Faced by the withdrawal of African American freedom, the terrorism of white southern racists, and Booker T. Washington's seeming acceptance of this turn of events, Turner sought to organize blacks for a mass return to Africa. As he frequently said in his speeches and writings, for blacks the choice was simple: "emigrate or perish."[7]

Turner was born a free man of color in 1834. A bishop of the African Methodist Episcopal church, he served as a chaplain in the Union army and as a member of the Reconstruction Georgia constitutional convention. Once Reconstruction ended, Turner attempted to organize a back-to-Africa movement. From 1890 until his death in 1915,

Turner organized numerous conferences and filed many petitions with Congress requesting support for his plan. He, for example, was the first African American leader to petition Congress for reparations, calling for a forty billion dollar payment to blacks for their two hundred years of slave labor.

Turner, like most advocates of back-to-Africa schemes, met with little success. Most African Americans—especially the small middle class—opposed Turner's efforts, apparently preferring to go along with the accommodationist approach of Booker Washington than to risk the perils of emigration across the Atlantic. This is an enduring dilemma of nationalist emigrationists; most African Americans do not wish to leave the United States. In addition, absence of support from middle-class blacks makes it difficult to finance emigration schemes. Turner did organize the Colored Emigration League, publish a monthly newsletter, and establish the Afro-American Steamship Company. For a time he was an honorary vice president of the American Colonialization Society, an organization of racists formed in the 1770s shortly after the Revolutionary War. This group favored emigration because, in its view, the United States should be a white man's country. Also, Turner was able to persuade several racist southern congressmen to introduce emigration legislation. This is another dilemma for black nationalist groups: Their potential white coalition partners tend to be racists and white supremacists. Marcus Garvey in the 1920s and more recently Louis Farrakhan have talked to representatives of the KKK and other racist groups about forming coalitions to secure emigration or separation.

Although Turner's movement ended with his death and with little success (it is estimated that perhaps a thousand blacks emigrated to Africa),[8] Turner's rhetoric (he was the first black leader to declare that God was black, a notion later advanced by Marcus Garvey and some sects of the Black Muslims) and strategy of organization was followed by subsequent nationalist leaders and organizations.

Marcus Garvey and the Universal Negro Improvement Association

The second major black nationalist movement was organized in Harlem by Marcus Garvey in 1914. Garvey's organization was called the Universal Negro Improvement Association. At its peak in the 1920s, it claimed a membership of two million in the United States and the West Indies.[9] Like Turner, Garvey declared that God, Jesus, and the angels were black, that whites were an inferior race, and that blacks should return to Africa and restore its past glories. He also founded a steamship company, a newspaper, and a number of small factories and businesses. A charismatic leader and powerful orator, like Louis Farrakhan today he would draw huge crowds to his rallies. An autocratic leader, in 1921 Garvey declared himself provisional president of Africa although he had never set foot on the continent and never would.

Like Turner's movement, Garvey's was opposed by most blacks, with his strongest base of support coming from among the poor and working classes of the big city ghettos of the North. Also, like Turner's movement, Garvey's was opposed by the mainstream, middle-class black leadership establishment (an especially bitter critic was W. E. B. Du Bois). Unlike Turner's movement, Garvey's attracted the attention of the federal government, since its mass following and radicalism appeared to be a threat to internal security. In 1925, Garvey and several of his associates were indicted on federal mail fraud charges of using the mail to sell phony stock in his steamship company. His associates were found not guilty, but Garvey was convicted, sentenced to prison for several years, then deported. He died in London in 1940. With his deportation in 1927, his organization and movement split into a number of small sects and factions and lost its effectiveness.

Louis Farrakhan and the Nation of Islam: The Resurgence of Black Nationalism in the Post–Civil Rights Era

The most influential black nationalist leader and organization of the post–civil rights era is Minister Louis Farrakhan and the Nation of Islam. The Nation of Islam—popularly known as the Black Muslims—was founded by W. D. Fard in 1931. After Fard's disappearance it was led by Elijah Muhammad until his death in 1976.[10] Like Garvey's movement, the Nation was based on racial chauvinism, glorifying everything black and condemning whites as devils.

The Nation grew slowly until the charismatic Malcolm X became its national spokesman in the 1960s. Malcolm helped to build a large following for the group among the urban poor and working class.[11] The Nation, like the Garvey movement, established chapters (mosques) throughout the country, operated small businesses and farms, and

Malcolm X with Elijah Muhammad, leader of the Nation of Islam.

published a weekly newspaper. Unlike the Garvey and Turner movements, the Nation did not establish a steamship line since it does not favor emigration to Africa. Instead, it desires the creation of a separate black nation within the boundaries of the United States.

When Elijah Muhammad died in 1976, the Nation of Islam split into a series of sects and factions; the main body of the group, led by Wallace Muhammad, Elijah Muhammad's son, was transformed into a mainstream, integrationist (including whites as members), orthodox Islamic group.[12] For a short time in the 1970s, the Nation of Islam disappeared. This was the objective of J. Edgar Hoover and the FBI. Sometime before the death of Elijah Muhammad (the date is not clear), Hoover sent a memorandum to the special agent in charge of the Chicago office which in part said:

> The NOI (Nation of Islam) appears to be the personal fiefdom of Elijah Muhammad. When he dies a power struggle can be expected and the NOI could change direction. We should be prepared for this eventuality. We should plan now to change the philosophy of the NOI to one of strictly religious and self-improvement orientation, deleting the race hatred and the separate nationhood aspects. In this connection Chicago should consider what counter intelligence action might be needed now or at the time of Elijah Muhammad's death to bring about such a change in the NOI philosophy. Important considerations should include the identity, strengths and weaknesses of any contender for NOI leader. The alternative to changing the philosophy of the NOI is the destruction of the organization. This might be accomplished through generating factionalism among the contenders for Elijah Muhammad's leadership or through legal action in probate court.[13]

For a while Minister Farrakhan acquiesced in the transformation of the Nation into a strictly religious, integrationist organization. However, after a year or so, he set about to rebuild the Nation on the basis of the original principles of Elijah Muhammad.[14] However, in his clearest break with the traditions of the Nation, Farrakhan in 1993 abandoned the doctrine of nonparticipation in American electoral politics. Under Elijah Muhammad, members of the Nation were strictly forbidden to participate in American politics, which he described as the "devil's" system. Farrakhan abandoned this position first by encouraging his followers to register and vote for Chicago mayoral candidate Harold Washington in 1983 and then by supporting Jesse Jackson's campaign for president in 1984.

Unlike most African American organizations, the Nation of Islam receives no money from white corporations or businesses. It has approximately 120 mosques in various cities around the country, operates a series of modest small business enterprises, and has a somewhat effective social welfare system for its members. It publishes a weekly newspaper—*The Final Call*—and Farrakhan may be seen and heard on more than 120 radio and television stations around the country. The organization does not reveal the size of its membership, but it is estimated at no more than 20,000. However, the Nation and Farrakhan have millions of followers. A 1994 *Times* magazine poll found that 73 percent of blacks were familiar with Farrakhan, making him, with Jesse Jackson, the best-known African American leader. And most blacks familiar with Farrakhan view him favorably, with 65 percent saying he was an effective leader, 63 percent that he speaks the truth, and 62 percent that he was good for black America.[15] The *Time* poll that produced these figures was taken prior to Farrakhan's success in calling the Million Man March, the largest demonstration in Washington in American history.

Black Nationalism and the Million Man March

Most African Americans are integrationists. That is, they believe that universal freedom and equality are possible in the United States and that blacks should struggle to achieve these goals. Yet, as a sentiment, nationalism is an enduring force in African American society, invoking as it does historical consciousness of race oppression, race solidarity, and collective race responsibility. Aspects of this nationalist sentiment may be observed in the data reported in Table 8.4. (See also Table 5.6.)

First, although only 23 percent of the African American population accept the fundamental nationalist belief that "equality will never be achieved in America," 77 percent agree that "American society is not fair to blacks." There is strong support for a black political party, for all-male black public schools, and for the idea that blacks should control the economy and government in predominantly black communities. Ironically, support for the most extreme nationalist sentiment—a separate black nation—has nearly doubled since the end of the black power movement. In 1968 at the peak of the black power movement only 7 percent of blacks supported the idea of a separate black nation,[16] but in the 1993–94 survey this support had doubled to 14 percent. And while most blacks reject the idea of the creation of a separate black nation, almost half (49%) embrace the sentiment that blacks in America are a people apart, a "nation within a nation."

According to Professor Michael Dawson, who conducted the survey reported in Table 8.4, support for black nationalist sentiments has increased in the last decade,

---
TABLE 8.4

Attitudes of Black Americans toward Elements of Black Nationalist Ideology, 1993–1994

STATEMENTS FROM SURVEY[a]	PERCENT AGREEING
Equality will never be achieved in America	23
American society is not fair to blacks	77
Blacks should form their own political party	50
Blacks should always vote for a black candidate	26
Blacks should support creation of all-male black public schools	62
Blacks should control the economy in predominantly black communities	74
Blacks should form a nation within a nation	49
Blacks should have their own separate nation	14

Source: Michael Dawson and Ronald Brown, "Black Discontent: The Preliminary Report of the 1993–94 National Black Politics Study," Report #1, University of Chicago. Results are based on a representative, randomly selected sample of the national black population. Percentages are of respondents agreeing with the statements.

Nation of Islam Minister Louis Farrakhan addressing the Million Man March.

especially among middle-class blacks.[17] Sensing this growth in black nationalist sentiments, Minister Farrakhan called on a million black men to march on Washington on
October 16, 1995. The figures are in dispute, but it is probable that a million men
(and several thousand women) did march on Washington.[18] Most of the mainstream
press ignored the march, and many prominent blacks and virtually all whites who
made comments attacked the march because it was led by Farrakhan, whom they described as a "racist, sexist, anti-semitic, homophobic demagogue." Nevertheless, as
the day of the march approached, it was endorsed by Jesse Jackson and many other
prominent blacks, including the poet Maya Angelou and a number of other well-
known black women.

According to Farrakhan, the purpose of the march was moral: a call for atonement,
reconciliation, and the acceptance by black men of responsibility for family and community. Farrakhan is usually portrayed in the mainstream press as a radical extremist; but
in his emphasis on moral reform and traditional values with respect to family life, sex,
and alcohol and drug use as well as his condemnation of welfare dependency, he is
rather conservative. Thus, the moral basis of the march is quite consistent with the philosophy of Farrakhan and the tradition of the Nation of Islam.

On the day of the march, two surveys were conducted: one by the *Washington Post*
and the other by a group of Howard University political scientists. Both show similar results in terms of the backgrounds of the marchers and their social and political atti-

tudes.[19] The Howard University survey team interviewed 1,070 men. Its results show that the men who attended the march were primarily from the middle and upper-middle class of the black community, were middle-age, married, and mostly Christian (only 8% were muslims).[20] Ideologically, 31 percent identified themselves as liberal, 21 percent as moderate, 13 percent as conservative, 11 percent as nationalist, and 4 percent as socialist (21% used some other ideological label).[21] These men were also extraordinarily politically active; 86 percent were registered to vote, 55 percent had lobbied a public official, 87 percent had signed a petition, and 45 percent had worked in political campaigns.[22] When asked why they attended the march, 88 percent cited improving moral values in the black community, 77 percent mentioned moral atonement and reconciliation, but others also expressed nationalist reasons. Eighty-five percent said the march encouraged black self-determination and unity, and 75 percent said they attended as a way to promote independent economic development.[23]

Black nationalist movements tend to come in cycles. Bracey, Meier, and Rudwick suggest that there have been four relatively distinct periods when nationalism was especially salient in African American politics and society, each coinciding with especially difficult or disappointing times for the race.[24] The extraordinary success of the Million Man March (a million men represents more than 10 percent of the black male population), consisting of mostly middle-class and politically active individuals, suggests that we may be on the verge of a new cycle of nationalism (see Box 8.3). The conditions are certainly ripe for such a new cycle. After a period of optimism about the possibility of universal freedom and equality following the success of the civil rights movement, many blacks now sense a turning back of the clock, a sense that history may be repeating itself in terms of a second Reconstruction. This sense of pessimism is fueled by the ongoing Reagan revolution as reflected in the election of a Republican congressional majority, the conservative tilt of the Clinton administration, and a series of adverse Supreme Court decisions on affirmative action and the Voting Rights Act. It is also fueled by a growing sense that the mainstream, establishment black leadership of elected officials and civil rights leaders has no plan, program, or strategy to deal with the deteriorating conditions of poor black communities.[25]

━━━━━━━━━━━━━━━ **BOX 8.3** ━━━━━━━━━━━━━━━

The African American Reparation Movement

In the post-Reconstruction era, Bishop Henry M. Turner was the first African American leader to demand reparation—repayment for the damages of slavery—from the American government. After the Civil War, there was talk of providing a kind of reparation to blacks in the form of "forty acres and a mule." In the 1865 Freedmen's Bureau Act, Congress included a provision granting blacks forty acres of abandoned land in the southern states. President Andrew Johnson, however, vetoed the bill, arguing that to take land from the former slave owners was "contrary to that provision of the Constitution which declares that no person shall

(Continued)

BOX 8.3 Continued

'be deprived of life, liberty and property without due process of law.' "[a] The closest the United States government ever came to paying reparation was General William Sherman's Special Order #15 issued on January 16, 1865.[b] It provided forty acres to black families living on the Georgia and South Carolina coasts (some of the descendants of these families still live or own property on these lands). Blacks, however, never abandoned their claims for reparation, and the recent payment by the Congress and several American cities of reparation to Japanese Americans for their World War II incarceration has led to the rebirth of an African American movement seeking similar renumeration.

The contemporary reparation movement is led by Imari Obadele, a professor of political science at the historically black Prairie View A & M University and the former provisional president of the Republic of New Africa. The Republic of New Africa is a black nationalist organization founded in 1968 by Obadele (who was then known as Richard Henry). The organization favors the creation of a separate, all-black nation in the southern part of the United States. In 1989 Obadele and others formed the National Coalition of Blacks for Reparations (NCOBRA), a nonprofit coalition of black religious, civic, and fraternal organizations. Since its formation the coalition has engaged in a variety of tactics to advance the cause of reparation, including petitions to Congress and the president, lawsuits, and protest demonstrations at the White House.

African American supporters of reparation cite a number of precedents regarding reparation.[c] But the one cited most frequently and the one that gave impetus to this new movement was the decision by Congress in 1988 to issue an apology and pay $20,000 to each Japanese American (or his or her survivors) incarcerated during World War II.[d] Earlier the cities of Los Angeles and San Francisco had taken similar actions. Using the Japanese case as a precedent, NCOBRA has made a proposal to Congress, called "An Act to Stimulate Economic Growth in the United States and Compensate, in Part, for the Grievous Wrongs of Slavery and the Unjust Enrichment Which Accrued to the United States Therefrom." The proposal indicates no dollar amount for payment (suggesting that the figure be established by an independent commission, as was done in the Japanese American case) but requires that one-third of the payment go to each individual African man, woman, and child; one-third to the Republic of New Africa; and one-third to a national congress of black church, civic, and civil rights organizations.[e]

In the Japanese case, the first step was the appointment by the Congress of a commission to study the issue. Thus, in 1995, Congressman John Conyers, an African American, and Congressman Norman Mineta, a Japanese American, introduced a bill to establish a "Commission to Study Reparations for African Americans."[f] Also, in 1995 several African Americans filed a suit in federal court in California asking the court to direct the government to pay reparation. The Court of Appeals of the Ninth Circuit rejected the suit, holding that the United States could not be sued unless it waived its "sovereign immunity" and that the "appropriate forum for policy questions of this sort . . . is Congress rather than the courts."[g]

This new reparation movement is just getting under way, and given the present climate of race relations in the United States, the prospects for its success do not appear good.[h] Recently, however, the state of Florida, after appointing a study commission, agreed to pay reparation to the survivors and descendants of blacks who lived in the town of Rosewood. In 1923, a white mob burned the black town of Rosewood, Florida, and drove out all its citizens.

The police did nothing to stop this violence. After the study commission's report, the Florida Legislature agreed to pay the nine survivors $150,000 each. The seventy descendants are scheduled to receive between $145 and $5,000.[i]

[a]The text of the Freedmen's Bureau bill and President Johnson's veto message are in *The Forty Acres Documents*, Introduction by Amitcar Shabazz (Baton Rouge, LA: The House of Songhay, 1994): 65, 74, 75–94.

[b]The text of Sherman's Order is also in *The Forty Acres Document*, pp. 51–58.

[c]See Boris Bittker, *The Case for Black Reparations* (New York: Random House, 1973) and Daisy Collins, "Reparations for Black Citizens," *Howard University Law Review* 82 (1979).

[d]Tom Kenworthy, "House Votes Apology, Reparations for Japanese Americans," *Washington Post*, September 18, 1987, p. A1.

[e]Chokwe Lumumba, Imari Obdele, and Nkechi Taifa, *Reparations NOW!* (Baton Rouge, LA: The House of Songhay, 1995): 67.

[f]The text of the Conyers-Mineta bill is in Lumumba, Obadele, and Taifa, *Reparations NOW!*, pp. 97–107.

[g]*Cato et al. v. United States of America*, United States Circuit Court of Appeals, 9th Circuit #94-17102 (1995): 15162.

[h]An ABC News poll found that overall 77 percent of Americans were opposed to reparation for blacks. Sixty-five percent of blacks supported the idea, while it was opposed by 88 percent of whites. See ABC News *Nightline*, July 7, 1997.

[i]The Rosewood, Florida, case is discussed in Lumumba, Obadele, and Taifa, *Reparations NOW!*, pp. 95–96.

SELECTED BIBLIOGRAPHY

Garson, G. David. *Group Theories of Politics*. Beverly Hills: Sage, 1978. A review and critique of the major theories and the research on the interest group basis of American politics.

Hamilton, Dana, and Charles Hamilton. *The Dual Agenda: Social Policies of Civil Rights Organizations from the New Deal to the Present*. New York: Columbia University Press, 1996. Although they do not use the terms *rights based* and *material based*, this book is an exhaustive study of the dual agenda of black Americans.

Lowi, Theodore. *The End of Liberalism*. New York: Norton, 1979. An influential study of how interest groups manipulate public policy making in pursuit of narrow, parochial interests.

Pinderhughes, Dianne. "Collective Goods and Black Interest." *Review of Black Political Economy* 12 (Winter 1983): 219–36. A largely theoretical analysis of the role of black interest groups in pursuing the multiple policy interests of blacks in an environment of resource constraints.

Pinderhughes, Dianne. "Black Interest Groups and the 1982 Extension of the Voting Rights Act" (pp. 203–24). In Huey Perry and Wayne Parent, eds. *Blacks and the American Political System*. Gainesville: University Press of Florida, 1995. A case study of African American interest group politics in the context of the contemporary civil rights coalition.

Smith, Robert C. *We Have No Leaders: African Americans in the Post–Civil Rights Era*. Albany: State University of New York Press, 1996. A detailed study of the transformation of the 1960s African American freedom struggle from movement to interest groups politics, focusing on African American interest groups, the Congressional Black Caucus, black presidential appointees in the executive branch, and Jesse Jackson's Rainbow Coalition.

Stuckey, Sterling. *The Ideological Origins of Black Nationalism*. Boston: Beacon, 1972. A seminal study that includes some of the classic black nationalist writings.

NOTES

1. Harold Wolman and Norman Thomas, "Black Interests, Black Groups and Black Influence in the Federal Policy Process: The Cases of Housing and Education," *Journal of Politics* 32 (November 1970): 875–97.
2. Dianne Pinderhughes, "Racial Interest Groups and Incremental Politics" (unpublished paper, University of Illinois, Urbana, 1980): 36.
3. A substantial part of the budgets of both the NAACP and the Urban League comes from contributions by white foundations and corporations. See Robert C. Smith, *We Have No Leaders: African Americans in the Post–Civil Rights Era* (Albany: State University of New York Press, 1996), 86–96.
4. Ibid., p. 122.
5. Edwin Redkey, "The Flowering of Black Nationalism: Henry McNeal Turner and Marcus Garvey," in Nathan Huggins, Martin Kilson, and Daniel Fox, eds., *Key Issues in the Afro-American Experience*, vol. 2 (New York: Harcourt Brace Jovanovich, 1971): 115.
6. On the historical origins of black nationalist thought, see Sterling Stuckey, *The Ideological Origins of Black Nationalism* (Boston: Beacon, 1972), and Sterling Stuckey, *Slave Culture: Foundations of Nationalist Thought* (New York: Oxford, 1967).
7. Stuckey, *The Ideological Origins of Black Nationalism*.
8. Ibid., p. 114.
9. See Edmund Cronon, *Black Moses: The Story of Marcus Garvey and the Universal Negro Improvement Association* (Madison: University of Wisconsin Press, 1955).
10. Claude Andrew Clegg, *An Original Man: The Life and Times of Elijah Muhammad* (New York: St. Martin's Press, 1997).
11. Bruce Perry, *Malcolm: The Life of a Man Who Changed Black America* (Barrytown, NY: Station Hill Press, 1991).
12. Don Terry, "Black Muslims Enter Islamic Mainstream," *New York Times*, May 3, 1993.
13. The Hoover memorandum is quoted in Imam Sidney Sharif, "Hoover Plotted against Muslims," *Atlanta Voice*, February 22, 1986.
14. On Farrakhan's strategy to revitalize the Nation of Islam, see Smith, *We Have No Leaders*, pp. 99–100; Lawrence Mamiya, "From Black Muslim to Bialian: The Evolution of a Movement," *Journal for the Scientific Study of Religion* 21 (1982): 141; and Mattias Gardell, *In the Name of Elijah Muhammad: Louis Farrakhan and the Nation of Islam* (Durham, NC: Duke University Press, 1996). Gardell's work contains a detailed analysis of the theological underpinnings of the Nation of Islam.
15. William Henry, "Pride and Prejudice," *Time*, February 28, 1994, p. 22.

16. Angus Campbell and Howard Schuman, *Racial Attitudes in Fifteen American Cities* (Ann Arbor: University of Michigan, Institute for Social Research, 1971): 18.

17. Michael Dawson, "Structure and Ideology: The Shaping of Black Public Opinion," paper prepared for presentation at the 1995 Annual Meeting of the Midwest Political Science Association, Chicago, p. 29.

18. "Million Man March Draws More Than 1 Million Black Men to Washington," *Jet*, October 30, 1995, pp. 3–11. A good documentary record of the march including the full program, the major speeches, mission statement, and selected press commentary is in Haki Madhubuti and Ron Karenga, eds., *Million Man March/Day of Absence* (Chicago: Third World Press, 1996).

19. For the *Washington Post* survey, see "Million Man March Survey," October 17, 1995, p. A23.

20. Lorenzo Morris et al., "Million Man March: Preliminary Report on the Survey" (Washington, DC: Howard University, 1995): 2–3. See also Joseph P. McCormick, "The Message and the Messengers: Opinions from the Million Men Who Marched," *National Political Science Review* 6 (1997): 142–64.

21. Morris, "Million Man March: Preliminary Report on the Survey," pp. 4–5.

22. Ibid.

23. Ibid., p. 6. In November 1997 a million black women gathered in Philadelphia to promote unity and community development. See "Million Woman March," *Jet*, November 10, 1997, pp. 5–18.

24. John Bracey, Jr., August Meier, and Elliot Rudwick, *Black Nationalism in America* (Indianapolis: Bobbs-Merrill, 1970): xxx–liii. The four time periods are the 1770s, 1840s, 1880s, and late 1960s.

25. Smith, *We Have No Leaders*, especially chap. 11.

CHAPTER 9

Political Parties

Conventional wisdom abounds with the argument that the 1964 presidential election was the "turning point" for African American partisans; this was the year that black voters switched from Republican to Democrat after the Democrats passed into law the most sweeping civil rights laws ever. All the books and articles that rely on polling and survey data argue that at the individual, attitudinal level, the vast majority of African American partisans came to identify with the Democratic party. Typical of the political scientists who promote this thesis are Edward Carmines and James Stimson. They write, "The 1964 presidential election thus marked the decisive turning point in the political evolution of racial issues . . . [and] this . . . led to the severing of the historic ties between the Republican party and the black electorate."[1] By 1996 this line of reasoning was argued by Donald Kinder and Lynn Sanders: "The dramatic switch in the position of the parties expressed so vividly in the 1964 election included predictable alterations in the partisanship of American voters. . . . Black Americans moved almost unanimously to the Democratic party."[2]

African American political scientist Katherine Tate proffered: "Black identification with the Democratic party did not reach its peak until the 1964 presidential election."[3] Yet the truth is more complex than this explanation.

Table 9.1, which relies on Gallup polling data from 1951 to 1960, reveals that African American partisans became majority Democrats sometime between 1951 and 1955, the period in which Truman and Eisenhower were presidents. Thus, the turning point occurred in the mid-fifties. However, Table 9.2, which also uses Gallup polling data, albeit in a much more systematic fashion, demonstrates that the major shift in African American party identification came in the 1948 presidential election. This was the year that President Truman launched his civil rights initiatives, issued an executive order that desegregated the armed services, and assisted in convincing his party to adopt a civil rights plank at the national convention that year—which precipitated a walkout by the southern Democrats. (This group reconvened in Birmingham, Alabama, renamed themselves the Dixiecrats, and nominated their own presidential and vice-presidential candidates.)

──────────────── **TABLE 9.1** ────────────────

Percentage of African American Partisans by Region: 1951, 1955, and 1960

YEARS/ REGION	Partisanship			
	DEMOCRATS	REPUBLICANS	INDEPENDENTS	TOTAL
1951				
South	48	35	17	100
Non-South	49	26	25	100
1955				
South	62	20	18	100
Non-South	56	22	22	100
1960				
Nationwide	54	23	23	100

Source: Adapted from Hazel Gaudet Erskine, "The Polls: Race Relations," *Public Opinion Quarterly* 26 (Spring, 1962): 146.

Of this 1948 partisan turning point, Everett Ladd and Charles Hadley say, "By the Truman years, however, the conversion was complete. Data on the partisan self-perception of blacks after 1948 reveal as decisive a commitment to the Democracy as does actual electoral performances."[4]

Why this confusion and multiple turning points? Here is how Ladd and Hadley explained it when they discovered these empirically based discrepancies: "The Survey

──────────────── **TABLE 9.2** ────────────────

Percentage of African American Partisans in Presidential Elections: 1937–1960

REGION	DEMOCRAT	REPUBLICAN	INDEPENDENT	TOTAL
1937[a]	44	37	19	100
1940	42	42	16	100
1944	40	40	21	100
1948	56	25	19	100
1952	66	18	16	100
1956	56	24	20	100
1960	58	22	20	100

[a]Not a presidential or congressional year. This is the earliest year for data on party identification inside the African American community. It is therefore a benchmark year.

Source: Everett Ladd, Jr., and Charles Hadley, *Transformation of the American Party System: Political Coalitions from the New Deal to the 1970s* (New York: Norton, 1975): 60, 112.

Research Center of the University of Michigan (NES), found the black vote for Democratic congressional candidates in 1960 considerably higher than that reported by Gallup, 83 as against 69 percent. Such variations inevitably occur when the number of cases (in national surveys) is small."[5]

If one moves away from individual-level survey and polling data and relies upon election return data that provides group-based insights, the crucial turning point came in the New Deal year of 1936. This shift began at first in the northern cities, slowly moved to the national level, and reached a climax in 1936. In short, blacks did not become Democrats because of the New Deal; they became "National Democrats during the New Deal."[6]

Election data taken from the African American wards and precincts in the major urban centers in the North, Midwest, and South,[7] revealed in Table 9.3, demonstrate that if one uses the African American voter turnout as the base of empirical insights (instead of responses to surveys and polls), the critical turning point was in 1936. This was the year that the majority of African American partisans became Democrats.

At best, these turning points are not some deterministic and causal moment in time, but key and important points on a *single* time continuum. *The 1936 point represents a moment of interparty realignment, the shift of African Americans from the Republican to the Democratic party at least on the national level.*[8] The 1948 and 1964 points represent intraparty realignment and must be interpreted in this light and not as some unique, singular, and exceptional period in African American party history.

TABLE 9.3

Percentage of Voters in Selected African American Precincts Voting for the Democratic Party in 1932, 1936, and 1940

URBAN AREAS	1932 VOTE %	1936 VOTE %	1940 VOTE %
Baltimore	46	55	64
Boston	12	31	37
Chicago	23	49	53
Columbus	26	47	54
Detroit	50	75	78
Kansas City, Kansas	42	61	60
Kansas City, Missouri	71	79	66
New Haven	40	61	59
Pittsburgh	53	77	77
Wilmington	28	40	42
MEAN	39	58	59

Source: Adapted from Gunnar Myrdal, *An American Dilemma: The Negro Problem and Modern Democracy* (New York: Harper and Brothers, 1944): 496, Table 1, for all the cities except Boston. The Boston data were taken from Gerald Gann, *The Making of New Deal Democrats: Voting Behavior and Realignment in Boston, 1920–1940* (Chicago: University of Chicago Press, 1989): 97. Calculations were done by the authors.

AFRICAN AMERICAN PARTY BEHAVIOR:
THE GROUP AND INDIVIDUAL DIMENSIONS

The study of partisanship in the African American community has followed the basic research routes mapped out for the studies of parties in general by political scientists. Initially, the focus was only on macro-level analysis, exploring parties as organizations and institutions. This methodological focus probed the internal structure of the party, such as the relationship between local structures (precincts, wards, county chairs), state party organizations, and national committees and conventions. This approach tended to downplay the role of blacks, except as party supporters and voters.[9]

The American Voter, which appeared in 1960, developed an individual micro-level approach for studying party behavior. The authors saw partisanship as involving psychological ties to the parties, ties that could exist without formal party membership or a consistent record of party support.[10] This psychological identification was measured by asking respondents in the NES, "Generally speaking do you think of yourself as a Republican, Democrat, Independent, or what?" While this approach did not downplay or ignore the role of black partisans, the problem was that subsamples of blacks in the NES were very small.

However, with this new shift in focus, the micro-assessment of African American partisanship could now get under way. But the lack of a sufficiently large African American subsample hindered the process. Nevertheless, numerous race relations studies—those comparing African American and white partisans—did generate what is now the conventional wisdom about African American partisans. All these studies, however, built their findings on remarkably small subsamples and numbers of cases. Hence, the interpretations derived from these studies must be treated like the "turning point" arguments and viewed with more than a little doubt.

There is another problem with the small numbers of cases. They do not permit any grasp of or any understanding of intraparty dynamism.[11] At best, the small numbers can only describe movement in and between the Democratic and Republican parties. Small numbers do not allow political scientists to tell us about those individuals who reenter the electoral process and vote for the "first" time for the Democrats, as well as those who became disgusted with the policies of Roosevelt, Truman, Kennedy, Johnson, Carter, and Clinton and simply dropped out.[12] This group of "inners-and-outers" who create the dynamism in African American Democratic partisanship are never picked up, and their omission permits the creation of a static and one-dimensional portrait of Democrats in particular and partisanship in general.

In *Hope and Independence: Black Response to Electoral and Party Politics,* Gurin, Hatchett, and Jackson write: "Blacks bring into their political ideologies ideas and feelings about their group membership and the group's status in society."[13] It is this group political consciousness that African Americans use to create their psychological tie to American political parties. And these "psychological resources" are part of African American politically motivated partisanship.

Gurin, Hatchett, and Jackson state further: "Even close party competition, which should have given blacks some electoral clout, usually did not help them." Thus, "the history of the black electorate is characterized by blacks' continual commitment to the electoral system and repeated rejection by one or the other party." Hence, "Black leaders have persistently searched for strategies that would make the party system work for the black electorate."[14] Therefore, in selecting an identification as a party partisan, African Americans carry these realities into their psychological resource makeup. And it is this psychological makeup that is reflected in their party identification.

BOX 9.1
Beyond the Two-Party System?

Recent polls indicate that more than half the public, black as well as white, are dissatisfied with the two-party system and would like to see another party or parties in addition to the Democrats and Republicans. In spite of this discontent, the structure of the electoral system makes the emergence of a viable third party extremely unlikely. The American electoral structure involves two distinct features that discourage the formation of third parties. The first is the *winner take all* method of allocating electoral college votes for president, in which the candidate with the most votes gets all a state's electoral college votes. (Thus, in 1992 Bill Clinton got 43 percent of the popular vote in California but 100 percent of that state's 52 electoral votes.) The second is the *single-member district* system used in electing members of the House, in which voters vote for only one congressman and the winner needs only a plurality to win. By contrast, virtually every other democratic country uses some form of **proportional representation** that encourages the formation of third or minor parties, since their candidates have a chance to win. A system of proportional representation in the United States would allocate electoral college votes to a candidate according to the proportion of the popular vote that candidate won. Had such a system been in effect in 1992, Ross Perot, who received 20 percent of the vote, would have been awarded 108 electoral votes (20% of 538) instead of the zero he got. Similarly, a **multimember district** system for House elections could allow a minor party to win because seats in the House would be determined by each party's percentage of the vote. For example, if there were a ten-member district and the Democrats won 40 percent of the vote, they would get four seats; the Republicans, with 40 percent, would get four seats, and Ross Perot's Reform Party, with 20 percent of the vote, would get two seats.

There is some discussion in academic circles about reform of the American electoral system to encourage proportional representation and a multiparty system;[a] former Congressman and 1980 third-party presidential candidate John Anderson is the head of a group—the Center for Voting and Democracy—that is trying to build public support for the idea, and African American congresswoman Cynthia McKinney (Democrat, Georgia) has introduced a bill to provide for proportional representation in House elections. However, unless a massive grassroots movement develops, these reform ideas will probably not go very far since the Democrats and Republicans will not easily yield their shared monopoly on political power.

[a]See Lani Guinier, *The Tyranny of the Majority: Fundamental Fairness in American Democracy* (New York: Free Press, 1994); Douglas Amy, *Real Choices/New Voices: The Case for Proportional Representation Elections in the United States* (New York: Columbia University Press, 1993); and Kay Lawson, "The Case for a Multiparty System," in Paul Herrnson and John Green, eds., *Minor Parties in American Politics: Performance, Promise, Prospects and Possibilities* (Boulder, CO: Rowman, Littlefield, 1999).

Michael Dawson continues the empirically based findings about African American individual-level partisanship. From a historical perspective, Dawson finds: "The African-American political world view forged during Reconstruction, which emphasized the importance of collective interests, has continued to shape African Americans' orientation toward the political parties to the present day."[15] Because of this worldview, African Americans from the Civil War to the New Deal identified, at least on the national level, with the Republicans. But "both major parties continued to disassociate themselves from African Americans in the period following World War I."[16] In fact, for the Democrats, this distancing posture began in the formative years of the party; for Republicans, it started in the post-Reconstruction era. By the turn of the century, it was clearly evident in both organizations (see Box 9.1).

However, in the 1950s, after the number of African American voters had risen significantly and the parties had realigned, Republican party ambivalence and southern Democratic hostility to the incipient civil rights movement led to a significant erosion of black Democratic support and increased volatility in the black vote.[17] Thus, by the 1980s if not before, "African Americans' allegiance to the two major political parties depends on their perceptions of each party's responsiveness to the needs and interests of the black community."[18] Thus, Dawson concludes that it is these group-based perceptions, not individual-level perceptions, that determine African American Democratic partisanship. Put differently, at the individual level, African Americans hold a group-based perception, a concern over which party will help and advance the group, that determines their partisan identification. In a different and separate analysis, Tate arrives at a similar conclusion about African American Democratic partisanship. *Emanating from all three of these pioneering empirical analyses of the psychological bases of African American partisanship is one singular reality: Racial identification determines African American Democratic partisanship.* But this common finding itself is something of a mystery. In the words of Tate, these "recent empirical studies of black partisanship have failed to explain why the majority of blacks are Democrats. Researchers have been unable to find, in fact, any crucial demographic differences between Black Democrats and Black Republicans."[19]

African American Partisanship in Presidential and Congressional Elections, 1952–1996

To overcome the problem of the small subsamples as well as address several other missing pieces of the puzzle at the individual level, we have pooled all the NES presidential surveys—1952–1996—in Table 9.4. This compilation provides a fairly reliable estimate of the diversity of African American partisans. Even so, with the pooled subsamples from twelve presidential and congressional elections, the numbers for partisan categories other than Democrats is still small. Using the number of cases in these pooled samples, there is a great similarity in the nature of African American partisanship in both presidential and congressional elections. About three-fourths of the African American electorate identify with the Democrats and one-tenth with the Republican. About one-tenth call themselves independent, meaning that in any election they can support either party or move toward a third party. Some 6 percent of African Americans captured in the NES surveys did not designate any party identification.

-- **TABLE 9.4** --

Partisan Identification of African Americans
in Presidential and Congressional Elections: 1952–1996

PARTISAN IDENTIFICATION	PRESIDENTIAL ELECTIONS (ALL YEARS: 1952–1996)	CONGRESSIONAL ELECTIONS (ALL YEARS: 1954–1994)
Democrat	75% (1,787)	77% (1,579)
Republican	10% (238)	9% (185)
Independent	9% (214)	8% (164)
Apolitical/Don't Know	6% (143)	6% (123)
TOTAL N	(2,383)	(2,050)

Source: National Election Studies Cumulative File (1952–1996).

To offer additional insight into partisanship beyond that of African American Democrats, Table 9.5 indicates the support that individual African Americans gave to the Republican party candidate George Bush in 1992 and Robert Dole in 1996. In addition, there is the support for Ross Perot. In 1992, Ross Perot's third party was called the "United, We Stand America"; in 1996 it was called the "Reform party." There were differences in African American party identification in these two elections, as the number of Ross Perot party supporters declined. Moreover, among the activists in the African American community there are data to suggest that this group of Perot supporters were disaffected Democrats, unhappy with the lack of explicit reform proposals by Clinton to address the problems of the African American community.[20] At the mass level, Tate shows that "Black men were more likely than Black women to have voted for Perot over Clinton . . . [and] Perot's Black supporters were more likely to be self-identified independents or Republicans."[21] Tate continues,

> In 1992 Blacks who voted for Perot are more detached from the Democratic party than
> are Jesse Jackson's supporters. They are also more ideologically diverse, leaning toward
> conservatism, whereas Jackson's strongest level of support came from those Blacks who
> identify themselves as liberals and are strongly race-conscious. Like Jackson's Black

-- **TABLE 9.5** --

African American Vote in the 1992 and 1996 Presidential Elections

PRESIDENTIAL CANDIDATES	% VOTE 1992	% VOTE 1996
Clinton	82	84
Bush/Dole	11	12
Perot	7	4
Total	100	100

Source: Adapted from "The 1992 Elections: Portrait of the Electorate," *New York Times*, November 5, 1992, and the Voter News Service Exit Poll of November 5, 1996, as reported by ABC News.

supporters, Black Perot voters, nevertheless, appear to be searching for an alternative to the Democratic party.[22]

However, by the 1996 election, African Americans voting for Perot's Reform Party declined from 7 percent to 4 percent.

African American Party Behavior and Presidential Primaries

Another aspect of African American partisanship can be seen in the respective parties' presidential nomination primaries. To date, two African Americans—Congresswoman Shirley Chisholm in 1972 and the Reverend Jesse Jackson in 1984 and 1988—have run in the Democratic presidential primaries; media commentator and radio talk show host Alan Keyes in 1996 ran in the Republican primaries. Although Arthur Fletcher, former director of the United States Commission on Civil Rights, announced in 1996 that he would be a candidate in the Republican primaries, he did not enter the race. Thus, there have been three African Americans running in four different presidential primaries.

Prior to the 1972 presidential primaries, African Americans had to vote either for all white candidates or an occasional favorite son candidate like Congressman Louis Stokes in Ohio or former state senator Julian Bond, who led a contested delegation from Georgia at the 1972 Democratic Convention.

A look at past white presidential hopefuls and African American voting patterns is revealing. The data in Table 9.6 show (using Georgia as a case) that African American Democratic partisans have been quite able to select and choose between the different types of presidential primary candidates, given the issues, the types of candidates, the intensity of endorsements, and the interaction of the candidates with the African American community.

A review of voting patterns for African American presidential hopefuls is also informative. The data in Table 9.7 are quite revealing and instructive about African American turnout and partisan voting for these candidates. The Shirley Chisholm and Alan Keyes votes are nearly the same. Neither of these candidates remotely approach the vote totals or the percentages that Jesse Jackson attained in the 1984 and 1988 presidential primaries.

However, Chisholm and Keyes have one important trait in common: They were pioneers. Chisholm was the first African American to enter the Democratic primaries, and Keyes was the first African American Republican to seek his party's nomination.

Chisholm's initial campaign was a liberal left one. Keyes ran as a conservative right-wing candidate. He was perhaps further to the right than all the 1996 Republican candidates, except Patrick Buchanan. In fact, of Keyes's right-wing campaign, observers have noted he was "a prophet in the political desert [and that] his chances of being considered a serious presidential contender in these elections are quite seriously . . . nil."[23] These observers continue,

> Alan Keyes, forty-three, is Catholic, conservative, and the nation's must articulate and intellectual anti-abortion advocate. Except for his Harvard Ph.D. in government, and the fact that he's not Irish, Alan Keyes could be Bob Dornan's ideological twin. [Dornan

──────────────────── **TABLE 9.6** ────────────────────

Voting Behavior of Voters in Primarily African American Precincts in the Democratic Presidential Primaries in Georgia: 1976–1996

	Urban		Rural
CANDIDATES	ATLANTA	SAVANNAH	HANCOCK COUNTY
	1976 Election Year		
Carter	92.4	89.5	74.5
Udall	4.1	0.7	2.0
Others	3.5	9.8	23.5
	1980 Election Year		
Carter	64.6	77.6	80.2
Kennedy	20.4	18.7	10.9
Others[a]	15.0	3.7	8.9
	1984 Election Year		
Jackson	58.4	71.5	66.5
Mondale	34.9	20.3	15.7
Hart	5.4	4.7	7.0
Others[b]	1.3	3.4	10.8
	1988 Election Year		
Jackson	93.1	89.4	79.7
Dukakis	3.5	4.2	1.7
Gore	1.8	2.1	8.1
Others	1.7	4.3	10.5
	1992 Election Year		
Clinton	72.7	65.8	68.0
Tsongas	14.3	14.9	13.6
Brown	6.5	10.0	10.2
Others	6.4	9.3	7.3
	1996 Election Year		
Clinton[c]	100.00	100.00	100.00

[a]Others included Paul Simon, Gary Hart, Bruce Babbit and Dick Gephardt.

[b]Others included Tom Harkin and Bob Kerry.

[c]Clinton was the only candidate in the preference primary.

Source: The 1976, 1980, 1984 data are taken from Hanes Walton, Jr., *Invisible Politics: Black Political Behavior* (Albany: State University of New York Press, 1985): 96 and 100. The 1988, 1992, and 1996 data are from precinct returns supplied by the Fulton County Registration Office, and the 1988 Hancock County data are from the Georgia State Archives. The 1992 and 1996 data are from the Election Division of the Georgia Secretary of State. The 1988, 1992, and 1996 Fulton County precinct returns came from those that were 90%–100% African American. Hancock County is 75% African American, which means some of the voters are nonblack. In Savannah, the county returns are reported by County Commissioner Districts. The district returns are from the three County Commissioner districts that are 65% or more African American. Calculations were prepared by the authors.

━━━━━━━━━━━━━━━━━━ **TABLE 9.7** ━━━━━━━━━━━━━━━━━

Vote Percentages for African American Candidates
in the Democratic and Republican Presidential Primaries

PRIMARY STATES	1972 VOTE % SHIRLEY CHISHOLM		1984 VOTE % JESSE JACKSON	1988 VOTE % JESSE JACKSON	1996 VOTE % ALAN KEYES
New Hampshire	*		5	8	3
South Dakota	*		5	5	3
Vermont	*		8	26	
Alabama	*		20	44	
Arkansas	*		*	17	
Florida	4		12	20	
Georgia	*		21	40	
Kentucky	*		*	16	
Louisiana	*		43	36	
Maryland	2		26	29	
Massachusetts	4		5	19	
Mississippi	*		*	45	
Missouri	*		*	20	
North Carolina	8		25	33	
Oklahoma	*		*	13	
Rhode Island	*		*	15	
Tennessee	4		25	21	
Texas	*		*	25	
Virginia	*		*	45	
Illinois	*		21	32	4
Connecticut	*		12	28	
Wisconsin	1		10	28	3
New York	*		26	37	
Pennsylvania	*		16	27	
Indiana	*		14	23	
Ohio	*		16	27	3
District of Columbia[a]	*		67	80	
Nebraska	1		9	26	
West Virginia	*		7	14	
Oregon	1		9	38	
Idaho	*		6	16	
California	4		18	35	4
Montana	*		11	22	
New Jersey	67		24	33	7
New Mexico	2		12	28	
North Dakota	*		0	15	3
Michigan	28		*	*	3
Nevada	*		*	*	1
Washington	*		*	*	5
Arizona	*		*	*	1
Delaware	*		*	*	5
Total	430,703	3	3,282,380 18	6,685,699 29	436,262 3

[a]Chisholm was not a candidate in 1972 District of Columbia primary and Keyes was not a candidate in the 1996 primary.

Note: Asterisk indicates the state did not hold a primary, or data are not available.

Source: Richard Simmon and Alice McGillvray, eds., *America Votes* (Washington, DC: Congressional Quarterly, 1989): 49, 51, 56. The Alan Keyes data were taken directly from data sent to the authors by the various Secretaries of States. Calculations prepared by authors.

was a right-wing congressman from California, who also ran in the 1996 Republican primaries.] Both have passion and the ability to move audiences with their oratory.[24]

In fact, in the 1996 primaries, "both could be cast as 20th century John the Baptist, verbally flogging an inattentive and licentious populace to change their hedonist ways and restore moral and personal order to their lives, their communities and the nation."[25] Not only did Keyes lose; he secured only ten delegates. In 1988, President Reagan, who sponsored his career in the subcabinet, permitted him to address the Republican National Convention in prime time. In 1992 George Bush and in 1996 Robert Dole would not even continue this courtesy.

AFRICAN AMERICAN PARTY CONVENTION BEHAVIOR

Although both the Democratic and Republican parties have been holding national nominating conventions since their initial contest in 1856, "the Republicans had black delegates only from the South in 1868 and none from the North until 1916; the Democrats had none from either the North or the South until 1936."[26]

However, as the data in Table 9.8 indicate, the number and percentage of African American Democratic delegates have dramatically increased while the number and

New York congresswoman Shirley Chisholm, the first African American to seek a major party presidential nomination, appears on "Meet the Press" in 1972, with the other candidates, George McGovern, Hubert Humphrey, Edmund Muskie, and Henry Jackson.

──────────────────── **TABLE 9.8** ────────────────────

Number and Percentage of African American Delegates
to the Republican and Democratic National Conventions: 1868–1996

YEAR	Republican		Democratic	
	NUMBER	%	NUMBER	%
1868	4			
1872	27			
1876	24			
1880	21			
1884	20			
1888	17			
1892	13			
1896	9			
1900	12			
1904	12			
1908	10			
1912	65	6		
1916	35	4		
1920	39	3		
1924	39	4		
1928	49	4		
1932	26	2	0[a]	
1936	45	5	12	.1
1940	32	3	7	.6
1944	18	2	11	.9
1948	41	4	17	1
1952	29	2	33	3
1956	36	3	24	2
1960	22	2	46	3
1964	14	1	65	3
1968	26	1	209	7
1972	56	4	452	15
1976	76	3	323	11
1980	55	3	481	14
1984	69	3	697	18
1988	61	3	962	23
1992	107	5	771	18
1996	52	3	908	21

[a]There were some alternate delegates to this convention.

Source: For the data from 1868–1972, see Hanes Walton, Jr., and C. Vernon Gray, "Black Politics at National Republican and Democratic Conventions: 1868–1972," *Phylon* (September, 1975): 269–78. The data from 1976 to 1996 were obtained from the Joint Center for Political Studies.

percentage of African American Republican delegates to the national conventions have dramatically declined. Two things have assisted these major trends. First, after African American challenges in 1944, 1948, 1956, 1964, and 1968 through the South Carolina Progressive Democratic party, the Mississippi Freedom Democratic Party in 1964 (see Box 9.2), and the National Democratic Party of Alabama in 1968, the Democratic party engaged in a reform effort led by George McGovern in 1972, which sought to provide equitable representation to minorities. These internal reforms, coupled with the Voting Rights Act of 1965 and the increasing number of African American elected officials, resulted in a significant increase in black delegate representation. That is, a change in the rules has made for a change in the number of African American delegates to the Democratic convention.

This increase in black delegates at Democratic party conventions has been significant. In general, blacks constitute about 20 percent of the party's national voters, 15 percent to 20 percent of convention delegates, 20 percent or more of the Democratic National Committee. They hold important positions in the party and convention hierarchies (such as chairs or co-chairs of convention platform, rules, and credential committees). And in 1989, Ronald Brown was elected chair of the Democratic National Committee, becoming the first African American to head one of the two major parties.

As for the Republican party, its sharp turn to the right in 1964 with Barry Goldwater as the presidential nominee (Goldwater denounced the 1964 Civil Rights Bill) has led to fewer and fewer African American supporters and therefore fewer and fewer delegates. This process continued with the nominations of Reagan and Bush and to a lesser extent Dole. The party's embrace of a right-wing ideology and conservative policies have led to an exit rather than an increase in support from the African American community—and thus, to a further decline in convention delegates.[27] Today, there are fewer black delegates to the Republican National Convention than in the days after the Civil War. Ideology, not the rules, has diminished delegate totals at Republican conventions.

If in their struggle for universal freedom African Americans have made herculean efforts to gain representation at the national conventions, the present situation reflects partisan identification within the African American community as well as the impact of structural rules and ideology. Thus, African Americans have resorted to running their own candidates in an effort to influence the outcome of these national conventions, but the result is that of the four presidential candidacies, only Jackson had nominal or symbolic influence on the outcome of party behavior. Chisholm was, like Keyes, ignored even in a symbolic role and function.

And at the delegate level, since Jesse Jackson's 1984 convention effort, African American convention delegates have become "captives" of their candidates, unable to support insurgent individuals like Jackson. To become more effective, convention delegates will have to devise a new convention strategy beyond running a primary candidate.

African American Partisanship in a One-Party System

African American partisans have employed the party system in their quest for universal freedom. For a permanent racial minority, this has been no small task. And in this role, there have been both limited successes and setbacks. As Republican partisans, African

BOX 9.2

"No Two Seats"

In 1964, a poor sharecropper from Mississippi challenged Lyndon Johnson and the Democratic party and helped to set in motion a process that fundamentally changed the relationship of the Democratic Party and African American voters.

Fannie Lou Hamer was born in rural Mississippi in 1917, the youngest of twenty children. She spent most of her life working as a sharecropper; in 1962 her life was changed forever when she was inspired by a civil rights rally to attempt to register to vote. For this she was fired and ordered off the plantation. From this point until her death at the age of fifty-nine in 1977, she was a major leader of the southern civil rights movement.

In 1964 Fannie Lou Hamer was a co-founder of the Mississippi Freedom Democratic party, an interracial party that challenged the white supremacist, all-white regular Mississippi Democratic party. In 1964 the Mississippi Freedom Democratic party (MFDP) challenged the seating of the all-white Mississippi delegation at the Democratic convention. Mrs. Hamer, the party's co-chair, in dramatic, nationally televised testimony, recounted the atrocities committed against Mississippi blacks who tried to register and vote, including a vivid description of her own brutal beating in a Mississippi jail. Despite the eloquence of her testimony, the convention, under instructions from President Johnson, rejected the MFDP chal-

Fannie Lou Hamer, speaking at the 1964 Democratic National Convention in behalf of the Mississippi Freedom Democratic party.

lenge, voted to seat the all-white delegation and as a compromise offered the MFDP two honorary "at large" seats. The MFDP, despite the urgings of Martin Luther King, Jr., and white liberal leaders such as Hubert Humphrey, rejected the compromise because, as Mrs. Hamer said, it represented "token rights" and "we didn't come all this way for no two seats." Later, she led a demonstration on the convention floor, protesting the compromise and singing freedom songs.

Although Mrs. Hamer and the MFDP did not succeed in 1964, they were seated at the 1968 convention, and it was their uncompromising position at the 1964 convention that helped to spark the reforms of 1972 that eventually opened the Democratic party to full or universal participation by all Americans. In 1977 Fannie Lou Hamer died, poor and humble despite her fame and still uncompromising in the struggle for universal freedom.[a]

[a]See Mamie Locke, "Is This America? Fannie Lou Hamer and the Mississippi Freedom Democratic Party," in Vicki Crawford et al., eds., *Women in the Civil Rights Movement: Trailblazers and Torchbearers, 1941–1965* (Brooklyn: Carlson Publishing, 1990): 27–37. See also Kay Mills, *This Little Light of Mine: The Life of Fannie Lou Hamer* (New York: Dutton, 1993).

Americans saw ratification of the Thirteenth, Fourteenth, and Fifteenth Amendments to the Constitution that reestablished the concept of universal equality put forth by the Declaration of Independence, embedding it in the Constitution's vision. As Republican partisans, African Americans helped to complete the unfinished business launched by the framers of the Constitution. They helped to expand the nature and scope of the Constitution to include universal freedom.[28]

Eventually, the Republican Party abandoned its African American partisan supporters and left their newly won constitutional freedoms to the politics and the political machinations of the day. By the 1890s, all that had been won was lost.[29] The revolution had gone backward, and in the words of historian Rayford Logan, the "betrayal of the Negro" was complete.

Out of this failed Republican partisan identification, African Americans renewed their quest for universal freedom through another partisanship. The northern migration of African Americans occurred at the same moment that Democratic political machines were taking over the large urban centers in the nation. And these machines, in their effort to control the cities, vigorously recruited African Americans as voters and subordinate machine operatives.[30] Initially this process sent African Americans to state legislatures, to city councils, and eventually in 1928 to Congress. And ultimately, it transformed African American Republican partisans into Democratic ones. Between 1936 and 1948, African American Democratic activists and their liberal allies transformed the party of slavery and segregation into an organization that desegregated federal and state employment, the armed services, and the public facilities of the country and secured voting rights. Partisan identification had once again enlarged the national scope and legal parameters of universal freedom. In addition, African American partisan efforts helped expand rights for women, consumers, peace advocates, public interest groups, and students. But once again, partisan identification could not forestall the race-based decline of the New Deal coalition and a Republican led counter-revolution that undercut the African American advancement of universal freedom (see Box 9.3).

BOX 9.3

The Rise and Fall of a Material-Based Coalition: The New Deal, 1932–1968

The New Deal, inaugurated with the election of Franklin Roosevelt, was a material-based coalition. When Roosevelt ran for president in 1932 in the midst of the Great Depression, he ran as a cautious, budget-balancing centrist rather than as a liberal reformer. However, once elected, he proposed a series of policies that laid the foundation for the American welfare state. Although many of the New Deal reforms were severely compromised and undermined by southern conservatives and business interests, several important universal programs were adopted, including Social Security, the right of collective bargaining for trade unions, work relief programs, and the minimum wage. In the 1960s, Lyndon Johnson, a protege of President Roosevelt, expanded the logic of New Deal universalism with his Great Society, which extended material benefits on a universal basis in areas such as health care for the elderly and poor and access to higher education. In establishing and consolidating the New Deal as a ma-terial-based coalition, Roosevelt resolutely refused to embrace the African American rights-based civil rights agenda, arguing that to do so would jeopardize support among southern whites for his material-based agenda. Initially, therefore, African Americans were reluctant to join the New Deal coalition; however, by Roosevelt's second election, African American lead-ers and voters began to shift allegiance from the party of Lincoln to the Democrats, tem-porarily subordinating their rights-based agenda to embrace the universalism of Roosevelt's material-based agenda. The shift was gradual, but by the time of Roosevelt's death in 1945, a majority of blacks who could vote voted Democratic. With the entry of blacks into the New Deal coalition, it became inherently unstable and subject to collapse. The coalition Roosevelt patched together included the industrial working class of the Northeast and Midwest, with such ethnic immigrants as Poles, Italians, and the Irish; it also had Jews, liberal intellectuals, white Southerners, and African Americans. This coalition of opposites—African Americans and southern white supremacists—was held together by a common interest in universal ma-terial benefits. However, once the Democratic party embraced the African American civil rights agenda—first in 1948 under President Truman and then in the 1960s under Presidents Kennedy and Johnson—the New Deal coalition began to fall apart. In 1948, southern white supremacists and racists left the New Deal coalition and formed a third party—the Dixecrats. With South Carolina's Strom Thurmond as its presidential candidate, the new party carried five deep South states. In 1964, southern racists again left the New Deal coalition—this time to support Barry Goldwater, the Republican nominee who had opposed the 1964 Civil Rights Act. Goldwater, like Thurmond in 1948, carried the deep South states. In 1968, southern whites supported segregationist Alabama governor George Wallace, and in 1972 southern whites supported Republican Richard Nixon. By 1972, the New Deal coalition was effectively dead; southern whites were defecting along with members of the northern industrial working class who supported Wallace in 1968 and Nixon and Ronald Reagan in subsequent elections. By 1980 the Republican party had consolidated itself as the conservative party of racial reac-tion. Meanwhile the African American electorate had become overwhelmingly Democratic, since 1964 voting nearly 90 percent in favor of the party on the basis of New Deal—Great Society material benefits and the party's embrace of the rights-based agenda of civil rights.

The New Deal coalition collapsed for one simple reason: racism. Many whites, especially in the South, were unwilling to be a part of a broad material-based coalition if that coalition also embraced the historic quest of African Americans for equality and universal freedom.

This context helps explain the African American party behavior that we have de-tailed empirically. It exists in both the group and the individual dimensions. In either di-mension, there is a skewed partisanship inside the African American community. One party at a time will be hegemonic in the black electorate. One party will have more indi-viduals attached to it and voting for it than another. But as was made clear, such one-sided partisanship does not negate the possibility of some voter attachment to other par-ties, third parties like H. Ross Perot's Reform party or the conservative-led Republican party.

Despite diversity in partisan tendencies, the historical reality is that African American partisan activists in coalition with others have only been able to transform one party at a time. Hence, *the two-party system in America has been and is essentially a one-party system or at best a modified one-party system for African Americans. There has never been a functional two-party system for African Americans* (Box 9.4). And this systemic and contextual reality raises questions about the psychological basis of African American partisanship.

Among all who have studied the individual-level dimension of partisanship, only one scholar has raised and examined this fundamental reality. Lorenzo Morris writes,

> The expectation that blacks, like whites, will identify with major political parties feeds on the myth that these parties have no concrete historical character, and, therefore, no independent political identity of their own, except, of course from the character they are thought to capriciously acquire from their ever flexible constituents.[31]

Morris continues this insight: "Black Democrats or Republicans may, for example, know nothing of the compromise of 1877, but they cannot help but know and feel that both parties have always represented something exclusionary of blacks."[32] Therefore, he concludes: "If, for example, blacks do not feel a psychological tie to the major parties, but rather choose among them out of a helpless fear that they must choose among evils presented by an alien system, they might well continue to do so for years without upsetting

---

BOX 9.4

"The Republican Party Is the Deck, All Else the Sea": The African American Voter and the One-Party System

---

Most American political scientists are committed to the two-party system as indispensable to the effective operation of the American democracy. The essence of that commitment, according to political scientist Leon Epstein, is the theory "that voters should be able to choose between recognizable competing leadership groups" that offer alternative programs and policies addressing citizen needs and interests.[a] The two-party system historically has worked reasonably well for white Americans, offering reasonable alternative candidates, programs, and policies from which they could choose. For African Americans, however, this has rarely been the case; on the contrary, since blacks obtained the vote in the Reconstruction era, they have essentially had to operate in a one-party system.

In the Reconstruction era, as blacks first began to vote, Frederick Douglass is said to have told a group of black voters that the "Republican party is the deck, all else the sea." What Douglass meant was that only one of the two parties was willing to offer any kind of program or policy to address the interests of African American voters. The second party—the Democrats—was unrelentingly hostile. Since the Douglass days, except for a brief period hardly anything has changed; one party is the deck, the other is the sea—except today the deck is Democratic.

For the brief period between the 1930s and 1960s, African Americans did enjoy the benefits of a two-party system, as both the Democrats and Republicans competed for the black vote with policy pledges, promises, and patronage. And the black vote oscillated between the two parties; as late as 1960, for example, Republican nominee Richard Nixon received as much as one-third of the black vote against the Democrat John Kennedy. Since the 1960 election, however, the American party system has returned to its normal status for African Americans—one partyism. As Gurin, Hatchett, and Jackson noted, "The history of the black electorate is characterized by blacks' continued commitment to the electoral system and repeated rejection by one or the other party."[b] From the 1860s to the 1930s, it was the Democrats who rejected blacks; since the 1960s, it has been the Republicans. This means that black voters, relative to whites, are of marginal political value, since they are not offered alternative candidates and policies that address their needs.

For example, in 1980, black Americans, like their fellow white citizens, had become dissatisfied (although for different reasons) with President Carter and his policies and programs, sensing his budget and social policies represented a shift to the right. Thus, Carter's job approval rating among blacks fell to the same low level as among whites.[c] Yet unlike whites, who could and did express their dissatisfaction with Carter by voting for Ronald Reagan and the Republicans, blacks could not change parties since the Republicans ignored them by refusing to offer any reasonable alternative to Carter's rightward drift. Thus, African American voters had no choice—as in a one-party system—except to stay at home or vote for Carter, their dissatisfaction with him notwithstanding. And of those blacks who voted in 1980, 85 percent voted for Carter.

[a]Leon Epstein, "The Scholarly Commitment to Parties," in Ada Finifter, ed., *The State of the Discipline* (Washington: American Political Science Association, 1983): 129.

[b]Patricia Gurin, Shirley Hatchett, and James Jackson, *Hope and Independence: Black Response to Electoral and Party Politics* (New York: Russell Sage, 1991): 259.

[c]Gallup poll data at the opening of the 1980 campaign year showed Carter's job approval rating among blacks at 30 percent and among whites at 29 percent. The data are reported in *The Ladd Report* (New York: Norton, 1991): 13.

---

hard data."[33] This is what Tate meant when she wrote: "Recent empirical studies of Black partisanship have failed to explain why the majority of Blacks are Democrats."[34] Such studies have empirically demonstrated that of all of the relevant independent variables, "race identification" is the major determinant of partisanship. They leave undiscussed and unremarked, however, the "historical" character of the parties and the one-party nature of the party system for African Americans—thus, the significance of Jesse Jackson's campaigns for the Democratic nomination. Again to quote Morris, "By his presence, if not his words, Jackson asked voters to be conscious of their race in the course of political party participation. However, white Americans had long ago rejected race as part of their political party consciousness."[35] Perhaps in the future, African American party activists and voters will have to find a tool other than the major parties to assist them in their struggle for freedom.

SELECTED BIBLIOGRAPHY

Chisholm, Shirley. *The Good Fight*. New York: Harper & Row, 1973. A memoir of her run for the presidency in 1972.

Davis, Benjamin. *Communist Councilman from Harlem*. New York: International Publishers, 1969. Memoir of a Republican turned communist.

Frady, Marshall. *Jesse: The Life and Pilgrimage of Jesse Jackson*. New York: Random House, 1996. A comprehensive, full-length biography of the civil rights leader and presidential candidate.

Jack, Hulan. *Fifty Years a Democrat: The Autobiography of Hulan E. Jack*. New York: The New Benjamin Franklin House, 1982. Memoir of the Democratic party activist and first president of the Borough of Manhattan.

Key, V. O. *Politics, Parties and Pressure Groups*. New York: Crowell, 1942. A still useful study of the American party system.

Ladd, Everett C., and Charles Hadley. *Transformation of the American Party System: Political Coalitions from the New Deal to the 1970s*. New York: Norton, 1975. An analysis of the decline of the New Deal coalition.

Lawson, Kay, ed. *Political Parties and Linkage*. New Haven, CT: Yale University Press, 1980. A collection of papers examining the decline of political parties as the linkage between citizens and government.

Mills, Kay. *This Little Light of Mine: The Life of Fannie Lou Hamer*. New York: Dutton, 1993. A biography of the famous Mississippi freedom fighter.

Morris, Lorenzo. "Race and the Rise and Fall of the Two Party System." In Lorenzo Morris, ed. *The Social and Political Implications of the 1984 Jesse Jackson Campaign*. New York: Praeger, 1990. An important article analyzing the functional limitations of the two-party system in terms of black voter choice.

Reid, Willie. *Black Women's Struggle for Equality*. New York: Pathfinder Press, 1976. A memoir of the African American Socialist Workers Party's 1976 candidate for vice president.

Walter, John C. *The Harlem Fox: J. Raymond Jones and Tammany Hall*. Albany: State University of New York Press, 1989. A memoir of the first African American head of Tammany Hall, the New York City Democratic party organization.

Walton, Hanes, Jr. *Black Political Parties: A Historical and Political Analysis*. New York: Free Press, 1972. A comprehensive analysis of African American political parties.

Walton, Hanes, Jr. "Democrats and African Americans: The American Idea." In Peter Kover, ed. *Democrats and the American Idea*. Washington: Center for National Policy Press, 1992. A brief history of African Americans in the Democratic party.

Weiss, Nancy. *Farewell to the Party of Lincoln: Black Politics in the Age of FDR*. Princeton, NJ: Princeton University Press, 1983. A historical account of the shift of blacks from the Republican to the Democratic party.

NOTES

1. Edward Carmines and James Stimson, *Issue Evolution: Race and the Transformation of American Politics* (Princeton, NJ: Princeton University Press, 1989): 47.

2. Donald Kinder and Lynn Sanders, *Divided by Color: Racial Politics and Democratic Ideals* (Chicago: University of Chicago Press, 1996): 208.
3. Katherine Tate, *From Protest to Politics: The New Black Voters in American Elections* (enlarged ed.) (Cambridge, MA: Harvard University Press, 1994): 62.
4. Everett Ladd, Jr., and Charles Hadley, *Transformation of the American Party System: Political Coalitions from the New Deal to the 1970s* (New York: Norton, 1975): 113.
5. Ibid., Note 24.
6. Hanes Walton, Jr., *Black Politics: A Theoretical and Structural Analysis* (Philadelphia: J. B. Lippincott, 1972): 100.
7. The data for nine of the ten urban centers were taken from the Gunnar Myrdal volume because his tabular data cover three of the four major regions of the country. There is another tabular listing of the African American Democratic vote percentages but it is confined to ten northern cities and therefore does not provide the reader with an inter-regional analysis—particularly the South. See Nancy Weiss, *Farewell to the Party of Lincoln: Black Politics in the Age of FDR* (Princeton, NJ: Princeton University Press, 1983): 30–31, 206–207.
8. Hanes Walton, Jr., "Black Presidential Participation and the Critical Election Theory," in Lorenzo Morris, ed., *The Social and Political Implications of the 1984 Jesse Jackson Presidential Campaign* (New York: Praeger, 1990): 49–62.
9. See Edward M. Sait, *American Parties and Elections* (New York: Century Company, 1927): pp. 49–55. See also V. O. Key, Jr.'s influential textbook *Politics, Parties, and Pressure Groups* (New York: Crowell, 1942).
10. Angus Campbell, Phillip Converse, Warren Miller, and Donald Stokes, *The American Voter* (New York: Wiley, 1960): 87.
11. Walton, *Invisible Politics* (Albany: State University of New York Press, 1985): 121–124.
12. A good study of the "inner and outer" voters in the Democratic party is by Michael Preston, "The Election of Harold Washington: An Examination of the SES Model in the 1983 Chicago Mayoral Election," in Michael Preston, Lenneal Henderson, Jr., and Paul Puryear, eds., *The New Black Politics*, 2nd ed. (New York: Longman Press, 1987): 139–163.
13. Patricia Gurin, Shirley Hatchett, and James Jackson, *Hope and Independence: Black Response to Electoral and Party Politics* (New York: Russell Sage, 1991): 64.
14. Ibid., p. 259.
15. Michael Dawson, *Behind the Mule: Race, Class and African American Politics* (Princeton, NJ: Princeton University Press, 1994): 101.
16. Ibid., p. 102.
17. Ibid., p. 105.
18. Ibid., p. 112.
19. Tate, *From Protest to Politics*, p. 63.
20. Hanes Walton, Jr., "African Americans, H. Ross Perot and Image Politics: The Nature of African American and Third Party Politics," in Hanes Walton, Jr., *African American Power and Politics: The Political Context, Variable* (New York: Columbia University Press, 1997), chap. 17.

21. Tate, *From Protest to Politics*, pp. 197–198.
22. Ibid., p. 198.
23. See Ralph Hallow and Bradley O'Leary, "Alan Keyes: A Prophet in the Political Desert," in Ralph Hallow and Bradley O'Leary, *Presidential Fellows: Those Who Would Be President and Those Who Should Think Again* (Dallas, TX: Brown, 1995): 103. See also Alan Keyes, *Masters of the Dream: The Strength and Betrayal of Black America* (New York: Morrow, 1995).
24. Ibid.
25. Ibid.
26. Walton, *Black Politics*, p. 119.
27. For data on this exit for ideological reasons, see Pearl Robinson, "Whither the Future of Blacks in the Republican Party?" *Political Science Quarterly* 97 (Summer, 1952): 217; and J. Clay Smith, Jr., "A Black Lawyer's Response to the Fairmont Paper," *Howard Law Journal* 26 (1983): 195–225.
28. For this interpretation, see the comments of Supreme Court Justice Thurgood Marshall, "Racial Justice and the Constitution: The View of the Bench," in J. H. Franklin and Genna Rae MacNeil, eds., *African Americans and the Living Constitution* (Washington: Smithsonian Institution, 1995): 314–18.
29. Bess Beatty, *A Revolution Gone Backward: The Black Response to National Politics, 1876–1896* (Greenwood, CT: Greenwood Press, 1987).
30. For a discussion of the machines, see Walton, *Black Politics*, pp. 56–69; and William Grimshaw, *Bitter Fruit: Black Politics and the Chicago Machine, 1931–1991* (Chicago: University of Chicago Press, 1992).
31. Lorenzo Morris, "Race and the Rise and Fall of the Two-Party System," in Morris, *The Social and Political Implications of the 1984 Jesse Jackson Presidential Campaign*, p. 78.
32. Ibid., pp. 78–79.
33. Ibid., p. 77.
34. Tate, *From Protest to Politics*, p. 63.
35. Morris, "Race and the Rise and Fall of the Two-Party System," p. 88.

CHAPTER 10

Voting Behavior and Elections

Table 10.1, based on a rare composite of Gallup polling data from 1950 through 1960, permits the reader to view individual African American voters in the decade preceding the passage of the Voting Rights Act of 1965 and on the eve of the publication of *The American Voter*, the book that would forever change how academics and journalists would analyze the voting behavior of all Americans. These data also provide an even rarer opportunity to offer commentary on African American voters as they were about to become fully enfranchised citizens.

The data in Table 10.1 reveal that long before the Democratic Congress and president passed the 1964 Civil Rights Act, two-thirds to three-fourths of African Americans voted for Democrats. And this voting pattern and tendency occur during the Republican control of the White House with President Eisenhower as well as with the

TABLE 10.1

Percentages of African American Democratic and Republican Voters in Presidential and Congressional Elections: 1950–1960

YEARS	REPUBLICAN	DEMOCRATIC
1950 (C)	37	63
1952 (P)	21	79
1954 (C)	22	78
1956 (P)	39	61
1958 (C)	31	69
1960 (P)	32	68

C = Congressional Elections

P = Presidential Elections

Source: Adapted from Hazel Gaudet Erskine, "The Polls: Race Relations," *Public Opinion Quarterly* 26 (Spring, 1962): 147.

election of the Democratic President Kennedy in 1960. Overall, the table reveals a tendency among African American voters toward the Democratic party. Additional demographic data in Table 10.2 permit an enhancement of our descriptive analysis. Table 10.2 provides regional demographic data for all elections through the 1960 presidential election. With this information it is possible to further profile the African American voters of the decade 1950–1960. For instance, the regional demographic variable demonstrates that southern African American voters had a much weaker Democratic partisan identification than those outside the South. A partial explanation for this regional differential in party identification is that during this decade, the southern Democratic party was the party of segregation, states' rights, and racial demagogues, like George Wallace. This was also the period of massive southern resistance to school de-

---

TABLE 10.2

Demographic Correlates of African American Voters in Presidential and Congressional Elections: 1950–1960

DEMOGRAPHIC VARIABLES	TYPES OF ELECTION	Partisan Percentages	
		DEMOCRATIC	REPUBLICAN
REGIONS			
South			
November, 1958	Congressional	64	36
November, 1960	Presidential	67	33
Non-South			
November, 1952	Presidential	79	21
July, 1956	Congressional	77	23
November, 1956	Presidential	66	34
November, 1958	Congressional	72	28
November, 1960	Presidential	68	32
Data for November, 1960: Presidential Only			
Age			
Under 50 years		71 (634)	29 (259)
51 +		63 (563)	37 (330)
Sex			
Female		70 (625)	30 (268)
Male		66 (589)	34 (304)
City Size			
Under 500,000		60 (536)	40 (357)
500,000 +		74 (661)	26 (232)
Union			
Members		76 (679)	24 (214)
Nonmembers		NA	NA

Note: The number of African Americans in the 1960 poll data was 893.

Source: Adapted from Hazel Gaudet Erskine, "The Polls: Race Relations," *Public Opinion Quarterly* 26 (Spring, 1962): 147. Calculations prepared by authors

segregation. In this era, African Americans found few positive things about the Democratic party in the South.

Moving beyond the regional demographics and exploring the 1960 presidential election, the bottom part of Table 10.2 tells us that younger voters, women, urban dwellers, and union members identified more strongly with the Democratic party than did older individuals, men, and rural dwellers. On the Republican side, the table shows that in cities with populations under 500,000 there is a strong identification with the Republican party (the GOP). In short, city size, at least in the 1960 presidential election, correlated with African American Republican voting.

Collectively, Tables 10.1 and 10.2 offer a rare glimpse into the voting behavior of African Americans in both the congressional and presidential elections long before the energizing and consciousness raising marches of Dr. Martin Luther King, Jr. With these data, good empirical description emerges. But with the publication of *The American Voter*, political science demanded not only empirically based descriptive accounts of voting behavior but also empirically supported explanations. Thus, it is to these twin concerns of both description and explanation that we now turn.

Theories of Voter Choice

Social scientists have developed four major theories to explain individual voter choice. The first is the *sociological theory of vote choice* developed by Bernard Berelson and his colleagues and explained in two books: *Voting: A Study of Opinion Formation in a Presidential Campaign,* published in 1954, and *The People's Choice: How the Voter Makes Up His Mind in a Presidential Campaign,* published in 1944.[1] This theory contends that an individual's social characteristics determine his or her political preferences. Here's how this theory is explained in *The People's Choice*.

> As the social characterization of the respondent becomes more detailed a closer relationship to political affiliation can be established. The wealthier people, the people with more and better possessions, the people with business interests—these people were usually Republicans. The poorer people, the people whose homes and clothes were of lower quality, the self-acknowledged laboring class—they voted Democratic. Different social characteristics, different votes.[2]

In other words, social class and related group memberships largely determined voter choice.

In *The Voter Decides* published 1954 and *The American Voter* in 1960, the *psychological theory of vote choice* was launched.[3] It combines the social characteristics of the individual with her or his psychological identification with or orientation toward the political parties, issues debated in the campaigns, and the candidates running for office.

The third approach is the *political theory* of vote choice advanced by V. O. Key in his 1966 book *The Responsible Electorate*.[4] Key argued that the American voter was not guided solely by social or psychological factors but rather by responsible choice among issues and candidates. Key concluded that the American "electorate is moved by concern about the central and relevant questions of public policy, of government performance and executive personality."[5] Voter choice was determined by public policy concerns, not psychology or group affiliations.

The fourth approach to explaining voting behavior is the *economic theory* of *vote choice*. First advanced by Anthony Downs in 1957 in *An Economic Theory of Democracy* and revised and updated by rational choice theorists such as William Riker,[6] this theory contends that "ordinary voters are prone to weighing costs and benefits when they make their candidate or issue choices in elections, or when they decide about whether to participate at all."[7] Dennis sums up the theory this way: "Downs (and his current disciples) thus postulates that voters are able and willing to employ voting calculus by which they weigh each party's promises for future policy initiatives against the record of past performance relative to their own needs, for maximization of utility."[8] Votes are thus like dollars invested for some anticipated return.

African Americans and the Major Theories of Vote Choice

Where is the African American voter in all this electoral theorizing? For the most part, this voter is almost invisible. But before we show that reality, it must be said that each of the four theories states either explicitly or implicitly that each one of them holds for subgroups in the American political process as it does for the dominant white majority. The sociological theory holds that social variables determine and cause the vote intentions and/or preferences of African American voters. The psychological theory holds that party identifications and one's subjective orientation to politics determine the African American voter choice. From the economic theory of voter choice and the political theory there are similar conclusions. Each theoretical perspective offers its own specific reason as to why African Americans as individuals tend to vote as they do. Four different theories; four different explanations.

Table 10.3 shows the number of African Americans in the surveys used in each of these books and the percentage of African Americans in each study. Overall, the table demonstrates that *these empirically based theories of voting behavior rest on woefully small and deficient numbers of African Americans to produce reliable estimates*. At best, the findings in these landmark voting studies are not empirically sound but merely suggestive and impressionistic. Hence, the early voting studies generated some questionable and highly unreliable theories about the voting behavior of the African American community. *They also failed to include in their theoretical equations the unique features of the African American voting experience.*

The Historical and Systemic Dimensions of African American Voting Behavior

As demonstrated throughout much of this book, the acquisition of the right to vote for African Americans has been extraordinarily difficult. Racism has prevented and denied African Americans this simple citizenship right. Moreover, shortly after America began, the African American population was bifurcated into a free population and a slave population. The latter, without any freedom, simply were not citizens, and the former, while quasi-citizens, were rarely given the right to vote.

If prior to the formation of the federal system African Americans, even the free ones, could not uniformly vote in the thirteen colonies (and eventual thirteen states),

─────────────────────── **TABLE 10.3** ───────────────────────

Number and Percentage of African Americans in Surveys Reported in the Four Books Used to Generate Four Theories of American Voting Behavior

THEORY CATEGORIES & MAJOR BOOKS	NUMBER OF AFRICAN AMERICANS	% OF AFRICAN AMERICANS
1. SOCIOLOGICAL THEORY		
The People's Choice (Berelson et al.)	0	0
Pre-election survey	17	1.6
Post-election survey	150[a]	12.7
2. PSYCHOLOGICAL THEORY		
The Voter Decides (Campbell et al.)		
Pre-election survey	61	9.2
Post-election survey	157	9.7
The American Voter[b] (Campbell et al.)		
1952 Pre-election survey	171	9.5
1952 Post-election survey	—	
1956 Pre-election survey	146	8.3
1956 Post-election survey	—	
3. POLITICAL THEORY		
The Responsible Electorate (Key)		
Pre-election survey	────[c]	────[c]
4. ECONOMIC THEORY		
An Economic Theory of Democracy (Downs)	0	0

[a]Supplemental sample

[b]*The American Voter* doesn't specify the exact number of African Americans. However, the book relied primarily upon the 1952 and 1956 University of Michigan national election surveys. Therefore, the numbers of African Americans in these surveys were taken directly from the codebooks for those surveys.

[c]Key does not provide a composite total of African Americans in his study. However, Tables 4.1, 4.6, and 5.1 in *The Responsible Electorate* do provide numbers by his functional categories.

Source: Adapted and revised from Hanes Walton, Jr., *Invisible Politics: Black Political Behavior* (Albany: State University of New York Press, 1985): Table 5.1, p. 79.

this reality persisted throughout antebellum America until the end of the Civil War. Hence, between the Constitutional Convention of 1787 and the end of the Civil War in 1865, only six states permitted the "Free" Negroes to vote. The Revolutionary War, with all its discussion of freedom, did not change the nonvoting status of African Americans. In fact, between the Revolutionary and Civil Wars, Tennessee in 1834, North Carolina in 1835, and Pennsylvania in 1838 all withdrew the right to vote from "Free Negroes."

New York, on the other hand, did not deny the right; rather, it restricted voting by requiring that "Free Negroes" show ownership of property valued at 200 hundred dollars. When this rule went into effect, the number of voters dropped. Yet what happened afterward is absolutely incredible. New York subsequently held three statewide suffrage referenda in which the state's white voters were asked to decide whether to give "Free

Negroes" full, universal voting rights. The first referendum was held in 1846, the second in 1860, and the third in 1869. Table 10.4 reveals the vote for and against these referenda. All three were voted down by the state electorate. And although the percentage of whites voting to give African Americans this aspect of universal freedom continued to increase, the opponents were always in the majority. The state became a systemic force in disallowing the vote.

New York electorate's refusal to grant universal suffrage rights to "Free Negroes" must be seen in the context that this state was a strong supporter of abolitionism, and a state with a significant "Free Negro" population. Moreover, although after the Revolutionary War the state moved to emancipate its slaves, and while it fought in behalf of African American universal freedom in the Civil War, it could not after both wars grant African Americans this basic right of citizenship. These three different failed statewide referenda votes demonstrate that the majority of whites in the state never envisioned African Americans as equal. And this is in spite of a strenuous one-year-long statewide African American campaign to galvanize support for the suffrage referendum that preceded each of the three statewide votes.[9]

Led by Frederick Douglass, the African American community lobbied not only the white community but the state legislature, governor, and the African American community as well.[10] One scholar declares: "The most dedicated group supporting equal suffrage proved to be New York's black community. Not only did they actively lobby the (state Constitutional) Convention itself, but they also issued public addresses and letters throughout the referendum campaign to explain why they wanted and needed the franchise."[11] Each time, the African American lobbying efforts failed to garner enough support to have voting rights extended to the community in an unrestricted fashion.[12]

But the New York example is just one of many in which the black leadership and community struggled to gain the ballot in the antebellum North and Midwest. William Gillette, writing on the many African American lobbying efforts prior to the Civil War

---
TABLE 10.4

Results of Three Statewide Suffrage Rights Referenda in New York: 1846, 1860, and 1869

TOTAL VOTES	VOTES FOR	% FOR	VOTES AGAINST	% AGAINST
The 1846 Statewide Referendum				
309,742	85,406	28%	224,336	72%
The 1860 Statewide Referendum				
543,680	197,889	36%	345,791	64%
The 1869 Statewide Referendum				
532,205	249,802	47%	282,403	53%

Source: Adapted from Phyllis Field, *The Politics of Race in New York: The Struggle for Black Suffrage in the Civil War Era* (Ithaca, NY: Cornell University Press, 1982): 61, 127, and 199.

either to gain or regain the ballot, observed the following about these failures: "Voters in the North, in referendum after referendum, rejected Negro suffrage by a generally substantial vote. Such unmistakable opposition, nearly always in the majority, understandably intimidated Republican politicians (who supported these measures), for in state after state the verdict was the same."[13] In fact, "during 1865 [alone] five jurisdictions voted down Negro suffrage in popular referendums."[14]

In the meantime, state-by-state lobbying did not exhaust all the efforts of African Americans.

> In October, 1864, at Syracuse, New York, blacks established the National Equal Rights League to obtain universal suffrage rights for all blacks. The president of the League, Frederick Douglass, called on President Andrew Johnson to give blacks full enfranchisement. Johnson refused but a group of radical Republicans were receptive to Douglass' plea. With this backing, the 15th Amendment was adopted on March 30, 1870.[15]

With this constitutional amendment, African Americans were now entitled to universal suffrage.

However, if the northern and midwestern states opposed a simple aspect of universal freedom like voting rights prior to the Civil War and thereafter, the South would become the central opponent after the Civil War until the present day. Beginning with the Compromise of 1877, which the South brought about through the fraud, corruption, and violence of the 1876 election, African Americans' newly won voting rights were once again restricted and curtailed, the Fifteenth Amendment notwithstanding. The South's drive to eliminate African Americans from the ballot box culminated in the "era of disenfranchisement" (1890–1901), when all eleven of the states of the old Confederacy adopted new state constitutions that either prevented, prohibited, or manipulated African Americans out of their voting rights. Because of a series of inventive, innovative, and amazingly effective devices like the Grandfather's Clause, White Primaries, pre-primaries, poll taxes, reading and interpretation tests, multiple ballot boxes, single-month registration periods, party- instead of state-administered primaries, single-state party systems, evasion, economic reprisals, terror, fraud, corruption, violence, mayhem and murder, African Americans found it exceedingly difficult to register, much less to vote.[16] In Louisiana, one of the eleven southern states where voter registration data were kept by race, it is possible to see in empirical terms just how effective these tactics were in crippling African American voters. Figure 10.1 shows percentages for an entire century comparing the eligible African American voting-age population with those who overcame the obstacles and became registered voters. African American registered voters plummeted from a high of 130,444 in 1897 to a low of 5,320 in 1910. Clearly the new state constitution in Louisiana disenfranchised, in a very short span of time, more than 95 percent of the entire African American electorate. Nearly the same reality prevailed in the other states of the old Confederacy.

But as had happened in the antebellum period, African Americans once again organized and lobbied to regain their suffrage rights, and they did so from 1895 to 1965. With the NAACP taking the lead nationally and numerous courageous individuals and groups spearheading efforts at the local and state levels, the drive to regain the ballot met with some success. Although the success was uneven and painfully slow and in numerous places quite deadly, some partial success was achieved.

Figure 10.1 The Percentage of African American Registered Voters in Louisiana: 1867–1964

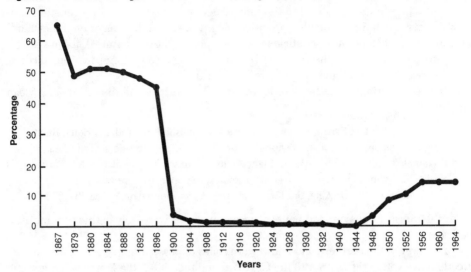

Source: Adapted from *Annual Cyclopaedia and Register of Important Events of the Year 1867,* Vol. VII (New York: D. Appleton and Company, 1869), p. 461 for the year 1867; Perry H. Howard, *Political Tendencies in Louisiana,* revised and expanded (Baton Rouge: Louisiana State University Press, 1971), pp. 421–422 for the years 1879–1964. Calculations prepared by authors.

Initially, victories came from Supreme Court cases, like *Guinn and Beal v. U.S.* (1914), which declared the Grandfather Clause unconstitutional; *Lane v. Wilson* (1939), which voided the single-month registration scheme; *Smith v. Allwright* (1949), which outlawed white primaries; *Terry v. Adams* (1953), which eliminated party-administered elections; and a federal district court decision in 1949 that declared "understanding and explaining clauses" to be unconstitutional.[17]

Later, congressional legislation assisted the court decisions. The Civil Rights Acts of 1957 and 1960 and Title I of the 1964 Civil Rights Act added limited federal protection for African American voting rights. Then in 1965, Congress passed the 1965 Voting Rights Act, which was renewed in 1970, 1975, and 1982. This law permitted a federal registrar to go into the states covered by the law and register African Americans to vote. However, by the 1960s, the African American community in the South had lost considerable political clout. For example, as Table 10.5 shows, in Mississippi and South Carolina in 1900 blacks were a majority of the population, but by the 1960s they constituted less than a third. Similar declines in voting power between 1900 and 1970 are observed in Louisiana, Georgia, Alabama, and Florida.

ELECTORAL POWER: THE THEORY AND PRACTICE OF THE "BALANCE OF POWER" CONCEPT

At this point, the following question can be raised: Why did African Americans continue their incessant struggle for ballot and voting rights? First, the ballot is both a character-

──────────────── **TABLE 10.5** ────────────────

Percentage of African Americans of Voting Age
In the Southern States: 1900–1990

SOUTHERN STATES	1900	1910	1920	1930	1940	1950	1960	1970	1980	1990
Alabama	43.9	41.7	37.7	35.6	33.4	29.5	26.2	21.1	22.5	23.2
Arkansas	27.8	28.2	27.4	26.6	24.6	20.5	18.5	14.8	13.9	13.6
Florida	44.2	42.0	34.0	29.0	26.0	20.1	15.2	11.9	11.6	11.9
Georgia	44.6	43.0	39.8	36.6	32.8	28.6	24.5	22.7	23.9	24.5
Louisiana	45.4	42.2	38.2	36.6	34.4	30.3	28.5	26.0	27.3	28.0
Mississippi	56.9	54.9	51.3	49.4	47.1	41.3	36.1	30.3	31.2	31.7
North Carolina	30.7	29.4	28.1	27.2	25.6	23.8	21.6	18.7	19.6	20.2
South Carolina	54.0	50.5	47.2	42.0	38.7	33.9	29.2	25.4	27.7	27.5
Tennessee	23.1	21.6	19.9	19.2	18.1	16.1	15.0	13.4	14.0	14.7
Texas	18.7	16.7	15.4	14.6	14.0	12.3	11.7	11.0	11.7	11.4
Virginia	32.7	30.5	28.8	25.3	23.1	21.1	18.9	16.2	17.4	17.8

Source: Adapted from U.S. Bureau of the Census, *Statistical Abstract of the United States: 1910–1990* (Washington, DC: Government Printing Office, 1911–1990). Calculations prepared by the authors.

istic of citizenship and it is one of the few tools which a racial minority can use to obtain power in a democratic system. Former NAACP publicist Henry Moon, writing in 1948, said: "Intent upon attaining full equality of citizenship in his native land, the Negro American today sees in the ballot his most effective instrument in the long and hazardous struggle toward this goal. From such equality, he realizes, flow all the good things of life in a democratic society—the freedoms and enjoyment long denied him."[18]

Thus what was needed was not only the ballot but a theoretical or strategic rationale about the use of the ballot so that it could become a tool for freedom. The second reason for a theory or strategy is the minority status of the African American electorate. As a permanent racial minority, the group could never hope to outvote the white majority except in a few black-belt counties and all-Negro towns. Thus justifications had to be offered to support and undergird the efforts that members and organizations in the community had to put forth to attain and/or regain the ballot. The theory became the "balance of power" concept.

This theory was first discussed and advanced in the pamphlet *The Negro in Politics* issued in 1886.[19] Discussion would continue through W. E. B. Du Bois's arguments in *The Crisis* and in the works of early black political scientists, like William Nowlin in *The Negro in American National Politics*,[20] and Edgar Lee Tatum in *The Changed Political Thought of the Negro: 1915–1948*.[21] However, in 1948 Moon's book would map out this underdeveloped theory. *Essentially, the balance-of-power theory posits that in any local, congressional, state, or national election in which the white vote is evenly divided, the African American vote cast as a solid bloc can determine the outcome of the electoral contest.*

Here is how Moon described the theory:

> The size, strategic distribution, and flexibility of the Negro vote lend it an importance which can no longer be overlooked. As significant as was this vote in the 1944 elections—and without it Franklin D. Roosevelt could hardly have been re-elected—it can, with wise and independent leadership, be even more important in the 1948 elections, and in the future.[22]

And, "unlike the southern vote, the Negro vote is tied to no political party. It cannot be counted in advance."[23] In the presidential elections of 1948 and 1960, when Harry Truman and John Kennedy narrowly won the presidency, the Negro vote provided the margin of victory. Now, the theory seemingly had great validity.

However, by 1968 when the Republicans led by Richard Nixon captured the White House, with African American voters vehemently opposed to him, African American journalist Chuck Stone criticized the balance-of-power theory as being inadequate.[24] He urged black leaders and the black community to drop their adherence to the theory. As Stone saw it, the theory was dysfunctional. Its day had passed. Stone advanced a new theory dubbed "Black Politics: Third Force." His concept called for an oscillating strategy by African American voters. They should switch from one major party to the other, depending on the political deal they could make and how well it was kept.[25] While Stone proffered his new theory as the ultimate voting strategy and tool for the African American electorate, it was not a *new* theory but a warmed-over version of Moon. Moon, as indicated earlier, called on the African American voter to be independent of the two parties.

Ronald Walters, in *Black Presidential Politics in America: A Strategic Approach*, which appeared forty years after Moon's book and twenty years after Stone's, revisited the balance of-power theory at the end of two Republican presidential victories and with a third one in the making. Since the African American vote could not halt Reagan's electoral landslides (as it could not Nixon's victories in 1968 and 1972), Walters saw the balance-of-power strategy and theory as deficient.

With Reagan's elections and his attempted rollback of civil rights gains, Walters rethought the problem of theory and strategy:

> I consider that the "balance-of-power" concept has served more as philosophy than strategy, but that this philosophy has been correct, not only because it has conformed to the logic of the Black political relationship with both major parties, but also because of the perception that it has occasionally provided the leverage which has given substance to Black public policy demands.[26]

Walters felt that the theory needed a "more rigorous tactical formulation" given "the decline in the Black voters' recent policy influence."[27] He argued, "It is my conclusion that the 'balance-of-power' strategy, as it has been implemented thus far, possessed serious limitations in the pursuit and achievement of political objectives, due, in part, to the use of dependent-leverage politics as the major implementing tactic."[28] Hence, he put forth his own reformulation of the theory and his proposal: "It will focus here on correcting the deficiencies of dependent-leverage tactics by recourse to independent-leverage" strategy.[29]

Why did Walters advance a challenge and modification to the theory called dependent-leverage? Because while Moon saw African Americans as independent voters, Walters declared that the theory had become almost completely associated with and dependent upon the Democratic party. Here is how he summed things up: "It has now become apparent that the euphoric pronouncements of the political 'independence' of the

Black vote in the 1930s and 1940s was somewhat premature, in that it has since settled comfortably into a reverse pattern of Democratic party dependency, rather than becoming a true 'swing vote.'"[30] Herein lies the Achilles heel. Thus, for Walters, the 1972 presidential campaign of Congresswoman Shirley Chisholm, and the 1984 and 1988 presidential campaigns of Jesse Jackson were dependent-leverage strategies and could not, no matter how successful, achieve but so much.[31] Walters urged an *independent-leverage strategy,* which would involve the building of a third multi-ethnic party, an African American party, or moving in and between the two major parties. Here are shades of both Moon and Stone again.

Consistent with Walters's new theoretical reformulation, presidential candidate Bill Clinton in 1992 and throughout his first term could virtually dismiss and downgrade Jesse Jackson because African American voters were still using a *dependent-leverage strategy* within the Democratic party. And while Clinton in his 1992 campaign did make a number of pledges to deal with issues important to the black community (national health care, incentives for investments in inner-city communities, an increase in the minimum wage, full funding for Head Start, and a national public works and infrastructure program), in general the 1992 campaign involved a strategically calculated effort to distance the candidate and the Democratic party from blacks while appealing to the concerns of disaffected "Reagan Democrats" and the white middle class generally.[32] In the 1996 campaign Clinton avoided altogether discussion of issues of direct concern to blacks while signing into law a welfare reform bill opposed by virtually all black interest groups and thirty-five of the thirty-seven Democratic members of the House Black Caucus (on the welfare bill, see chapter 15).

By 1996, at the Democratic National Convention in August in Chicago, the Reverend Jackson arose and spoke on the second day, offering the president a "black" agenda. Prior to his nationally televised speech, Jackson had issued a detailed proposed agenda in a Rainbow Coalition news release entitled, "32 Years Later: We Still Have a Dream."[33] President Clinton, on the last night of the convention, when he accepted his party's nomination for a second term, made no mention at all of any program for America's urban areas, nor any specific effort for African Americans. In Walters's schema of things, the dependent-leverage strategy was simply not working and it promised to be even more ineffective in the president's second term.

AFRICAN AMERICAN VOTING BEHAVIOR: EMPIRICAL RENDERINGS

Theory and the state of that theory not withstanding, African Americans are currently registering and voting. Data from the Bureau of the Census (which collects racial voting statistics through surveys) permit us to compare voter registration to actual voting in Table 10.6. From the mid-sixties until the present, nearly two-thirds of the African American community have registered to vote. And with the exception of the 1976 presidential election, more than half of all African American registered voters voted in presidential elections. There is, however, an almost 10 percent gap between African American registered voters and those who actually vote.

Figure 10.2 permits us to further delineate the total African American voting pattern by focusing on presidential and congressional voting. Although African Americans

──────────────── **TABLE 10.6** ────────────────

Percentage of African Americans Registered and Voting, 1964–1996

YEAR	PERCENTAGE REGISTERED	PERCENTAGE VOTING
1964	60[a]	59
1966	60	42
1968	66	58
1970	61	44
1972	66	52
1974	55	34
1976	59	49
1978	57	37
1980	60	51
1982	59	43
1984	66	56
1986	64	43
1988	65	52
1990	39	39
1992	64	54
1994	59	37
1996	64	51

[a]Estimated Data

Source: For the presidential election data, see Jerry T. Jennings, *Voting and Registration in the Election of November 1992: Current Population Reports, Population Characteristics P20–422* (Washington, DC: Government Printing Office, 1993); for congressional election data, Jerry T. Jennings, *Voting and Registration in the Election of November 1990: Current Population Reports, Population Characteristics P10–453* (Washington, DC: Government Printing Office, 1991).

Figure 10.2 The Percentage of African Americans Voting Democratic and Republican in Presidential and Congressional Elections: 1950–1960

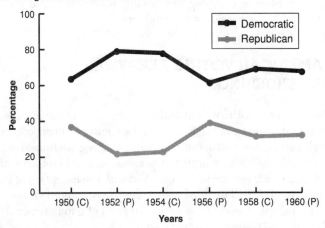

C = Congressional elections, P = Presidential elections.

Source: Adapted from Hazel Gaudet Erskine, "The Polls: Race Relations," *Public Opinion Quarterly* 26 (Spring 1962): 147.

can vote for African American candidates in the congressional elections, more African Americans, like whites, turn out in the presidential elections than in congressional ones. On average, more than 14 percent more African Americans tend to vote in presidential elections than in nonpresidential ones. Table 10.7 reveals the demographic correlates of the 1992 and 1996 black vote. African American voters tend to be female and over forty-five years of age. The majority live in the South. Three-fourths have a high school education or higher; about two-thirds are working, earning less than $25,000 per year, and the majority own their own homes.

TABLE 10.7

Demographic Correlates of African American Voters in the 1992 and 1996 Presidential Elections

DEMOGRAPHIC VARIABLES	% OF 1992 VOTERS	% OF 1996 VOTERS
Sex		
Male	42.1	40.9
Female	57.9	59.1
Age		
Under 45	41.5	63.5
Over 45	58.5	36.5
Region		
Northeast	16.8	16.6
Midwest	21.1	21.0
South	54.1	55.6
West	8.1	7.1
Education		
Grade school	23.5	19.4
High school	34.7	32.4
Some college	26.9	30.4
College	14.9	17.7
Labor		
Employed	61.6	64.4
Unemployed	6.8	4.7
Not in labor force	31.7	31.2
Family Income		
Under 25,000	63.6	40.9
25,000 to 49,999	24.8	28.3
50,000 and above	3.8	23.1
Not reported	7.9	7.7
Tenure		
Owner occupied	60.5	60.7
Renter occupied	39.5	39.3

Source: Adapted from U.S. Bureau of the Census, *Current Population Reports,* Series P20–466, "Voting and Registration in the Elections of November 1992" (Washington, DC: 1994), and Current Population Survey, "Voting and Registration in Elections of November 1996," Series P20–504 (Washington, DC: 1998). Calculations prepared by the authors.

The African American Vote in the Clinton Era

The data reported in Table 10.8 show that despite President Clinton's timid responsiveness to African American policy concerns and his strategy of moving to the right to coopt Republican issues, the African American vote in 1996 remained loyal to the president and the Democratic party. Clinton enjoyed the support of most African American leaders who, although dissatisfied with Clinton, were apparently more frightened of Newt Gingrich and the Republican revolution. Thus, they argued that a vote for Clinton was the only way to halt the Republican revolution.

Although the African American presidential vote between 1992 and 1996 remained essentially unchanged (82% and 84%), there was a fairly large (10%) increase in the African American congressional vote—from 82 percent to 92 percent. This increased congressional vote for the Democrats in all likelihood reflects the enormous fear generated in the African American community by Newt Gingrich and his "Contract with America." Although the Democrats did not regain control of the House, the Republicans did lose ten seats, reducing their margin of control.

The 1998 elections took place in the midst of the scandals involving allegations that President Clinton had lied under oath about a sexual relationship with a young White House intern. Several weeks before the election, the House of Representatives had voted to open an inquiry on whether the president should be impeached. The African American community and its leadership strongly opposed the move to impeach the president. The Congressional Black Caucus unanimously opposed the impeachment inquiry, and public opinion polls showed more than 90 percent of blacks opposed impeachment. In this context, the Democratic party engaged in a major effort to mobilize black voter turnout in the 1998 election.

Although exit polls indicated that black turnout at 10 percent of the electorate was about what it was in the 1994 midterm elections, it apparently was somewhat higher in the South, contributing to Democratic gains of five seats in the House, reducing the Re-

---
TABLE 10.8

The African American Vote in the Presidential and Congressional Elections, 1992, 1994, 1996, and 1998

	The Presidential Vote		
	1992	1996	
Clinton	82%	84%	
Bush/Dole	11	12	
Perot	7	4	
	The Congressional Vote		
	1994	1996	1998
Democrat	82%	92%	88%
Republican	18	8	11

Source: Exit poll by the Voter News Service as reported in various issues of the *New York Times.*

publican majority to a narrow 223–211 margin (one House member is an Independent who votes with the Democrats).[34] The partisan makeup of the Senate (55 Republicans, 45 Democrats) was unchanged, although the only African American in the Senate, Carol Mosley-Braun of Illinois, was defeated in her bid for a second term. Also, as a result of the Republican losses, House Speaker Newt Gingrich, leader of the conservative Republican takeover in 1994, was forced to resign by his disgruntled Republican House colleagues.

SELECTED BIBLIOGRAPHY

Guinier, Lani. *The Tyranny of the Majority*. New York: Free Press, 1994. President Clinton's failed nominee for assistant attorney general for civil rights explains the limitations of the Voting Rights Act and blacks' use of the ballot to achieve race reform.

Jarvis, Sonia. "Historical Overview: African Americans and the Evolution of Voting Rights." In R. Gomes and L. Williams, eds. *From Exclusion to Inclusion: The Long Struggle for African American Political Power*. Westport, CT: Greenwood Press, 1992. A concise overview of the long struggle of blacks to obtain the ballots.

Ladd, Everett C., and Charles Hadley. *Transformation of the American Party System: Political Coalitions from the New Deal to the Present*. New York: Norton, 1975. An excellent analysis of the decline of the New Deal coalition during the 1960s and 1970s.

Pinderhughes, Dianne. "The Role of African American Political Organizations in the Mobilization of Voters." In R. Gomes and L. Williams, eds. *From Exclusion to Inclusion: The Long Struggle for African American Political Power*. Westport, CT: Greenwood Press, 1992. A study of the role that black political organizations play in registering and turning out the black vote.

Reid, John. "The Voting Behavior of Blacks." *Intercom* 9 (1981): 8–11. A brief but very useful analysis of the factors shaping the black vote.

Tate, Katherine. *From Protest to Politics: The New Black Voter*. Cambridge, MA: Harvard University Press, 1994. A sophisticated study of the black vote intention and the vote itself, focusing on their determinants.

Walters, Ronald. *Black Presidential Politics: A Strategic Approach*. Albany: State University of New York Press, 1988. An important and influential study of the strategic uses of the black vote in presidential elections.

Walton, Hanes, Jr. "Black Voting Behavior in the Segregationist Era." In Hanes Walton, Jr. *Black Politics and Black Political Behavior: A Linkage Analysis*. Westport, CT: Praeger, 1994. An examination of how blacks registered and voted in Georgia during the era of disenfranchisement.

NOTES

1. Bernard Berelson, Paul Lazarsfeld, and William McPhee, *Voting: A Study of Opinion Formation in a Presidential Campaign* (Chicago: University of Chicago

Press, 1954); Paul Lazarsfeld, Bernard Berelson, and Hazel Gaudet, *The People's Choice: How the Voter Makes Up His Mind in a Presidential Campaign* (New York: Columbia University Press, 1994).

2. Lazarsfeld, Berelson, and Gaudet, *The People's Choice*.

3. Angus Campbell, Gerald Gurin, and Warren Miller, *The Voter Decides* (Evanston, IL: Row, Peterson, 1954); Angus Campbell, et al., *The American Voter* (New York: Wiley, 1960).

4. V. O. Key, *The Responsible Electorate: Rationality in Presidential Voting* (Cambridge, MA: Harvard University Press, 1966).

5. Ibid., pp. 7–8.

6. Anthony Downs, *An Economic Theory of Democracy* (New York: Harper & Row, 1957); William Riker, "A Theory of the Calculus Voting," *American Political Science Review* 62 (1968): 25–42.

7. Jack Dennis, "The Study of Electoral Behavior," in William Crotty, ed., *Political Science: Looking to the Future*, vol. 3 (Evanston, IL: Northwestern University Press, 1991): 62.

8. Ibid.

9. Phyllis Field, *The Politics of Race in New York: The Struggle for Black Suffrage in the Civil War Era* (Ithaca, NY: Cornell University Press, 1982): 59, 124–126, 198.

10. Ibid., p. 52.

11. Ibid.

12. Ibid. See the following work for documents of the various Black State Constitution Conventions, Philip Foner and George Walker, eds., *Proceedings of the Black State Conventions, 1840–1865* (Philadelphia: Temple University Press, 1979), vols. I & II.

13. William Gillette, *The Right to Vote: Politics and the Passage of the Fifteenth Amendment* (Baltimore: Johns Hopkins University Press, 1969): 25.

14. Ibid.

15. Hanes Walton, Jr., *Black Politics: A Theoretical and Structural Analysis* (Philadelphia: J. B. Lippincott, 1972): 35.

16. On these various schemes used in the South to deprive blacks of the vote, see Walton, *Black Politics*.

17. For citations to and discussions of these cases, see Walton, *Black Politics*, pp. 33–40.

18. Henry Lee Moon, *Balance of Power: The Negro Vote* (New York: Doubleday, 1948): 7.

19. Hanes Walton, Jr., Leslie Burl McLemore, and C. Vernon Gray, "The Pioneering Books on Black Politics and the Political Science Community, 1903–1965," *National Political Science Review* 1 (1990): 196.

20. William Nowlin, *Negro in American National Politics* (Boston: Stratford, 1931).

21. Edgar Lee Tatum, *The Changed Political Thought of the Negro: 1915–1948* (New York: Exposition Press, 1951).

22. Moon, *Balance of Power*, p. 10.

23. Ibid., p. 11.

24. See Chuck Stone, *Black Political Power in America* (New York: Bobbs-Merrill, 1968).
25. Chuck Stone, "Black Politics: Third Force, Third Party or Third Class Influence?" *The Black Scholar,* 1 (December, 1969).
26. Ronald Walters, *Black Presidential Politics in America: A Strategic Approach* (Albany: State University of New York Press, 1988): 185.
27. Ibid., p. 185.
28. Ibid., p. 110.
29. Ibid.
30. Ibid.
31. Ibid., p. 27. Walters was a major strategy adviser to Jesse Jackson in his two presidental campaigns.
32. On Clinton's 1992 strategy of symbolic distance from blacks and embrace of the white middle class, see Kenneth O'Reilly's *Nixon's Piano: Presidents and Racial Politics from Washington to Clinton* (New York: Free Press, 1995): chap. 9, and Robert C. Smith, *We Have No Leaders: African Americans in the Post–Civil Rights Era* (Albany: State University of New York Press, 1996): chap. 10, especially pages 263–74.
33. Jackson News Release.
34. Kevin Sack, "Democrats in Political Debt for Black Turnout in South," *New York Times,* November 6, 1998. The relatively high black turnout in the South is credited with the election of Democratic governors in South Carolina and Alabama, the defeat of Senator Lauch Faircloth in North Carolina, and the reelection of Senator Ernest Hollings in South Carolina. Blacks were also elected to several statewide offices including attorney general of Georgia, lieutenant governor of Colorado, and secretary of state in Ohio and Illinois. See "How Blacks Fared in Recent Elections," *Jet,* November 23, 1998, pp. 4–13.

PART IV

Institutions

CHAPTER 11

The Congress and the African American Quest for Universal Freedom

The framers of the Constitution intended for Congress to be the dominant branch of the government. Of the legislative power, John Locke had written, it "is not only the supreme power of the commonwealth, but sacred and unalterable in the hands where the community have once placed it."[1] Following Locke's logic the framers made the Congress the first branch of government (Article I), preceding the presidency (Article II) and the judiciary (Article III). Article I is also by far the longest of the three articles, specifying in detail the broad powers of the United States government.

Legislation is understood as a general rule of broad application *enacted by a broadly representative body*.[2] We emphasize the words to make the point that in democratic societies, legislation and representation are closely connected, such that a defining property of a legislative institution is the extent to which it fairly represents the people. The English philosopher John Stuart Mill stated the case for the necessary relationship between legislation, representation, and democracy in his 1869 book *Considerations on Representative Government:*

> In a really equal democracy, every or any section would be represented, not disproportionately, but proportionately. A majority of electors would always have a majority of the representatives but a minority of electors would always have a minority of representatives, man for man, they would be as fully represented as the majority; unless they are, there is not equal government, but government of inequality and privilege: one part of the people rule over the rest: There is a part whose fair and equal share and influence in representation is withheld from them contrary to the principle of democracy, which professes equality as its very root and foundation.[3]

177

THE REPRESENTATION OF
AFRICAN AMERICANS IN CONGRESS

Given that in a democracy the legislature should represent the people equally, a first question becomes, How representative of African Americans is the Congress? Political scientists usually measure the representativeness of a legislative institution on the basis of three criteria: descriptive, symbolic, and substantive.[4] *Descriptive representation* is the extent to which the legislature looks like the people in a demographic sense. *Symbolic representation* concerns the extent to which people have confidence or trust in the legislature, and *substantive representation* asks whether the laws passed by the legislature correspond to the policy interests or preferences of the people. We discuss the extent to which Congress represents the substantive interests of African Americans later in this chapter. With respect to symbolic representation, African Americans, like white Americans, have relatively low levels of confidence or trust in Congress.[5]

Historically, the Congress has not been descriptively representative of African Americans. Of more than 11,000 persons who have served in the Congress, only 102 have been black (98 in the House, 4 in the Senate).[6] From 1787, the year of the first Congress, until 1870, no African American served in Congress. In 1870–71 six blacks were seated in the House of Representatives. From the 1870s to 1891, blacks averaged two representatives in the House, and in the next decade there was only one black congressman to represent the nation's population of more than eight million blacks. In 1901 George White of South Carolina became the last Reconstruction era African American to serve in Congress. In his farewell speech, White told his white colleagues, "This, Mr. Chairman, is perhaps the Negroes' temporary farewell to the American Congress; but let me say like the Phoenix he will rise again. These parting words are in behalf of an outraged, heart broken, bruised and bleeding but God fearing people, faithful, industrious loyal, rising people—full of potential force."[7]

From 1901 to 1931 no blacks served in the Congress. In 1928 Oscar DePriest was elected from Chicago, and in 1944 Adam Clayton Powell was elected from Harlem. Until the post–civil rights era, only five blacks served in the House. Then in 1969 and again in 1992 there was a fairly rapid rise in black representation in the House, reaching an all-time high of thirty-nine in 1993. The growth in black representation is a function of several factors; the concentration of blacks in highly segregated urban neighborhoods, the Supreme Court's "one person, one vote" decisions in *Baker v. Carr* and *Wesberry v. Sanders,* and the implementation of the 1965 Voting Rights Act.[8] These gains in black representation are jeopardized, however, by a series of Supreme Court decisions beginning with *Shaw v. Reno* in 1993 suggesting that many of the districts represented by blacks may be unconstitutional (these cases are discussed in chapter 13).

In the Senate's more than two hundred years, only four blacks have served in it: Hiram Revels and Blanche K. Bruce from Mississippi during Reconstruction; Edward Brooke from Massachusetts, who served from 1966 to 1978; and Carol Mosley Braun, elected in 1992 from Illinois but defeated for reelection in 1998. Senators are elected on a statewide basis, and since no state has a black majority, it has been very difficult for blacks to win Senate seats. Because of racist and white supremacist thinking, whites have been reluctant to vote for black candidates (of the thirty-eight blacks in the House, four are elected from majority white districts: Democrats Julia Carson of Indiana, Cynthia McKinney and Sanford Bishop from Georgia, and Republican J. C. Watts from Oklahoma).

Although blacks have made substantial progress in achieving fair and equitable representation in the House, the Congress, as Table 11.1 shows, is still best described as a body of middle-age, middle-class, white men. In the House and Senate, Asian Americans are reasonably represented, in part because they are a voting plurality in Hawaii. However, blacks and Latinos are not equitably represented; African Americans, for example, are 12 percent of the population but 0 percent of the Senate and 9 percent of the House. Women, who constitute more than half the population, are only 10 percent of the House and 9 percent of the Senate. These numbers for women are small, but they are much better than the numbers of a decade ago when there were only one or two female senators and women constituted only 5 percent of the House. The nation's major religious groups—Protestants, Catholics, and Jews—are equitably represented in both the House and the Senate. (Jews to some extent are "overrepresented," constituting less than 3 percent of the population but about 6 percent of the House and 9 percent of the Senate.) In sum, the Congress is not a representative body insofar as its African American, Latino, and female citizens are concerned.

TABLE 11.1

Selected Demographic Characteristics of Members of the 105th Congress, 1997–1999

% POPULATION	DEMOGRAPHIC CHARACTERISTICS	HOUSE	SENATE
	Race		
75.2	White	86%	96%
12.1	Black	9	1
9.0	Latino	4	0
2.9	Asian American	0.9	2
0.8	Native American	0	1
	Religion[a]		
62	Protestant	55	64
27	Catholic	33	22
2.5	Jewish	6	9
	Education		
23	College	96	91
77	Noncollege	4	3
	Average Age		
32.8		52	58

[a]6% of House members and 5% of the senators are members of other religious faiths, mainly Mormon and Greek Orthodox.

Source: Calculations by authors from Michael Barone and Grant Ujifusa, *The Almanac of American Politics, 1996* (Washington, DC: National Journal, 1997).

CONGRESSIONAL ELECTIONS
AND AFRICAN AMERICANS

Reapportionment and Redistricting

The Constitution requires that every ten years the government conduct a census, an "enumeration" of the population. The primary constitutional purpose of the census is to provide a basis for reapportioning seats in the House. The size of the House is fixed by law at 435. *Reapportionment* involves the allocation of these 435 seats among the fifty states on the basis of changes in population—for example, the movement of the population in the last four decades from the "snowbelt" states of the Midwest and Northeast to the "sunbelt" states of the South and West. After reapportionment, the states then engage in the process of *redistricting*, the allocation of seats within a state on the basis of populations within each congressional district, with each district containing roughly 600,000 persons. The census is therefore important as a basis of allocating political power among and within the states. This has particular implications for America's racial minorities since it is well known that the census regularly undercounts blacks and Latinos, thereby depriving them of a fair share of political power as well as other social and economic benefits that are allocated on the basis of population. In the 1990 census, an estimated 4.8 percent of the black population and 5.2 percent of the Latino population were not counted.[9] Although it is possible for the Census Bureau to "statistically adjust" the census count to include those left out, the Supreme Court has held that such an adjustment is not required by the Constitution.[10] However, for the 2000 census, the Census Bureau agreed to employ statistical sampling as a means to count those persons most often missed by traditional methods of counting. The Republican leadership in the House pledged to block this change, saying the plan violated the Constitution's requirement that there be an actual "enumeration" of the population; also, it would likely help Democrats by increasing the number of minority and urban dwellers.

However, in January 1999 the Supreme Court ruled that federal law bars the use of statistical sampling for apportioning seats in the House. Instead, the Court, in a 5–4 decision upholding the ruling of a special three-judge federal district court in Richmond, Virginia, said that while sampling could be used for other purposes (such as redistricting state legislatures and allocating federal money to the states), Congress had mandated that an actual enumeration or "head count" be used in congressional reapportionment. The decision split the Court on ideological lines with the four more liberal justices dissenting, holding that while sampling could not be a substitute for an enumeration it was a permissible "supplement" to "achieve the very accuracy that the census seeks and the Census Act itself demands."[11]

Black Congressional Districts, Campaigns, and Elections

Of the thirty-eight congressional districts represented by blacks in the House, four are majority white and the rest are either majority black or majority minority (blacks and Latinos).[12] Except for one, each of these districts is represented by Democrats. Until 1992, virtually all the black majority districts were urban, northern, and disproportion-

Members of the Congressional Black Caucus meeting at the White House with President Clinton.

ately poor.[13] As a result of the 1992 redistricting, the large southern (52% of the total) and rural (25%) black population is now represented in the House (all the southern states except Arkansas send at least one black to the House).[14]

The black districts are overwhelmingly Democratic in party registration and invariably elect Democrats. Like most members of the House, blacks once elected are routinely reelected. The *advantages of incumbency*—name recognition, congressional staff, free mailing privileges, and campaign finance contributions—make it virtually impossible to defeat an incumbent congressman; more than 90 percent who seek reelection are reelected. A major advantage of incumbency is PAC campaign contributions, and black congresspersons even more than whites rely heavily on PAC contributions, mostly from labor unions but also from corporate and trade groups.[15] Of the thirty-nine blacks seeking reelection in 1998, all won; more than half ran without opposition in the primaries (primaries are the potentially competitive elections in the one-party dominant black congressional districts) and those who had an opponent won by an average of 75% of the vote.

Finally, except for their race and the greater representation of women, blacks in Congress are quite similar to whites: well-educated, middle-class men. Women, however, are better represented, constituting 20 percent of the black congressional delegation compared to about 10 percent among white women.[16]

AFRICAN AMERICAN POWER IN THE HOUSE

Power or influence in the House of Representatives is best gauged by committee and subcommittee assignments, seniority, and party leadership positions.[17] In addition, in the last two decades House members have increasingly attempted to exercise power outside the formal committee and party leadership positions by forming caucuses of like-minded members.

The Congressional Black Caucus

There are now more than one hundred legislative caucuses in the House. These groups are organized by members with a common interest or policy agenda so that they can exchange research and information, develop legislative strategies, and act as a unified voting bloc to bargain in support of or against particular bills and amendments.[18]

The Congressional Black Caucus (CBC) is one of the oldest House caucuses, formed in 1969 as an outgrowth of the black power movement's call for racial solidarity and independent black organization. In addition to its role as an internal House legislative caucus, the CBC also plays an external role by forming coalitions with interest groups outside the Congress and operating as one of the two or three major African American interest organizations in Washington.[19] The work of the caucus includes such activities as lobbying the president, presenting various black legislative agendas and alternative budgets in floor debates, and holding its annual legislative weekends. The legislative weekends, held in the fall of each year, usually bring several thousand African American scholars, elected officials, and civil rights leaders to Washington to participate in panels and workshops on issues affecting African Americans.

Until the election of the Republican congressional majority in 1994, the Caucus was supported by contributions of $4,000 from each of its members' official office accounts. In addition to all the black members except one,[20] the Caucus has an "associate member" category for whites who wish to join. As associates, whites may not attend or vote at closed meetings and dues are $1,000 rather than $4,000. (As of 1990, forty whites had become associate members.) These member contributions allowed the Caucus to maintain a small staff and research operation. However, in 1995 the Republican congressional majority led by Speaker Newt Gingrich adopted rules prohibiting House caucuses from receiving dues from members or from using House office space, staff, or equipment. As a result, the CBC as an official House caucus no longer exists. The Congressional Black Caucus Foundation (a separate tax-exempt organization formed in 1982) continues to operate, funded by tax-deductible contributions and the Caucus's annual fund-raising dinner, held during its legislative weekends. Nevertheless, the action of the Republican majority in cutting off funds to the caucuses (which may be reversed if the Democrats again become the majority) undermines the capacity of the group to do its work in the House.

More important than the loss of financial support is the loss of Democratic majority control in the House. Since power in the House is based primarily on party, blacks in Congress, who are almost all Democrats, lost considerable influence and power when Republicans became the majority. First, as a result of their seniority, blacks in the Democratic Congress had chaired three committees and seventeen subcommittees. When the Republicans took the majority, these leadership positions went to white conservative Republicans. Equally important, when the Democrats lost their majority, the Caucus lost its principal source of influence in congressional decision making—its capacity as a *unified minority within the majority to develop legislative packages that balance liberal and conservative elements in a coalition that could get the support of the Democratic majority*. That is, as a unified liberal bloc within the Democratic party, the Caucus, by threatening to withhold its vote in the House, was able throughout the 1980s to get the House majority to adopt more liberal positions on issues like welfare, crime, and the budget (the welfare reform bill signed by President Clinton in 1996, for example, would not have passed if the House had been controlled by the Democrats). With a Republican majority, the Black Caucus becomes a *minority within a minority with little bargaining power, since the conservative Republican majority will ignore the liberal minority just as the Democratic majority ignored the Republican minority when it controlled the House*. Thus, as long as Republicans have a majority in the House, the Congressional Black Caucus will have much less power and influence.

AFRICAN AMERICANS IN THE CONGRESSIONAL POWER STRUCTURE

Party Leadership

The principal members of the Democratic party power structure in the House are the Minority Leader, the Minority Whip, the deputy whips, the members of the Steering and Policy Committee (which makes committee assignments and establishes broad party policy), and the officers of the Democratic Caucus. From 1989 to 1991 when he resigned to become president of the United Negro College Fund, Pennsylvania congressman Bill Gray served as Majority Whip, the number three leadership position behind the Speaker and the Majority Leader. In the 104th Congress (1995–1996), John Lewis of Georgia served as one of the four deputy whips, and four blacks served on the twenty-four-member Steering and Policy committee.

In 1999, third-term congressman J. C. Watts of Oklahoma was elected chairman of the Republican Party Conference, the fourth-ranking position in the Republican leadership structure in the House. This was widely interpreted as a move by the party to reach out to black and other minority voters. Watts's selection marked the first time an African American had held a leadership position in the House Republican party.

Committees and Committee Leadership

In the 104th Congress, blacks served on every standing committee of the House except one (Natural Resources). In Table 11.2, data are displayed on black membership and seniority on the major or "power" committees of Congress and on those committees that are especially important to black interests. The major or power committees are the ones dealing with money: the Budget Committee, the Committees on Ways and Means (taxes) and Appropriations (spending); the Rules Committee; the Commerce Committee (because of its broad jurisdiction under the commerce clause); and the National

Security Committee (because of the importance of military policy and the size of the military budget). The Judiciary Committee is important to black interests because of its jurisdiction over civil rights legislation; the Financial Services Committee because of its jurisdiction over urban and housing policy; and the Economic and Educational Opportunities Committee because of its jurisdiction over education, labor, and parts of welfare policy.[21]

Table 11.2 shows that African Americans are represented on each of the major or power committees except Rules, and they are heavily represented on those committees of special relevance to black interests—Judiciary, Financial Services, and Economic and

―――――――――――――――――― **TABLE II.2** ――――――――――――――――――

African American Members of the House, Assignments on Major/Power Committees and Committees of Special Interest to Blacks, 105th Congress

MAJOR/POWER COMMITTEES	DEMOCRATIC MEMBERS	BLACK MEMBERS AND RANK
Appropriations	24	
		Dixon (8)[c]
Budget[a]	18	Meek (16)
Commerce	21	Towns (9)
		Rush (17)
National Security	25	McKinney (25)
Rules	4	NONE
Ways and Means[b]	15	Rangel (1)
		Lewis (13)
Committees of Special Interest to Blacks		
Banking and Financial Services	22	Waters (8)
		Wynn (16)
		Watt (17)
Economic and Educational Opportunities	19	Clay (1)
		Owens (5)
		Payne (7)
		Scott (14)
Judiciary	15	Conyers (1)
		Watt (10)
		Jackson Lee (14)
		Waters (15)

[a]The Budget Committee prepares the annual congressional budget, setting targets for taxation, spending, and borrowing.

[b]In addition to its power to impose taxes on personal, corporate, and other income, the Ways and Means Committee also has responsibility for Social Security, Medicare, Medicaid, welfare, and international trade.

[c]The number in parentheses represents the member's rank or seniority among Democratic members of the Committee.

Educational Opportunities. Blacks are also the senior Democrats or *ranking members* on one of the power committees, Ways and Means (arguably the most powerful committee in the Congress), and two of the interest committees, Judiciary and Economic and Educational Opportunities. As the ranking members, these persons are in line to become chairmen of these committees when Democrats again become the majority party in the House. The ranking member of a committee or subcommittee sets the agenda for the minority party, hires and directs the staff for the party, and plays a role in shaping committee hearings and floor debate. In addition to serving as ranking members on these three full committees, African Americans are the ranking members on fourteen subcommittees, including two on the powerful Appropriations Committee.

Because of the operation of the seniority system and the ability of African Americans to be routinely reelected to the Congress, these members have gained considerable power in the House—power that will be increased if and when the Democrats regain a majority (see Box 11.1).

CONGRESSIONAL RESPONSIVENESS TO THE AFRICAN AMERICAN QUEST FOR UNIVERSAL RIGHTS AND FREEDOM

Rights-Based Issues: From Arguing about Slavery to the Civil Rights Act of 1991

Like each of the major institutions of the American government, the Congress's response to the black demand for universal freedom and equality has been hesitant, tentative, and unstable. Interestingly, the first congressional response to the African American demand for universal freedom was a debate over whether the Congress should listen—simply hear—let alone respond to the demand for African freedom. From 1835 to 1844, Congress debated whether it should even receive African American petitions for freedom. Until 1835, black petitions to end slavery were received, printed in the record, and referred to committee. But in 1835 Congressman James Hammond of South Carolina demanded that these petitions not even be received by Congress because to do so was an unconstitutional infringement on slavery. For nine years the House debated this "gag rule," with the opponents (led by former president John Quincy Adams, by then a House member) arguing that to ban slave petitions was a violation of the First Amendment right of petition, which, they claimed, should be accorded even to slaves. In 1844, the House finally defeated the gag rule on slave petitions.[22]

Before Congress enacted the first wave of civil rights legislation during Reconstruction, it took three other actions dealing with the issue of slavery. First, in 1787 in the Northwest Ordinance Act, Congress banned slavery in the new territories of the upper Midwest, which prevented the spread of slavery into places like Illinois and Indiana.[23] Second, in 1808 Congress abolished the slave trade. Although this was an important law, the illegal importation of an estimated additional thousand slaves actually continued until the Civil War.[24] But this was much less than the scores of thousands imported prior to the law. Finally, in 1862 in the middle of the Civil War, Congress abolished slavery in the District of Columbia.

BOX 11.1

Term Limits, Seniority, and African American Power in the House

For decades, more than 90 percent of the members of the House who have sought reelection have won. The advantages of incumbency—name recognition, access to the media, staff support, and campaign contributions—make it virtually impossible to defeat an incumbent congressperson. Even with the massive turnover in Congress after the Republican victory in 1994, 93 percent of the incumbents running for reelection won. As a result, in recent years a movement has developed that would limit the terms of members of Congress by law (usually the proposal is that members of the House be limited to six 2-year terms and members of the Senate to two 6-year terms). The Supreme Court, in the 1995 case *U.S. Term Limits, Inc. vs. Thornton,* held that the terms of members of Congress could be limited only by an amendment to the Constitution, not by actions of the states or the Congress. In 1995 the House voted on a term-limits amendment to the Constitution, but it failed to get the necessary two-thirds majority (227–204).

Proponents of term limits argue that members who serve long periods of time lose touch with their constituents back home, becoming "professional" rather than "citizen" legislators and eventually becoming the captives of the Washington interest group establishment. Opponents of term limits argue that it would result in an inexperienced Congress that could easily be dominated by special interest groups, the media, and the bureaucracy. Often overlooked in the debate on term limits is the effect on African American political power in the House. Black members of the House are more likely to be reelected than whites, as a result, they have greater seniority (in the 104th Congress, seven of the fourteen most senior House Democrats were African American), and seniority translates into power in terms of committee leadership. Thus, blacks in the House hold major leadership positions on some of that body's most important committees and are the most senior Democrats on more than fifteen House subcommittees. Not everyone in Washington is pleased with this development. After the Republican victory in 1994, two prominent Washington columnists, Cokie and Steven Roberts, wrote that blacks have too much power in the House and "accordingly, the Democratic leadership in the House will become increasingly weighted toward minorities and thus toward liberal ideas and principles. And to party moderates, this is exactly the wrong direction."[a]

It is the wrong direction, the Robertses argue, because the presence of so many blacks in powerful positions sends the wrong signal to suburban white voters. All African American Democratic members of the House voted against the term limit amendment in 1995, perhaps because they saw it as a means to deprive them of power. The political scientist Bruce Oppenheimer wrote, "Although I would be among the first to resist conspiratorial explanations for the recent popularity of congressional term limits, it is ironic that one clear effect of its adoption would be to deprive nonwhites of the only power base advantage they currently have in American government."[b]

[a]Cokie and Steven Roberts, "Democrats Must Face Race Issue," *West County Times*, December 16, 1994, p. A11.

[b]Bruce Oppenheimer, "House Term Limits: A Distorted Picture," *Social Science Quarterly* 76 (December 1995): 728.

Congressional responsiveness to the African American agenda of universal rights and freedom occurred in two periods: the 1860s during Reconstruction and the 1960s during the civil rights movement. (See Box 11.2.) As Table 11.3 shows, from 1866 to 1875 Congress passed six civil rights bills including three civil rights enforcement acts. Between 1957 and 1968 the Congress passed seven civil rights bills, including the crucially important Civil Rights Act of 1964, the Voting Rights Act of 1965, and the Fair Housing Act of 1968.

In many ways the civil rights laws of the 1960s simply duplicate those passed in the 1860s. The Supreme Court invalidated the 1860s laws as unconstitutional or declined to require their enforcement; thus, the Congress in the 1960s had to repass them, which again shows the tenuousness and instability of rights-based coalitions. Similarly, the Civil Rights Restoration Act of 1985 and the Civil Rights Act of 1991 were passed to overturn Supreme Court decisions that made parts of the 1964 Act difficult to enforce (see chapter 13). In addition to these major civil rights laws, Congress in the 1970s passed a series of amendments to the 1964 act allowing the government to engage in affirmative action to achieve equality in employment for African Americans, other minorities, and women.[25] (See Box 12.3.)

Civil Rights in the Republican Congress

When the Republicans took control of the Congress in 1995, black leaders expressed alarm that they might roll back civil rights gains, especially affirmative action. However, in 1998 both the House and Senate rejected amendments to the transportation bill that would have prohibited the use of a 10 percent "goal" in the allocation of contracts to

──────────────**TABLE 11.3**──────────────

List of Civil Rights Laws Enacted by Congress: Reconstruction Era, Civil Rights Era, and Post–Civil Rights Era

Reconstruction Era

Civil Rights Act, 1866
Civil Rights Act, 1870
Civil Rights Act, 1875
Enforcement Act, 1870
Enforcement Act, 1871
Enforcement Act, 1875

Civil Rights Era

Civil Rights Act, 1957
Civil Rights Act, 1960
Civil Rights Act, 1964
Voting Rights Act, 1965
Fair Housing Act, 1968

Post–Civil Rights Era

Equal Employment Opportunity Act of 1972
Civil Rights Restoration Act, 1988
Civil Rights Act of 1991

━━━━━━━━━━━━━━━━ **BOX II.2** ━━━━━━━━━━━━━━━━

Two Massachusetts Senators[a] and the
African American Quest for Universal Freedom

Massachusetts is often referred to as "freedom's birthplace" and as the "citadel of American liberalism." Whether this reputation is deserved or not, in Senator Charles Sumner and in Senator Edward "Ted" Kennedy,[a] Massachusetts has sent to the Senate two men who have distinguished themselves in the African American quest for universal freedom.

Frederick Douglass described Senator Sumner as the greatest friend the Negro people ever had in public life. Born in 1811, Sumner served in the Senate from 1852 until his death in 1874. During his career in the Senate he was that body's most outspoken champion of the freedom of the enslaved African. In an 1856 Senate speech he bitterly attacked two of his colleagues for their support of slavery. Two days later Congressman Preston Brooks entered the Senate chamber and nearly beat Sumner to death, arguing that his remarks were a libel on the South. After a three-year recovery period, Sumner returned to the Senate to continue his struggle for black freedom, both rights and material based.

Sumner made his greatest contribution to the African American freedom struggle after the Civil War. With Congressman Thaddeus Stevens, he led the fight in Congress for civil rights legislation and passage of the Fourteenth and Fifteenth amendments. Stevens and Sumner were also responsible for the idea of "forty acres and a mule," introducing legislation to confiscate the slaveholders' plantations, divide them up, and give them to the slaves as compensation or reparation and as a means to punish the slaveholders for treason.

At the time of his death, Sumner was fighting for a civil rights bill that would have banned discrimination and segregation in every public place in the United States—from schools to churches, from cemeteries to hospitals. On his deathbed, surrounded by Frederick Douglass and other African American leaders, Sumner's last words were said to have been, "Take care of my civil rights bill—take care of it—you must do it."

One hundred years later another Senator from Massachusetts took up Sumner's cause. Senator Edward Kennedy, elected to the Senate in 1962 to take the seat vacated by his brother when he became president, is the second most senior Democrat in the Senate. Throughout his more than three decades in the Senate, Kennedy has been a leader in the passage of every civil rights bill, from the Civil Rights Act of 1964 to the Civil Rights Act of 1991. Especially after the murder of his brother Robert in 1968, Kennedy made the cause of the poor and racially oppressed his cause. As the senior Democrat on both the Labor and Public Welfare Committee and the Judiciary Committee, he has led the fight for minimum wage legislation, national health insurance, immigration reform, and education and employment legislation. In 1993, his Labor and Public Welfare Committee was the only committee to report and send to the floor national health insurance legislation, largely due to his leadership as chair. In 1996 he was the floor leader of the fight to increase the minimum wage, to provide health coverage for laid-off workers, and to ban discrimination in employment against homosexuals.

Perhaps the Senate's most famous member, Kennedy is regarded as one of the body's most passionate and skilled legislators on issues of civil rights and social justice. In 1980 he challenged President Jimmy Carter for renomination, charging that the president had abandoned the liberal cause. After his loss to Carter, Kennedy returned to the Senate where he became a leading opponent of the Reagan administration's civil rights and social welfare policies. Although his goal of succeeding his brother as president was not to be, he has left his mark, as there is no major piece of civil rights or liberal reform legislation of the last three decades that was not influenced by the Senator from Massachusetts.

^aOn Sumner, see Frederick Blue, *Charles Sumner and the Conscience of the North* (New York: Norton, 1976), and on Kennedy, see James MacGregor Burns, *Edward Kennedy and the Legacy of Camelot* (New York: Norton, 1976).

---

minority- and female-owned businesses. The amendment was rejected in the Senate by a vote of 58 to 37, with all Democratic senators voting no except one (Senator Ernest Hollings of South Carolina) and with fifteen of the fifty-five Republican Senators also opposing the amendment. In the House, the amendment was defeated by a vote of 225 to 194. All except three House Democrats opposed the amendment and it was also opposed by twenty-nine Republicans. Note that this amendment was supported by Republican congressional leaders, including House Speaker Gingrich, who made a passionate floor speech calling on his colleagues to end this form of affirmative action.

Several weeks later the House also defeated by an even larger margin an amendment prohibiting colleges and universities from using affirmative action in their admission policies if they receive federal funds. The vote was 249 to 171. Although Republican leaders supported the amendment, fifty-five Republicans joined with 193 Democrats to defeat the legislation.[26]

MATERIAL-BASED RIGHTS: FROM FORTY ACRES AND A MULE TO THE HUMPHREY-HAWKINS FULL EMPLOYMENT ACT

If Congress has been reluctant and tentative in terms of responsiveness to the rights-based black agenda, it has been even less responsive to the material-based agenda. The Constitution, after adoption of the Fourteenth Amendment, may be interpreted to guarantee universal civil and political freedoms; however, many, perhaps most, Americans tend to think that access to material benefits (land, health care, jobs) should not be universal but rather individual. That is, in a free enterprise, capitalist system, it is up to each individual to get his own land, health care, and employment. This view was expressed very clearly by President Andrew Johnson when he vetoed the Freedmen's Bureau Act, which, in addition to granting blacks land, also provided other welfare and educational benefits to the former slaves. In his veto message the President wrote, "The idea on which the slaves were assisted to freedom was that on becoming free they would be a self-sustaining population. Any legislation that shall imply they are not expected to attain a self-sustaining condition must have a tendency injurious alike to their character and their prospects."[27] The ideas of President Andrew Johnson are echoed today by Newt Gingrich and Bill Clinton, who argue that welfare is injurious to the character, individual responsibility, and sense of self-reliance of the African American community.

The Humphrey-Hawkins Act

The 1963 March on Washington during which Dr. King gave his famous "I Have a Dream" speech was a march for "Jobs and Freedom." However, as we pointed out in chapter 7, rights-based demands usually take precedence over material-based ones. Thus, the demand for jobs had to await the gaining of freedom in the form of the 1960s civil rights laws. But the problem of joblessness was clearly a major problem in the African American community, especially in the cities of the North where blacks already had basic civil and political rights. Since the end of the Depression, African Americans have never experienced full employment (see chapter 15). In general, in the post–World War II era, black unemployment has been twice that of whites, generally at about 10 percent of the adult labor force.[28] Thus, at the end of the civil rights era, the material-based demand for jobs—full employment guaranteed by the federal government—became the principal African American demand, the priority item on the black agenda.

At the time of his death in 1968, Dr. King was planning to lead a multiracial coalition of poor people to march on Washington, the principal demand of which was a guaranteed job or income. After Dr. King's death this demand for jobs became the principal priority of African American interest groups.[29] In the late 1960s the Congressional Black Caucus, under the leadership of California congressman Augustus Hawkins, developed a broad coalition of blacks, liberal, labor, and religious groups to try to persuade Congress to pass legislation "guaranteeing a job to all willing and able to work." Once before, in 1946, a broad liberal-labor coalition had sought similar legislation. By the time the bill was passed as the Employment Act of 1946, however, the job guarantee provision had been deleted and the act was little more than a policy planning mechanism, creating the President's Council of Economic Advisors and a Joint Economic Committee in the Congress.[30]

Critics of the Employment Act of 1946 including business leaders, academic economists, and the mainstream media and conservative politicians argued that the idea of full employment guaranteed by the federal government was "socialistic," "anti–free enterprise," "utopian," "un-American," and would result in "runaway inflation." Similar criticisms were made of the 1978 legislation introduced by Congressman Hawkins and Senator and former vice president Hubert Humphrey. The bill, "The Full Employment and Balanced Growth Act," as originally introduced provided each American citizen with a legal right or entitlement to a job and required the Congress, if necessary, to create public sector jobs if an individual could not find a job in the private economy. By the time the bill was passed and signed by President Carter, these provisions, as was the case in 1946, had been deleted, making the bill little more than a symbolic statement of principles.[31]

In the Clinton administration, the black unemployment rate fell below 10 percent for the first time since the Vietnam War (the comparable white unemployment rate was 4%). Generally, economists have considered 5 percent to 5.5 percent unemployment to be "full employment"—the rate reached during the Clinton administration. But this leaves large numbers of adult blacks unemployed. Thus, even in relatively good economic times the African American community remains in a recession. And the fate of the Humphrey-Hawkins Act suggests that there is little that can be done about it. We discuss this problem in chapter 15 dealing with domestic public policy.

SELECTED BIBLIOGRAPHY

Baker, Ross. *House and Senate,* 2nd ed. New York: Norton, 1995. A comparative analysis of the two houses focusing on how the differences in their sizes affect their operations.

Barone, Michael, and Grant Ujifusa. *The Almanac of American Politics 1996.* Washington: National Journal, 1995. The biannual compilation of data on the districts and members of the House and Senate.

Berg, John. *Unequal Struggle: Class, Gender and Race in the U.S. Congress.* Boulder, CO: Westview Press, 1994. A perceptive analysis of how the structure of the capitalist economy constrains progressive action that would benefit minorities, workers, and women.

Champagne, Richard, and Leroy Rieselbach. "The Evolving Congressional Black Caucus: The Reagan-Bush Years." In Huey Perry and Wayne Parant, eds. *Blacks and the American Political System.* Gainesville: University Press of Florida, 1995. A historical survey of the Caucus from its founding in 1969 to the last years of the Bush administration.

Congressional Quarterly. *Origins and Development of Congress.* Washington: Congressional Quarterly, 1976. A concise account of the historical development of Congress.

Congressional Quarterly. *Powers of Congress.* Washington: Congressional Quarterly, 1976. A concise account of the historical development of Congress.

Graham, Hugh Davis. *The Civil Rights Era: Origins and Development of National Policy.* New York: Oxford University Press, 1990. A comprehensive study of the passage and implementation of the 1960s civil rights laws.

Jones, Charles E. "An Overview of the Congressional Black Caucus, 1970–85." In F. Jones et al., eds. *Readings in American Political Issues.* Dubuque, IA: Kendall/Hunt, 1987. An overview of the caucus's operations from its founding through the middle Reagan years.

Loevy, Robert, ed. *The Civil Rights Act of 1964: The Passage of the Law That Ended Racial Segregation.* New York: State University of New York Press, 1996. Firsthand, behind-the-scenes accounts of how the Civil Rights Act was passed.

Singh, Robert. *The Congressional Black Caucus: Racial Politics in the U.S. Congress.* Thousand Oaks, CA: Sage, 1998. An analysis of the limited effectiveness of the caucus as a lobby for black interests in Congress.

Swain, Carol. *Black Faces, Black Interests: The Representation of African American Interests in Congress.* Cambridge, MA: Harvard University Press, 1993. A controversial analysis suggesting that whites in Congress represent the interests of blacks as well as do blacks.

Wilson, Woodrow. *Congressional Government: A Study in American Politics.* Gloucester, MA: Peter Smith, 1956. The 28th president's still-insightful study of how the organization and procedures of Congress make it an inefficient, irresponsible, and ineffective legislative institution.

NOTES

1. John Locke, *The Second Treatise of Government,* edited by Thomas Peardon (Indianapolis: Bobbs-Merrill, 1952): 75.

2. Benjamin Akzin, "Legislation: Nature and Function," *International Encyclopedia of the Social Sciences* (New York: Free Press, 1972): 223.

3. John Stuart Mill, *Considerations on Representative Government* (Indianapolis: Bobbs-Merrill, 1869, 1952): 146.

4. Hanna Pitkin, *The Concept of Representation* (Berkeley: University of California Press, 1972): 5.

5. In the most recent survey, only 14 percent of Americans said they have a "great deal" or "quite a lot" of confidence in Congress. See *Why Don't Americans Trust the Government* (Cambridge, MA: *The Washington Post*/Kaiser Family Foundation/Harvard University Survey Project, 1996): 3. For detailed data on African American attitudes toward Congress, refer to chapter 3, Table 3.3.

6. For a list and biographical and related information on each person who has served in the Congress, see *Biographical Directory of the American Congress, 1774–1996* (Washington, DC: Congressional Quarterly, 1998).

7. Quoted in Rayford Logan, *The Betrayal of the Negro* (New York: Collier Books, 1965): 98.

8. In *Baker v. Carr* (369 US 186, 1962), the Supreme Court held that the Fourteenth Amendment's equal protection clause required that state legislative districts be equal in population, and that each legislator represent roughly the same number of people. In *Wesberry v. Sanders* (376 US1, 1964), the Court applied this equality in representation principle to congressional districts.

9. Linda Greenhouse, "Supreme Court Agrees to Hear Case on Government's Refusal to Adjust Census," *New York Times*, September 28, 1995, p. A14.

10. *Wisconsin v. City of New York* #94–1614, 1996 (slip opinion).

11. Linda Greenhouse, "In Blow to Democrats, Court Says Census Must Be by Actual Count," *New York Times on the Web* (January 26, 1999).

12. Congresswoman Eleanor Holmes Norton, who is black, represents the District of Columbia. Each of the U.S. territories—Puerto Rico, Guam, the Virgin Islands, and American Samoa—are allowed to send delegates to the House. These delegates are allowed to vote in committees and participate in floor debates but they are not allowed to vote on the floor. The delegate from the Virgin Islands is also black.

13. Robert C. Smith, "The Black Congressional Delegation," *Western Political Quarterly* 34 (June 1981): 204–05.

14. David Bositis, *The Congressional Black Caucus in the 103rd Congress* (Washington: Joint Center for Political and Economic Studies, 1994): 10–12.

15. Robert C. Smith, "Financing Black Politics: A Study of Congressional Elections," *Review of Black Political Economy* 17 (Summer 1988): 5–30. See also Bositis, *The Congressional Black Caucus in the 103rd Congress*, pp. 28–30.

16. Smith, "The Black Congressional Delegation," pp. 209–13, and Bositis, *The Congressional Black Caucus in the 103rd Congress*, Table 4, pp. 82–83.

17. Richard Fenno, "The Internal Distribution of Influence: The House," in David Truman, ed., *The Congress and America's Future* (Englewood Cliffs, NJ: Prentice Hall, 1965): 52.

18. Susan Webb Hammond, Daniel Mulhollan, and Arthur Stevens, "Informal Congressional Caucuses and Agenda Setting," *Western Political Quarterly* 38 (1985):

583–605; Burdett Loomis, "Congressional Caucuses and the Politics of Representation," in Lawrence Dodd and Bruce Oppenheimer, eds., *Congress Reconsidered* (Washington: Congressional Quarterly, 1981): 204–20.

19. On the Congressional Black Caucus's origins and evolution, see Charles Jones, "An Overview of the Congressional Black Caucus," in Franklin Jones et al., eds., *American Political Issues* (Dubuque, IA: 1987): 219–40; Richard Champagne and Leroy Rieselbach, "The Evolving Congressional Black Caucus," in Huey Perry and Wayne Parant, eds., *Blacks and the American Political System* (Gainesville, FL: University Press of Florida, 1995): 130–61, and Robert Singh, *The Congressional Black Caucus: Racial Politics in the U.S. Congress* (Thousand Oaks, CA: Sage, 1998).

20. Oklahoma Congressman J. C. Watts, a black Republican, refused to join the Caucus when he took office in 1995.

21. Four blacks serve on the International Relations Committee. While not as important as its Senate counterpart, the House committee plays a role in shaping congressional decision making on foreign policy.

22. The story of the battle to lift the gag rule on slave petitions is told in William Lee Miller, *Arguing about Slavery: The Great Battle in the United States Congress* (New York: Knopf, 1995).

23. William Freehling, "The Founding Fathers and Slavery," *American Historical Review* 77 (1972): 87. To get around the law, Illinois and Indiana passed black indentured servant laws; these, although not law, in effect legalized African slavery.

24. Ibid.

25. Robert C. Smith, *We Have No Leaders: African Americans in the Post–Civil Rights Era* (Albany: State University of New York Press, 1996): chap. 6. The Senate during the 1970s also passed in close votes or blocked through filibusters House-passed bills that would have banned school busing for purposes of school desegregation.

26. A "dear colleague" letter from J. C. Watts, the only House black Republican, was said to have been influential in persuading some Republican members to oppose the amendment. See Juliet Eilperin, "House Defeats Bill Targeting College Affirmative Action," *Washington Post*, May 7, 1997, p. A4.

27. Veto message of President Andrew Johnson, The Freedmen Bureau's Act, February 19, 1966, as reprinted in *The Forty Acres Documents*, ed. Amilcar Shabazz (Baton Rouge: House of Songhay, 1994): 84.

28. On black joblessness and its effects on the origins of the so-called black underclass, see William Wilson, *The Truly Disadvantaged* (Chicago: University of Chicago Press, 1987).

29. C. Hunter-Gault, "Black Leaders Agree Full Employment Is Overriding Issue of the 1970s," *New York Times*, August 31, 1977, p. A1.

30. Stephen K. Bailey, *Congress Makes a Law: The Story Behind the Employment Act of 1946* (New York: Vintage Books, 1964).

31. For a detailed case study of the Humphrey-Hawkins Act, see Smith, *We Have No Leaders*, chap. 7.

CHAPTER 12

The Presidency and the African American Quest for Universal Freedom

My paramount object in this struggle is to save the union, and is not either to save or destroy slavery—If I could save the union without freeing any slave I would do it, and if I could save it by freeing all the slaves I would do it; and if I could save it by freeing some and leaving others alone I would also do that—what I do about slavery and the colored race, I do because I believe it helps to save the union—I shall do less whenever I shall believe what I am doing hurts the cause, and I shall do more whenever I shall believe doing more will help the cause—I shall try to correct errors when shown to be errors; and I shall adopt new views so fast as they shall appear to be true views—I have here stated my purpose according to my view of official duty; and I intend no modification of my oft-expressed personal wish that all men everywhere could be free.

Abraham Lincoln (1862)[1]

We begin this chapter with the famous quotation from Abraham Lincoln's letter to newspaper editor Horace Greeley. We do so first because Lincoln was the first American president to deal in a positive, antiracist way with the African American quest for universal freedom. And second, in his timid, cautious, moderate approach to dealing with the freedom of African Americans, Abraham Lincoln is the paradigmatic president, setting an example—a pattern or model—for the handful of other American presidents who have dealt in a positive way with the African American freedom quest.[2]

ABRAHAM LINCOLN: THE PARADIGMATIC PRESIDENT

Horace Greeley, a former congressman and liberal reform leader (best known for his famous saying, "Go West, young man"), urged President Lincoln to turn the Civil War into a moral crusade against slavery. Lincoln refused. Writing to Greeley that while he personally opposed slavery and supported universal freedom for all men everywhere, his principal objective in the war, according to his view of "official duty" as president, was to save the Union, and that what he did about slavery was secondary to this "paramount objective." What President Lincoln was saying and what all other American presidents from George Washington to Bill Clinton have said is that the problem of African American freedom must take second place to what is good for the nation—the Union—as a whole.

Lincoln, as his most recent biographer shows in detail, was a skilled politician, despite his reputation as a back-country lawyer from Illinois.[3] Thus, he might also have said that what he did about slavery was also secondary to what was good for him as a politician in terms of public opinion (white public opinion) and his chances for reelection. While American presidents perhaps should attempt to lead public opinion on issues important to the nation's well-being—and occasionally some have done so—most have not, choosing instead to follow rather than lead. This may be an enduring dilemma of the American democracy on all kinds of issues but especially on issues of race and racism where Bryce's description of presidential leadership is apt: "timid in advocacy . . . infertile in suggestion . . . always listening for the popular voice, always afraid to commit himself to a point of view which may turn out unpopular."[4] Alexis de Tocqueville's *Democracy in America,* published in 1835, is generally considered the most perceptive and prophetic book ever written on the subject of America's democracy. In it he argued that universal freedom and equality for blacks and whites were unlikely to occur in any country, but it was especially unlikely in the United States precisely because of its democracy. Tocqueville wrote:

> I do not imagine that the white and black races will ever live in any country upon an equal footing. But I believe the difficulty to be still greater in the United States than elsewhere. . . . A despot who should subject the Americans and their former slaves to the same yoke, might perhaps succeed in commingling the races, but as long as the American democracy remains at the head of affairs, no one will undertake so difficult a task; and it may be foreseen that the freer the white population of the United States becomes, the more isolated it will remain.[5]

One hundred fifty years after Tocqueville's pessimistic assessment, political scientist Richard Riley writes of the history of the presidency and the African American struggle for freedom:

> These incentive structures made it extremely unlikely that someone fervently committed to racial equality would rise through the popularly based electoral process to the presidency in the first place, or that, once there he or she would feel free (or compelled) to invest presidential power in the controversial enterprise. . . . At bottom, on the question of African American rights, the presidency became an agency of change only when movements for equality had successfully reoriented the incumbent's perception of those role requirements, by preparing public opinion and illuminating the risks of inequality in periods of heightened danger to the nation's peace and security.[6] (See Box 12.1.)

━━━━━━━━━━━━━━━━━━━━━ **BOX 12.1** ━━━━━━━━━━━━━━━━━━━━━

Executive Power, Executive Orders, and Civil Rights[a]

Executive orders have been frequently employed by American presidents in the development of civil rights policy. Although the legislative power is vested exclusively in the Congress, presidents since Lincoln have claimed the right to issue directives of broad and general application that have the same legal effect as a law passed by Congress. Presidents trace their authority to engage in this kind of quasi-legislative activity to the general grant of the "executive power" to the president and to the command of Article II: "He shall take care that the laws be faithfully executed." The Supreme Court has upheld this broad interpretation of presidential power by holding that executive orders have the full force of law unless they conflict with a specific provision of the Constitution or of the law. Presidents use executive orders to establish policies when Congress refuses to do so. For example, when Congress refused to pass legislation prohibiting businesses from firing workers who go on strike, President Clinton issued an executive order prohibiting businesses with government contracts from doing so (most large corporations and many small companies have contracts with the federal government to deliver products or services).[b]

Until the 1960s, the Congress refused to legislate in the area of civil rights; thus, presidents, beginning with Franklin Roosevelt, began to use executive orders as a way to get around congressional inaction on civil rights policy. Below are the most important executive orders (E.O.s) dealing with civil rights:

E.O. 8802 (1941): Establishes policy of nondiscrimination in employment by companies with defense contracts and creates the Committee on Fair Employment Practices—Franklin Roosevelt

E.O. 9980 (1948): Establishes policy of nondiscrimination in government employment and creates a Fair Employment Board within the Civil Service Commission—Harry Truman

E.O. 9981 (1948): Establishes policy of nondiscrimination in the armed forces and creates the President's Committee on Equality of Treatment and Opportunity in Armed Services—Harry Truman[c]

E.O. 10479 (1953): Establishes Government Contract Committee to ensure that government contractors and subcontractors comply with nondiscrimination provisions in employment—Dwight Eisenhower

E.O. 10925 (1961): Establishes President's Committee on Equal Employment Opportunity and requires government contractors to take "affirmative action to ensure that applicants are treated equally during employment, without regard to their race, creed, color or national origin"—John Kennedy

E.O. 11063 (1962): Prohibits discrimination in federally assisted housing and creates President's Committee on Equal Housing—John Kennedy

E.O. 11246 (1965): Requires government contractors to take affirmative action as a prerequisite to the award of a contract and requires the Labor Department to enforce the order—Lyndon Johnson

E.O. 11245 Revised (1971): Requires government contractors to develop affirmative action plans with goals and timetables for hiring, training, and promoting African Americans and other minorities—Richard Nixon[d]

Executive orders are an easy way for a president to establish public policy; however, Congress, if it wishes, may vote to overturn such orders. Since they are the policy decisions of a single individual, what one president gives, another may take away by a simple "stroke of his pen."

[a]On the use of executive orders to make civil rights policy from the Roosevelt to the Johnson administration, see Ruth Morgan, *The President and Civil Rights: Policy Making by Executive Order* (New York: St. Martin's Press, 1970).

[b]A three-judge federal appeals court in Washington ruled that President Clinton's striker replacement order was illegal because it conflicted with federal labor law. The administration declined to appeal this ruling to the Supreme Court, fearing the conservative court might issue a sweeping ruling undermining the president's power to issue executive orders. See "Clinton Accepts Defeat on Strikers' Protection," *San Francisco Chronicle*, September 10, 1996, p. A9.

[c]President Truman based this order on his authority as commander in chief as well as the executive power and the "take care" clause.

[d]This order is the basis and model for affirmative action programs and policies discussed in Box 12.3.

Lincoln, Emancipation, and Colonialization

The historian George Fredrickson describes President Lincoln as a "pragmatic white supremacist."[7] Throughout his public career, Lincoln opposed slavery—because he thought it was morally wrong but also because he thought it was economically unwise, favoring instead "free labor on free soil."[8] But Lincoln also was a white supremacist, holding that the African people were "inferior in color and perhaps moral and intellectual endowment."[9] And while Lincoln was antiracist in his attitudes toward slavery, he was racist in the sense that he, like the overwhelming majority of northern whites, opposed social and political equality for blacks. Whether Lincoln's views on racial equality were sincere or simply politically expedient is not known. However, as Frederick Douglass said, "Clearly, if opposition to black equality constituted a strong and general conviction of the white community, Lincoln would be prepared to accept it as a fact of life, not readily altered even if morally wrong."[10] (See Box 12.2.)

As Lincoln told Greeley in his letter, if he could save the Union without freeing any slave he would do it; if he could do it by freeing some he would do it; and if he could do it by freeing some and leaving others alone he would do that. As the war progressed, Lincoln eventually concluded that to save the Union, he must *promise* freedom to *some* of the slaves. Thus, on January 1, 1863, the president, using his authority as commander in chief of the army and navy, issued the Emancipation Proclamation. The Proclamation was issued as a war measure, a measure necessary to win the war. Lincoln called it a "fit and necessary war measure for suppressing said rebellion."[11] The Emancipation Proclamation applied only to those parts of the country under Confederate control—"the states and parts of states . . . wherein the people are this day in rebellion."[12] It specifically exempted Union border slave states such as Maryland and those parts of the South controlled by the Union army (New Orleans, for example). Thus, at the time the Emancipation Proclamation was issued, it freed very few slaves.[13] Rather, it was important as a

━━━━━━━━━━━━━━ **BOX 12.2** ━━━━━━━━━━━━━━
The First Thirteenth Amendment[a]

As the prospects of secession and civil war increased, the House and Senate appointed special committees to investigate the situation and make recommendations that might avoid war. Among the recommendations proposed by the House committee was an amendment to the Constitution that would have prohibited any amendment to the Constitution granting the Congress the power to interfere in any way with slavery in any state. The text of the Amendment read:

> No amendment shall be made to the Constitution which will authorize or give to Congress the Power to abolish or interfere, within any state, with the domestic institutions thereof, including that of persons held to labor or service by the laws of said state.

This extraordinary amendment, intended to freeze slavery into the Constitution forever, was adopted on March 2, 1861, by a Congress that was overwhelmingly northern, since by that time the senators and representatives from seven southern states that had already seceded were not present. President Lincoln took the extraordinary and completely unnecessary step of personally signing the amendment, the first and only time a president has signed a constitutional amendment. Three states—Ohio, Illinois, and Maryland—quickly ratified the amendment. However, the attack one month later on Fort Sumter that brought on the Civil War ended any prospect of preserving the Union by preserving slavery, and no other state ratified this first Thirteenth Amendment. Ironically, the second Thirteenth Amendment, adopted four years later, abolished slavery throughout the United States.

[a]For a history of the first Thirteenth Amendment and an analysis of whether it would have been constitutional if it had been ratified, see Mark Brandon, "The 'Original' Thirteenth Amendment and the Limits to Formal Constitutional Change," in Sanford Levinson, ed., *Responding to Imperfection: The Theory and Practice of Constitutional Amendment* (Princeton, NJ: Princeton University Press, 1995).

war measure to encourage blacks in the South to rise and join the struggle because once the war was won, the Proclamation promised that they "henceforward shall be free." In addition to being a war measure, the Proclamation had a diplomatic purpose, which was to encourage European support for the Union cause by transforming the war into a moral crusade against slavery.

Lincoln's use of the commander-in-chief clause to promise freedom to the slaves was unprecedented and of questionable constitutionality since it may have violated the Fifth Amendment provision against the "taking of private property without just compensation."[14] The Thirteenth Amendment, however, settled the question of the constitutionality of the Proclamation. What should be done with the African Americans, once they were free, became the central question before the president and the country.

Lincoln's position was similar to that of Thomas Jefferson and it was clear and long-standing: colonialization. Once freed, the Africans should be deported out of the coun-

President Lincoln reading the draft Emancipation Proclamation to his Cabinet on July 22, 1862.

try. In his first message to Congress, Lincoln urged recognition of Liberia and Haiti and colonialization of blacks there or in some other places where the climate is "congenial to them."[15] Why colonialization? Why not instead integration and universal freedom? Lincoln's response was public opinion, telling a delegation of black leaders at the White House that "insurmountable white prejudice made racial equality impossible in the United States."[16] And "on this broad continent, not a single man of your race is made the equal of a single man of ours. Go where you are treated the best and the ban is still on you."[17] Colonialization was an impractical scheme, costly and complex. Thus, nothing ever came of it although Lincoln supported it until the day of his death.

Lincoln was the first president to act decisively in favor of African American freedom, but his actions were partial (promising limited rather than universal freedom), limited by his own prejudices, by public opinion, and by the exigencies of winning the war. Lincoln is universally considered the nation's greatest president. Yet, in his approach to the problem of race, he was timid and cautious, "always listening for the popular voice, always afraid to commit himself to a point of view which may turn out unpopular." This is how it has always been with American presidents and race—and perhaps, as Tocqueville said, must be. Frederick Douglass summed up the paradigmatic Lincoln in a speech unveiling a monument to the president on April 14, 1876. He told the whites in the audience, "You are the children of Lincoln, we are at best his step-children," but Douglass said:

> Viewed from the genuine abolition ground, Mr. Lincoln seemed tardy, cold, dull and in-
> different, but measuring him by the sentiment of his country, a sentiment he was bound
> as a statesman to consult, he was swift, zealous, radical and determined.[18]

Lincoln himself could not have summed it up better.

THE RACIAL ATTITUDES AND POLICIES OF AMERICAN PRESIDENTS FROM GEORGE WASHINGTON TO BILL CLINTON

The American presidency is an office of great power and majesty, and therefore the racial attitudes and policies of American presidents have been a crucial factor in the African American quest for universal freedom.

Of the forty-two men who have served as president, very few have been allies in the African American freedom struggle. On the contrary, most have been hostile or at best neutral or ambivalent. Table 12.1 lists the American presidents in terms of their racial attitudes and policies. Twenty-three (more than half) were white supremacists, includ-ing, as we have said, Abraham Lincoln. Eighteen have also been racists, supporting ei-ther slavery (including eight slave owners) or segregation and racial inequality. Thirteen have been neutral or ambivalent in their attitudes toward African American freedom. Nine—Lincoln, Grant, Benjamin Harrison, Truman, Kennedy, Johnson, Nixon, Carter, and Clinton—have pursued antiracist policies in terms of emancipation of the slaves and their freedom and equality in the United States. And although we classify Lincoln as an antiracist president on the basis of the Emancipation Proclamation, as we indi-cated, he was ambivalent, favoring freedom for the slaves but not racial equality and universal rights. Table 12.1 also shows that with the exception of Lincoln, Grant, and Harrison, all the antiracist presidents have served in the mid-twentieth century, most since the 1960s.[19] Of the ten greatest American presidents, according to the most recent poll of American historians—Lincoln, Washington, Franklin Roosevelt, Jefferson, Jack-son, Theodore Roosevelt, Wilson, Truman, Polk, and Eisenhower—eight were white supremacists, six were racists, and only two—Lincoln and Truman—were antiracists.[20]

THE PRESIDENCY AND THE AFRICAN AMERICAN QUEST FOR UNIVERSAL FREEDOM: FROM THE REVOLUTIONARY ERA TO THE POST–CIVIL RIGHTS ERA

This part of the book is necessarily brief since, as we indicated in the previous section, most American presidents have been unresponsive to the African American quest for universal freedom.

The Revolutionary Era

Perhaps all the early American presidents supported the institution of slavery because they thought it was economically necessary or because doing so was politically expedient.

TABLE 12.1

A Typology of the Racial Attitudes and Policy Perspectives of American Presidents, from George Washington to William Clinton[a]

WHITE SUPREMACIST[b]	RACIST	RACIALLY NEUTRAL	RACIALLY AMBIVALENT	ANTIRACIST
George Washington (1789–1797)	George Washington[c]			
	John Adams (1798–1801)			
Thomas Jefferson (1801–1809)	Thomas Jefferson[c]			
James Madison (1809–1817)	James Madison[c]			
James Monroe (1817–1825)	James Monroe[c]			
	John Q. Adams (1825–29)			
Andrew Jackson (1829–1837)	Andrew Jackson[c]			
Martin Van Buren (1837–1841)	Martin Van Buren			
William H. Harrison (1841)	William H. Harrison			
John Tyler (1841–1845)	John Tyler			
James Polk (1845–1849)	James Polk[c]			
Zachary Taylor (1849–1850)	Zachary Taylor[c]			
Millard Fillmore (1850–1853)	Millard Fillmore			
Franklin Pierce (1853–1857)	Franklin Pierce			
James Buchanan (1857–1861)	James Buchanan			
Abraham Lincoln (1861–1865)				Abraham Lincoln
Andrew Johnson (1865–1869)	Andrew Johnson[c]			Ulysses S. Grant (1869–1877)
			Rutherford B. Hayes (1877–1881)	
		Chester Arthur (1881–1885)	James Garfield (1881)	
Grover Cleveland (1885–1889, 1893–1897)		Grover Cleveland		Benjamin Harrison (1889–1893)
William Mckinley (1897–1901)		William Mckinley		
Theodore Roosevelt (1901–1909)	Theodore Roosevelt	William H. Taft (1909–1913)		
Woodrow Wilson (1913–1921)	Woodrow Wilson			

(Continued)

TABLE 12.1 (Continued)

WHITE SUPREMACIST[b]	RACIST	RACIALLY NEUTRAL	RACIALLY AMBIVALENT	ANTIRACIST
Warren G. Harding (1921–1923)		Warren G. Harding		
		Calvin Coolidge (1923–1929)		Harry S. Truman
		Herbert Hoover (1929–1933)		
		Franklin D. Roosevelt (1933–1945)		John F. Kennedy (1961–1963)
				Lyndon B. Johnson (1963–1969)
				Richard Nixon (1969–1974)
Harry S. Truman (1945–1953)			Dwight Eisenhower	
Dwight Eisenhower (1953–1961)				Jimmy Carter (1977–1981)
Richard Nixon (1969–1974)			Gerald Ford (1974–1977)	
			Ronald Reagan (1981–1989)	William Clinton (1993–2000)
			George Bush (1989–1993)	

[a] We classify a president as a white supremacist if the historical record indicates that he held a belief in the inferiority of the African people. A racist is one who supported the institutions of slavery and segregation. A racial neutral is a president whose record shows no positions on racial issues, while a racial ambivalent is a president whose actions on race issues vary from antiracist to racial neutral. An antiracist president is one whose record is characterized by actions to dismantle at least parts of the system of racial subordination. All presidents until Lincoln were racist since they defended the institution of slavery, as sanctioned by the Constitution. After Lincoln, we do not classify presidents as racists or white supremacists unless there is evidence in the historical record that they believed blacks were an inferior people or they supported racial segregation and inequality. There is unavoidably some ambiguity in these classifications. For example, as president, John Q. Adams took no antiracist or antislavery actions, but he was not personally racist; after leaving the presidency, Adams, as a congressman, was a vigorous opponent of slavery and the slave trade. Or Jefferson—clearly a white supremacist and a racist—acted as soon as the Constitution permitted to abolish the slave trade.

Information on the attitudes and racial policies of the presidents were obtained from various biographical sources including the entire University Press of Kansas American Presidency series and the summary works of George Sinkler, *Racial Attitudes of American Presidents: From Abraham Lincoln to Theodore Roosevelt* (Garden City, NY: Doubleday, 1971), Kenneth O'Reilly, *Nixon's Piano: Presidents and Racial Politics from Washington to Clinton* (New York: Free Press, 1995), and Richard Riley, *The Presidency and the Politics of Racial Inequality: Nation-Keeping from 1831 to 1965* (New York: Columbia University Press, 1999).

[b] Years in parentheses indicate tenure in office.

[c] Indicates slave owners.

O'Reilly in his book on the racial attitudes of American presidents indicates that several revolutionary era presidents (Washington, Jefferson, Madison, and John Q. Adams) saw slavery as morally wrong and hoped that it would wither away.[21] Yet, none of these early presidents favored universal freedom for blacks; rather, they, like Lincoln, tended to favor colonialization.[22] The only action against slavery by an American president during this period was Jefferson's decision to stop the slave trade as soon as the Constitution permitted. In fact, he proposed to end slavery in 1807, one year before the constitutionally permissible year of 1808. In his annual message to Congress on December 2, 1806, Jefferson wrote,

> I congratulate you fellow citizens on the approach of the period when you may interpose your authority constitutionally [to stop Americans] from further participation in those violations of natural rights which have been so long continued on the unoffending inhabitants of Africa, and which the morality, reputation and best interests of our country have long been eager to proscribe.[23]

The Antebellum Era

None of the nine presidents who served during the antebellum era (1830–1860) took any actions in response to the African American quest for universal freedom, ignoring or attempting to repress the increasingly militant demands for freedom coming from the abolitionist movement.

The Reconstruction Era

Andrew Johnson, who succeeded Lincoln after his murder, was one of the more racist of American presidents in his attitudes and policies. A white supremacist, racist slave owner from Tennessee, Johnson vetoed civil rights legislation and the Freedmen's Bureau Act. When Congress overrode his vetoes, he refused to faithfully carry out the law as required by the Constitution—one of the factors that led to his impeachment by the House (he came within one vote of being convicted in the Senate and removed from office). By contrast, Ulysses S. Grant, Johnson's successor, was one of the most antiracist presidents in American history. Although he owned one slave, Grant freed him early, and once Grant became president he attempted to enforce the civil rights laws vigorously, urging his white countrymen to grant African Americans universal suffrage and equality under the law. Grant also appointed blacks to federal office for the first time. Frederick Douglass said of Grant that he never exhibited "vulgar prejudices of any color."[24] Even so, when Grant left office, most of the southern states were under the control of white racists and the tide of public opinion in the North was shifting against his policies.

Grant was followed in office by Rutherford B. Hayes. While antiracist in his personal convictions, Hayes, to win the presidency, agreed in the famous "compromise of 1877" to withdraw federal troops from the South, effectively bringing the brief era of Reconstruction to an end.[25]

The Post-Reconstruction Era

Most presidents after Hayes ignored the problems of race and racism. White public opinion was indifferent or hostile to the African American quest for freedom, and

American presidents, whatever their personal attitudes, followed rather than led during this period: 1880s–1930s. Presidents Grover Cleveland and Theodore Roosevelt were attacked because they had eaten dinner with blacks. Cleveland denied it and Roosevelt, who invited Booker T. Washington to the White House for dinner, promised never to do it again. Woodrow Wilson, the first Democratic candidate for president to receive significant black support, nevertheless once in office immediately sought to impose racial segregation throughout the federal workplace in Washington (see chapter 14).

Benjamin Harrison was the first antiracist president since Grant and the last before Truman. Among his antiracist policies was a proposed constitutional amendment to overturn the Supreme Court decision invalidating the Civil Rights Act of 1883; legislation to allow the federal government to enforce African American voting rights in the South; and antilynching legislation.[26] Harrison also responded to the material-based interests of blacks by supporting legislation—the Blair Act—that would have provided large sums of federal money to improve southern schools.

From Benjamin Harrison to Franklin Roosevelt, American presidents were largely silent on the issues of race and racism. Roosevelt, the first Democratic president to receive a majority of the black vote, is typical of the political expediency of American presidents on issues of race and racism. In more than thirteen years in office, Roosevelt never took any stand on issues of racial discrimination, refusing, despite the urging of his wife Eleanor, even to speak out against lynchings. Like President Kennedy a generation later, Roosevelt's response was always, "I can't take the risk."[27] That is, the president argued that he could not risk losing the support of the powerful white supremacist southern Democrats for his New Deal economic program. Thus, he was willing to sacrifice or trade off the civil rights of blacks to obtain material benefits for all Americans. Blacks benefited from Roosevelt's material-based reforms—public works, housing, and agricultural programs—although the programs were administered on a racially discriminatory basis.

Roosevelt was also concerned that support for civil rights would jeopardize his renomination and reelection, since southern whites controlled an important bloc of votes at the Democratic convention and in the electoral college.

Roosevelt did respond to one black demand during his term in office. This was the material-based demand for jobs in the war industries, but he did so only after the threat of a massive march on Washington by African American workers. Charging that there was widespread discrimination in the growing war industries, A. Phillip Randolph threatened to bring hundreds of thousands of blacks to Washington in a massive protest demonstration. To convince Randolph to call off the march, Roosevelt in June 1941 issued Executive Order 8802, prohibiting discrimination in employment of workers in industries with government contracts. The order also created a committee on Fair Employment Practices; however, it was poorly funded and staffed and was not very effective in ending employment discrimination.[28]

The Civil Rights Era

Although President Truman shared the same white supremacist views of his native Missouri, as president he took a strong antiracist position. He did so for two reasons. First, faced with a third party challenge from the liberal, progressive Henry Wallace, Truman judged that a strong civil rights program would help him rally the black vote in the big cities of the electoral vote-rich northeastern and midwestern states. Second, Truman judged that support for civil rights was a cold war imperative. That is, as the leader of the "free world," the United States would be embarrassed and ridiculed by the Soviet Union if it continued to adhere to racism as a national policy.[29]

Thus, President Truman became the first president in history to propose a civil rights reform agenda to the Congress, including a ban on employment discrimination, antilynching legislation, and a proposal to end the poll tax. President Truman also issued Executive Order 9981 banning discrimination in the armed services; ordered an end to discrimination in federal employment; was the first president to address an NAACP convention; and directed the Justice Department to file a brief in support of school de-segregation cases then pending before the Supreme Court. Although the Congress did not pass Truman's civil rights proposals, his administration was the first in fifty years to place the issue of civil rights on the national agenda.[30]

Two minor civil rights bills passed during the administration of President Eisen-hower (the first since Reconstruction); however, his support for them was reluctant. Eisenhower was a white supremacist and a race ambivalent, preferring to avoid taking any actions on civil rights or race-related issues if at all possible. He did issue executive orders prohibiting discrimination in government employment and by companies with government contracts, and he appointed a few blacks to minor positions in his adminis-tration. The major civil rights issue during the Eisenhower administration was the Supreme Court's *Brown* desegregation decision. Eisenhower opposed the Court's deci-sion and was reluctant to enforce it. However, when Arkansas Governor Orval Faubus used the state's national guard to block the admission of nine black schoolchildren to Little Rock's Central High School, Eisenhower felt he had no choice as president but to "take care that the laws be faithfully executed." Thus, he reluctantly dispatched the United States Army to enforce the Court's order that the black children be admitted.

John F. Kennedy would not have won the closest election in American history with-out the support of black voters. But like Franklin Roosevelt, he was reluctant to risk los-ing the support of white Southerners by introducing civil rights legislation. Only after the civil rights demonstrations led by Dr. King created a national crisis did Kennedy fi-nally propose civil rights legislation. In his 1963 speech proposing what was to become the Civil Rights Act of 1964, Kennedy became the first American president to declare that racism was morally wrong.

President Kennedy also appointed a number of blacks to high-level posts in his ad-ministration and was the first president to openly entertain blacks at the White House. He also reluctantly issued Executive Order 11063 banning discrimination in federally assisted housing. During the 1960 campaign, Kennedy had promised with a "stroke of the pen" to end discrimination in the sale and rental of housing. Yet, he delayed, causing blacks to send hundreds of pens to the president in case he had misplaced his. Finally, in late 1962, he signed the order, but it was limited, excluding all existing housing and covering only housing owned or directly financed by the federal government. Also, President Kennedy, like President Eisenhower, reluctantly sent the Army into Missis-sippi to enforce a court order desegregating the state's university.

Unlike Presidents Kennedy and Roosevelt, President Johnson was willing "to take the risk" of losing the support of white southern Democrats by enthusiastically and

President Johnson signing the Civil Rights Act of 1964.

unequivocally supporting civil rights legislation (when he signed the 1964 Act he told his aides, "We have just lost the South for a generation"). In addition to signing three major civil rights bills, Johnson also initiated the Great Society and the "war on poverty" designed to deal with the material-based needs of urban and rural poor people, many of whom were African Americans. Johnson also made a number of historic appointments, placing the first black in the cabinet and the first black on the Supreme Court.

The Post–Civil Rights Era

Although Richard Nixon was a white supremacist and his 1968 campaign was based on a strategy of attracting the white racist vote in the South,[31] as the first post–civil rights era president he presided over the successful desegregation of southern schools, the renewal of the Voting Rights Act in 1970, implementation of Executive Order 11246 establishing affirmative action, and the appointment of scores of blacks to high-level positions in the government. In addition Nixon proposed a far-reaching material-based reform—the Family Assistance Plan—that would have guaranteed an income to all families with children. Although this reform was defeated by an odd coalition of blacks and liberals (who thought the income guarantee was too low) and conservatives (who wanted no guarantee at all), if it had passed it would have substantially raised the income of poor families, many of whom were black.[32] Historians are unclear as to why Nixon took such a strong civil rights policy stance (especially on affirmative action),[33] but the political climate in the late 1960s probably made such positions seem politically expedient.

In his year and half in office, President Gerald Ford distinguished himself on race by appointing the second black to the cabinet and by waging a year-long campaign to get the courts and the Congress to end busing for purposes of school desegregation.

Jimmy Carter appointed a number of blacks to high-level positions in his administration and to the federal courts,[34] supported affirmative action in the form of the *Bakke* case (see Box 12.3), and reorganized the civil rights enforcement bureaucracy.[35] However, he rejected an ambitious proposal by his African American Housing Secretary Patricia Roberts Harris for a new urban, antipoverty program,[36] and supported only a watered-down version of the Humphrey-Hawkins full employment bill.

Ronald Reagan's two terms in office were characterized by ambivalence on race. He came into office determined to dismantle the Great Society and affirmative action programs. Several Great Society programs were eliminated and the budgets for others were substantially cut. But Reagan also signed a twenty-five-year extension of the Voting Rights Act, strengthened the Fair Housing Act, and (reluctantly) signed the Martin Luther King, Jr., holiday bill. He also refused to issue an executive order eliminating affirmative action, as he had implied he would during the 1980 campaign (see Box 12.3).

George Bush's administration was also characterized by ambivalence on civil rights. In 1990 he vetoed the Civil Rights Act (designed to overturn several Supreme Court decisions that made it difficult to enforce employment discrimination laws), calling it a "quota bill," but in 1991 he signed essentially the same bill he had vetoed a year earlier.[37] Bush also appointed the second black to the Supreme Court, but the appointee was a man described by most black leaders as an "Uncle Tom" and a "traitor to the race."[38] Justice Thomas was also accused by Anita Hill, a former black female employee, of sexual harassment. Additionally, Bush rejected proposals by his aides for new antipoverty programs, arguing that they were too expensive and too liberal.[39]

Bill Clinton is arguably the first authentically nonracist, non–white supremacist president in American history. American presidents are a product of the culture and socialization process of their time, and Bill Clinton is the first president to come of age in

---

BOX 12.3

African Americans and Presidential Policy Making: The Case of Affirmative Action

---

Affirmative action—a variety of programs and policies designed to enhance the access of racial minorities and women to education, employment, and government contracts—is one of the most controversial civil rights policies of the day, as it has been since it was created by African American policy makers in the Johnson and Nixon administrations. Although affirmative action as national policy was developed by African Americans and is widely supported by African Americans and their leaders, in the Carter administration African American policy makers sought to abolish such programs.

(Continued)

BOX 12.3 Continued

Late in the Johnson administration, Edward Sylvester, an African American who headed the Labor Department's office of Federal Contract Compliance, developed the "Cleveland Plan" designed to assure equal employment opportunity for blacks in the Cleveland, Ohio, construction industry. The Cleveland Plan required that construction companies with government contracts develop detailed plans specifying the precise number of blacks they planned to hire in all phases of their work. This plan brought protests from labor unions, business groups, conservatives, and liberals who argued that it established racial hiring quotas. Eventually, the comptroller general (head of the General Accounting Office, the congressional watchdog agency) ruled that the plan was illegal, not because it required quotas but because it violated standard contract bidding procedures. Thus, Sylvester's plan was dropped. To the surprise of most observers, Sylvester's plan was resurrected in the conservative, business-oriented Nixon administration, again under the policy leadership of African Americans. President Nixon appointed Arthur Fletcher as an assistant secretary of Labor and John Wilks as director of the Office of Federal Contract Compliance. Immediately these two African Americans set about to revive Sylvester's plan. Using Philadelphia as the model city, the "Philadelphia Plan" required government contractors to set specific numerical goals for the employment of minority workers. Unlike Sylvester's Cleveland Plan, the Philadelphia Plan complied with standard contracting procedures but the comptroller general again ruled it was illegal, this time because it used race as a factor in determining employment. President Nixon, however, rejected the comptroller general's ruling, arguing that as president he had the inherent "executive power" to implement the Philadelphia Plan by executive order (E.O. 11246). The Senate later passed an amendment upholding the comptroller general's decision, but after intense lobbying by President Nixon and his secretary of labor, George Shultz, the House by a vote of 208 to 156 rejected the Senate's amendment and affirmative action effectively became the law of the land. Ironically, given Democratic support for affirmative action and Republican opposition to it today, in 1971 a majority of Democrats in Congress voted against affirmative action while it was supported by a majority of Republicans.

The Philadelphia Plan became the model for affirmative action throughout American society, including admission to colleges and universities. In the late 1970s the University of California at Davis established an affirmative action program at its medical school in order to increase the number of minority students enrolled there. Under its plan, sixteen of its 100 openings were set aside for minorities only. Allan Bakke, a white applicant who was rejected for admission, sued the university, arguing that for a university to consider race in making its admission decisions was a violation of the Civil Rights Act of 1964 and the Fourteenth Amendment's equal protection clause The California Supreme Court in the case of *Regents of the University of California vs. Bakke* (1978) declared the Davis plan unconstitutional. The university appealed this decision to the United States Supreme Court.

A sharply divided Supreme Court upheld the university's right to use race in making admission decisions but agreed that setting a quota of sixteen slots for minorities only was unconstitutional. We discuss the details of the Court's opinion in *Bakke* and other affirmative action cases in chapter 15; here we focus on the role of African American policy makers. In important cases, the Supreme Court will "invite" the administration to submit an amicus curiae ("friend of the court") brief explaining how it thinks the case should be decided. In the Carter administration, the two policy makers responsible for preparing the administration brief were Wade McCree, who was solicitor general, and Drew Days, III, assistant attorney general for civil rights (and later solicitor general in the Clinton administration). In the first draft of the brief prepared by the solicitor general, the very principle of affirmative action—that race could be considered in admissions or employment decisions—was rejected as a violation of the equal protection clause. It read "we doubt that it is *ever* proper to use race to close any portion of the class for competition by members of all races" and that "racial classifications favorable to minority groups are presumptively unconstitutional."[a] If this position had been adopted by the Court, affirmative action would have been eliminated, not just in university admissions but in employment and government contracting. McCree's brief, however, was leaked to the press and after intense lobbying by the NAACP, the Congressional Black Caucus and others, President Carter instructed the attorney general to request the solicitor general to rewrite the brief. Although McCree was reportedly outraged by what he considered unseemly political pressure, the brief was rewritten upholding the right of the university to use race in its admissions decisions. Again, the irony here is that affirmative action created by black men serving in a conservative Republican administration was almost eliminated by black men serving in a liberal Democratic administration.

Three decades after the Philadelphia Plan and two decades after *Bakke,* affirmative action is still under attack. President Reagan implied during the 1980 campaign that he would abolish affirmative action in the federal government by revoking Nixon's 1971 order. But he backed off at the urging of former Nixon administration Labor Secretary George Shultz (then Reagan's secretary of state) and Samuel Pierce, the secretary of housing and urban development and the only African American in his cabinet. In his review of affirmative action policy—a review led by Christopher Edley, an African American White House staff assistant—President Clinton concluded that while some reforms might be appropriate, affirmative action programs were still necessary to assure equal opportunities for minorities and women. Thus, his formulation: "mend it, don't end it."[b]

However, Republican congressional leaders are opposed to affirmative action; 1996 Republican presidential nominee Bob Dole also opposed affirmative action; the Supreme Court in a series of cases has been edging away from the principle of affirmative action (led by African American Justice Clarence Thomas); and in 1996, the trend-setting voters of California—by 56 percent to 44 percent—approved Proposition 209, the ballot initiative ending affirmative action in that state's education, employment, and contracting.[c] A leader of the California anti-affirmative action initiative was Ward Connerly, an African American.

[a]Quoted in Robert C. Smith, *We Have No Leaders: African Americans in the Post–Civil Rights Era* (Albany: State University of New York Press, 1996): 149–50. For a detailed analysis of the evolution of affirmative action from the Kennedy to the Nixon administration, see Hugh Davis Graham, *The Civil Rights Era: Origins and Development of National Policy* (New York: Oxford, 1990): chaps. 10–13; on policy developments from the Nixon to the Bush administration, see Smith, *We Have No Leaders,* chap. 5.

[b]See "Remarks by the President on Affirmative Action," The White House, Office of the Press Secretary, July 19, 1995. The Clinton administration's detailed review of affirmative action is "Affirmative Action Review: Report to President Clinton" (Washington: Bureau of National Affairs, 1995). This report was prepared by White House advisors George Stephanopoulos and Christopher Edley, Jr.

[c]Several days after Proposition 209 was approved, Federal District Court Judge Thelton Henderson suspended its implementation because he said it probably violated the Fourteenth Amendment's equal protection clause. Judge Henderson's order was later reversed by the Ninth Circuit Court of Appeals and the proposition took effect in the late summer of 1997. See John Bourdeau, "Appeals Court Upholds Support for Prop. 209," *West County Times,* August 22, 1997,: p. A1.

the nominally nonracist, non–white supremacist post–civil rights era. By all accounts, Clinton is as free of racist and white supremacist thinking as any white person can be.[40] Yet, to win the presidency, Clinton ran on a strategy of deliberately distancing himself from black voters in order to win over the so-called Reagan Democrats who had voted Republican because of the Democrats' close identification with African Americans.[41]

In his first term in office, Clinton appointed a large number of blacks to high-level positions in the administration (one-fourth of the cabinet) and to the courts. He also refused to support proposals to eliminate affirmative action (see Box 12.3) and was responsive to black concerns to use military force to restore the democratically elected president to office in Haiti (see chapter 16). On material-based issues, Clinton proposed a complicated yet comprehensive plan to guarantee health care to all Americans. Although Clinton's plan was not enacted, if Congress had passed it, it would have universalized access to health care and been of enormous benefit to African Americans (see chapter 15).

However, if Clinton sought to universalize health care and establish it as a right for all citizens, he did the exact opposite with respect to welfare. During the 1992 election, Clinton campaigned on the pledge, "End Welfare as We Know It," by imposing a two-year time limit on eligibility for Aid to Families with Dependent Children. The Congress did not act on Clinton's welfare bill in his first two years in office. But once the Republicans took control of Congress, they enacted a much more radical proposal; one that abolished the sixty-year-old New Deal guarantee of welfare as a universal, federally guaranteed right. Clinton vetoed two versions of this bill, but as the 1996 election approached, he was persuaded (against the advice of his policy advisers on welfare) by his political advisers that the politically expedient and popular thing to do was sign the bill. So, in July of 1996 he signed this radical reform bill (we discuss the welfare reform bill in detail in chapter 15). Clinton's major initiative on race during his second term was to propose a dialogue on race and to make a historic visit (the first by an American president) to several African countries.[42]

Clinton's initiative on race included a series of speeches and town meetings on race and the appointment of a seven-member advisory board to study the problem of race and ethnicity in the United States. Headed by the distinguished African American historian John Hope Franklin, the board, after a year's work, issued its report. Among its major recommendations was a call for the creation of a permanent body, called the President's Council for One America, to promote harmony and dialogue among the nation's racial and ethnic groups. The Board also supported the President's "Mend It, Don't End It" policy on affirmative action; urged presidential support for reducing the disparity in sentences for cocaine and crack; and proposed studies of media stereotyping and police misconduct toward minorities.[43] President Clinton accepted the board's report in a White House ceremony, but declined to commit his administration to accepting its recommendations.

SELECTED BIBLIOGRAPHY

Donald, David. *Lincoln*. New York: Simon & Schuster, 1995. The most recent and one of the best biographies of the sixteenth president.

Fehrenbacher, Don. "Only His Stepchildren: Lincoln and the Negro." *Civil War History* 12 (1974): 293–309. A generally favorable analysis of the president's posture toward African Americans.

Fredrickson, George. "A Man Not a Brother: Abraham Lincoln and the Negro." *Journal of Southern History* 41 (1975): 39–58. A balanced assessment of the subject.

Holden, Matthew, Jr. "Race and Constitutional Change in the Twentieth Century: The Role of the Executive." In John Hope Franklin and Genna Rae MacNeil, eds. *African Americans and the Living Constitution.* Washington: Smithsonian Institution Press, 1995. An analysis of the policy initiatives on race of American presidents, focusing on the context of presidential decision making.

Morgan, Ruth. *The President and Civil Rights: Policy Making by Executive Order.* New York: St. Martin's Press, 1970. A study of presidential use of executive orders to advance civil rights.

O'Reilly, Kenneth. *Nixon's Piano: Presidents and Racial Politics from Washington to Clinton.* New York: Free Press, 1995. A useful study of the subject.

Quarles, Benjamin. *Lincoln and the Negro.* New York: Oxford University Press, 1962. The definitive study of the subject.

Riley, Richard. *The Presidency and the Politics of Racial Inequality: Nation-Keeping from 1831 to 1965.* New York: Columbia University Press, 1999. The most recent booklength study of the subject.

Rossiter, Clinton. *The American Presidency,* rev. ed. New York: Harcourt Brace Jovanovich, 1960. The standard study of the role of the president and the presidency's central role in American politics.

Sinkler, George. *The Racial Attitudes of American Presidents: From Abraham Lincoln to Theodore Roosevelt.* Garden City, NY: Doubleday, 1971. A comprehensive analysis of the subject.

Walton, Hanes, Jr. *African American Power and Politics: The Political Context.* New York: Columbia University Press, 1996. A detailed study of how the Reagan and Bush presidencies changed the political context of discussions on race.

NOTES

1. Letter to Horace Greeley, *Abraham Lincoln: Collected Works,* vol. V, pp. 388–89.
2. Richard Riley explains the role of the president on issues of race in terms of "Nation-Maintaining." He writes, "The central finding of this study is that the presidency has routinely served as a nation-maintaining institution on the issue of racial inequality. Indeed, the evidence arrayed here strongly suggests that one of the enduring roles each president is required to execute is that of nation-keeper, a protector of the inherited political and social order and a preserver of domestic tranquility." See *The Presidency and the Politics of Racial Inequality: Nation-Keeping from 1831 to 1965* (New York: Columbia University Press, 1999): 10.
3. David Donald, *Lincoln* (New York: Simon & Schuster, 1995).
4. As quoted in George Sinkler, *The Racial Attitudes of American Presidents: From Abraham Lincoln to Theodore Roosevelt* (Garden City, NY: Doubleday, 1971): 11.

5. Alexis de Tocqueville, *Democracy in America*, ed. by Phillips Bradley (Garden City, NY: Doubleday, 1848, 1969): 356.

6. Riley, *The Presidency and the Politics of Racial Inequality,* pp. 18–19.

7. On Lincoln's racial attitudes, see Benjamin Quarles, *Lincoln and the Negro* (New York: Oxford University Press, 1962); George Fredrickson, "A Man Not a Brother: Lincoln and the Negro," *Journal of Southern History* 41 (1975): 39–58; and Don Fehrenbacher, "Only His Stepchildren: Lincoln and the Negro," *Civil War History* 12 (1974): 293–309.

8. Lincoln did not favor the abolition of slavery (frequently calling abolitionism "dangerous radical utopianism") but rather opposed its extension beyond the South to the Midwest and the West because he wanted these lands preserved for free (white) labor on free land. See Eric Foner, *Free Soil, Free Labor: The Ideology of the Republican Party before the Civil War* (New York: Oxford University Press, 1970).

9. Fredrickson, "A Man Not a Brother," p. 46.

10. Quoted in Fredrickson, "A Man Not a Brother," p. 45.

11. Abraham Lincoln, "The Emancipation Proclamation," in Kermit Hall, William Wiecek, and Paul Finkelman, eds., *American Legal History: Cases and Materials* (New York: Oxford University Press, 1991): 224.

12. Ibid.

13. A standard study of the Emancipation Proclamation is John Hope Franklin, *The Emancipation Proclamation* (Garden City, NY: Doubleday, 1963).

14. The commander-in-chief clause was used by Franklin Roosevelt to incarcerate Japanese Americans as a World War II measure, which at the time was held to be constitutional by the Supreme Court although it was a clear violation of the Fifth Amendment prohibition on the deprivation of liberty without a trial.

15. Fredrickson, "A Man Not a Brother," p. 45.

16. Ibid., p. 48.

17. Fehrenbacher, "Only His Stepchildren," p. 307.

18. *The Life and Times of Frederick Douglass written by Himself,* introduction by Rayford Logan (London: Collier Books, 1892, 1962): 485, 489.

19. Matthew Holden, Jr., "Race and Constitutional Change in the Twentieth Century: The Role of the Executive," in John Hope Franklin and Genna Rae MacNeil, eds., *African Americans and the Living Constitution* (Washington: Smithsonian Institution Press, 1995): 117–43.

20. Arthur Schlesinger, Jr., "Rating the Presidents: From Washington to Clinton," *Political Science Quarterly* 112 (1997): 179–90.

21. Kenneth O'Reilly, *Nixon's Piano: Presidents and Racial Politics from Washington to Clinton* (New York: Free Press, 1995). O'Reilly argues that Andrew Jackson was the "first (and arguably the only) chief executive in American history not to consider slavery a moral evil" (p. 31).

22. Ibid., chap. 1.

23. Quoted in William Freehling, "The Founding Fathers and Slavery," *American Historical Review* 77 (1972): 396.

24. O'Reilly, *Nixon's Piano*, p. 135.

25. Samuel Tilden, governor of New York, apparently won a majority of the vote for president but the Republicans controlled enough southern electoral votes to

give the presidency to Hayes in exchange for his promise to withdraw federal troops and leave the South alone with respect to the treatment of blacks. See C. Vann Woodward, *Reunion and Reaction: The Compromise of 1877 and the End of Reconstruction* (Garden City, NY: Doubleday, 1956).

26. Harrison's support for antilynching legislation came about not as a result of the lynching of blacks, but rather after eleven Italian citizens were lynched in New Orleans. The Italian government filed a strong protest and Harrison responded with his proposed legislation. See O'Reilly's *Nixon's Piano*, p. 59.

27. Ibid., p. 111. Roosevelt was even reluctant to send a written message to the annual NAACP convention.

28. Louis Ruchames, *Race, Jobs and Politics: The Story of FEPC* (New York: Columbia University Press, 1953).

29. See Mary Dudziak, "Desegregation as a Cold War Imperative," *Stanford Law Review* 41 (1988): 1147–75.

30. As Franklin Roosevelt had feared, Truman's support did cost him the support of white southern Democrats, who walked out of the 1948 convention, formed a third party, and ran Strom Thurmond for president. Thurmond carried five deep southern states.

31. See John Ehrlichman, *Witness to Power* (New York: Auburn House, 1982): 222–23, and O'Reilly, *Nixon's Piano*, chap. 7.

32. Daniel P. Moynihan, *The Politics of a Guaranteed Income: The Nixon Administration and the Family Assistance Plan* (New York: Vintage Books, 1973).

33. O'Reilly, *Nixon's Piano,* chap. 7, and Hugh Davis Graham, *The Civil Rights Era: Origin and Development of National Policy* (New York: Oxford University Press, 1990): chaps. 12–14.

34. Robert C. Smith, "Black Elected Officials: A Neglected Category of Political Participation Research," *Journal of Black Studies* 14 (March 1984): 369–88.

35. Eleanor Holmes Norton, "The Role of Black Presidential Appointees," *Urban League Review* 9 (Summer 1985): 108–09.

36. Harold Wolman and Astrid A. E. Merget, "The President and Policy Formulation: President Carter and Urban Policy," *Presidential Studies Quarterly* 10 (1980): 402–15, and Robert C. Smith, *We Have No Leaders: African Americans in the Post–Civil Rights Era* (Albany: State University of New York Press, 1996): 149–51.

37. On Bush's flip-flop on the 1990 and 1991 civil rights bills, see Smith's, *We Have No Leaders*, pp. 170–82.

38. Arch Parsons, "Thomas Nomination Divides the Black Community," *West County Times*, July 28, 1991.

39. Robert Pear, "Administration Rejects Proposals for New Anti-Poverty Programs," *New York Times*, July 6, 1990.

40. O'Reilly, *Nixon's Piano*, chap. 9.

41. See O'Reilly, *Nixon's Piano,* and Smith, *We Have No Leaders*, chap. 9, for discussion of Clinton's electoral strategy.

42. "President Clinton Journeys to Africa," *Jet*, April 20, 1998.

43. "Presidents' Panel on Race, Issues Report: Urges U.S. to Face Up to Legacy of Racism," *Jet*, October 5, 1998, pp. 4–6.

CHAPTER 13

The Supreme Court and the African American Quest for Universal Freedom

The question is simply this: can a Negro, whose ancestors were imported into this country, and sold as slaves, become a member of the political community formed and brought into existence by the Constitution of the United States, and as such become entitled to all the rights, and privileges, and immunities, granted by that instrument to the citizens. . . . We think they are not, and they are not included, were not intended to be included, under the word "citizen" in the Constitution, and can therefore claim none of the rights and privileges which that instrument provides for and secures to citizens of the United States. On the contrary, they were at that time [1787] considered as a subordinate and inferior class of beings, who had been subjugated by the dominant race, and, whether emancipated or not, yet remained subject to their authority, and had no rights or privileges but such as those who held the power and the government might choose to grant them.

—Chief Justice Roger B. Taney[1]

We begin this chapter with an excerpt from Chief Justice Taney's remarkable opinion in *Dred Scott v. Sanford.* The Dred Scott decision is historically important because that case marks the first time in the seventy-year history of the Court that it squarely addressed the rights of the African people in the United States, holding that they had no rights—none whatsoever—except those that white people might choose to give them.[2] For the next seventy years of its history, the Court ignored the rights and freedoms of Africans, in spite of the adoption of the Civil War amendments to the Constitution, which granted citizenship to blacks and guaranteed universal rights and freedoms.[3] Then beginning in the 1940s and lasting until the 1980s, the Supreme Court in a series of cases began slowly to enforce the Constitution's guarantees of universal rights and freedoms. Except for this remarkable forty-year period—1940s–1980s—the Supreme

214

Court historically has been a racist institution, refusing to support universal freedom for African Americans. On the contrary, as in the Dred Scott case, for much of its more than two hundred years the Court has taken the position that the rights of African Americans were not universal but rather existed only as whites might "choose to grant them." And it now appears, as the Court approaches its third century, that it may once again be reverting to its racist past.[4]

The Supreme Court of the United States is a political institution. That is, unlike the courts in most nations, the courts in the United States are not simply legal institutions deciding questions of innocence or guilt in criminal cases or liability in civil cases. Rather, as Professor Robert Dahl writes, "To consider the Supreme Court of the United States strictly as a legal institution is to underestimate its significance in the American political system. For it is also a political institution, an institution, that is to say, for arriving at decisions on controversial questions of national policy."[5] And in its decisions on controversial issues of national policy, the Court responds slowly but surely to public opinion and the fundamental currents of national election majorities. Thus, if the Supreme Court is reverting to racism, it may be reflecting its understanding of public opinion and the outcome of five of the last seven presidential elections, which were won by candidates hostile to the black quest for universal freedom. Or in the famous words of humorist Finley Peter Dunne's "Mr. Dooley," "The Supreme Court follows the election returns."

The Warren Court (circa 1960), the most pro–universal freedom Court in the history of the United States.

JUDICIAL APPOINTMENTS AND AFRICAN AMERICANS

President Franklin Roosevelt was the first president to appoint a black person to the federal courts, naming William Hastie as a judge in the Virgin Islands. President Kennedy appointed three black judges to the federal courts; President Johnson named seven; and President Nixon, three.[6] Generally, appointments to the courts are based on party and ideology. That is, American presidents and senators tend to select judges of their party, who share their ideology whether liberal or conservative. This means that African Americans who tend to be liberal Democrats are more likely to receive judicial appointments from Democratic presidents. This trend is shown in Table 13.1. In the Carter administration, 13.9 percent of all judicial appointments were black, and in the Clinton administration's first term, the figure was 19.5 percent. In the Reagan administration, however, 2.1 percent of the appointees were black, and in the Bush administration the figure was 6.8 percent.

HOW SHOULD THE CONSTITUTION BE INTERPRETED: JUDICIAL RESTRAINT VERSUS JUDICIAL ACTIVISM AND THE IMPLICATIONS FOR UNIVERSAL FREEDOM

Throughout the Court's history, but especially in the twentieth century, there has been a debate between scholars, politicians, and judges over how the Constitution should be interpreted. Conservative scholars and jurists tend to favor *judicial self-restraint* or "strict constructionism." That is, they argue that justices and judges should look to the intent of the framers of the Constitution and precedents in interpreting the Constitution rather than applying their own political values or changing the Constitution to fit the needs of a changing society. By contrast, liberal scholars and jurists tend to favor *judicial activism* or "loose constructionism." That is, they argue that the intent of the framers on many issues is vague and unclear, and that the framers designed the Constitution as a "living" document to be interpreted broadly to fit the needs of a changing society.[7]

Although an important legal and political debate, it is in some ways misleading since at times liberals have favored judicial restraint and conservatives have favored

---

──────────────────────── **TABLE 13.1** ────────────────────────

Percentage of African American Appointees to the Federal Courts, from the Carter to the Clinton Administrations

Carter	13.9%	(28)[a]
Reagan	2.1	(6)
Bush	6.8	(10)
Clinton	19.5	(33)

[a]The numbers in parentheses represent the number of appointments of black judges in each administration.

Source: Sheldon Goldman and E. Slotnick, "Clinton's First Term Judiciary: Many Bridges to Cross," *Judicature* 80 (1997): 254–73.

activism. For example, an important principle of conservative jurisprudence is that the courts should adhere to precedent (stari decisis) and not overturn the decisions of democratically elected legislative bodies unless they clearly violate the Constitution. Yet, the current conservative majority on the Supreme Court has in recent years been active in overturning precedents and congressional and state legislative acts in the areas of commerce, affirmative action, and voting rights. The liberal bloc led by Justice John Paul Stevens, on the other hand, in its dissents has called for restraint, adherence to precedents, and deference to legislative majorities. Thus, whether one is for "strict" or "loose" interpretation depends, as the saying goes, "on whose ox is gored."

Table 13.2 lists the number of federal and state laws declared unconstitutional from 1800 to 1990. The data in the table show that there have been two periods of

TABLE 13.2

Number of Federal, State, and Local Laws Declared Unconstitutional by the Supreme Court, 1800–1990

YEARS	FEDERAL LAWS	STATE AND LOCAL LAWS
1800–1809	1	1
1810–1819	0	7
1820–1829	0	8
1830–1839	0	3
1840–1849	0	9
1850–1859	1	7
1860–1869	4	23
1870–1879	7	36
1880–1889	4	46
1890–1899	5	36
1900–1909	9	40
1910–1919[a]	6	118
1920–1929	15	139
1930–1939	13	93
1940–1949	2	58
1950–1959[a]	5	60
1960–1969	16	149
1970–1979	20	193
1980–1990	18	125
TOTAL	126	1,151

[a]Periods of judicial activism.

Source: Calculated by the authors from Lawrence Baum, *The Supreme Court,* 4th ed. (Washington: Congressional Quarterly Press, 1992).

sustained judicial activism: from 1910 to 1940, and from 1950 to 1990. In the first period, a conservative Supreme Court declared unconstitutional twenty-six federal laws and 350 state laws. This represents 26 percent of all the federal laws and 30 percent of all the state laws declared unconstitutional in the entire history of the Court. This spate of judicial activism involved a conservative Court overturning a series of progressive reforms regulating private property and the industrial economy. The second period of judicial activism involved a liberal Supreme Court overturning state and federal laws that restricted civil rights, liberties, and freedoms. In this period, forty-one federal laws and 402 state laws were declared unconstitutional, representing 32 percent and 35 percent, respectively, of all federal and state laws declared unconstitutional by the Court.

For African Americans and their quest for universal freedom, the debate on how the Constitution should be interpreted depends on the context and the times. In the post-Reconstruction era, when the Court ignored the intent of the framers of the Fourteenth and Fifteenth Amendments and declared unconstitutional several civil rights laws, black interests would have been served by judicial self-restraint. But in the 1960s and 1970s, black interests were served when the Court for the first time began to enforce the Fourteenth and Fifteenth Amendments by declaring state laws unconstitutional and upholding federal civil rights laws. As a result of the activism of the Court under Chief Justice Warren's leadership, liberals and progressives came to view the Court as a defender of minority rights. Historically, however, the Warren Court is an anomaly since for much of the Court's history it has been a racist, antifreedom institution. The legal scholar Girardeau Spann argues that this racist, antiminority stance of the Court is "structurally" inevitable. He writes:

> My argument is that, for structural reasons, the institutional role that the Court is destined to play within our constitutional scheme of government is the role of assuring the continued subordination of racial minority interests. I believe that this subordination function is inevitable; that it will be served irrespective of the Court's composition at any particular point in time; and that it will persist irrespective of the conscious motives of the individual justices.[8]

THE SUPREME COURT AND AFRICAN AMERICANS: RIGHTS-BASED AND MATERIAL-BASED CASES

The Supreme Court was transformed into a liberal institution beginning with the New Deal. President Roosevelt appointed nine justices to the Court and his successor President Truman appointed four. Most of the Roosevelt and Truman appointees were more or less liberal, as were the four appointees of President Eisenhower, including Chief Justice Warren. This liberal tendency of the Court was consolidated by the four appointments of Presidents Kennedy and Johnson. Among the leading liberal jurists appointed to the Court from the 1930s to the 1960s were Hugo Black, William O. Douglas, William Brennan, Arthur Goldberg, Thurgood Marshall, and Abe Fortas. As a result, by the late 1940s the Court was in the process of shifting its jurisprudence from a focus on protecting property rights and business interests toward a concern with individual civil liberties and the civil rights of minorities.[9]

Simultaneous with this transformation of the Court, the NAACP transformed its approach to civil rights from lobbying to litigation. In 1939 the NAACP Legal Defense Fund was created and under the leadership of Thurgood Marshall it developed a systematic strategy of using the courts to achieve social change and racial justice, a strategy later employed by many other American groups (see Box 13.1). This strategy was enormously successful, as the Court during the 1960s and early 1970s issued a number of landmark rulings expanding the rights of blacks, other ethnic minorities, women, atheists, communists, and persons accused of crimes.

These successes, however, brought reactions from conservative and racist forces (during the 1950s and 1960s there were billboards throughout the South reading "Impeach Earl Warren"), and conservative Republican presidents began to campaign against the Court's "liberal activism" and promise to appoint "strict constructionists" as justices. Between 1969 and 1991, Presidents Nixon, Ford, Reagan, and Bush appointed eleven justices to the Court. By the late 1980s, as a result of these appointments, the Supreme Court had a narrow five-person conservative majority (see Table 13.3). Immediately, this majority, led by Chief Justice William Rehnquist, began to retreat from the civil rights reforms of the 1960s and 1970s (see Box 13.2, Box 13.3). We examine this retreat on rights and material-based cases in an analysis of the last three decades of Supreme Court decision making on school desegregation, voting rights, and affirmative action.

─────────────── **TABLE 13.3** ───────────────

Justices of the Supreme Court by Ideological Inclination, 1996–1997

JUSTICE	NOMINATED BY
STRICT CONSERVATIVE[a]	
Chief Justice William Rehnquist	Ronald Reagan (1986)
Antonin Scalia	Ronald Reagan (1986)
Clarence Thomas	George Bush (1991)
MODERATE CONSERVATIVE	
Sandra Day O'Connor	Ronald Reagan (1981)
Anthony Kennedy	Ronald Reagan (1988)
MODERATE LIBERAL	
John Paul Stevens	Gerald Ford (1975)
David Souter	George Bush (1990)
Ruth Bader Ginsberg	Bill Clinton (1993)
Stephen Breyer	Bill Clinton (1994)

[a]These classifications are not fixed or inflexible; rather, they vary to some extent by the type of case. But on civil rights cases, the five conservatives and four moderate liberals vote as fairly consistent blocs. On other cases (abortion, for example), Justices O'Connor and Kennedy are frequently the swing votes. The year in parentheses refers to the year of the justice's appointment.

━━━━━━━━━━━━━━━━━━━━ **BOX 13.1** ━━━━━━━━━━━━━━━━━━━━

Litigation and Social Change: The Legacy of *Brown*

In chapter 7 we discussed how the African American civil rights and black power movements of the 1960s and 1970s sparked and served as a model for social movements among women, gays, and other minorities. The success of the NAACP Legal Defense Fund's litigation strategy in the *Brown v. Board of Education* case also led other groups in the United States to create organizations and develop strategies using litigation to bring about social change.[a]

Thurgood Marshall, George Hayes, and James Nabrit outside Supreme Court after it announced its landmark decision in *Brown* v. *Board of Education.*

Following the NAACP model, in the late 1960s scores of groups organized legal defense funds—women, Mexican Americans, Puerto Ricans, Asian Americans, gays and lesbians, and evangelical Christians. Once organized, these groups followed the strategy pioneered by Thurgood Marshall of bringing a series of well-researched, strategically selected "test cases" before the Court to force the Supreme Court to establish new rights and expand the idea of freedom.

Supreme Court Justice Ruth Bader Ginsberg is sometimes referred to as the "Thurgood Marshall of the women's movement" for her work as an attorney on women's legal projects in the 1960s and 1970s; these were projects that led to an expansion of women's rights and freedoms, including the critical right of a woman to choose an abortion. As a result of the litigation, new rights have been established for the elderly, the poor, language minorities, immigrants, environmentalists, and the handicapped.

The NAACP turned to the Courts in the 1930s to pursue its civil rights agenda because its leaders felt relatively powerless in the ordinary politics of lobbying Congress and the president. Other groups, also feeling powerless and seeing the success of the NAACP in *Brown,* also turned to the Courts, and the process significantly expanded the idea of universal freedom.[b]

---

[a]See Clement Vose, "Litigation as a Form of Pressure Group Activity," *The Annals of the American Academy of Social and Political Science* 319 (September 1958): 20–31, and Karen O'Connor, *Women's Organizations' Use of the Courts* (Lexington, MA: Lexington Books, 1980).

[b]In recent years, right-wing conservative and religious groups have also adopted the NAACP approach to litigation, filing strategic test cases, for example, on voting rights and affirmative action.

═══════════════ **BOX 13.2** ═══════════════

To Be Young, White, and Male:
The Supreme Court Record on Equal Employment Opportunity

A principal responsibility of the Supreme Court in the post–civil rights era is to decide cases involving implementation of the 1964 Civil Rights Act's prohibition on employment discrimination. And in its affirmative action jurisprudence, the Court has to deal with issues of "diversity"—the extent to which universities and employers may take race and gender into account in creating a workplace and university class that reflects the diverse ethnic and racial makeup of the nation.

Although the Supreme Court is the ultimate judge of equal employment and affirmative action for the nation, its own record on these matters is itself suspect. Indeed, under ordinary circumstances, the Court's record might lead to its being sued for violations of the Civil Rights Act and for failure to achieve a diverse workplace (the Court is, of course, exempt from such suits).

Each year, each of the nine justices is allowed to select up to four clerks to serve for a one-year term. These young persons—usually selected from among the best students at the nation's elite law schools—play an influential role in screening cases the Court will hear, in doing research, and in writing draft opinions for the justices. Thus, these clerks play powerful behind-the-scenes roles in shaping the kinds of cases the Court will hear and the legal rationales and scope of its opinions.[a]

In 1998, *USA Today* conducted the first ever demographic study of Supreme Court law clerks.[b] The study found that this elite of the Court's workforce was largely composed of young white males. Specifically, the study found that of the 394 clerks hired during the tenure of the current justices (from 1972 to 1998), 1.8 percent were black, 1 percent were Latino, and 4.5 percent were Asian Americans.[c] Four of the nine justices (including the chief justice, who has served on the Court for more than a quarter of a century) have never hired a black clerk. The table below shows the percentage of white clerks appointed by the current justices.

Percentage of Whites Hired as Clerks by Justices of the Supreme Court[*]

JUSTICE	NUMBER OF CLERKS	PERCENTAGE WHITE
Rehnquist	79	99%
Stevens	58	86
O'Connor	68	91
Scalia	48	100
Kennedy	45	91
Souter	31	94
Thomas	29	86
Ginsberg	20	90
Breyer	16	80

[*]The Justices are listed by length of service on the Court. These data are reported in Tony Mauro, "Schools Urged to Press for Diversity in Court Clerkships," *USA Today*, May 8–10, 1998, p. 4A. In the 1997–98 term, none of the clerks were black.

(Continued)

BOX 13.2 Continued

[a]The screening of cases is an especially important role. For example, typically more than 5,000 cases are appealed to the Court annually but it usually hears fewer than a hundred.

[b]In 1996, as part of the research for this book, we tried unsuccessfully to obtain data on the racial composition of the Court's clerks. We were told by the Office of the Clerk of the Court that such information was not available either from the Clerk's office or the chambers of the individual justices. The results of the USA Today study are reported in Tony Mauro, "Court Faulted on Diversity," May 8–10, 1998 p. A1.

[c]Seventy-five percent of the clerks during this period were men.

BOX 13.3
The Chief Justice and Race Matters

William Hubbs Rehnquist, chief justice of the United States, is a man with long-held and consistent views on race matters, and those views have been consistently hostile to the quest of African Americans for universal freedom and equality. Appointed associate justice by Richard Nixon in 1972 and chief justice by Ronald Reagan in 1986, Rehnquist, in his twenty-five years on the Court, has consistently ruled against the rights of African Americans and working people. His hostile views on race matters may be traced to his days as a young law school graduate serving as a clerk to Justice Robert Jackson in 1953, the year the *Brown v. Board of Education* was argued.

When Rehnquist was nominated to the Court, *Newsweek* published a memorandum written by Rehnquist titled "A Random Thought on the Segregation Cases." In it the future chief justice argued that the Supreme Court could not protect the rights of minorities and that the Court should vote to uphold *Plessy v. Ferguson* and the principle of racial segregation. Specifically the memorandum read, "I realize it is an unpopular and unhumanitarian position, for which I have been excoriated by 'liberal' colleagues but I think *Plessy v. Ferguson* was right and should be re-affirmed."[a] When this memorandum became public, there was substantial and growing opposition to Senate approval of the Rehnquist nomination. He, therefore, sent a letter to the Senate admitting that he had written the memorandum but that it was written at Justice Jackson's request to reflect Jackson's, not his, views (Justice Jackson was by now deceased). Rehnquist also told the Senate that in *1971* he supported the *Brown* decision. But after careful study of the evidence, Richard Kluger, the historian of the *Brown* decision, concluded that the chief justice probably lied to the Senate. Kluger writes, "Taking the careers and judicial assertions of both men in their totality, one finds a preponderance of evidence to suggest that the memorandum in question—the one that threatened to deprive William Rehnquist of his place on the Supreme Court—was an accurate statement of his views on segregation, not those of Robert Jackson, who by contrast was a staunch libertarian and humanist."[b] Kluger's conclusion is also supported by Rehnquist's statement to the Senate that he supported *Brown* in 1971, not necessarily in 1953 or 1954. In addition, in 1986 during his confirmation hearings to become chief justice, Rehnquist told an astonished Senator Joseph Biden, chairman of the Judiciary Committee, that he was not convinced that *Brown* was correctly decided and moreover was not certain how he would have voted on the case if he had been on the Court in 1954.

Other evidence of the chief justice's racial animus include his opposition to a Phoenix public accommodation bill because it deprived white property owners of the "liberty" to choose their customers; his opposition in 1967 to the desegregation of the Phoenix schools; and his participation in a program to intimidate minority voters in Arizona. And as an assistant attorney general in the Nixon administration, Rehnquist drafted a memorandum calling for a constitutional amendment banning busing for purposes of school desegregation.

aQuoted in Richard Kluger, *Simple Justice: The History of* Brown v. Board of Education (New York: Vintage Books, 1977): 606.
bIbid., p. 609.

RIGHTS-BASED CASES

School Desegregation

In 1954 the Supreme Court, in a unanimous decision written by Chief Justice Warren, in effect overruled its decision in the 1896 *Plessy v. Ferguson* case by declaring that, at least in the area of public education, the principle of "separate but equal" violated the equal protection clause of the Fourteenth Amendment.[10] "Separate educational facilities," the Chief Justice wrote are *"inherently unequal"* (emphasis added). The *Plessy* decision dealt with segregation on railroad cars but thereafter it was applied to all areas of southern life, including public schools.

Although, according to the Court, separate was constitutionally permissible only if facilities for blacks and whites were equal, the equality part of the principle was never enforced. Three years after *Plessy* in *Cummings v. Richmond County Board of Education,* the Court held that it was permissible to provide a high school for whites but not for blacks.[11] Thus, the doctrine of equality in *Plessy* was a lie. *African Americans in violation of the Court's own decision were relegated to separate and unequal schools and other facilities.* The initial strategy of the NAACP, therefore, was to attack not the practice of segregation itself but rather the absence of equality in the education of blacks.

This attack on unequal educational opportunities began at the graduate and professional levels. In 1938 in *Missouri ex rel. Gaines v. Canada,* the Court invalidated Missouri's policy of excluding blacks from its law school and instead offering to pay for their attendance at out-of-state law schools.[12] In *Sweatt v. Painter* (1939) the Court found that Texas's all-black law school was "inherently inferior" to its school for whites and ordered the admission of blacks to the white school.[13] And in *McLaurin v. Oklahoma State Regents,* the Court ruled that Oklahoma State University's practice of segregating black students in its graduate school was unconstitutional.[14] After these victories at the graduate level, the NAACP, after extensive research and debate, changed its strategy and decided to launch a direct attack on the doctrine of separate but equal.[15] The result was the Court's 1954 *Brown* decision.

When the Court declared that segregated schools were unconstitutional it did not order the schools to be integrated. Rather, a year later, in what is called *"Brown II,"* the Court ordered the states practicing segregation in public education to "desegregate" with "all deliberate speed."[16] In other words, the states were told to take their time; to desegregate the schools, but slowly. It was not until 1969 in *Alexander v. Holmes County Board of Education* that the Court ordered the states to desegregate the schools "at once."[17] Only after this decision—some fifteen years after *Brown*—did most southern school begin to desegregate their separate and unequal schools.[18]

In 1971, in *Swann v. Charlotte Mecklenburg,* the Court ordered school districts to use busing to achieve racial balance or quotas so that "pupils of all grades be assigned in such a way that as nearly as practicable the various schools at various grade levels have about the same proportion of black and white students."[19] Then, in *Keyes v. School District #1, Denver, Colorado,* the Court ruled that even if a school district had never practiced de jure (legal) segregation, it could violate the principles of *Brown* by practicing de facto segregation—that is, segregation in practice or fact. Specifically, in a 7–1 decision (with Justice Rehnquist dissenting and Justice White not participating because he was a former Colorado resident), the Court held that although Denver had never maintained de jure segregation, it had deliberately created a separate and unequal school system through a strategy of locating schools and drawing boundary lines in such a way as to place blacks in separate schools with the oldest books and the least experienced teachers.[20] The Court then ordered, as it had in the *Swann* case, that Denver bus black and white students to achieve racial balance in all its schools. The principles of the *Keyes* case were soon applied nationwide, leading to an enormous political controversy and eventually a decision by the Court to reverse its position and put an end to school busing.[21]

Busing for purposes of school desegregation was overwhelmingly opposed by white Americans (in the range of 75% to 80%); African American opinion was about equally divided, with polls showing about half supporting busing. In many cities, court-ordered busing led to mass protests by whites, boycotts, violence, and "white flight" to private or suburban schools. George Wallace, Richard Nixon, and Ronald Reagan made opposition to busing a major theme in their presidential campaigns, and conservative and liberal members of Congress, north and south, began to introduce legislation to stop the courts from ordering busing. Presidents Nixon and Ford proposed similar legislation, and in 1974, the House, by a vote of 281 to 128, passed a bill prohibiting the courts from ordering busing for purposes of school desegregation. It also required the courts to re-open any existing case, no matter how long settled, that did not comply with this prohibition. The Senate in a narrow 47 to 46 vote rejected the House bill and instead adopted an amendment prohibiting busing unless the courts found that it was "needed to guarantee a black child his constitutional rights"—a prohibition that in effect transformed the House bill into a nonbinding suggestion to the courts.[22]

In *Milliken v. Bradley,* the Supreme Court took the Senate's suggestion and began the process of dismantling busing for purposes of desegregation. Specifically, the Court overturned a lower court order that required busing between largely black Detroit and the largely white surrounding suburbs. The Court majority agreed that Detroit's schools were unconstitutionally segregated but held that cross-district busing between city and suburbs was not required to comply with *Brown*.[23] In an angry dissenting opinion, Justice

Thurgood Marshall accused his colleagues of bowing to political pressure and of being unwilling to enforce school busing because it was unpopular with the white majority.

Since *Milliken,* the court has continued to retreat from busing as a device to desegregate the schools. In Denver, for example, although the schools are more segregated now than when the *Keyes* decision was handed down in 1973, a federal judge (with the approval of the Supreme Court) has allowed the city to abandon its twenty-year-old school busing program and return to neighborhood schools.[24] And in *Missouri et al. v. Jenkins,* a narrow 5 to 4 majority overruled a lower court ruling requiring the Kansas city school district to increase teacher salaries and fund remedial "quality" education programs to attract white students into the system.[25]

Because of white flight to the suburbs, America's urban school systems cannot be desegregated unless there is cross-district busing between city and suburbs. The Supreme Court, however, will not permit this. Thus, forty years after *Brown,* most African American school children remain in schools that are separate and unequal—inequalities that are so great that one observer describes them as "savage."[26]

Because school integration cannot be achieved, a number of black educators are now calling for a return to separate, adequately funded all-black schools.[27] This is not a new idea. As early as 1970 black nationalist groups like CORE called for separate black schools as an alternative to busing, rejecting the idea of Chief Justice Warren that separate schools are "inherently unequal."[28] What is new is the rejection of the ideal and goal of school integration by mainstream establishment black educators and political leaders. In his concurring opinion in *Missouri v. Jenkins,* Justice Clarence Thomas wrote:

> Mere de facto segregation (unaccompanied by discriminatory inequalities in educational resources) does not constitute a continuing harm after the end of de jure segregation. Racial isolation itself is not a harm; only state enforced segregation is. After all, if separation itself is harm, and if integration therefore is the only way that blacks can receive a proper education, then there must be something inferior about blacks. Under this theory segregation injures because blacks when left on their own, cannot achieve. To my way of thinking, that conclusion is the result of a jurisprudence based on a theory of black inferiority.[29]

Apparently, the goal of a common, universal school system for all Americans without regard to race is an idea whose time has come and gone. This means that for the foreseeable future, neither the country nor the courts are prepared to end the practice of racially separate and unequal education.[30]

Voting Rights and Racial Representation

Prior to the passage of the Voting Rights Act in 1965, very few African Americans were elected to office in the United States. In that year, approximately 280 blacks held elected office in this country, including six members of Congress. Today there are more than 7,000 black elected officeholders, including thirty-eight members of Congress.[31] Thus, blacks in the last twenty-five years have made considerable progress in their quest for public office; however, 7,000 offices constitute a minuscule 1.5 percent of the more than 500,000 elective offices in the United States. And even this tiny number of blacks holding elected office may be in jeopardy as a result of recent Supreme Court interpretations of the Voting Rights Act.

When the Voting Rights Act was passed, it was initially used to guarantee southern blacks the simple right to cast a vote. However, in the late 1960s, the Supreme Court issued a series of decisions interpreting various provisions of the Act as guaranteeing not just the simple right to vote but also the right to cast an effective vote—a vote that would allow African Americans to choose candidates of their choice, presumably one of their own race.[32] The key case in this regard is *United Jewish Organizations v. Carey.*[33]

In 1972, the New York State Legislature redrew Brooklyn's state senate and assembly districts so that several would have black and Puerto Rican majorities ranging from 65 percent to 90 percent. In doing this, the Legislature divided a cohesive community of Hasidic Jews between separate assembly and senate districts in the Williamsburg section of Brooklyn, where previously they had been located within single districts. The Hasidic Jews alleged that the creation of the majority-minority districts was "reverse discrimination" against whites, and the United Jewish Organizations of Williamsburg filed suit, claiming that the New York Legislature's actions violated the Fourteenth Amendment's equal protection clause.

In a 7–1 decision (Chief Justice Warren Burger dissenting), the Supreme Court rejected the claims of the Hasidic Jews, holding that deliberate creation of majority-minority legislative districts was not reverse discrimination and therefore did not violate the equal rights of Brooklyn's white voters. Writing for the majority, Justice White noted that whites made up 65 percent of Brooklyn's population and were majorities in 70 percent of its senate and assembly districts. Therefore, "as long as whites, as a group, were provided with fair representation, we can not conclude that there was a cognizable discrimination against whites or an abridgment of their right to vote."[34] In 1993 in *Shaw v. Reno,* the Supreme Court in effect reversed its holding in *Carey,* deciding that the deliberate creation of majority black districts might indeed violate the equal protection rights of white voters.[35]

After the 1990 census, most of the southern states, following the precedent established in *Carey,* created twelve new majority black congressional districts. These districts in turn elected twelve new black congresspersons. In several states (North Carolina, South Carolina, Florida, Alabama, and Virginia) this was the first time a black had been elected to Congress since Reconstruction. In North Carolina, several white voters sued, alleging as did the Hasidic Jews in Brooklyn two decades earlier, that the creation of the black districts was "reverse discrimination" and a violation of the Fourteenth Amendment's equal protection clause.

In *Shaw,* a narrow 5 to 4 majority of the Court agreed with North Carolina's white voters. Writing for the majority, Justice O'Connor held that the North Carolina districts were unconstitutional because they were irregularly shaped. (The 12th district in North Carolina stretches approximately 160 miles along Interstate 85 and for much of its length is no wider than the I-85 corridor.) Justice O'Connor said the districts were "so extremely irregular on [their] face . . . that they rationally can be viewed as an effort to segregate the races for purposes of voting." Such segregation, Justice O'Connor wrote, "reinforces the perception that members of the same racial group—regardless of their age, education, economic status or the community in which they live—think alike, share the same political interests and will prefer the same candidate. We have rejected such perceptions elsewhere as impermissible racial stereotyping."[36]

Justice White, who wrote the majority opinion in *Carey*, said in his dissent in *Shaw* that his colleagues chose "not to overrule but side step" the *Carey* precedent. Justice White rejected the claims of North Carolina whites for the same reason he rejected the claims of white voters in Brooklyn in 1977. He wrote "under the state's plan, they [whites] still constitute a voting majority in 10 (or 83 percent) of the 12 congressional districts. Though they might be dissatisfied at the prospect of casting a vote for a losing candidate—a lot shared by many, including a disproportionate number of minority voters—surely they can not complain of discriminatory treatment."[37] In his dissent, Justice Stevens pointed out the irony and perversity of the situation in which the Fourteenth Amendment, which was enacted to protect the rights of African Americans, was being used in this case to deny them rights and representation. He wrote:

> If it is permissible to draw boundaries to provide adequate representation for rural voters, for union members, for Hasidic Jews, for Polish Americans or for Republicans, it necessarily follows that it is permissible to do the same thing for members of the very minority group whose history in the United States gave birth to the Equal Protection clause. A contrary conclusion could only be described as perverse.[38]

Following the *Shaw* decision, the lower federal courts began to strike down majority black districts throughout the South, including congressional districts in Texas, Georgia, Florida, and Louisiana.[39] As a result, five of the twelve new black congressional districts created in 1992 have been eliminated. If the Court's majority follows the logic of *Shaw* as it hears redistricting cases from other states, possibly more than a third of the thirty-eight existing majority black congressional districts could be eliminated. If this occurs, black representation in the House would be reduced from its 1992 high of 9 percent to about 5 percent or 6 percent, compared to a black population of 12 percent.[40]

The principles of *Shaw* are applicable to congressional districting but also to state and local offices. Thus, the consequence of the decision could be to reduce sharply the tiny 1.5 percent of blacks holding elected office. For example, in 1992 a federal judge acting under provisions of the Voting Rights Act ordered the state of Arkansas to create twelve majority black judicial districts. Prior to this decision, no African American had been elected as a judge in Arkansas in more than a hundred years. Since the decision, twelve have been elected. However, once *Shaw* was decided, these judicial districts were challenged (the suit was filed by two white lawyers on behalf of a Chinese American) on the basis of the equal protection clause. The Arkansas suit goes further than similar cases challenging majority black districts. It asks the Court to declare the entire Voting Rights Act unconstitutional.[41]

MATERIAL-BASED CASES: AFFIRMATIVE ACTION

The Supreme Court in the 1990s, like its counterpart in the 1880s, is clearly retreating from enforcement of the voting rights of African Americans as these relate to the right of African Americans to elect candidates of their choice to represent them.

The Court also appears to be in the process of dismantling affirmative action. Affirmative action encompasses a variety of policies and programs designed to assure African Americans (and other minorities and women) access to material benefits or rights in the areas of education, employment, and government contracts. These programs and policies were put into place in the late 1960s and early 1970s by the courts, Congress, the president, and many of the states for one or more of the following reasons: (1) to remedy or compensate African Americans for past discrimination, (2) to enforce or implement provisions of the 1964 Civil Rights Act, and (3) to create diversity in education, employment, and government contracting. These programs are now under attack by the conservative Republican leadership in Congress and at the state and local levels.[42] Leading this attack is the Supreme Court's five-person conservative majority. Below, we review the history of Supreme Court decision making on affirmative action in cases dealing with education, employment, and government contracting.

Education

In *Regents of the University of California v. Bakke,* the Supreme Court in a split decision upheld the constitutionality of affirmative action.[43] The case involved two issues: first, whether it was constitutionally permissible for a state to take race into account in allocating material benefits—in this specific case, access to medical school; second, if the use of race was permissible, whether the state could use a numerical racial quota to allocate these benefits (in *Bakke* this involved setting aside 16 of 100 slots for minority students only). In deciding the case, the Court was deeply divided, issuing six separate opinions. Four conservative justices led by Justice Rehnquist argued that the University of California program violated Title VII of the 1964 Civil Rights Act (which prohibits discrimination by institutions receiving federal funds) as well as the equal protection clause of the Fourteenth Amendment. In the view of these four justices, taking race into consideration in allocating material benefits was never permissible. Four liberal justices led by Justices Brennan and Marshall held that a state, in order to remedy past discrimination or create ethnic diversity, could take race into consideration in allocating benefits and could, if it wished, use a fixed quota. Justice Lewis Powell, the Court's only Southerner, split the difference between his liberal and conservative colleagues by holding that a state could use race for purposes of diversity but that a fixed quota was illegal and unconstitutional. Until recently this was the state of the law on affirmative action: affirmative action, yes; quotas, no.[44]

As a result of *Bakke,* colleges and universities across the country adopted affirmative action admission programs for African Americans, women, and other racial minorities. These programs are now in jeopardy as a result of two recent Supreme Court decisions. First, the Court declined to hear and therefore upheld the decision of the Fourth Circuit Court of Appeals that the University of Maryland's use of race to allocate scholarships was unconstitutional.[45] Second, the Court refused to hear an appeal of *Hopwood v. Texas;* this was a case decided by the Fifth Circuit Court of Appeals that declared unconstitutional the admission program for minorities of the University of Texas Law School. With this decision, the judges of the Fifth Circuit explicitly overruled *Bakke* by declaring that "*any* consideration of race or ethnicity for the purpose of achieving a diverse student body" is a violation of the Fourteenth Amendment (emphasis added).[46]

Despite the urgings of the Clinton administration, the Court refused to hear Texas's appeal of the case (often the Court will take cases if urged to do so by an administration). Thus, it may be that the Court's conservative majority agrees with the Fifth Circuit's overruling of *Bakke*. This position, however, is unclear since by the time the case reached the Court, Texas had changed its minority admissions program. The change led Justices Ginsberg and Souter to issue an unusual one-paragraph statement explaining that the Court refused to hear the case because it was "moot," noting that the law school had changed its affirmative action program.[47] Whether Justices Ginsberg and Souter are correct is not clear; in the meantime, the Fifth Circuit's decision abolishing affirmative action stands for Texas, Louisiana, and Mississippi, the three states covered by the circuit.

Employment

The equivalent to the *Bakke* case in the area of employment is *Griggs et al. v. Duke Power Company,* decided in 1971.[48] In this case, a unanimous Supreme Court struck down educational and test requirements that had a discriminatory impact on blacks seeking employment, unless such requirements could be shown to be necessary to the performance of the job. In *Wards Cove v. Atonio,* decided in 1989, the Supreme Court by a 5 to 4 vote in effect overruled *Griggs,* holding that a business could engage in racially discriminatory hiring practices if they served "legitimate employment goals."[49] Unlike the Court's decisions in the areas of affirmative action involving education and government contracts, which involved interpreting the Constitution, the employment cases involve interpreting a statute or law (specifically Title VII of the 1964 Civil Rights Act). Thus, the Congress could change the Court's decision by simply passing a new law. This it did in the 1991 Civil Right Act. Specifically, with respect to *Wards Cove,* the Congress reinstated the principles of *Griggs* by requiring that employee qualifications be nondiscriminatory and "job related for the position in question and consistent with business necessity."[50] However, the language of the 1991 Act is, according to lawyers specializing in employment discrimination, so riddled with confusing, contradictory, and ambiguous provisions that sorting it out will take years.[51] But since the Supreme Court's misinterpretation of the existing law is what made the 1991 act necessary in the first place, the Court may read the ambiguous new law in a way adverse to the interests of African Americans. Indeed, in 1993 the Court in *St. Mary's Honor Center v. Hicks* once again overturned two twenty-year-old precedents involving employment discrimination, leading Justice Souter in a dissenting opinion to warn his colleagues that they were ignoring the intent of Congress as expressed in the 1991 Civil Rights Act.[52] (See Box 13.4.)

Government Contracts

In 1977, to increase minority access to government contracts, Congress added a provision to the Public Works Act requiring that at least 10 percent of federal funds granted for local projects be awarded to minority-owned businesses. White businessmen challenged this 10 percent set-aside as an unconstitutional racial quota, but the Court in *Fullilove v. Klutznik* rejected their claims.[53] In *Fullilove* the Court held that

━━━━━━━━━━━━━━━━━ **BOX 13.4** ━━━━━━━━━━━━━━━
Buying Justice?

Although the Supreme Court's narrow five-person majority is clearly hostile to affirmative action, it has not completely repudiated the principle that the government may in limited circumstances take race and gender into account in allocating certain material benefits. African American leaders, however, apparently believe the current Court will do so if it gets the appropriate case. And apparently they thought the case of *Piscataway v. Taxman* was an appropriate case—a case the Court would use to declare the principle of affirmative action unconstitutional.

In 1989, the Board of Education in the Township of Piscataway, New Jersey, was forced to lay off one tenured teacher, for budgetary reasons. At the time, two of the teachers in the school's business department were equally qualified and had equal seniority, having been hired nine years earlier on the same day. One of the two, Debra Williams, was black; the other, Sharon Taxman, was white. In order to maintain "diversity" in the department, the board of education decided to lay off Taxman rather than Williams (if Williams had been dismissed, the school's eleven-person business department would have become all white). Taxman sued, claiming that the board's decision was based on race and was discriminatory and therefore violated Title VII of the 1964 Civil Rights Act and the equal protection clause of the Fourteenth Amendment. Both the federal district court and a divided Third Circuit Court of Appeals agreed with Taxman and ordered the board of education to rehire her and pay her $433,500 in back pay and legal fees. The Piscataway Board appealed this decision to the Supreme Court.

By the time the case reached the Supreme Court, Ms. Taxman had been rehired; thus, the only issue was the money she claimed in back pay and legal fees. Fearing that the Court would use this case to issue a broad ruling striking down all affirmative action programs, public and private, black leaders raised the more than 400,000 to persuade Taxman to drop the case. She took the money and the case was dropped.[a]

Although African American leaders anticipated an unfavorable decision in this case, what the Court would have decided is not clear. For example, two months after the *Piscataway* case was dropped, the Court, without comment, turned down the appeal of Yvette Farmer, a white college professor at the University of Nevada, who argued that she was the victim of illegal racial discrimination when the university deferred hiring her for a year in order to hire a black man. In rejecting her claims, the Nevada Supreme Court said the university was a "white enclave" and should be allowed the flexibility to take race into account to achieve a diverse faculty.[b] In any event, black leaders bought only a little time (perhaps hoping that the seventy-three-year-old chief justice will die or retire and be replaced by a more sympathetic Clinton appointee); eventually, another case will appear whose plaintiff cannot be bought. Indeed, there are several well-financed conservative foundations that are openly searching for test cases that will allow the Court to strike the final blow to affirmative action, if that is its inclination.

[a]Steven Holmes, "Rights Groups Work to Keep Preferences," *West County Times,* November 23, 1997.
[b]*Farmer v. University of Nevada,* #97-1104 (1997).

Congress, to remedy past discrimination, had the authority to establish the 10 percent set-aside as a reasonable method to assure minority access to contracts. In 1989 in *Metro Broadcasting v. Federal Communications Commission,* the Court upheld similar minority set-aside programs in the allocation of broadcast licenses.[54] Both these decisions have been overruled by the current conservative Court majority.

In 1983, Richmond, Virginia, established a minority set-aside program for its contracts modeled on the plan passed by Congress and approved by the Supreme Court in *Fullilove.* In *J. A. Croson v. City of Richmond,* the Court in a 5 to 4 decision declared the Richmond plan unconstitutional.[55] Writing for the majority, Justice O'Connor declared that Congress as a co-equal branch of government had the authority to establish such set-asides but the states and localities were prohibited by the Fourteenth Amendment's equal protection clause from doing so unless the plans were "narrowly tailored" to meet identified discriminatory practices. In one of his many angry dissents during his last years on the Court, Justice Marshall described his colleagues' overturning of Richmond's set-aside program as a "deliberate and giant step backward in this Court's affirmative action jurisprudence" that assumes "racial discrimination is largely a phenomenon of the past, and that governmental bodies need no longer preoccupy themselves with rectifying racial injustice."[56]

In *Croson,* Justice O'Connor implied that Congress had the authority to do what the city of Richmond could not do in remedying racial discrimination. Six years later, in *Adarand Constructors v. Pena,* she rejected this view and ruled that Congress had to follow the same strict standards as the states.[57] In *Adarand,* the Court, again by 5 to 4, overturned the *Fullilove* and *Metro Broadcasting* precedents. As a result of the Croson decision there has been a dramatic decline in minority access to contracts in Richmond and other states and localities.[58] A similar result may follow in the wake of *Adarand.* For example, after *Adarand,* President Clinton suspended most federal affirmative action programs that reserved contracts exclusively for minorities and women.[59]

SELECTED BIBLIOGRAPHY

Abraham, Henry. *The Judicial Process,* 4th ed. New York: Oxford University Press, 1980. A general overview of the judicial process in the United States, including local, state, and federal courts.

Dahl, Robert. "Decision Making in a Democracy: The Supreme Court as a National Policy Maker." *Journal of Public Law* 6 (Fall 1957): 257–88. A classic analysis of the Court's role in the political process.

Hall, Kermit, William Wiecek, and Paul Finkelman. *American Legal History: Cases and Materials.* New York: Oxford University Press, 1991. A nearly comprehensive collection of cases and commentary on the development of law in the United States, focusing on all areas of law including race and civil rights.

Howard, John R. *The Shifting Wind: The Supreme Court and Civil Rights from Reconstruction to Brown.* Albany: State University of New York Press, 1999. A sprightly and often moving analysis of the Court's role in pushing and subverting the African American quest for freedom. Especially valuable for its insights into the internal dynamics of Supreme Court decision making.

Leuctenburg, William. *The Supreme Court Reborn: The Constitutional Revolution in the Age of Roosevelt*. New York: Oxford University Press, 1995. A lucid account of the transformation of the Supreme Court into a liberal reform institution beginning with the New Deal and ending with the Warren Court.

Rosenberg, Gerald. *The Hollow Hope: Can Courts Bring about Social Change*. Chicago: University of Chicago Press, 1996. An analysis of the limited capacity of the courts to foster social change, including detailed study of school desegregation.

Spann, Girardeau. *Race against the Court: The Supreme Court and Minorities in America*. New York: New York University Press, 1993. An argument that the Supreme Court will enforce minority rights only to the extent that whites are not disadvantaged.

Vose, Clement. "Litigation as a Form of Pressure Group Activity." *The Annals of the American Academy of Political and Social Science* 319 (September, 1958): 20–31. The classic analysis of the use of litigation as a means of influencing the making of public policy.

Walton, Eugene. "Will the Supreme Court Revert to Racism?" *Black World* 21 (1972): 46–48. A cogent analysis of the racist history of the Court.

NOTES

1. *Dred Scott v. Sanford* 19 Howard (60 U.S.) 393, 1857, as cited in Kermit Hall, William Wiecek, and Paul Finkelman, eds., *American Legal History: Cases and Materials* (New York: Oxford University Press, 1991): 208.

2. Dred Scott was a slave residing in Illinois, a free state. When his owner returned to Missouri, a slave state, Scott argued that as a result of living in Illinois he had become free and remained free even in Missouri. The Supreme Court of Missouri rejected Scott's claims and he appealed to the Supreme Court of the United States, which upheld the decision of the Missouri court. Historians contend that this decision (described by Horace Greeley at the time as "wicked," "atrocious," "abominable" and "detestable hypocrisy") was one of the factors that helped to cause the civil war. Greeley is quoted in Hall, Wiecek, and Finkelman, *American Legal History*, p. 213.

3. J. Morgan Kouser, *Dead End: The Development of Nineteenth Century Litigation on Racial Discrimination* (New York: Oxford University Press, 1986).

4. Eugene Walton, "Will the Supreme Court Revert to Racism?" *Black World* 21 (1972): 46–48.

5. Robert Dahl, "Decision Making in a Democracy: The Supreme Court as a National Policy-Maker," *Journal of Public Law* 6 (Fall 1957): 281. In his analysis of the Court, Dahl concluded that its main function is to confer legitimacy on decisions taken by the political branches.

6. Robert C. Smith, "Black Appointed Officials: A Neglected Category of Political Participation Research," *Journal of Black Studies* 14 (March 1984): 375.

7. On this debate, see Edwin Meese (Reagan's attorney general, for the judicial self-restraint view), *The Great Debate: Interpreting Our Written Constitution*

(Washington: Federalist Society, 1986), and William Brennan (the former justice, for the activism view), *The Great Debate: Interpreting Our Written Constitution* (Washington: Federalist Society, 1986).

8. Girardeau Spann, *Race against the Court: The Supreme Court and Minorities in Contemporary America* (New York: New York University Press, 1993).
9. William Leuchtenburg, *The Supreme Court Reborn: The Constitutional Revolution in the Age of Roosevelt* (New York: Oxford University Press, 1995).
10. *Brown v. Board of Education,* 347 U.S. 483 (1954).
11. 175, U.S. 528 (1899).
12. 305 U.S. 337 (1938).
13. 339 U.S. 629 (1950).
14. 339 U.S. 737 (1950).
15. For detailed analysis of this strategy shift, see Richard Kluger, *Simple Justice: The History of* Brown v. Board of Education (New York: Vintage Books, 1977).
16. *Brown v. Board of Education,* 349 U.S. 294 (1955).
17. 392 U.S. 430 (1969).
18. In addition to the impact of the Court's unequivocal order in *Alexander v. Holmes,* southern school districts began to rapidly desegregate, because the 1964 Civil Rights Act provided that schools practicing racial segregation could not receive federal financial assistance. In 1969 the Nixon administration began to enforce this provision vigorously.
19. 402 U.S. 1 (1971).
20. 413 U.S. 189 (1973).
21. See Nicholas Mills, ed., *The Great School Bus Controversy* (New York: Teachers' College Press, 1973).
22. Spencer Rich, "Bus Ban Defeated 47 to 46," *Washington Post,* May 16, 1974, p. A1.
23. *Milliken v. Bradley* 418 U.S. 717 (1974).
24. James Brooke, "Court Allows Denver to End 21 Year Busing Experiment and Return to Neighborhood Schools," *New York Times,* September 17, 1995, p. A13.
25. *Missouri et al. v. Jenkins,* 115 S.Ct. 2038 (1995).
26. Jonathan Kozol, *Savage Inequalities: Children in America's Schools* (New York: Crown, 1991).
27. Derrick Bell, "The Case for a Separate Black School System," in W. Smith and E. Chunn, eds., *Black Education: A Quest for Equity and Excellence* (New Brunswick, NJ: Transaction, 1989): 136–45.
28. See Congress of Racial Equality, *A True Alternative to Segregation: A Proposal for Community School Districts* (New York: Congress of Racial Equality, 1970).
29. *Missouri et al. v. Jenkins.*
30. Georgia Persons, "Is Racial Separation Inevitable and Legal," *Society,* March/April 1996, pp. 19–24.
31. On the growth of black elected officials since the Voting Rights Act, see Theresa Chambliss, "The Growth and Significance of African American Elected Officials,"

in R. Gomes and L. Williams, eds., *From Exclusion to Inclusion* (Westport, CT: Praeger, 1992): 53–70.

32. For a review of these cases, see Robert C. Smith, "Liberal Jurisprudence and the Quest for Racial Representation," *Southern University Law Review* 15 (Spring 1988): 1–51.

33. 430 U.S., 144 (1977).

34. Ibid.

35. *Shaw v. Reno* 509 U.S. 690 (1993).

36. Ibid.

37. Ibid.

38. Ibid.

39. Linda Greenhouse, "High Court Voids Race Based Plans for Gerrymandering," *New York Times,* June 14, 1996, p. A1; and Kevin Sack, "Court Draws Georgia Map of Congressional Districts," *New York Times,* December 14, 1995, p. A14.

40. In the 1996 elections, each of the five black representatives in newly redrawn majority white districts were reelected. Perhaps the major reason for their electoral successes are the advantages of incumbency. Congresswoman Cynthia McKinney, reelected in Georgia, said that she would never have been elected without the advantages of incumbency deriving from her initial election in a majority black district. See Donna Brit, "Crossover Appeal Elected a Black Rep.," *West County Times,* November 21, 1996, p. 37.

41. Ronald Smothers, "Arkansas Plan to Promote Election of Black Judges Brings a Familiar Challenge," *New York Times,* December 14, 1995, p. A14.

42. In Louisiana, after his election in 1995, Republican governor Mike Foster issued an executive order banning affirmative action in state government.

43. 438 U.S. 265 (1978).

44. The Supreme Court has permitted the use of quotas in a limited number of cases to compel obedience among recalcitrant states and private institutions to the antidiscrimination provisions of the 1964 Civil Rights Act. See *Sheetmetal Workers International Association et al. v. EEOC* 478 U.S. 421 1986 (requiring a quota in the employment of black craft workers) and *United States v. Paradise* 480 U.S. 92, 1987 (requiring a quota in the hiring of Alabama highway patrolmen).

45. Steven Holmes, "Minority Scholarship Loans Are Dealt Setback by Court," *New York Times,* May 23, 1995, p. A1.

46. Quoted in Peter Applebome, "Ruling Threatens College Policies on Racial Entries," *New York Times,* March 21, 1996, p. A1.

47. Linda Greenhouse, "Court Says It Will Not Hear Appeal on Affirmative Action," *New York Times,* July 2, 1996, p. A1.

48. 401 U.S. 424 (1971).

49. Another important affirmative action case in the area of employment is *Steelworkers v. Weber* (99 S.Ct. 2721, 1979). In this case, the Court approved a plan by the steelworkers' union and Kaiser Aluminum that set aside half the slots in a training program for skilled and craft workers for African Americans. This decision too is jeopardized by the Supreme Court's recent line of decisions.

50. "The Compromise on Civil Rights," *New York Times,* December 12, 1991.

51. Steven Holmes, "Lawyers Expect Ambiguities in New Rights Law to Bring Years of Lawsuits," *New York Times,* December 12, 1991.
52. 90-602, 1993 (slip opinion).
53. 448 U.S. 448 (1980).
54. 110 S.Ct. 2997 (1990).
55. 488 U.S. 469 (1989).
56. Ibid.
57. 903-1841, 1995 (slip opinion). This case involved a suit by white contractors challenging a minority set-aside in federal highway construction.
58. Augustus Jones and Clyde Brown, "State Responses to *Richmond v. Croson:* A Survey of Equal Employment Opportunity Officers," *National Political Science Review* 3 (1992): 40–61. See also W. Avon Drake and Robert Holsworth, *Affirmative Action and the Stalled Quest for Racial Progress* (Urbana: University of Illinois Press, 1996): chap. 7.
59. Steven Holmes, "White House to Suspend a Program for Minorities," *New York Times,* March 8, 1996, p. A1, and Steven Holmes, "Administration Cuts Affirmative Action While Defending It," *New York Times,* March 16, 1998, p. A17.

CHAPTER 14

The Bureaucracy and the African American Quest for Universal Freedom

President Clinton's former chief of staff Leon Panetta was socialized by an African American woman. Ruby Martin was director of the Office for Civil Rights in the Department of Health, Education and Welfare (HEW) when Richard Nixon won the presidency in 1968. President Nixon appointed Robert Finch as his new HEW Secretary. With Finch in place, Southerners led by Senator J. Strom Thurmond went to see Nixon about easing the government's desegregation enforcement policies. Southern states had abandoned the Hubert Humphrey-led Democratic party in the presidential election and supported Nixon, and their electoral support had helped him win. To garner that support Nixon had promised Southerners that he would address their heightened concerns about the pace of civil rights and desegregation. After the Thurmond-Nixon meeting, HEW under Robert Finch began a "slow down" approach in desegregating southern schools and colleges.[1]

Ruby Martin felt that a stronger, swifter, and more dramatic federal enforcement effort was needed. Finch resisted. Eventually, Martin resigned in protest. Once on the outside, Martin staged protest demonstrations at the Justice Department and wrote exposé pieces about the new "slow down" approach from her position at the Washington Research Group—a liberal think tank.

Robert Finch brought in Leon Panetta to replace Martin as the new director of the Office for Civil Rights. Martin, in numerous meetings with Panetta, told him of the negative consequences of the "slow down" approach and how it violated both the spirit and letter of the 1964 Civil Rights Act.[2] Martin gave Panetta a new perspective. He too resigned in protest.

These two dramatic examples raise the questions, What is the federal bureaucracy? What role does the bureaucracy play in the African American quest for universal freedom?

236

THE NATURE OF THE FEDERAL BUREAUCRACY

In his classic studies, Max Weber defined bureaucracy as a form of power based on knowledge—rationally and hierarchically organized. In other words, bureaucracy is a system of bureaus and agencies that carry out laws and policies on a routine, day-to-day basis, using a hierarchy, standardized procedures, knowledge, and a specialization of duties.[3]

What are the functions of the bureaucracy? Essentially, the bureaucracy serves three major functions. First, it must execute the law. Second, it must write the rules so as to execute the law. And finally, it must adjudicate between claimants and resolve disputes when disagreements arise about proper procedures, regulations, guidelines, and federal practices. Collectively, these three major functions are subsumed under the rubric of *implementation*. Hence, the purpose of the federal bureaucracy is to implement the laws of the land.

Table 14.1 shows the structure, organization, and types of federal agencies and bureaucracies. Basically, the bureaucracy can be grouped into five major categories. First, the agencies within the *Executive Office of the President*, such as the Office of Management and Budget and the National Security Council. Second are the fourteen *cabinet departments*. There are also numerous *independent agencies* such as the Environmental Protection Agency, the National Aeronautics and Space Administration, and the Social Security Administration.

In addition to these administrative units, there are the *government corporations*, which can function like private corporations. Examples are the United States Postal Service, Amtrak, and the Resolution Trust Corporation.

Finally, there are the *independent regulatory commissions*, which are supposed to be beyond presidential and congressional influence. Members of these commissions serve for fixed terms and therefore may not be fired by the president, so these commissions may in theory act in the public interest without political pressure. Table 14.1 shows only two of the sixty-one independent commissions and government corporations that deal explicitly with issues of race or civil rights: the Civil Rights Commission and the Equal Employment Opportunity Commission. They represent 3.3 percent of the total commissions and corporations.

CREATING A BUREAUCRACY WITH RACE AS A MISSION: THE ROLE OF NECESSITY

In March 1865, the Bureau of Refugees, Freedmen and Abandoned Lands, better known as the Freedmen's Bureau, was established.[4] Here is John Hope Franklin and Albert Moss's description of this first race bureaucracy:

> With officials in each of the Southern states, the bureau aided white refugees and former slaves by furnishing supplies and medical services, establishing schools, supervising contracts between ex-slaves and their employers, and managing confiscated or abandoned lands, leasing and selling some of them to former slaves.[5]

They continue:

TABLE 14.1

Structure of the Federal Bureaucracy

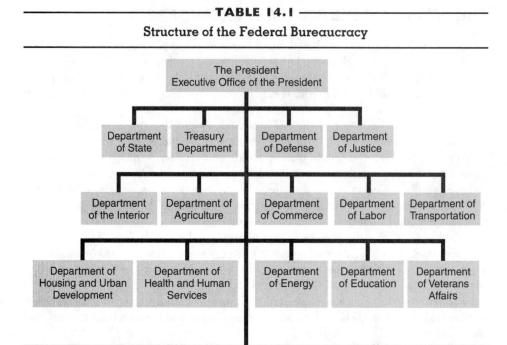

Independent Establishments and Government Corporations

ACTION
Administrative Conference of the U.S.
African Development Foundation
Central Intelligence Agency
Commission on the Bicentennial of the U.S. Constitution
Commission on Civil Rights
Commodity Futures Trading Commission
Consumer Product Safety Board
Defense Nuclear Facilities Safety Board
Environmental Protection Agency
Equal Employment Opportunity Commission
Export-Import Bank of the U.S.
Farm Credit Administration
Federal Communications Commission
Federal Deposit Insurance Corporation
Federal Election Commission
Federal Emergency Management Agency
Federal Housing Finance Board
Federal Labor Relations Authority
Federal Maritime Commission
Federal Mediation and Conciliation Service

Federal Mine Safety and Health Review Commission
Federal Reserve System, Board of Governors of the Federal Retirement Thrift Investment Board
Federal Trade Commission
General Services Administration
Inter-American Foundation
Interstate Commerce Commission
Merit Systems Protection Board
National Aeronautics and Space Administration
National Archives and Records Administration
National Capital Planning Commission
National Credit Union Administration
National Foundation on the Arts and the Humanities
National Labor Relations Board
National Mediation Board
National Railroad Passenger Corporation (Amtrak)
National Science Foundation
National Transportation Safety Board
Nuclear Regulatory Commission

Occupational Safety and Health Review Commission
Office of Government Ethics
Office of Personnel Management
Office of Special Counsel
Oversight Board
Panama Canal Commission
Peace Corps
Pennsylvania Avenue Development Corporation
Pension Benefit Guaranty Corporation
Postal Rate Commission
Railroad Retirement Board
Resolution Trust Corporation
Securities and Exchange Commission
Selective Service System
Small Business Administration
Tennessee Valley Authority
U.S. Arms Control and Disarmament Agency
U.S. Information Agency
U.S. International Development Corporation Agency
U.S. International Trade Commission
U.S. Postal Service

Source: United States Government Manual, 1990–91 (Wallington: Government Printing Office).

There can be no doubt that the Freedmen's Bureau relieved much suffering among blacks and whites. Between 1865 and 1869, for example, the bureau issued 21 million rations, approximately 5 million going to whites and 15 million to blacks. By 1867, there were forty-six hospitals under the bureau staffed by physicians, surgeons, and nurses. . . . The death rate among former slaves was reduced, and sanitary conditions were improved.[6]

Besides health matters, the bureau assisted African American with jobs and labor contracts. "The bureau sought to protect blacks in their freedom to choose their own employers and to work at a fair wage.[7] The Bureau's commissioner, General Oliver Howard, reported that there were no less than fifty thousand labor contracts in each of the southern states.

In addition to health and employment, the Bureau provided land and free transportation. Although abandoned and confiscated lands were generally restored to their owners under the amnesty proclamations of Presidents Lincoln and Johnson, "the bureau distributed some land to former slaves. . . . Small parcels of land were first allotted and then leased to them for management and cultivation."[8]

To help resolve disputes between former slaves and their masters, the Freedmen's Bureau established courts and arbitration boards that had legal jurisdiction in both civil and minor criminal matters. The attainment of justice, equity, and fair play was the concern of this function of the Bureau.

Last, the Bureau struggled to provide education to the former slaves, implementing a twofold approach to the problem of illiteracy. First, the Bureau itself created all types of schools, from the elementary to the college level. Second, it entered into joint and cooperative ventures with religious and philanthropic organizations to provide education. The result was a panoply of African American colleges and universities. The most notable of these creations was Howard University (named after the first director of the Freedmen's Bureau, General Oliver O. Howard).

Thus, the initial federal bureaucracy with the concerns of race as a mission was the Freedmen's Bureau. It was a relief agency created out of *military necessity*. This human welfare agency came to an end on June 30, 1872, a little more than seven years after its creation. Amid charges of corruption and inefficiency, southern hostility, northern claims of high cost and expenses, and a general outcry that this was not the proper role for the federal government, the first federal welfare bureaucracy disappeared. But the groundwork or pattern of response by such an agency was established.

After the Compromise of 1877, *military necessity* had given way to *political necessity* in the creation of a federal bureaucracy with a race mission. This compromise gave the white South "home rule" and permitted whites to "redeem" the southern governments and the political process for "whites only." To obtain their goals of white supremacy, the southern whites instituted fraud, political corruption, economic peonage, and violence that ignored both the spirit and the letter of the law as put forth in the Thirteenth, Fourteenth, and Fifteenth Amendments. These developments forced a reluctant federal government to address the problem by giving the Justice Department power to investigate and prosecute those who violated African American civil rights. Now instead of a new agency like the Freedmen's Bureau, Congress gave an old agency new duties and responsibilities. However, because of hostility from southern whites and northern disinterest, the new mission of the Justice Department was quietly discontinued.[9] The second federal bureaucracy to help African Americans address the question of universal freedom came to the same end as the Freedmen's Bureau. And the pattern of response for ending these agencies, despite their differences in structural arrangements, was starting to solidify. Vigorous protest by whites could bring these agencies to a standstill.

Thus, prior to the turn of the century, necessity, both *military* and *political*, had caused the creation of two federal bureaucracies with a race mission; but protests by southern whites led to their demise. This is basically where matters stood until 1939. At this time the federal government was jolted out of its cautious tradition when Attorney General Frank Murphy issued an order establishing a civil liberties unit in the Department of Justice. The "Order of the Attorney General No. 3204" was issued on February 3, 1939.[10] According to Robert Carr, Murphy "created the civil liberties unit as a warning that the weight of the United States government was on the side of oppressed people in protecting their civil liberties."[11]

Then, in the 1957 Civil Rights Act, Congress created the Commission on Civil Rights—a fact-finding agency that made recommendations to the president—(presidents could and frequently did reject their recommendations and refuse to accept their reports).[12] In addition, this new law upgraded the civil rights unit in the Justice Department to a full-fledged Civil Rights Division (CRD).

Congress followed up with the 1960 Civil Rights Act that expanded the power of the CRD of the Justice Department. By 1964, the Civil Rights Act with its eleven titles created three new race-oriented federal bureaucratic units, although with different structural arrangements. Title VI created inside all federal agencies, departments, and commissions an Office of Civil Rights Compliance (OCRC), which monitored state and local governments to ensure that they did not spend federal funds in a racially discriminatory fashion. The office of Federal Contract Compliance (OFCC) was also created in the Department of Labor to assure nondiscrimination and affirmative action by employers with government contracts.

Title VII created the Equal Employment Opportunity Commission (EEOC) to ensure nondiscrimination in federal employment and in private employment with companies holding federal contracts. In 1972, congressional legislation sponsored by African American congressman Augustus Hawkins made the Equal Employment Opportunity Commission (EEOC) a completely independent commission.

Title X of the 1964 Act created the Community Relations Agency, a federal bureaucracy designed to improve race relations in communities having racial conflicts. The agency was empowered to use the carrot-and-stick approach: provide money and assistance, and also use legal recourse to minimize racial conflict. Eventually this agency was reduced in size and shifted to unit status within the Justice Department.

The 1965 Voting Rights Act created a unit inside the Justice Department's CRD to handle matters of racial discrimination in voter registration and voting, particularly in the southern states where efforts have been persistent in denying African Americans their voting rights. Hence, because of legislation, the Justice Department has had to increase its functions, adding civil rights and voting rights units along with the community relations unit.

Last, in 1984 Congress created the Martin Luther King, Jr., Federal Holiday Commission and eventually provided some small funding to it, empowering it to help in the celebration and promotion of the King holiday.

Thus, necessity forced the government to create two types of federal agencies with a racial mission: (1) relief agencies (material based) and (2) protection agencies (rights based). Both types have faced strong public criticism, driven in part by southern racial hostilities. By the time of the Reagan administration, the president himself attacked these agencies.[13] First, President Reagan appointed members to the Commission on Civil Rights who were hostile to civil rights, including its African American chairman Clarence Pendelton. Second, Attorney General Edwin Meese and the Assistant Attorney General for Civil Rights William Bradford Reynolds attempted to undermine civil rights enforcement. Clarence Thomas at EEOC did the same thing. Thus, Reagan's ideological appointees diminished the enforcement role of the bureaucracy. President Bush followed Reagan's approach, and Clinton moved away from appointing anyone who had an activist orientation toward promoting a stronger and better civil rights enforcement effort.

Overall, there are four federal bureaus devoted to an explicitly racial mission: (1) the Commission on Civil Rights, (2) the Equal Employment Opportunity Commission, (3) the Martin Luther King, Jr., Federal Holiday Commission, and (4) the Civil Rights and Voting Rights unit in the Justice Department. Each of these bodies, as President Reagan showed, are subject to political influences and pressures (as well as budgeting ones) that can reduce their enforcement effectiveness. Thus, the federal bureaucracy has not been a consistently useful tool in the African American quest for universal freedom, and occasionally it has been hostile to that quest (see Boxes 14.1 and 14.2).

RUNNING THE BUREAUCRACY:
AFRICAN AMERICAN POLITICAL APPOINTEES

When one analyzes and evaluates the federal bureaucracy, however, the entire story is not captured by focusing on federal agencies designed to deal with race and race relations. An important part was played by African Americans who obtained leadership roles in the federal bureaucracy in general.

During the New Deal, Mary McLeod Bethune announced, "My people will not be satisfied until they see some black faces in high places."[14] When she uttered these words, no African American had ever headed a federal agency or bureau.

More than three decades after her comment, there had still been no African American in such a capacity (although President Roosevelt did appoint Mrs. Bethune director of the Division of Negro Affairs of the National Youth Administration). Although President Eisenhower made a couple of token appointments, this situation would not change until the administration of President Kennedy in 1962. Thus, for the greater part of America's history, African Americans, though subject to the federal bureaucracy, were outside it. Therefore, the first quest of African Americans in terms of the bureaucracy was to make it representative of all the people. Access was the necessary first step, achieved through patronage politics.

====================== **BOX 14.1** ======================

The Bureaucracy at Work:
Dr. Martin Luther King, Jr., and the FBI

The Federal Bureau of Investigation, a part of the Justice Department, is the nation's principal law enforcement and investigative agency, made famous in scores of television programs and movies. This agency, charged with enforcing the civil and constitutional rights of citizens, consistently failed to provide protection to civil rights workers in the South during the 1960s, claiming, in the words of its director, J. Edgar Hoover, that it was not a police force and therefore could not protect the civil rights of southern blacks. Yet the FBI and Hoover set about to systematically harass, discredit, and destroy America's preeminent civil rights leader.

From 1963 until Martin Luther King, Jr.'s death in 1968, the FBI systematically attempted to destroy his effectiveness as leader of the civil rights movement. According to the FBI agent in charge, "No holds were barred. We have used [similar] techniques against Soviet agents. [The same methods were] brought home against any organization which we targeted. We did not differentiate. This is a rough, tough business."[a] Among the many "rough, tough" tactics used against Dr. King were efforts to prove that he was a communist or that he was being manipulated by communists: wiretaps and microphone surveillance of his home, office, and hotel rooms; attempts to prove he had secret foreign bank accounts; attempts to prove that he had numerous affairs with women; and attempts to prevent him from publishing his books and from receiving the Nobel Peace Prize. Derogatory information about Dr. King's private life was given to members of Congress, the press, university and church leaders (including the Pope), and other leaders of the civil rights movement. Finally, in an act of desperation, the FBI sent a letter to Dr. King urging him to commit suicide or face exposure as a "liar" and "pervert," leading Dr. King to exclaim that the FBI, the nation's chief law enforcement bureaucracy, was "out to break me."

To his eternal credit, Dr. King did not yield to the efforts of the FBI. However, for a time the Bureau's dirty tricks caused deep distress for Dr. King, his family, and his associates. The FBI's attempt to destroy Dr. King is thoroughly documented in the Senate's investigation and in David Garrow's *The FBI and Martin Luther King, Jr.*[b] Many critics of the FBI's campaign against Dr. King contend that it was a product of J. Edgar Hoover's paranoia and a bureaucracy gone amok; however, Garrow, a political scientist, argues that this view is not correct. Granted, the FBI under Hoover had unprecedented power and autonomy; even so, the presidents and members of Congress in Hoover's time were mostly white men of narrow conservative views,[c] and Garrow contends that the FBI faithfully represented these same American values and was not an out-of-control bureaucracy. Garrow concludes, "The Bureau was not a renegade institution secretly operating outside the parameters of American values, but a virtually representative bureaucracy that loyally served to protect the established order against adversary challenges."[d]

[a]*Supplementary Detailed Staff Reports on Intelligence Activities and the Rights of Americans, Book III.* Final Report of the Select Committee to Study Government Operations with Respect to Intelligence Activities, United States Senate, 94th Congress, April, 1976, p. 81.

[b]David Garrow, *The FBI and Martin Luther King, Jr.* (New York: Penguin Books, 1983).

[c]Ibid., pp. 224–25.

[d]Ibid., p. 213.

━━━━━ BOX 14.2 ━━━━━
The Bureaucracy at Work: The CIA and the Crack Connection

As the FBI is the nation's principal domestic investigative and law enforcement bureaucracy, the Central Intelligence Agency (CIA) is the nation's principal foreign investigative and intelligence gathering bureaucracy. An independent agency with a secret budget, the CIA also engages in what is euphemistically called "covert operations," secret plots and counterplots to assist America's friends and to neutralize or destroy its enemies. If a three-part investigative report in the *San Jose Mercury News* is to be believed, in the 1980s one of the CIA's covert operations involved helping drug pushers in San Francisco turn powdered cocaine into crack and then sell it by the tons to the Crips and Bloods, Los Angeles street gangs.[a]

According to the *San Jose Mercury News*, during the 1980s, in order to raise money to support the U.S.-backed "Contras" (an anticommunist insurgent group in the Central American nation of Nicaragua), the CIA facilitated the sale of illegal drugs in Los Angeles. Over the objections of President Reagan, the Congress cut off funds for the Contras, leading the Reagan administration to trade arms to Iran illegally so as to raise the funds to finance the Contras. The Iran-Contra affair precipitated a major scandal and crisis, leading to the resignation and indictment of several top-level Reagan administration officials.[b] The *San Jose Mercury News* reports suggest that in addition to selling arms to Iran, the CIA also sought money for the Contras by developing a new, cheap drug and mass marketing it to the African American community. Since the 1980s, use of crack has reached nearly epidemic proportions, with devastating consequences for black America.

When the *San Jose Mercury News* story was published, John Deutch, the CIA director, denied the CIA crack connection. Most African Americans and their leaders did not believe him and called for an independent investigation of the charges. African Americans have long believed that the U.S. government was involved in the drug trade. For example, a *New York Times* poll in 1990 found that 60 percent of blacks (compared to 16 percent of whites) believed it might be true that the government had deliberately made sure drugs were easily available in the black community.[c] The allegations about the CIA's crack connection, whether true or not,[d] are surely going to reinforce this sense of alienation and distrust of the government that is already widespread in the African American community.

---

[a]The three-part *San Jose Mercury News* series on the CIA and crack was reprinted in a number of newspapers, including the *West County Times*. See Gary Webb, "State Drug Rings Linked to CIA," September 8, 1996, p. 48; Gary Webb, "Unlikely Trio Created Market for Crack," September 9, 1996, p. A1; Gary Webb, "Ex-Bay Area Man Stumbled into Gun, Drug Ties to Contras," September 10, 1996, p. 4A.

[b]Ernest J. Wilson, III, "The Iran-Contra Affair: Errant Globalism in Action," *National Political Science Review* 1 (1989): 110–13.

[c]Jason DeParle, "Talk of Government Out to Get Blacks Falls on More Attentive Ears," *New York Times*, October 19, 1990.

[d]After much criticism, the *San Jose Mercury News* conducted an internal reexamination of Webb's story and concluded that parts of it were an "oversimplification," and that there was not "proof" that "top CIA officials" knew the Contras were getting money from Los Angeles drug dealers. See Richard Zoglin, "Not So Hot Copy," *Newsweek*, May 26, 1997, pp. 81–82. Webb, however, continues to maintain that his story is accurate. Indeed, he documents it in greater detail in his book *Dark Alliances: The CIA, the Contras and the Crack Cocaine Explosion* (New York: Seven Stories Press, 1998).

President Grant began the initial process of appointing African American Republican leaders to minor federal posts in Washington, D.C., and the southern states, and to diplomatic posts in African and Caribbean nations. Posts such as custom collector and minister to foreign countries became the manner in which the Republican party enhanced and enlarged its alliance with the African American electorate.

The first Democratic president to deal with patronage appointments was Grover Cleveland, elected in 1884. Lawrence Grossman states:

> President Cleveland recognized blacks in his appointments to the diplomatic corps. He adhered to the tradition, instituted by Republican presidents, of appointing blacks as ministers to the black nations of Haiti and Liberia and named another black as consul in Luanda. [Domestically, he also] nominated James Matthews, a black lawyer from Albany, New York, to replace Frederick Douglass as Recorder of Deeds in the District of Columbia.[15]

But no matter whether the appointments were by the Democratic or the Republican parties, they were based on a single reality: "The . . . strategy was to identify and then latch onto a black leader who could coalesce a potentially powerful black vote."[16] Hence, "the motives of the Republicans (or Democrats) who aligned themselves with blacks were utilitarian and shortsighted."[17] Listen as one politico writes President Grant urging the appointment of an African American state leader to an ambassadorial post. In a letter dated January 28, 1871, Carmen A. Newcombe, a party faithful and personal friend of the president's, wrote:

> If [James Milton Turner] can go to Liberia for two years he will gain a national reputation which will make him the universally trusted leader of the colored men in the campaign of [18]72. . . . He can come back in '72 and take his place as the chosen leader of his race and whose [sic] claims to leadership will not be disputed.[18]

Simply put, African American political appointees in the bureaucracy had the exposure to make them trusted leaders in their own communities.

However, in the midst of such political appointments, white Southerners took over the southern governments and displaced most African American state and local appointive officials by violence, fraud, and corruption. These displaced officials then turned to Presidents Grant, Arthur, and Harrison "as a source of federal appointments" and "patronage positions."[19] Thus, what started out as a trickle of federal jobs emerged into a full-fledged effort to find employment for black party loyalists.

In sum, the Republican party's need for the black vote launched African Americans into the federal bureaucracy. Eventually this trend, coupled with the need for political jobs for the African American community, made federal patronage appointments all the more important and useful for the African American community. Thus, political patronage became a way in which they could gain access to the federal bureaucracy. Necessity again proved vital in forging a connection between the African American community and the budding federal bureaucracy. These two links—the party's need for votes and the community's need for employment—continued and expanded. The period of greatest expansion came in the New Deal era, 1932–1945. Here is how it has been described:

> One of the most important factors in the achievements of political respectability on the part of blacks was the New Deal policy of securing the assistance of African-American

specialists and advisers in various governmental departments. Seeking the advice of blacks was not a Roosevelt innovation. Other presidents had sought the pulse of the black population through one or more leaders of the black community. . . . Roosevelt's group of black advisers differed from the others in several important respects. In the first place, the number of black cabineteers was fairly large, in contrast to the smaller number on whom previous presidents had relied for advice. . . . Roosevelt's black advisers . . . were placed in positions of sufficient importance that both the government and the African American population generally regarded the appointment as significant . . . and it could not be said that they were brought in because of faithful political service during campaigns. . . . They were highly intelligent and highly trained people who were called in to perform specific functions.[20]

The New Deal formalized the role of African American advisers to presidents, which had started with Frederick Douglass, who advised Presidents Lincoln and Grant, and continued with Booker T. Washington, who advised Cleveland, Harrison, Theodore Roosevelt, and Taft. These individuals, however, had served in informal, nebulous, and unofficial positions. Roosevelt was the first to give his political appointees and advisers institutional positions in the bureaucracy.

Following the New Deal, the next great step came with Presidents Kennedy and Johnson, who appointed a number of blacks to high-level positions. In 1966, President Johnson became the first president to appoint an African American to cabinet rank, as Robert Weaver became secretary of Housing and Urban Development (HUD). President Gerald Ford appointed William Coleman secretary of Transportation. President

Mary MacLeod Bethune, the informal leader of FDR's black cabinet.

Carter placed Patricia Harris first at HUD then at HEW and appointed Andrew Young and later Donald McHenry as UN ambassadors; Reagan named Samuel Pierce secretary of HUD.

In 1992, President Clinton broke new ground. Usually African Americans were given one cabinet position, frequently at HUD or HEW (now HHS). Clinton placed four blacks in his cabinet—at Energy, Agriculture, Veterans Affairs, and Commerce, and named numerous ones to subcabinet positions. Between 1966, when one black was appointed, and 1992, when four were appointed, Democratic presidents made the largest number of political appointments. Toward the end of his first term, Clinton named an African American—Franklin Raines—to head (with cabinet rank) the powerful Office of Management and Budget. Clinton also appointed blacks to head two important regulatory commissions: the National Labor Relations Board and the Federal Communications Commission. Table 14.2 shows the appointment patterns of recent American presidents.

Robert Weaver, the first African American in the Cabinet, with President Johnson who appointed him in 1965.

--------- **TABLE 14.2** ---------

Percentage of African American Political Appointees, from the Kennedy-Johnson Administrations to the Clinton Administration[a]

ADMINISTRATION	PERCENT[b]
Kennedy-Johnson	2
Nixon-Ford	4
Carter	12
Reagan	5
Bush	6
Clinton	13

[a]The Kennedy-Johnson administrations were treated as one.for purposes of data collection, as were the Nixon-Ford administrations.

[b]Percentages are based on all presidential appointments, excluding judges and military officers.

Source: Robert C. Smith, *We Have No Leaders: African Americans in the Post–Civil Rights Era* (Albany: State University of New York Press, 1996): 131.

President Clinton put more blacks on the federal bureaucracy than any previous president, including four cabinet secretaries. Here is a photo of some 60 blacks on the White House staff.

STAFFING THE BUREAUCRACY:
AFRICAN AMERICAN CIVIL SERVANTS

African American political appointees cannot, in and of themselves, do the job alone.[21] All political appointees are transients. The average length of service is twenty-two months out of a four-year cycle. Thus, to influence and impact bureaucratic rule making and policy, any group needs a continuing presence and permanency inside the bureaucracy, a day-to-day involvement. This means African Americans had to become permanent bureaucrats through the civil service process. Individuals hired through this process—*civil servants*—after a brief probationary period may not be fired. They become part of the *permanent government*.

When political scientists treat the federal bureaucracy and the question of race, their focus is usually on African American employment in this permanent bureaucracy. Although black employees were appointed after the Civil War, by the time of the passage of the Pendleton Act (which created the civil service), there were only 620 black civil servants in the federal government. By 1893, the report of the Civil Service Commission indicated that the number had risen to 2,393, but this 74 percent increase was to run headlong into southern opposition and the ideology of white supremacy and its emerging social and political context of segregation. Here is how an observer describes the influence of these southern realities of white supremacy and segregation on the federal system and eventually the bureaucracy:

> In practice, the price of the South's reintegration [into the political system] was the acceptance by the North of Southern race relations . . . [and] Federal politics tolerated and reproduced this Southern-originating pattern. From the 1880s national politics were progressively imbued with segregationists' views, whose origin lay in ante-bellum attitudes and arrangements, augmented by fresh prejudices propagated in the post-Reconstruction years.[22]

Therefore, segregation occurred in federal government departments before 1913, but it was limited, received little White House consideration, depended largely on individual administrations, and did not prevent some black Americans from gaining promotions.[23] However, this rising federal acceptance of the southern system of segregation started slowly and gradually to have an impact in the federal bureaucracy despite the civil service merit system. For instance, the percentage of black employees fell from 6 percent in 1910 to 4.9 percent in 1918.[24] But the influence of the gradual and evolving southern forces of white supremacy and segregation coalesced into a tidal wave with the election of a Democratic Congress and a southern Democratic president, Woodrow Wilson in 1912. As noted by Franklin and Moss,

> The election of a Democratic Administration and Congress in 1912 gave a fuller opportunity to the articulation and implementation of these views, but also to a full reorganization of the federal bureaucracy, the outcome of which happened to isolate Black American employees from their white peers and to consign them to the worst jobs.[25]

This turning point for African Americans in the bureaucracy was the Wilson presidency in 1913.

Southern forces started to work on President Wilson from the first day of his administration. Franklin and Moss wrote,

> Soon after Woodrow Wilson entered the White House in 1913, the Acting Secretary of the Treasury, J. S. Williams prepared a memorandum about the department's Bureau of Engraving and Printing . . . [noting] an arrangement . . . in the "sizing department" disturbing to his sensibilities: young white women and colored women were working together side by side and opposite each other.[26]

Thomas Dixon was the southern novelist who wrote the racist *Clansman,* which became D. W. Griffith's film, *The Birth of a Nation.* (President Woodrow Wilson saw this film at the White House and endorsed it, saying it was "history written with lighting.")[27] Dixon wrote President Wilson on his nomination of a black American to a post in the Treasury: "I am heartsick over the announcement that you have appointed a Negro to boss white girls as Register of the Treasury."[28] With these types of cries and pleas pouring in, President Wilson permitted most federal bureaucracies in 1913 to segregate African Americans from whites; even the toilets and restrooms were segregated.

In May 1914, the U.S. Civil Service Commission, finding itself in a changed political context and environment, "made photographs mandatory on all application forms. . . . [This practice became] an obvious instrument of discrimination in the appointment of applicants, since it abrogated the principle of merit."[29] With the president and the Commission supporting the segregation of the federal bureaucracy, in 1913 and 1914 Congress joined the process. First, southern Congressmen in 1913 formed the Democratic Fair Play Association (DFPA), made President Wilson an honorary member, and held numerous public meetings to discuss their central principle of "the segregation of the races in government employment" and "the reorganization of the civil service" in light of these principles.[30] Chief among the leaders of the DFPA were southern demagogues: Hoke Smith of Georgia, Benjamin Tillman of South Carolina, and James Vardaman of Mississippi. There was a similar group in the House of Representatives.

Public meetings were only part of the congressional strategy. There was the introduction of numerous bills and the monitoring of federal departments that did not maintain the "color line" by following a rigid policy of segregation. Leaders of such departments were publicly criticized and denounced and their budgets were threatened with severe reduction. Professor Desmond King states, "Individual members of Congress also kept a watchful and circumspect eye on the activity of Federal departments, alert to activities weakening segregated race relations."[31]

Overall, the federal government's embrace of segregation outlasted the Wilson administration, since the succeeding Republican presidencies continued Wilson's policies.[32] Thus, the federal government's acceptance of the policies of white supremacy and segregation "determined the relationship between Black Americans and the federal government for the ensuing fifty years."[33] Hence, the legacy the Wilson presidency left African Americans in the bureaucracy was devastating. Desmond King concludes, "After 1913 Black American employees in Federal Agencies were disproportionately concentrated in custodial, menial and junior clerical positions and were frequently passed over for appointment at all."[34] The federal bureaucracy became a pillar of segregated race relations.

African Americans, through the NAACP and various African American leaders, fought this trend; and while some of the worst features, such as photographs on applications, were removed in 1940, the final dismantling did not occur until the 1964 Civil Rights Act. Figure 14.1 displays the rise, fall, and gradual evolution of federal employment of African Americans. The graph shows that African Americans have slowly risen in the staffing of the federal bureaucracy, but their appearance and presence have not yet made the federal bureaucracy a representative of the nation's population.

Moreover, despite the gains brought by the 1964 and 1972 laws, significant reversals came in the Reagan years. If 1913 was a fateful year, so were Reagan's first and second terms. In his first term, President Reagan launched the Reduction in Force (RIF) policy that disproportionately reduced the number of African Americans in federal employment because of their lower seniority and their significant concentration in the job classifications most susceptible to the staff reductions.[35]

In his second term, Reagan established a policy that allowed senior-level bureaucrats to move around inside the bureaucracy without affecting their rank. That is, they could carry rank with them from agency to agency. Also, these Reagan bureaucrats could reorganize the department to suit their ideological leanings. Hence, even permanent African American civil servants now found themselves in an ideologically changed political context, with the top and middle-level administrators sponsoring conservative

Figure 14.1 Percentage of African Americans in the Federal Bureaucracy: 1881–1990

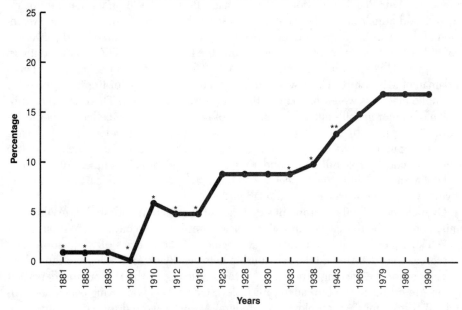

*These percentages were taken from the King Book cited below.

**These percentages are based on a partial survey covering only 44 federal agencies.

Source: Adapted from L. J. Hayes, *The Negro Federal Government Worker* (Washington, DC: The Graduate School, Howard University, 1941), pp. 1 and 153; and Desmond King, *Separate and Unequal: Black-Americans and the U.S. Federal Government* (London: Oxford University Press, 1995), pp. 81, 221–237.

rule making and regulations and opposing any civil rights initiatives.[36] President Bush basically continued the bureaucratic policies of the Reagan administration, although he did not insist as strongly on ideological conformity. In his first term, President Clinton left the Reagan-Bush bureaucratic thrust in place. And in the second term, President Clinton has instituted few changes. Thus, race remains a factor affecting the staffing of the federal bureaucracy; indeed, the very meaning of race in the United States is determined by federal bureaucrats (see Box 14.3).

BOX 14.3

The Bureaucracy and Your Race

In the United States—*and only in the United States*—a person of *any* known African ancestry is defined as black or African American. This peculiar definition of one's race was established early by the United States Bureau of the Census, which declared:

> A person of mixed white and Negro blood should be returned as a Negro, no matter how small the percentage of Negro blood. Both black and mulatto persons are to be returned as Negroes, without distinction. A person of mixed Indian and Negro blood should be returned as a Negro. . . . Mixtures of non-white races should be reported according to the race of the father, except that Negro Indian should be reported as Negro.[a]

At the founding of the Republic, the Census Bureau recognized three races: black, white, and red. However, as the nation became more ethnically diverse or multicultural, this definition became inadequate. Thus, the bureaucracy in 1977 changed the definition or meaning of race. The bureaucracy responsible for defining race is not the Census Bureau (an agency within the cabinet-level Department of Commerce) but the Office of Management and Budget (OMB), an agency within the Executive Office of the president, whose principal responsibility is to prepare the annual budget the president submits to Congress. In addition to its budget responsibilities, the OMB also has overall management or oversight responsibility for the federal bureaucracy. In this latter role, in 1977 it issued Statistical Policy Directive #15 defining the meaning of race for purposes of federal policy. According to this definition, there are four "races" in the United States: black, white, American Indian or Alaskan native, and Asian or Pacific Islander. To determine ethnic identification, black and white respondents are asked to check "Hispanic origin" or "not of Hispanic origin," in effect creating a fifth "race." The five categories are used by the Census Bureau and all other government agencies that collect statistical data. Such data are used to determine the racial composition of the country; to reapportion the House and state and local legislative bodies; to monitor enforcement of civil rights and affirmative action laws; and for other purposes.

In recent years, however, this bureaucratic definition of race has been challenged by many Americans, especially the growing number of biracial or mixed race couples. In 1967 the Supreme Court declared in *Loving v. Virginia* that a state was in violation of the Fourteenth Amendment's equal protection clause if it prohibited interracial or mixed marriages.[b] Since

(Continued)

BOX 14.3 Continued

that time the number of mixed black-white marriages has increased dramatically—from 149,000 to 964,000 (a 547 percent increase).[c] Increasingly, some of these mixed couples, their offspring, and others are demanding that OMB change its 1977 directive to include the category "mixed race" or "multiracial." According to a 1995 *Newsweek* poll, 49 percent of blacks but only 36 percent of whites support adding this new category.[d] However, most African American leaders and civil rights organizations have opposed the change, arguing that the new category will result in a loss of black political power, undermine affirmative action, and lead to increased discrimination and stigmatization of African Americans.[e]

In 1993 the OMB agreed to consider adding the multiracial category in time for use in the 2000 census. But a task force appointed to study the issue recommended that instead of a new multiracial category, people be allowed to check more than one race on the census questionnaire. The task force contended that a new multiracial category would "add to racial tensions and further fragmentation of our population."[f]

[a] This definition from the first census is quoted in Langston Hughes and Milton Meltzer, *A Pictorial History of the Negro in America* (New York: Crown, 1964): 2. On the historical origins of America's definition of race, see F. James Davis, *Who Is Black: One Nation's Definition* (University Park: Pennsylvania State University Press, 1991).

[b] 380 U.S. 1 (1967).

[c] See Michael Frisby, "Black, White or Other," *Emerge*, December/January, 1996, p. 49.

[d] Tom Morganthau, "What Color Is Black?" *Newsweek*, February 13, 1995, p. 65.

[e] Frisby, "Black, White or Other," p. 51.

[f] Steven Holmes, "Panel Balks at a Multiracial Census Category," *New York Times*, July 9, 1997, p. A8.

SHAPING BUREAUCRATIC POLICY: ANTIDISCRIMINATION RULE MAKING

Another characteristic of African Americans and the federal bureaucracy is their role in rule making, especially in antidiscrimination policy. The federal bureaucracy cannot protect, and promote African American civil and voting rights unless it has the rules and regulations in place to implement the laws. The federal bureaucracy is severely restricted in its role and function when these rules and regulations do not exist.

When the 1960s civil rights laws were passed, the federal bureaucracy could began writing antidiscrimination rules and regulations. Given the racial history of the federal bureaucracy, most departments did not move swiftly to develop and promulgate rules designed to achieve antidiscrimination in America. Rather, as Figure 14.2 shows, most of the federal bureaucracy was very slow in developing antidiscrimination rules and regulations. Even so, by the late 1970s, antidiscrimination rules and regulations were well established.

In the first week of his second term, President Reagan signed Executive Order #12498, which required all units of the federal bureaucracy to submit to OMB any rule or regulation that was being contemplated for approval.[37] With OMB in the Executive Office of the president, all antidiscrimination policies could be stopped even before they were drafted. And they were.[38]

Figure 14.2 Proposal Cycle: Title VI Regulations in the *Federal Register,* 1964–1984

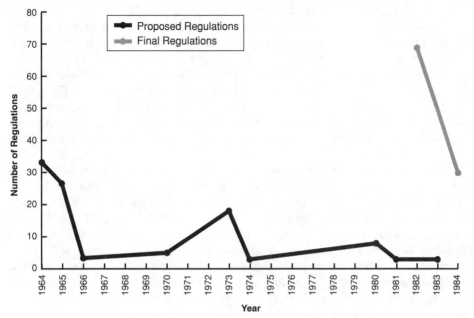

Source: Hanes Walton, Jr., *When the Marching Stopped: The Politics of Civil Rights Regulatory Agencies* (Albany: State University of New York Press, 1988), p. 93.

When President Bush entered the White House in 1988, he not only permitted the Reagan Executive Order to stand (presidential executive orders can be repealed or revoked by the next president),[39] but he also shifted federal regulations away from race to discrimination against the aged and handicapped. Few antidiscrimination civil rights rules and regulations were promulgated during the Bush presidency.

The Clinton administration took over in 1992 with four African American cabinet secretaries whereas Bush and Reagan had had only one. Did the presence of a Democratic president and four African American top political appointees change the civil rights regulatory policies of the Clinton administration? The answer is no. First, President Clinton, like Bush, permitted Reagan's Executive Order to continue in force. Second, the large number of African American cabinet secretaries had little impact or influence on antidiscrimination rule making. They simply did not advance such rules or regulations. Neither the Democratic president nor his African American appointees took any major initiatives to shift the rule-making process toward protection of the civil rights of African Americans.

THE CLINTON ADMINISTRATION AND CIVIL RIGHTS REGULATORY REFORM

President Clinton signed "Executive Order #12866—Regulatory Planning and Review" on September 30, 1993, a full nine months into his first term.[40] Clearly, regulatory reform and support of civil rights for African Americans were not priority agenda items for either President Clinton's transition team, or the president himself in the first two hundred days of the administration. President Reagan had used the regulatory powers of the federal bureaucracy to rescind and undercut the civil rights of African Americans. President Clinton's regulatory reform initiative did not seek to change this situation.

Moreover, President Clinton's executive order required agencies to publish agendas of all regulations under development or review rather than address the negative civil rights regulatory actions of the Reagan and Bush administrations. Also, the Clinton administration did not fashion any new regulatory efforts to enhance civil rights enforcement. The Clinton order merely set a cost-benefit and cost-effective strategy as the new criterion for developing regulations. Such an approach was not new; it had been initially used by President Ford.

However, shortly after issuing his executive order, President Clinton added a new twist. He held a series of meetings with Vice President Al Gore and ordered him, under the administration's "Reinvent Government" initiative, "to conduct a series of meetings with various agencies to develop additional reforms on both cross-cutting and sector-specific regulatory issues."[41] Nearly a year later, President Clinton formalized the "Reinvent Government" thrust with a memorandum, "Regulatory Reinvention Initiative."[42] All these actions ignored civil rights. As a result of this memorandum, Vice President Gore announced that "commitments to reinvent significant regulatory programs" in several federal agencies had been quite successful.[43] He summed up the matter:

> We announced new policies on enforcement and paperwork reduction. Enforcers have been encouraged to use their authority to waive up to 100 percent of punitive fines for small businesses that act in good faith so they can put their energy into fixing the problem, not fighting a regulator.
>
> We announced the results this past summer—16,000 pages to be eliminated from the Code of Federal Regulations and another 31,000 to be reinvented. . . . This is the right way to reform the regulatory system of this Nation.[44]

At least with respect to civil rights, Vice President Gore's conclusion is problematic. The regulatory reform initiative of the Clinton administration had no civil rights thrust at all nor did it make any exception for particular needs in this area. *In both the long and short run, the Clinton regulatory reform may impact the African American community more negatively than the Reagan and Bush ones.* The evidence presented in Table 14.3 dramatically demonstrates this possibility. First, the table separates the four Cabinet agencies headed by African Americans in the Clinton administration from the other ten departments. In addition, we separate the two bureaucracies in the federal government with a race-specific mission—the Commission on Civil Rights and the Equal Employment Opportunity Commission. Next, the table uses the categories of regulatory rules set in place by the executive order of President Reagan—that is, the pre-rule, the proposed rule, and the final rule stages. Beginning in 1993, the year in which the Clinton regulatory initiative was being developed, the departments initiating the greatest number of regulatory rules dealing with civil rights were headed by non-African Americans. Most of these rules were proposed by HUD, headed by Henry Cisneros, a Latino American. In 1995 when the Clinton-Gore initiatives were being put in place, and subsequently in 1995 and 1996, civil rights regulatory rules declined in number and the African American cabinet secretaries discontinued their rule-making efforts altogether.

In the cabinet bureaucracies where civil rights regulations did exist, they were shifted from the proposed rule stage to a new category called "long-term action." Hence, they did not move from the proposed to final rule stage. Long-term action meant that nothing was planned to move these rules forward any time in the near future.

Clearly President Clinton's regulatory reform initiative did not address the matter of civil rights. Table 14.3 also shows that he did not instruct his African American appointees to take independent action. And they could have, if one judges by the civil

---

TABLE 14.3

The Number and Stages of Civil Rights Regulations in Federal Departments/Agencies with and without African American Heads: 1993–1996

DEPARTMENTS HEADED BY AFRICAN AMERICANS	STAGES OF RULE MAKING[a]	1993	1994[b]	1995[c]	1996
Agriculture	Pre-Rule	0	0	0	0
	Proposed Rule	2	1	1	0
	Final Rule	0	0	0	0
Commerce	Pre-Rule	0	0	0	0
	Proposed Rule	0	0	0	0
	Final Rule	0	0	0	0
Energy	Pre-Rule	0	0	0	0
	Proposed Rule	0	0	0	0
	Final Rule	0	0	0	0
Veteran Affairs	Pre-Rule	0	0	0	0
	Proposed Rule	1	1	0	0
	Final Rule	0	0	0	0
	TOTAL	3	2	1	0
Ten Departments with Non-African American Heads					
	Pre-Rule	0	0	0	0
	Proposed Rule	2	5	1	0
	Final Rule	4	1	1	0
Role Mission Agencies[d]					
Commission on Civil Rights/EEOC	Pre-Rule	0	0	0	0
	Proposed Rule	2	0	0	0
	Final Rule	0	0	0	0
	TOTAL	8	6	2	0

[a]In the pre-rule stage, specific rules are simply considered. In the proposed rule stage, rules that were considered are actually drawn up and formalized. In the final rule stage, proposed rules are formalized and disseminated to guide bureaucratic actions.

[b]1994 is the first year of regulatory rule making under President Clinton's new Executive Order, 12498; 1993 is the last year of regulatory rule making under the Reagan and Bush procedures.

[c]1995 is the year President Clinton sent his regulatory memorandum on reinventing government to the entire bureaucracy. And this is the year in which all proposed civil rights regulating rules are shifted to "long-term action" status.

[d]The Commission on Civil Rights was headed by an African American; the EEOC was headed by a non-African American.

Source: Adapted from a content analysis of the semiannual regulatory agenda of the Federal Register 1993, 1994, 1995 and 1996. The numbers for each year were drawn from the last Register for that particular year. The Federal Register is the official publication for all federal rules and regulations.

rights regulatory initiative taken by Cisneros at HUD. But given the problems that surfaced around President Clinton's attempts to nominate individuals from the black community who had a strong commitment to civil rights (such as Lani Guinier), it appears that all the bureaucracies put their civil rights regulatory rules on hold. Thus, the overall effect of the Clinton-Gore regulatory reform initiative has been more crippling than conditions in the Reagan-Bush era. As Table 14.3 reveals, there are no pre-rule efforts and no final rules, and the proposed rules have been discontinued. A centrist Democratic administration has taken the federal bureaucracy out of an activist, antidiscrimination mode—what was left of this mode by the outgoing Reagan and Bush administrations.

However, in a 1998 Martin Luther King Jr. Day address, Vice President Gore, speaking at Dr. King's church, proposed a new civil rights enforcement initiative emphasizing "prevention" and nonlitigation remedies, as well as increased enforcement of antidiscrimination laws. The vice president also indicated that the 1999 budget for civil rights enforcement in the bureaucracy would be increased by 16 percent over the 1998 level.

BUREAUCRATIC IMPLEMENTATION: FEDERALISM AND STATES' RIGHTS

Ultimately, the bureaucracy must act as an implementor and manager of public policy. And to lower its effectiveness and efficiency in these rules, critics, particularly southern critics, have turned to the very nature of the American system—federalism—to support, undergird, and structure their attack.

As one scholar said, "Under the Federal principle of states' rights, each state's racial policy was considered its own business."[45] In his political statements in the 1830s and later in his original work on American political philosophy and theory, *Disquisitions on Government,* South Carolina senator John C. Calhoun equated the constitutional principle of federalism with the southern states' doctrine of states' rights that included slavery and later segregation. Hence, every attempt of the federal government in general and of the federal bureaucracy in particular to regulate these social systems has been met with protests about the intrusion on states' rights and the violation of the constitutional principle of federalism. When federal departments have been created with a racial mission, they have been denounced as a federal grab for power and the usurpation of states' rights. Hence, such agencies have tended to pursue only voluntary, cautious, temporary, and persuasive enforcement efforts. Political appointees cannot have or take aggressive stances toward protecting civil rights. This situation leads to the diminution of antidiscriminatory rules and regulations.

Federalism therefore has been used as a device to limit the influence and impact of the federal bureaucracy in advancing the quest for universal freedom of African Americans.

SELECTED BIBLIOGRAPHY

Altshuler, Alan, and Norman C. Thomas, eds. *The Politics of the Federal Bureaucracy.* New York: Harper & Row, 1977. A good collection of papers examining the structure and operation of the federal bureaucracy and its place in the political system.

Hayes, L. J. *The Negro Federal Government Worker*. Washington: Howard University Press, 1941. A pioneering work on the subject.

King, Desmond. *Separate and Unequal: Black Americans and the U.S. Federal Government*. London: Oxford University Press, 1995. A historical account of African Americans in the federal bureaucracy.

Krislov, Samuel. *The Negro in Federal Employment: The Quest for Equal Opportunity*. Minneapolis: University of Minnesota Press, 1967. Generally considered the standard work on the subject.

Smith, Robert C. "Black Appointed Officials: A Neglected Category of Political Participation Research." *Journal of Black Studies* 14 (March 1984): 369–88. A study of African American presidential appointees from the Kennedy to the Carter administrations.

Smith, Robert C. *We Have No Leaders: African Americans in the Post–Civil Rights Era*. Albany: State University of New York Press, 1996: chap. 5, "Blacks and Presidential Policy Making: Neglect, Policy Symbols and Cooptation." A study of the policymaking roles of black presidential appointees from the Nixon to Bush administrations.

Walton, Hanes, Jr. *When the Marching Stopped: The Politics of Civil Rights Regulatory Agencies*. Albany: State University of New York Press, 1988. A comprehensive study of the ups and downs of the implementation of the 1964 Civil Rights Act, from the Johnson to the Reagan administrations.

NOTES

1. Leon Panetta and Peter Gall, *Bring Us Together: The Nixon Team and the Civil Rights Retreat* (Philadelphia: J. B. Lippincott, 1984): 81.
2. Ibid.
3. See Max Weber, "Bureaucracy," in H. H. Gerth and C. Wright Mills, eds., *From Max Weber: Essays in Sociology* (New York: Oxford University Press, 1969).
4. John Hope Franklin and Alfred Moss, Jr., *From Slavery to Freedom: A History of African Americans*, 7th ed. (New York: McGraw-Hill, 1994): 228.
5. Ibid.
6. Ibid., p. 229.
7. Ibid., p. 230.
8. Ibid.
9. William Gillette, *Retreat from Reconstruction, 1869–1879* (Baton Rouge: Louisiana State University Press, 1979): 54.
10. Hanes Walton, Jr., *When the Marching Stopped: The Politics of Civil Rights Regulatory Agencies* (Albany: State University of New York Press, 1988): 60.
11. Robert Carr, *Federal Protection of Civil Rights* (Ithaca, NY: Cornell University Press, 1947): 24.
12. See Theodore Hesburgh, "Integer Vitae: Independence of the United States Commission on Civil Rights," *Notre Dame Lawyer* (Spring, 1971): 445–60.
13. Walton, *When the Marching Stopped*, p. 6.
14. Quoted in Hanes Walton, Jr., *Invisible Politics* (Albany: State University of New York Press, 1985): 262. See also Mary McLeod Bethune, "Certain Unalienable

Rights," in Rayford Logan, ed., *What the Negro Wants* (Chapel Hill: University of North Carolina Press, 1944): 248–58.

15. Lawrence Grossman, "Democrats and Blacks in the Gilded Age," in P. Kolver, ed., *Democrats and the American Idea* (Washington, DC: Center for National Policy Press, 1992): 149–61.

16. Gary Kremer, *James Milton Turner and the Promise of America: The Public Life of a Post–Civil War Black Leader* (Columbia: University of Missouri Press, 1991): 40.

17. Ibid.

18. Ibid., p. 53.

19. Ibid., p. 50.

20. Franklin and Moss, *From Slavery to Freedom*, p. 391–92. For more on the "Black Cabinet," see Robert Brisbane, Jr., *The Black Vanguard* (Valley Forge, PA: Judson Press, 1970).

21. For analysis of policy roles of black presidential appointees from the Nixon to the Bush administrations, see Robert C. Smith, *We Have No Leaders: African Americans in the Post–Civil Rights Era* (Albany: State University of New York Press, 1996): chap. 5.

22. Franklin and Moss, *From Slavery to Freedom*, p. 396.

23. Ibid., p. 9.

24. Ibid., p. 49.

25. Ibid., p. 9.

26. Ibid., p. 3.

27. Thomas Cripps, "The Reaction of the Negro to the Motion Picture, *The Birth of a Nation*," *Historian* 25 (May, 1963): 224–262.

28. Desmond King, *Separate and Unequal: Black Americans and the U.S. Federal Government* (Oxford: Imendan Press, 1995): 5.

29. Ibid., p. 48.

30. Ibid., p. 22.

31. Ibid., p. 25.

32. Ibid., pp. 20, 49.

33. Ibid., p. 20.

34. Ibid., p. 4.

35. Lenneal J. Henderson and Michael Preston, "Black Public Employment and Public Interest Theory," in M. Rice and Woodrow Jones, Jr., *Contemporary Public Policy Perspective and Black Americans* (Westport, CT: Greenwood, 1984): 40–42; *Impact of 1981 RIFs on Minorities and Women* (Washington, DC: Government Printing Office, 1983).

36. Joel Aberbach and Bert Rockman, "The Political Views of U.S. Senior Federal Executives: 1970–1992"(unpublished paper in Walton's files).

37. Walton, *When the Marching Stopped*, p. 134.

38. Ibid., pp. 135–36.

39. Ibid., pp. 137–57.

40. "Unified Agenda of Federal Regulations: Summary," *Federal Register*, 58 (October 25, 1993): 56002.

41. Al Gore, "Presidential Documents: Statement by the Vice President," *Federal Register*, 60 (November 28, 1995): 59503.
42. Ibid. See also "Department of Agriculture, Statement of Regulatory Priorities," *Federal Register*, 60 (November 28, 1995): 59510.
43. Ibid.
44. Ibid.
45. Samuel DuBois Cook, "Introduction: The American Liberal Democratic Tradition, the Black Revolution and Martin Luther King, Jr.," in Hanes Walton, Jr., *The Political Philosophy of Martin Luther King, Jr.* (Westport, CT: Greenwood, 1971): xiii–xxxviii.

Public Policy

CHAPTER 15

Domestic Policy and the African American Quest for Social and Economic Justice

In this chapter we examine the efforts by African Americans to secure universal freedom in terms of access to material benefits for all the people of the United States, focusing on the interrelated domestic policies of full employment and welfare reform. We examine these two issues because, along with national health insurance, they have consistently been priority items on the post–civil rights era black agenda (see chapter 8).

THE FEDERAL GOVERNMENT, THE ECONOMY AND THE WELFARE STATE

Until the Great Depression, the federal government took little responsibility for managing the economy or seeing to the security of its citizens. Rather, the generally accepted belief was that in a free enterprise, capitalist economy the government should follow Adam Smith's principle of "laissez-faire" (leave it alone). This meant that the economy should be self-regulating, without interference from the government, and that each individual should be responsible for his and his family's welfare. Thus, at the height of the Depression, with 13 million people—25 percent of the labor force—unemployed, President Hoover declined to propose any major plan or program to get the economy back on its feet or to help those in misery, arguing that the federal government lacked the constitutional authority to act and that, in any event, anything the government did would simply make things worse.

This view changed with the coming of the New Deal. Under Franklin Roosevelt's leadership, the federal government for the first time assumed responsibility for managing the economy, seeking full employment, and assisting in providing for the social security and welfare of the American people.[1] In the Employment Act of 1946, the law explicitly spells out the responsibility of the government to manage the economy in order "to promote maximum employment, production and purchasing power."[2] To achieve these objectives of the 1946 Act, the Congress created within the Executive Office of the president a three-person Council of Economic Advisors (staffed by academic economists) and directed the president to submit an annual economic report on his plans to achieve the act's objectives of economic growth, maximum employment, and price stability (low inflation). To oversee the president's economic report and plan, the Congress also created the Joint Economic Committee, which has members from both the House and the Senate.[3]

AFRICAN AMERICANS AND THE QUEST FOR FULL EMPLOYMENT

African Americans were strong supporters of the Employment Act of 1946 and its goal of universal employment.[4] As the scholar-diplomat (and later Nobel Peace Prize winner) Ralph Bunche wrote in 1939,

> There is an economic system, as well as a race problem in America and that when a Negro is unemployed, it is not just because he is a Negro but more seriously because of the defective operation of the economy under which we live—an economy that finds it impossible to provide adequate jobs and economic security for the population.[5]

Similarly, blacks were the principal sponsors and supporters of the Humphrey-Hawkins Act of 1978. This is to be expected, given the historically high rate of unemployment in the African American community since the end of World War II. In Table 15.1, data are displayed comparing the black-white unemployment rates for selected years since 1948. If an unemployment rate of 4 percent is considered full employment (the standard postwar measure) then in no year in the forty-year period 1948–1987 did black males experience full employment; the nearest was 4.8 percent unemployment in 1953. White males, on the other hand, have experienced this rate during several periods, falling to a low of 2.5 percent unemployment in 1953.

Viewed another way, if an unemployment rate of 5 percent plus is considered an indicator of recession, then in every selected year except 1953, black males have faced a recession; with the same criterion, white males experienced recessions in only four of the selected years. (The black-white unemployment gap for females is similar during this period.) In six of the ten years in the forty-year period (seven for females), black male unemployment reached double digits; in no year did this occur for white males or females. In two years—1963 and 1983—the black unemployment rate reached near depression levels. This long-term, persistent joblessness is *the* central explanation of the disabilities of black people in the United States today.[6] Thus, the African American quest is for jobs, jobs, and more jobs.

──────────────────── **TABLE 15.1** ────────────────────

Black and White Unemployment Rates Selected Years, 1948–1987ᵃ

YEAR	BLACK MALES	WHITE MALES	BLACK FEMALES	WHITE FEMALES
1948	5.8	3.4	6.1	3.4
1953	4.8	2.5	4.1	3.1
1958	13.8	6.1	10.8	6.2
1963	20.5	4.7	11.2	5.8
1968	5.6	2.6	8.3	4.3
1973	7.7	3.8	10.6	5.3
1978	11.0	4.6	13.0	6.2
1983	20.3	8.8	18.6	7.9
1986	14.8	6.0	14.2	6.1
1987	12.7	5.4	13.2	5.2

ᵃ1948–78 figures include blacks and other races; 1983–87 figures are for blacks only.

Source: U.S. Department of Labor, Bureau of Labor Statistics, *Employment and Earning Averages* (Washington, DC: Department of Labor, 1987).

THE FAILURE OF "UNIVERSAL" EMPLOYMENT

Can full or universal employment be achieved in the American economy? Some scholars suggest that through a combination of sound fiscal and monetary policies and targeted job creation, public works, and service programs, the American economy can be made to operate at full employment without unacceptably high levels of inflation.[7] Yet these scholars are a minority: Most economists and political leaders argue that full employment cannot be achieved in the United States without unacceptably high levels of inflation or some permanent system of government wage and price controls.

For example, during congressional hearings on the Humphrey-Hawkins Act, two leading liberal economists said flatly that full employment (defined as 4 percent unemployment) was not possible. Charles Shultz, later to become chair of President Carter's Council of Economic Advisors, told the Senate Labor committee that "the chief obstacle is inflation. I believe S. 50 [The Full Employment and the Balanced Growth Act] does not sufficiently recognize that fact, and hence needs to be changed in a number of important respects. Moreover, the combination of 'employer of last resort' provisions in this bill and the wage standards that go with it threaten to make the inflation problem worse."[8] Also, John Kenneth Galbraith, long-time liberal Democratic economist, presidential adviser, and Harvard professor, told the Senate Banking Committee:

> At a four percent unemployment rate, there is no question the American economy can be dangerously inflationary. . . . I must specifically and deliberately warn my liberal friends not to engage in the wishful economics that causes them to hope that there is still some undiscovered fiscal or monetary magic which will combine low unemployment and low inflation.[9]

In the decade and a half since passage of the Humphrey-Hawkins Act, neither the president, the Congress, nor the Federal Reserve have sought to use the planning process established by the act to move toward a 4 percent unemployment rate. As Congressman Hawkins woefully wrote in a 1986 article, "Since the passage of the Act, we have yet to see an economic report from the President, a Federal Reserve report or a Joint Economic Committee report that constructs the actual programmatic means for achieving full employment."[10] To the contrary, economic policy makers today generally consider 5 percent to 5.5 percent unemployment as the so-called natural rate of unemployment. This natural rate of unemployment, which translates into 10 percent to 12 percent for blacks, is accepted by Democrats and Republicans and liberals and conservatives—what one writer calls "a bipartisan fear of full employment."[11]

In 1998 the overall unemployment rate fell to 4.3 percent, the lowest rate in twenty-four years, which led immediately to fears that the Federal Reserve would raise interest rates to slow the growth of the economy and prevent a rise in inflation.[12] Yet, as the numbers in Table 15.2 show, this "dangerously low" level of unemployment still left the black community in a recession, with an adult unemployment rate of 7.7 percent; the black male teenage unemployment rate was 23.5 percent, compared to 11.6 percent for white teenagers. Meanwhile, whites were experiencing full employment at 3.6 percent as defined by the Humphrey-Hawkins Act. Since it is not likely that the Federal Reserve will permit the unemployment rate to fall much below 4 percent, blacks in this country will *never* experience full employment (on the role of race and racism on black unemployment (see Box 15.1).

One reason that blacks have more difficulty in finding employment than whites do is that employers increasingly locate businesses away from the central cities. For example, in testimony to Congress in 1998, HUD Secretary Andrew Cuomo reported that in the most recent growth cycle in the economy (1992–98), more than fifteen million new

---

TABLE 15.2

The Rate of Unemployment in the United States by Race, Gender, and Age, April 1999

OVERALL RATE	4.3%
Adult Whites	3.8
Adult White Men	3.0
Adult White Women	3.6
White Teenagers	11.6
Adult Blacks	7.7
Adult Black Men	6.1
Adult Black Women	6.8
Black Teenagers	23.5

Source: United States Department of Labor, Bureau of Labor Statistics, May 1999 press release. These data are seasonally adjusted. Adult is 20 years and older; teenager is 16 to 19.

jobs were created, but only 13 percent were located in central cities.[13] Recognizing this problem, late in his second term President Clinton undertook a "poverty tour" of central cities, Appalachia, and the Pine Ridge Indian Reservation in South Dakota. The president said the purpose of his three-day tour was to call attention to those "left behind" in the current prosperous economy and to encourage businesses to invest in the ghettos and other "pockets of poverty." In general, however, blacks criticized the president's tour as mere symbolism and as "too little, too late." Carl Rowan, the dean of African American columnists, for example, described the president's efforts as "an act of futility."[14]

BOX 15.1
Race, Racism, and African American Unemployment

Until the passage of the Civil Rights Act of 1964, it was perfectly legal for white employers to post signs or simply say to black job seekers, "We don't hire coloreds." Since the passage and implementation of the 1964 act and the development of affirmative action policies, racism has declined in the employment of blacks. However, studies still show continuing discrimination as African Americans seek work.

In 1991, the Urban Institute conducted a "hiring audit" to determine the degree of racial discrimination in entry-level employment in Washington and Chicago. The research used selected black and white "job testers" carefully matched in age, physical size, education (all were college educated), and experience, as well as such intangible factors as poise, openness, and articulateness. They were then sent to apply for entry-level jobs advertised in Washington and Chicago area newspapers. The study found what the authors call "entrenched and widespread" discrimination at every step in the hiring process, with whites three times as likely to advance to the point of being offered a job.[a]

Similarly, a study by Kirschenman and Neckerman, titled "We'd Love to Hire Them But . . .," found that Chicago area white employers were extremely reluctant to hire blacks, especially black men. Speaking of potential black workers, these employers told the researchers, "They are lazy; they steal; they lack motivation; they don't have a work ethic." Or "I need someone who will fit in"; "my customers are 95 percent white . . . I wouldn't last very long if I had a black," and "my guys don't want to work with blacks."[b] Finally, in a study of job losses during the 1990–91 recession, the *Wall Street Journal* found that African Americans were the *only* group to experience a net loss of jobs, losing 59,470 compared with *gains* of 55,104 by Asians, 60,000 by Hispanics, and 71,444 by whites.[c]

[a]Margery Turner, M. Fix, and R. Struyk, *Opportunities Denied, Opportunities Diminished: Discrimination in Hiring* (Washington: Urban Institute, 1991).

[b]Joleen Kirschenman and Kathryn Neckerman, "We'd Love to Hire Them But . . . The Meaning of Race for Employers," in C. Jencks and P. Peterson, eds., *The Urban Underclass* (Washington: Urban Institute, 1991).

[c]Rochelle Sharp, "Losing Ground: In Latest Recession Only Blacks Suffered Net Employment Loss," *Wall Street Journal*, September 14, 1993, p. A14.

CONSEQUENCES OF THE FAILURE OF FULL EMPLOYMENT ON THE AFRICAN AMERICAN COMMUNITY

What are the consequences of this long-term recession on the well-being of the African American community? First and most obviously, a job is a material benefit, providing the money necessary to support self and family. Less obvious but also important, a job is a psychic benefit, providing individuals with a sense of self-esteem, self-worth, and dignity. Thus, for many people, unemployment means not just a lack of money but lack of a sense of self-worth. We discuss the lack of money—enough money—in a moment, but first, what can be said about the impact of unemployment on things other than a person's pocketbook?

In 1984 Harvey Brenner, a sociologist, prepared a report for the Joint Economic Committee of Congress. In it, he showed that for every 1 percent increase in the rate of unemployment, there is an associated increase of 5.7 percent in murders, 4.1 percent in suicides, 1.9 percent in mortality, 3.3 percent in mental institutionalization, and a 4.7 percent increase in divorce and separation.[15] Other studies have found correlations between increases in unemployment and increases in child abuse, alcoholism,

Since the end of slavery, blacks have always faced a disproportionately high rate of unemployment. Indeed, blacks frequently say "The only time we had full employment was during slavery."

wife battering, and other individual and community pathologies.[16] Multiply Brenner's 1 percent increase by a factor of 10 over several generations to get a feel for the damaging consequences of long-term unemployment on the African American community (Box 15.2).

BOX 15.2

Crime and Punishment in Black and White

The United States imprisons more people than any other country in the world—in 1996 about 3 million people or about 3 percent of the population was incarcerated.[a] Nearly 40 percent of these people are African Americans, although blacks constitute little more than 12 percent of the population. Further, in 1995, more than 32 percent of young black men (20–29) were in jail or prison compared to only 7 percent of young white men. Astonishingly, the percentage of young black women in jail (5 percent) is almost as large as the percentage of jailed white men (only 1.5 percent of white women are jailed).[b] A partial explanation of this disproportionately high rate of black incarceration is that young black men who are poor commit more crimes than whites, but also important is the racial discrimination in the criminal justice system and unfairness in the punishment for use of illegal drugs. In 1995 the *Nashville Tennessean* analyzed all 1992–93 convictions in all federal district courts in the United States. The study found that the sentences of black criminals were up to 40 percent longer than those of white criminals in some courts, and that blacks are less likely than whites to get a break on their sentences. This racial disparity existed in all parts of the country, but it was highest in the West (California) and lowest in the South. And the disparity was only a black-white one, as Hispanics received the same sentences for the same crime as whites (there were too few Asians to make a comparison).[c]

Adding to this disparity in crime and punishment is the war on drugs. Under federal law, a person convicted of selling five grams of crack cocaine receives a mandatory five years in prison; a person would have to sell 250 grams of powdered cocaine to get a five-year sentence (a 100 to 1 ratio). Ninety percent of the persons convicted of selling crack cocaine are black; 90 percent of those convicted of selling powdered cocaine are white. Thus, blacks are given sentences five times as great as those of whites because their illegal drug of choice is crack rather than powdered cocaine. These racial sentencing disparities have been challenged and upheld in the federal courts, and shortly after the Million Man March on October 16, 1995, the House of Representatives voted down a Congressional Black Caucus bill that would have equalized sentences for powdered and crack cocaine.[d]

[a]"Justice System Holds about 3% of the U.S.," *New York Times*, July 2, 1996, p. A9.

[b]Marc Mauer, *Young Black Americans and the Criminal Justice System* (Washington: The Sentencing Project, 1995).

[c]Laura Frank, "U.S. Courts Give Blacks Longer Terms," *West County Times*, September 24, 1995, p. B1.

[d]President Clinton in August 1997 accepted the recommendation of Attorney General Janet Reno and "Drug Czar" Barry Mc-Caffrey and proposed to the Congress that those who sell 25 grams of crack and 250 grams of powdered cocaine receive the same five-year mandatory sentence, reducing the disparity to 10 to 1. See "President Clinton Supports Changes in Sentencing for Selling Cocaine," *Jet*, August 11, 1997, p. 39.

UNEMPLOYMENT, POVERTY, AND THE AFRICAN AMERICAN FAMILY

Using the government's official definition of poverty—in 1998 about $15,000 for a family of four—roughly a quarter of the African American community is poor. Only about 11% of the white population fits this definition. While there are more poor whites than blacks (about 20 million whites compared to 9 million blacks), poverty has a more devastating impact on the black *community* than on the white. For example, the impact of unemployment on the African American family has been nearly disastrous.

In 1965, Senator Daniel Patrick Moynihan, then an assistant secretary of labor, wrote a report on the "Negro" family in which he argued that high unemployment was leading to a breakup of the traditional two-parent family. Moynihan wrote that the "fundamental overwhelming fact" in the decline of the traditional African American family is that "Negro unemployment with the exception of a few years during the Korean War, has continued *at disastrous levels for 35 years*" (emphasis in original).[17] When Moynihan wrote his report, the percentage of female-headed households (father/husband absent) in the black community was about 30 percent. Today, consistent with the continued disastrous levels of high unemployment, the percentage is nearer 70 percent. This means that black families (mainly women and children) are much more dependent on government welfare programs than are whites. This is because white women are much more likely to find employed men to help support them and their children.

Persistently high unemployment is one important cause, if not the principal cause, of the high rate of divorce, separation, and out-of-wedlock births in the black community, a phenomenon traceable at least in part, as Senator Moynihan pointed out a generation ago, to the disastrously high levels of black male joblessness.[18] Black male unemployment is also one reason that African American families are so heavily dependent on welfare—Aid to Families with Dependent Children (AFDC)—and why the decision by President Clinton and the Congress to abolish AFDC as a universal (federal) benefit threatens to do such harm to the black community.

ENDING WELFARE AS WE KNOW IT

In his 1992 campaign, President Clinton pledged two major reforms in domestic social welfare policies: national health insurance and an "end to welfare as we know it." The president's complicated plan to provide health insurance for all Americans was not enacted by the Congress (on the impact of national health insurance on black Americans, see Box 15.3). However, he was able to keep his promise and end the sixty-year-old federal guarantee of aid to poor families with dependent children.

Ending Welfare as We Know It as Election Strategy

Historically, Americans have been reluctant to provide assistance to the poor, believing that it is up to individuals to provide (through hard work) for their own income and family welfare. Government "handouts" or the "dole" therefore are not generally acceptable because they contribute to laziness and individual irresponsibility. As shown by the data

===================== **BOX 15.3** =====================

African American Health and National Health Insurance

African Americans are not as healthy as whites. Two measures that frequently serve as summary measures of a people's health—the infant mortality rate and life expectancy—may be used to establish this point. The black infant mortality rate (the number of deaths per 1,000 live births before a child reaches one year of age) is 19.6, nearly twice that of whites, which is 10.1. The black life expectancy rate is 69.2 compared to 75.6 for whites. Why this enormous gap between the races in health? The most basic explanation is the lack of adequate care and health insurance among African Americans.[a]

Twenty percent of African Americans lack health insurance compared to 12 percent of whites. Studies have shown that this lack of health insurance is directly related to their health and life expectancy. For example, Eugene Schwarz and his colleagues examined the records of Americans age fifteen to fifty-four who died between 1980 and 1986 from twelve illnesses that normally are curable if treated: pneumonia, hernia, gallbladder, and influenza, among others. Between 1980 and 1986, nearly 18,000 persons died of these illnesses. More than 80 percent of the people who died in what Schwarz and his colleagues call "excess" deaths were black. The study concludes that blacks died of the diseases four times more frequently than whites because they did not receive adequate, routine health care. They did not receive health care, in large part, because they did not have health insurance.[b]

In the post–civil rights era, universal health insurance—after full employment—has been the major item on the African American leadership agenda. African American Congress members and interest groups were strong supporters of President Clinton's national health care legislation. The reason is obvious; for blacks, its defeat in the Congress is literally a matter of life and death.

[a]Brigid Schulte, "Americans Face Separate and Unequal Health," *West County Times,* August 21, 1998.

[b]Eugene Schwarz et al., "Black/White Comparisons of Deaths Preventable by Medical Intervention: United States and District of Columbia, 1980–86," *International Journal of Epidemiology* 19 (1970): 591–98.

reported in Table 15.3, Americans are dead last among the major nations of the world in believing it is the responsibility of the government to take care of the poor. Nearly two-thirds of the French, British, Spanish, Italians, and Russians believe that the government has such a role, compared to only 23 percent of Americans.

In addition to these negative attitudes toward government help for the poor in general, most white Americans are specifically hostile to welfare. Contrary to what the data in Table 15.4 show, they believe that most people on welfare are black and that blacks are lazy and prefer welfare to work. The truth is that blacks constitute 37 percent of AFDC recipients; Hispanics, 18 percent; Asians, 3 percent; others, 3 percent; and whites, 39 percent. Thus, there are more whites on welfare than blacks but blacks nevertheless are disproportionately more likely to be receiving welfare. (Roughly a third of black families compared to about 10 percent of white families depend on welfare.)

--- **TABLE 15.3** ---

Attitudes Concerning the Government's Responsibility to Take Care of the Poor: Selected Countries, 1991

	PERCENTAGE AGREEING THAT GOVERNMENT HAS RESPONSIBILITY TO CARE FOR POOR
Spain	70
Russia	70
Italy	66
France	62
Great Britain	61
Poland	56
East Germany[a]	64
West Germany	45
United States	23

[a]The poll was conducted prior to the formal unification of the two Germanies

Source: Times Mirror Center for the People and the Press. We are grateful to Professor David Tabb of San Francisco State University for making these data available to us.

Thus, the *perception* among whites that welfare is a black program is not wholly off the mark. And this perception profoundly affects attitudes about welfare.

According to the 1992 General Social Survey, 47 percent of whites believe that African Americans as a people are lazy, and 59 percent believe that blacks would prefer to live on welfare rather than work.[19] And these beliefs—that the majority of people on welfare are black and that blacks are lazy—profoundly affect how the public views welfare. Table 15.5 shows that those who believe most welfare recipients are white (18%)

--- **TABLE 15.4** ---

Recipients of Aid to Families with Dependent Children (AFDC) by Ethnicity, 1994

RECIPIENTS BY ETHNICITY	PERCENTAGE OF TOTAL CASELOAD[a]
White	39
Black	37
Hispanic	18
Asian	3
Other	3

[a]As of 1994, there were 14.1 million recipients of AFDC, at a total cost of $22.5 billion per year. In addition, most AFDC recipients (along with others) also received food stamps and Medicaid. In 1994, there were 27 million food stamp recipients and the program cost $25 billion. Medicaid's budget was $125 billion and had a total caseload of 32 million.

Sources: The House Ways and Means Committee, the Departments of Agriculture, and Health and Human Services, as reported in the *Orange County Register,* December 19, 1994, p. 6.

───────────────────── **TABLE 15.5** ─────────────────────

Attitudes of Americans toward Welfare According to Whether Respondent Believes Most Recipients Are Black: 1994

	Respondent believes most on welfare are:	
	BLACK (44%)	WHITE (18%)
WHY ARE PEOPLE ON WELFARE?		
Lack of effort	61%	38%
Circumstances beyond control	25	48
DO MOST PEOPLE ON WELFARE WANT TO WORK?		
Yes	29	51
No	65	43
DO MOST PEOPLE ON WELFARE REALLY NEED IT?		
Yes	34	48
No	60	49

Source: 1994 *New York Times* poll. We are again grateful to Professor David Tabb at San Francisco State University for sharing these data.

are more likely to think people on welfare want to work, that they are on welfare because of circumstances beyond their control, and that they really need help. On the other hand, those who think most recipients are black (44%) believe the opposite.

It is out of this historical and cultural context of individualism and white supremacist thinking that President Clinton developed his "end welfare as we know it" strategy, a strategy that Senator Moynihan—the leading congressional authority on welfare policy—called "boob bait for the bubbas." In 1992 President Clinton's strategist told him that to win back the so-called Reagan Democrats in the key battleground states of the midwest (Pennsylvania, Ohio, Illinois, and Michigan), he would have to take a tough antiwelfare stance. For example, a 1984 Democratic party poll concluded that the Democrats had lost the support of many whites because the party was viewed as the "giveaway party, giving white tax money to blacks and poor people."[20] Thus, in ads that ran in places like Pennsylvania and Ohio, Clinton pledged to end welfare as we know it by limiting assistance to two years and then forcing people to work. Also, in his campaign rhetoric, candidate Clinton attacked teenage pregnancy and out-of-wedlock births as evidence of the lack of "individual responsibility" and "family values" among the disproportionately African American recipients of welfare.

Ending Welfare as We Know It as Public Policy

Clinton's campaign rhetoric and ads suggested that people would be cut off welfare and forced to find a job or else. In fact, his proposal, based on the work of Harvard professor of public policy David Ellwood (who became a top welfare policy maker in the first two years of Clinton's administration) involved a broad program of expanded social services including job training, health, child care, and public sector jobs.[21] This proposal, which had the support of the Congressional Black Caucus, liberals, and children's advocacy groups, would have cost more than the existing welfare system, an estimated $30 billion. For almost two years Clinton delayed sending his welfare reform bill to Congress, focusing in his first year on his budget deficit plan and in the second year on health care. Meanwhile, his staff was working on ways to scale back the expensive Ellwood plan. Finally, late in 1994, Clinton submitted his plan, but it arrived too late in the session for the Congress to act.

When the Republicans in 1994 won majorities in the Congress, they took Clinton's campaign promise seriously and three times passed bills ending the 60-year-old federal welfare system, including food stamps, Medicaid and AFDC. Clinton vetoed the first two bills (forcing deletions in the third bill of the Medicaid and food stamp provisions), but as the 1996 presidential election got under way, Clinton—reluctantly he said—signed the Republican welfare bill.

The bill signed by Clinton was opposed by Senator Moynihan; Senator Tom Daschle, the Democratic leader; and Representative Richard Gephardt, the House Democratic leader. It was also opposed by half the Senate Democrats and all except two of the thirty-five black Democrats in the House (Congressman Albert Winn of suburban Maryland and Congressman Sanford Bishop of rural Georgia were the two black Democrats who supported the bill). Finally, the bill was opposed by *all* of Clinton's senior policy advisers on welfare; three of these—Wendel Primus, Mary Jo Bane, and Peter B. Edelman—resigned in protest after the president signed the bill.[22] Yet Clinton was told by his campaign strategists to sign the bill—although it was bad—because otherwise Republican candidate Dole would use the veto to undermine Clinton's support among Reagan Democrats in the fall campaign.[23] Clinton signed the bill, promising to "fix" those parts he did not like (mainly the provisions denying benefits to legal immigrants and the cuts in the food stamp budget).

The bill Clinton signed passed the House 256 to 170 and the Senate 74 to 26, with the near-unanimous support of Republicans in both the House and Senate. Just as President Clinton signed the bill for political rather than policy reasons, the handful of Democratic liberals who voted for it did so for the same reason. Here is New York Democratic Congressman Gary Ackerman's explanation of his vote:

> It was not a happy decision. *This is a bad bill but a good strategy.* In order to continue economic and social progress, we must keep President Clinton in office. And we are within striking distance of a majority in the House in this year's election. We had to show Americans that Democrats are willing to break with the past, to move from welfare to workfare. *Sometimes in order to make progress and move ahead, you have to stand up, do wrong.* If we take back the House, we can fix this bill and take out some of the draconian parts (emphasis added).[24]

Thus, the Democratic party and the president accepted a "bad bill" in order to win the election, in the process risking the welfare of perhaps millions of women and their children.[25]

The bill signed by the president amends Title IV of the Social Security Act of 1935. Its major provisions include these:

- The federal government's guarantee of aid to poor mothers and children is abolished, with the states given authority to decide their own welfare programs.

- Welfare is limited to five years but states could waive this requirement for up to 20 percent of recipients.
- States can deny benefits to unmarried mothers under 18.
- With a few exceptions, most adult recipients are required to work within two years.
- Legal immigrants would have to work in the United States for a minimum of ten years or become citizens before getting food stamps or Supplemental Security Income.
- The bill saves about $55 billion over six years through cuts in food stamps and aid to legal immigrants.

Since the federal government assumed responsibility for managing the economy to assure economic growth, employment, and price stability, full employment has been the top priority of African Americans and their leaders. It appears, however, that the American economy cannot be made to operate at full employment (without risking high inflation) except in times of war. Today, most economists assume that an unemployment rate of 5 percent to 5.5 percent is the normal, "natural rate" of unemployment. This rate translates into an ongoing recession in black America. Generations of recession-level unemployment rates of 10 percent or more have had devastating consequences for the African American family and community. Since 1935 the federal government has maintained AFDC as a federal, universal program of welfare for poor women and children who did not have employed husbands and who themselves could not find work at living wages. The abolition in 1996 of this sixty-year-old universal safety net, returning responsibility for welfare of poor children and women to the states, has raised the specter that millions of children and their parents might be thrown into increased poverty and misery.

This chapter has focused on the African American quest for universal freedom in terms of access to material-based benefits. This quest has met with limited success. African Americans are not likely to be satisfied with this limited success. How the African American community and its leaders and white society will deal with this dissatisfaction is one of the more fascinating and puzzling questions for the future of the African American freedom struggle.

SELECTED BIBLIOGRAPHY

Bailey, Stephen. *Congress Makes a Law*. New York: Vintage Books, 1964. A classic legislative case study, focusing on the Congress's first attempt to enact full employment legislation.

Edelman, Peter. "Clinton's Worst Mistake." *Atlantic Monthly,* May 1997. An incisive critique of the welfare reform bill signed by President Clinton.

Ellwood, David. *Poor Support: Poverty in the American Family*. New York: Basic Books, 1988. A detailed discussion of humane reforms in welfare by the Harvard professor and former Clinton administration welfare official.

Frendreis, John, and Raymond Tatalovich. *The Modern Presidency and Economic Policy*. Itasca, IL: F. E. Peacock, 1994. A descriptive analysis of how economic policy is made.

Harvey, Phillip. *Securing the Right to Employment: Social Welfare Policy and the Un-employed in the United States*. Princeton, NJ: Princeton University Press, 1989. An analysis with recommendations on how to achieve full employment.

Kirshernman, J., and K. Neckerman. "We'd Love to Hire Them But . . . The Meaning of Race for Employers." In C. Jencks, ed. *The Urban Underclass*. Washington: Brookings Institution, 1992. A study of the role of race and racism in the employment decisions of white employers.

Moynihan, Daniel P. *The Politics of a Guaranteed Income*. New York: Vintage Books, 1973. A study of the Nixon administration's failed attempt to enact a universal family assistance plan to replace AFDC.

Piven, Frances, and Richard Cloward. *Regulating the Poor: The Functions of Public Welfare*. New York: Vintage Books, 1971. A provocative analysis of how welfare is used as a mechanism to control the political behavior of the poor.

Schlesinger, Arthur. *The Coming of the New Deal*. New York: Houghton Mifflin, 1959. A classic account of the beginnings of the American welfare state.

Smith, Robert C. "The Humphrey-Hawkins Act as Symbolic Politics." In Robert C. Smith, *We Have No Leaders: African Americans in the Post–Civil Rights Era,* chap. 7. Albany: University of New York Press, 1996. A case study of Congress's second attempt to enact full employment legislation.

Wilson, William. *The Truly Disadvantaged: The Inner City, the Underclass and Public Policy*. Chicago: University of Chicago Press, 1987. A very influential study that focuses on the loss of industrial jobs as the key factor in the rise and growth of the underclass.

NOTES

1. See Arthur Schlesinger, Jr., *The Coming of the New Deal* (New York: Houghton Mifflin, 1959).

2. For a history of the 1946 act's adoption, see Stephen Bailey, *Congress Makes a Law* (New York: Vintage Books, 1964).

3. For a discussion of the economic policy-making apparatus, including the work of the president and his budget and economic advisers, the Congress, and the Federal Reserve Board, see John Frendreis and Raymond Tatalovich, *The Modern Presidency and Economic Policy* (Itasia, IL: F. E. Peacock, 1994).

4. Dana Hamilton and Charles Hamilton, *The Dual Agenda: Social Policies of Civil Rights Organizations from the New Deal to the Present* (New York: Columbia University Press, 1996).

5. Ralph Bunche, "The Programs of Organizations Devoted to the Improvement of the Negro," *Journal of Negro Education* 8 (1939): 542–43.

6. William J. Wilson, *The Truly Disadvantaged: The Inner City, the Underclass and Public Policy* (Chicago: University of Chicago Press, 1987); William J. Wilson, *When Work Disappears: The World of the New Urban Poor* (New York: Random House, 1996).

7. Phillip Harvey, *Securing the Right to Employment: Social Welfare Policy and the Unemployed in the United States* (Princeton, NJ: Princeton University Press,

1989); Richard Gill, *Economics and the Public Interest* (Pacific Palisades: Goodyear, 1968).

8. Committee on Labor and Public Welfare, Subcommittee on Employment, Poverty and Migratory Labor, Senate, *Hearings on S. 50 and S. 472*, May 14, 17, 18, 19, 1976, p. 141.

9. Quoted in the *Congressional Record—House*, March 8, 1978, p. 6122.

10. Augustus Hawkins, "Whatever Happened to Full Employment," *Urban League Review* 10 (1986): 11.

11. F. Thayer, "A Bipartisan Fear of Full Employment," *New York Times*, October 12, 1988.

12. Richard Stevenson, "Trying to Figure Out How Low Unemployment Figures Can Go," *New York Times*, September 7, 1996, p. 20.

13. Testimony of Secretary Cuomo, House Appropriations Subcommittee on VA, HUD, and Independent Agencies broadcast on C-Span, March 25, 1998.

14. Rowan is quoted in Jason Deparle, "Clinton's Poverty Tour Draws Skepticism and Indifference," *New York Times* on the Web, July 9, 1999.

15. Harvey M. Brenner, "Estimating the Effects of Economic Change on National Health and Social Well-Being," paper prepared for the Subcommittee on Economic Goals and Intergovernmental Policy, Joint Economic Committee, July 15, 1984.

16. Jeanne Prial Gordus and Sean McAliden, "Economic Change, Physical Illness and Social Deviance," paper prepared for the Subcommittee on Economic Goals and Intergovernmental Relations, Joint Economic Committee, July 14, 1994.

17. Daniel Patrick Moynihan, "The Negro Family: A Case for National Action," in Lee Rainwater and William Yancey, *The Moynihan Report and the Politics of Controversy* (Cambridge, MA: MIT Press, 1967): 369, 375.

18. M. Belinda Tucker and Claudia Mitchell-Kernon, eds., *The Decline in Marriage among African Americans* (New York: Russell Sage, 1995). We should note that divorce rates and the rate of out-of-wedlock births have gone up sharply among whites in the United States and throughout the Western industrial world. See Tamar Lewin, "The Decay of Families Is Global, Study Says," *New York Times*, May 30, 1995.

19. These data are reported in Robert C. Smith, *Racism in the Post–Civil Rights Era: Now You See It, Now You Don't* (Albany: State University of New York Press, 1995): 39. Although most whites view blacks as lazy and not willing to work, blacks have historically constituted a large proportion of the nation's working poor, doing much of America's "dirty" work as housecleaners, janitors, and hospital orderlies. See U.S. Department of Labor, *A Profile of the Working Poor* (Washington: Government Printing Office, 1983): Tables 3, 13.

20. Million Kolter and Nelson Rosenbaum, "Strengthening the Democratic Party through Strategic Marketing: Voters and Donors," a confidential report for the Democratic National Committee, Washington, D.C. On the background of the strategic approach followed by Clinton, see his campaign "bible" by Thomas Edsal and Mary Edsal, *Chain Reaction: The Impact of Race, Rights and Taxes on American Politics* (New York: W.W. Norton, 1992). See also Smith, *We Have No Leaders*, chap. 10.

21. David Ellwood, *Poor Support: Poverty and the American Family* (New York: Basic Books, 1988).

22. Bane, Primus, and Edelman were all assistant secretaries in the Department of Health and Human Services with responsibilities for welfare policy. They resigned, they said, because the bill would result in a huge increase in child poverty—by one estimate adding more than a million kids to the poverty rolls. See "Official Quits in Protest of Welfare Decision," *West County Times*, August 18, 1996, p. 3D, and "2 Clinton Aides Quit over Bill," *San Francisco Chronicle*, September 12, 1996, p. A3. During House consideration of the bill, Harvard's David Ellwood, who helped to design the Clinton administration's bill and then returned to his teaching post, wrote an op-ed essay urging a Clinton veto of the Republican bill. See "Welfare Reform in Name Only," *New York Times*, July 22, 1996, p. A15. See also Peter Edelman, "The Worst Thing Clinton Has Done," *Atlantic Monthly* (May, 1997): 7–23.

23. The principal political adviser urging the president to sign the welfare bill was Dick Morris, who subsequently was forced to resign from the campaign after it was learned he had fathered an out-of-wedlock child and was exposed (on the last night of the Democratic convention) as having a long-time sexual relationship with a prostitute. With an abundance of hypocrisy and hubris, Morris had urged Clinton to sign the bill because doing so would symbolize his support for "family" values and opposition to promiscuous sex and out-of-wedlock births. Morris also said he told the president that a veto of the welfare bill would cost him the election, transforming a 15 percent win into a 3 percent loss. See Dick Morris, *Behind the Oval Office: Winning the Presidency in the Nineties* (New York: Random House, 1997): 300.

24. Robert Pear, "Many Subtleties Shaped Welfare Vote," *New York Times*, August 4, 1996, p. A12.

25. After passage of the legislation, the welfare rolls begin to decline rapidly as recipients apparently were able to find jobs in the growing economy. However, the decline was greatest among whites so that two years after the bill was enacted, blacks and Latinos outnumber whites on welfare by a margin of 2 to 1. In addition, the welfare caseload more so than ever is concentrated in the central cities, where, as we pointed out earlier, job growth has been modest. See Jason Departes, "Welfare Race Gap Raises Fear," *New York Times*, July 28, 1998. Although it is too early for a comprehensive assessment of welfare reform, a summary of available studies by the Congress's General Accounting Office released in May of 1999 found that between 61 percent and 87 percent of those leaving welfare have found jobs but that many of the jobs are short-lived, the majority are low paying, and between 19 percent and 30 percent of the people who leave welfare soon return.

CHAPTER 16

The African American Quest for Universal Freedom and U.S. Foreign Policy

In the 1940s, Edith Sampson, an attorney in Chicago, was appointed by President Truman as a delegate to the United Nations General Assembly. Over the years she has been followed by Pearl Bailey, Zelma George, Marian Anderson, Coretta Scott King, and a host of others. Sampson became the first African American, male or female, to represent the United States at the United Nations.[1]

African Americans have served as consuls, ministers, and ambassadors to foreign capitals as well as the United Nations. African Americans have been employed as foreign service officers and career officials at the Department of State. Outside the bureaucracy, African Americans have served the nation in an ad hoc fashion. For example, in 1889, upon learning that historian-lawyer George Washington Williams would be making a visit to the Congo, President Benjamin Harrison asked him to gather information and submit a report on his return, which could be used in determining what this nation's policy should be toward the Congo.[2] President Jimmy Carter sent boxer Muhammad Ali on a goodwill tour of Africa, and President Clinton, during his first term, sent Jesse Jackson as a special representative to Nigeria and William Gray, a former congressman, as special envoy to Haiti. In addition to performing these short goodwill representative roles and functions, African Americans have been selected to serve and represent the nation on international commissions and tribunals. Fisk University president and sociologist Charles S. Johnson was appointed by President Herbert Hoover in 1929 to serve on the International Commission to Investigate Slavery and Forced Labor in Liberia and give a report to the State Department.[3]

There is one other role that African Americans have played in implementing United States foreign policy: as participants in all the nation's wars. Whether it was as buffalo soldiers in the Indian wars or as troops in the Spanish-American War, both world wars, the Korean conflict, Vietnam, the invasion of Grenada, Panama, or the Gulf War, African Americans have carried the sword in every military conflict.

Although they have played numerous roles and functions in implementing and managing American foreign policies, African Americans have also served as *creators* in foreign matters, particularly as America's policy has related to the Third World and Africa. In fact, in their role as creators, African Americans have been critics, as was the NAACP after its investigation of the U.S. Marine occupation of Haiti (1915–1934). African Americans have been innovators, as were Sylvester Williams and W. E. B. Du Bois in organizing the Pan-African Congresses; or William Monroe Trotter and Du Bois at the Paris Peace Conference in 1919; or Mary McCleod Bethune, Walter White, and Du Bois at the founding conference of the United Nations. William Patterson and Malcolm X presented petitions to the United Nations on human rights; and Randall Robinson had a leadership role in creating Trans Africa, a national foreign policy lobbying organization for African American interests. In addition, in this role as creators, African American foreign policy elites have developed numerous tactics and strategies to mobilize the masses to rally around issues, as did Trans Africa in the boycott of South Africa.[4]

Finally, in their role as creators, African Americans have slowly and gradually shaped and developed a reasonable and distinguishable foreign policy. Whether they were reacting and responding to short-term international crises and events, or long-term and continuing events like colonialism and the Cold War, certain trends and patterns have emerged as a discernible foreign policy. It is in this role that African Americans have served, in John Hope Franklin's words, as "ministers/diplomats without portfolio," or in the words of Karen Stanford, "citizen diplomats."

Thus, in their quest for universal freedom, African Americans, who were born in foreign affairs through African slavery and the slave trade, have turned to America's foreign policy to support foreign policies of human rights and humanitarianism. Any appreciation of the universal freedom thrust of African American politics must include an understanding of African Americans' role in foreign affairs.

AFRICAN AMERICANS AS FOREIGN POLICY IMPLEMENTORS/MANAGERS

In his study of African Americans in the foreign policy apparatus, Jake Miller made the following comments: "When one considers the input of Blacks into the Foreign policy-making machinery, the State Department immediately becomes the major part of the focus, since it is in this governmental department that foreign policy is traditionally formulated."[5] But looking at the State Department as late as 1998, only 2.7 percent of the entire Foreign Service Corps was African American.

Given this basic reality, Miller then asserted: "It can be concluded that decision-making powers in the State Department reside in a very limited number of officers, few of whom are Blacks."[6] (See Box 16.1.) However, "select groups often speak with commanding voices in this field . . . [but] Blacks . . . have tended to be among the least influential in the field of foreign affairs."[7] African Americans have not had the key positions in the bureaucracy, yet as an interest group they have had a recognizable and continuing role throughout their sojourn in America. And they have had to fashion this role inside the bureaucracy in a different manner from that used by other pressure groups.

═══════════════ **BOX 16.1** ═══════════════

Colin Powell

Although for much of its history the American foreign policy establishment was constituted almost exclusively of white male Protestants with Ivy League backgrounds, in recent years a handful of African American men have entered this elite circle of policy makers. Among this group is Carl Rowan, director of the United States Information Agency (the government's international information and propaganda agency) under President Lyndon Johnson and the first African American to sit on the high-level National Security Council. Two African Americans in the Carter administration served in the post of ambassador to the United Nations (Andrew Young and Donald McHenry), and Clifton Warton served briefly as deputy secretary of state in the Clinton administration, the number two diplomatic post in the government.

During the Reagan and Bush administrations, General Colin Powell reached the pinnacles of the American foreign policy establishment. General Powell's early career in the Army was distinguished, and in 1972 young Lieutentant Colonel Powell was awarded a prestigious White House Fellowship. These positions allow young professionals to work at the highest level of the executive branch for a year. From this point on, Powell's rise in military and diplomatic circles was meteoric. As a White House Fellow, Powell worked closely with Casper Weinberger when Weinberger was director of the Office of Management and Budget in the Nixon administration. After this, he was assigned as a military aide to the deputy secretary of defense and when Weinberger became defense secretary in the Reagan administration, he named Powell as his military aide. After six years in this post, Powell became deputy to Frank Carlucci, Reagan's National Security Advisor, and when Carlucci succeeded Weinberger as Secretary of Defense, Reagan appointed Powell National Security Advisor. The post of National Security Advisor—a job made famous by Henry Kissinger during the Nixon administration—is the third most important in the foreign policy-making bureaucracy (behind the secretaries of state and defense). The National Security Advisor is responsible for the coordination of all diplomatic, intelligence, and military data for presentation to the president on a daily basis, and is the principal "crisis manager" during periods of international conflict.

When George Bush was elected president, he reportedly offered Powell a choice of two other top foreign policy jobs, director of the CIA or deputy secretary of state. Powell declined both, opting instead to return to his career in the Army. He was immediately promoted to the rank of four-star general and commander in chief of the nation's Strategic Reserve Forces, one of only ten such

(Continued)

BOX 16.1 Continued

command posts worldwide. After only six months in this position, President Bush appointed Powell chairman of the Joint Chiefs of Staff, the highest-ranking post in the armed services and principal military adviser to the President. In naming Powell to this position, Bush passed over fifteen other more senior four-star generals, making Powell the youngest chair of the Joint Chiefs in history. Powell became well known to the public during the Persian Gulf War. Although he reportedly opposed immediately going to war in favor of the Democratic party leadership's economic sanctions strategy, once Bush made the decision, Powell oversaw the development and implementation of the rapid defeat of the Iraqi military. His poised and self-confident defense of the war on television and the quick victory of the American forces made Powell something of a national hero.

After two 2-year terms at the Joint Chiefs, Powell resigned from the Army, wrote his memoirs, engaged in a highly successful book tour, announced he was a Republican, and briefly considered running for president in 1996.[a]

[a]On Powell's career, see Bob Woodward, The Commanders (New York: Simon & Schuster, 1991), and Powell's memoir, My American Journey (New York: Random House, 1995).

Inside the bureaucracy, African Americans had to fashion their role from positions as ministers and ambassadors to small African nations. To locate and extrapolate this role, it is essential to probe and analyze the diplomatic correspondence of these individuals as well as their symbolic actions, "to protest and advance the cause of a black nationality, both on the continent of Africa and in the diaspora"[8] Elliot P. Skinner, African American scholar, former ambassador to the Republic of Upper Volta, and student of these early African American diplomats, notes that this collective role could be encapsulated in the concept of *black nationality*.[9] Skinner writes, "Diplomats such as J. Milton Turner, Henry H. Smyth and Ernest Lyon were openly confrontational with the State Department to achieve their objectives. They endeavored to prove that they could serve faithfully as American foreign service officers even while protecting the black nationality."[10] Many of these African American implementors of American foreign policy believed that by helping to create a strong and developed Africa, they would contribute to the solution of its people's problems the world over. And they would be helping to preserve the already existing nation-states of Liberia and Haiti. This was their expression of "black nationality" and they would leave it as a legacy to future African Americans coming into the foreign policy bureaucracy.

One of the roots of the black nationality began in Abraham Lincoln's annual message to Congress in December, 1861. President Lincoln announced, "If any good reason exists why we should persevere longer in withholding our recognition of the independence and sovereignty of Haiti and Liberia, I am unable to discern it."[11] At a National Convention meeting in Syracuse, New York, African Americans "passed a resolution praising Congress for honoring the President's request."[12] Senator Charles Summer of Massachusetts introduced the bill for the president; this bill authorized the president to appoint diplomatic representatives to Haiti and Liberia. It was attacked but eventually passed by 32 to 7 in the Senate and 86 to 37 in the House. The reality had been that "for decades southerners had blocked the formal recognition of Haiti and Liberia."[13] Thus, "when with secession these primary opponents of Haitian (and Liberian) recognition lost their posts of power within the federal government, they could no longer exercise a veto over the formulation of national policy."[14] But even with this action by President Lincoln, "the United States was the last of the western nations to open normal diplomatic relations with [these] African countries."[15]

After recognition of the two countries, the first African American diplomats to these "Negro" republics began to use their influence in the State Department on behalf of the new nations. Miller writes that an analysis of the diplomatic correspondence of the "black ministers accredited to Port-au-Prince . . . revealed that no issue tended to be more dominant than those involving the granting of asylum to Haitians and the protection of Americans and their interest in the Black Republic."[16] Clearly related to this issue was the question of political instability in the country.[17]

In Liberia, black ministers were preoccupied with the attempts by European powers to encroach on the territorial sovereignty of the young black republic. Their notes to the State Department reflected their concern with such matters as Liberian border frictions with England and France. With Haiti, political instability became the primary issue.

In pressing the concerns of Haiti and Liberia, diplomats in both these "Negro" republics found themselves in conflictual and confrontational stances with the State Department. Here is an example of bureaucrats opposing their own bureaucracy. As Miller writes: "The structural challenge for African Americans chosen as envoys (diplomats) was that they also had to serve a nation that denigrated them and Africa itself."[18] The first African American diplomat to Liberia, J. Milton Turner (1871–1878), realized that these black diplomats had to use "extreme prudence"; he designed his dispatches "as much . . . to educate the officials in the State Department about the realities of Liberia as to enlist the help of his government for the Liberians."[19]

However, not all the black diplomats took such a frontal and conflictual approach with the State Department. Some moved in fugitive, back-channel, and secretive manners, acting on their own and beyond the normal diplomatic channels. Of this tactic Miller writes that while most black ministers participated in the drive for greater Liberian security in a noncontroversial manner, the State Department has felt compelled to chastise some for overstepping guidelines.

An example was diplomat Ernest Lyon. Lyon, a protege of Booker T. Washington, became adept at "back-channel" manipulation; establishing important contacts outside the State Department in order to effect policy. Lyon knew how to exploit Booker T. Washington's strong support among both northern and southern African Americans and his accommodationist attitude toward the white power structure to accomplish his goals.[20] To achieve their aims and objectives, these back-channel diplomats used symbolic structures as a means of seeking to influence United States policy, toward Africa and its people. These "symbolic structures" were conferences and hortatory rhetoric, newspaper coverage, lectures, letters, and contact with interested and powerful white individuals and groups.[21] Symbolic structures were devices to mobilize public opinion and mass interest in both African American and white communities.

In sum, African American diplomats, ministers, envoys, and ambassadors found in their own individual manner, three discernible ways to articulate their concern for universal freedom and respect. First, they could be conflictual and confrontational with the State Department. This tactic was an effort to move the department toward a more positive policy in maintaining and enhancing the independence of these new black republics. The second technique was individual initiatives. Here, they took matters in their own hands, devising solutions independent of the State Department.

The third and final tactic was the back-channel technique. Here insiders passed vital information to elites inside the black community. This procedure, unlike the others, forged a link between the diplomats and the African American community, as well as with key individuals in the white community.

However, "almost all the early diplomats in Africa (and elsewhere) . . . badgered the United States to take a stronger stand in protecting the areas they served. These men understood fully the complexity of United States complicity in European imperialist designs rather than the country's national interest that dictated policy."[22] Overall, both these early and latter day diplomats, "in activities largely unknown to contemporaries and to later generations . . . collaborated in an attempt to use both their limited political power and their considerable symbolic means to influence United States policy toward Africa."[23]

These strategies may not have been as influential, but they perpetuated a legacy for the future. For instance, when African Americans served as delegates to the United Nations' General Assembly, they continued the tradition taken by the early diplomats. Alternate delegate Zelma George in 1960 "displayed contempt for the position taken by the United States when she stood and joined African and Asian representatives in applauding the adoption of the resolution calling for an end of colonialism—a resolution on which the United States had abstained."[24]

In 1971, U.N. delegate, Congressman Charles Diggs of Michigan, sent a telegram to Secretary of State William Rogers expressing his opposition to the United States position on apartheid and resigned from the delegation. In its response to Congressman Diggs, "the State Department noted that while it recognized the value of consultation, there was a need for the United States to speak with one voice in the United Nations General Assembly."[25]

AFRICAN AMERICANS AS FOREIGN POLICY DISSENTERS

However, black diplomats were not solely concerned with "Negro" Republics. Because of their posting to these nations, they could speak to only this one aspect. But the limitations of federal bureaucrats are not the limitations of the entire black community. Elites, organizations, and institutions inside the community also helped shape responses to a wider array of issues and concerns.

Paul Cuffe began an aspect of black nationality when in 1815 he took thirty-eight blacks to Africa at a personal expense of $3,000 or $4,000.[26] His African colonization plan was a critique of the treatment and possibilities of African American universal freedom in the United States. His critique was a harbinger of a new American policy of colonization, as well as an African American policy of emigration.

Cuffe's initial articulation through activism was taken up by Martin Delany and Robert Campbell when they launched a trip to explore the Niger River area as a site for emigration. But on their return to America, Delany and Campbell had to face the reality that it was not easy for African Americans to go to Africa.[27] After the Berlin Conference of 1884–1885, colonialism arrived full force in Africa and the visions created by Cuffe, Delany, and Campbell went sour under the terror brought on by some of the colonial powers. At the 1884–85 Berlin Conference, the Congo was given to King Leopold of Belgium, and he "instituted one of the harshest, cruelest and most violent systems of colonialism in Africa."[28] American foreign policy stood silent as the atrocities of King Leopold occurred on a daily basis.[29] George Washington Williams—historian, politician, and Ohio legislator—bitterly criticized King Leopold's policies in the Congo.[30] African American dissenters to American foreign policy now began to fashion a role in line with specific events and places. The actions by Williams were more specific and more focused than had been the work of Cuffe, Delany, and Campbell.

Many African American leaders (along with such whites as Henry David Thoreau and the young congressman Abraham Lincoln) were vigorous opponents of the Mexican-American War. Frederick Douglass, for example, was scathing in his criticism, writing in his newspaper *North Star* that the United States government had

> succeeded in robbing Mexico of her territory, and are rejoicing over their success under the hypocritical pretense of a regard for peace. Had they not succeeded in robbing Mexico of the most important and most valuable of her territory, many of those now loudest in their professions of favor for peace would be loudest and wildest for war.[31]

Following in the path blazed by Williams and Douglass was Bishop Alexander Walters of the National African American Council, who was strongly critical when the Americans annexed the Philippines during the Spanish-American War.[32] There, in the cause of white supremacy, the United States turned from a policy of cooperating with Tagalog insurgents against the Spanish colonial authorities to one of joining with the defeated Spaniards against the Filipinos.[33] Therefore, as a foreign policy dissenter, Walters noted that "had the Filipino been white and fought as brave as they have, the war would have been ended and their independence granted a long time ago."[34] But those in the Walters-led group were not the only dissenters. One of the African American troops sent the following letter to an African American newspaper, the *Wisconsin Weekly Advocate*, in Milwaukee, May 17, 1900:

> I have mingled freely with the natives and have had talks with American colored men here in business and who have lived here for years, in order to learn of them the cause of their (Filipino) dissatisfaction and the reason for this insurrection, and I must confess they have a just grievance. All this never would have occurred if the army of occupation would have treated them as people. The Spaniards, even if their laws were hard, were polite and treated them with some consideration; but the Americans, as soon as they saw that the native troops were desirous of sharing in the glories as well as the hardships of the hard-won battles with the Americans, began to apply home treatment for colored peoples: cursed them as damned niggers, steal [from] and ravish them, rob them on the street of their small change, take from the fruit vendors whatever suited their fancy, and kick the poor unfortunate if he complained, desecrate their church property, and after

fighting began, looted everything in sight, burning, robbing. . . . Heaven's sake, put the party [Democratic] in power that pledged itself against this highway robbery. Expansion is too clean a name for it.[35]

After analyzing the entire conflict, one historian noted:

By the time the black troops departed from the Philippines, it was generally agreed that their relationships with the natives were more cordial than those of white soldiers. When the Negro soldiers first arrived in the islands, Filipinos viewed them with awe and fear as an "American species of bete noir." A typical reaction was: "These are not Americans; they are Negritoes." But their fear quickly turned into friendliness and their awe into admiration. Filipinos came to accept black Americans as "very much like ourselves only larger" and gave them the affectionate appellation, "Negritos Americanos." Negro soldiers generally reciprocated the good will of peaceful natives and treated them with consideration and respect. In letters home they often referred to the contempt which white soldiers displayed toward all Filipinos and insisted that such an attitude underlay much of the natives' hostility to American rule.[36]

In the Boer War, where the British fought the white South Africans, and American foreign policy was one of solidarity with the British, African Americans spoke out,

denouncing the [British] act as aggression; the Afrikaners had looked to the United States for help. Their leader, Paul Kruger, appealed personally to the American government to protest the annexation. He received no response. Few Americans, other than attentive blacks, were interested in Africa at this time. As for the Anglo-American elite, it simply did not wish to become involved.[37]

At first blacks viewed the struggle as between whites with little interest to them. As they learned more of the racism in Afrikaner society, they became increasingly hostile to the Boers.[38] They also criticized America's foreign policy stance.

With the coming of World War I, African American socialists A. Philip Randolph and Chandler Owens demanded a change in America's foreign policy. They published a newspaper, *The Messenger*, in New York, and because of an article they wrote, "Pro-Germanism among Negroes," Randolph and Owens were sentenced to jail for two and one-half years and their second-class mailing privileges were revoked.[39]

The Paris Peace Conference, the Treaty of Versailles, and the founding of the League of Nations all gave African American elites an opportunity to further express their foreign policy concerns. Both W. E. B. Du Bois and William Monroe Trotter attended the Paris Peace Conference. While Du Bois was able to influence the creation of the League of Nation's mandate system for the colonial-held third world nations,[40] Trotter found that the State Department denied him a passport and thereby an official presence at the Conference.[41] Yet Trotter attended and wrote his critical observations in his newspaper, the *Boston Guardian*.[42] Du Bois's reflections appeared in the *Crisis*.

But it was the Italian invasion of Ethiopia that was the one single event and crisis that mobilized the African American community to action on foreign policy. Mussolini had come to power in Italy 1922 and by 1935 he was seeking to restore the Roman Empire by overrunning Ethiopia.[43] In the face of such naked imperialism, it could be expected that a few lonely voices and organizations might have spoken out. However, Franklin and

Moss write, "When Italy invaded Ethiopia African Americans protested with all the means at their command. Almost overnight even the most provincial among black Americans became international-minded. Ethiopia was a black nation, and its destruction would symbolize the final victory of white over blacks."[44] In opposition, "African-Americans held pro-Ethiopian demonstrations in Harlem, Chicago, Miami, Washington, and elsewhere; they sent money and medical supplies to Addis Ababa and boycotted Italian-made goods. They saw race as central to the dispute."[45] And "Ethiopia was the major concern of the black press in the 1930s with the *Crisis, Messenger, Opportunity* and most of the black weeklies criticizing the Italian invasion of this African Nation."[46] The *Pittsburgh Courier* assigned J. A. Rogers as a war correspondent to send the news on the war front back to the *Courier* readers; and there were pleas made both to Washington and the League of Nations. For instance, "the National Association for the Advancement of Colored People telegraphed the League of Nations on behalf of 12,000,000 American Negroes, demanding action to restrain dictator Benito Mussolini."[47]

In fact, all of this frenzied lobbying "set the African-Americans against outspoken Italian-American groups which, as a matter of ethnic pride, supported their ancestral homeland. In some eastern cities where Italian and black neighborhoods adjoined riots erupted."[48] However, in this intense and rising competition between the two groups "to affect policy toward the war, the African Americans (were) more successful than the Italian Americans . . . [because the] Roosevelt administration imposed an arms embargo on Italy."[49] The intensity as well as the strength of the African American reaction to the Italian invasion "helped considerably in arousing a general American sympathy for Ethiopia."[50] This time the outcry came from all quarters and sectors of African American society. In point of fact, the demand for help for Ethiopia was so systematic and comprehensive this time that in the midst of the conflict, in January 1937, African American leaders, founded the Council on African Affairs, a national organization to lobby for Africa—a forerunner of Trans Africa.

During World War II the global nature of the struggle and the indeterminate post–world war realities forced African Americans to "wage a Double V campaign, victory at home as well as abroad."[51] In World War II, African Americans "were willing to do their part and to make necessary sacrifice to ensure victory, but they never failed to remind the people of the United States that they resented all forms of mistreatment."[52] In addition to the Double V, the African American press simultaneously called for a new and more progressive approach to colonialism and the problems of Third World nations.[53]

With the coming of the Cold War era, African American leaders supported an independent Israel, but after the 1973 Yom Kippur war, increasing numbers of African Americans began to speak for the cause of Palestinian independence as well.

During 1946–47, leading black newspapers were opposed to the Cold War policies of the United States; however, in 1948 they shifted their attention from colonialism to communism. At the same time, these papers reminded Americans that the best defense against communism was universal freedom, at home and abroad.[54]

When the Korean conflict made the Cold War a hot war, white American soldiers "disparaged their opponents in racial terms, dismissing the North Koreans and the Chinese—even their own South Korean allies—with epithets such as 'barbarians,' 'beasts,' and 'gooks'. . . . [Being] aware of this attitude most African Americans analyzed the conflict from their own racial perspective. Many of them and their organization opposed it."[55] And during this conflict, African American dissenters had to fight the army to integrate its units, as stipulated in President Harry Truman's executive order in 1949. In the midst of the war, General Matthew Ridgeway received permission to integrate African Americans throughout his command. Between May and August 1951, the extent of troop integration in Korea increased from 9 percent to 30 percent.[56]

One of the crisis events of the Cold War that American policy makers had to cope with was the Nigerian civil war, better known as the Biafran secession, which emerged during the Nixon administration. President Nixon supported the Biafran secession, a position that put him at odds with the African American community.[57] From the outset, African Americans put their support behind the Nigerian federal government. Thus, when the Biafra secessionists surrendered in January, 1970, "the Nigerians . . . expressed gratitude toward African Americans who [sought] . . . to keep Washington committed to the one-Nigeria policy."[58] Like the situation in Ethiopia some three and a half decades earlier, blacks had helped to shape events in Nigeria in a way supportive of African nationality.

Muhammad Ali, Martin Luther King, Jr., and many other prominent blacks also voiced opposition to the Vietnam war. When Martin Luther King, Jr., dissented from the rising American consensus about the war, it divided the civil rights movement and angered liberals and President Johnson. Several African American leaders, notably Whitney Young of the Urban League, denounced King and supported President Johnson. But King's prestige made him a major voice in the anti-war movement.[59]

Inside the military, African American Vietnam veterans spoke out against both the racial epithets and some of the inhumane policies of American troops fighting there.

> Replacing the careerists were black draftees, many just steps removed from marching in the Civil Rights Movement or rioting in the rebellions that swept the urban ghettos from Harlem to Watts. All were filled with a new sense of black pride and purpose. They spoke loudest against the discrimination they encountered on the battlefield to protest these indignities and provide mutual support. And they called themselves "Bloods."[60]

When President Reagan ordered an invasion of the Caribbean island nation of Grenada in October 1984, five members of the Congressional Black Caucus moved to impeach the president while the entire caucus condemned the invasion as being nurtured essentially by white racism. African Americans also tended to oppose George Bush's Persian Gulf War.[61] Finally, African Americans lobbied the Clinton administration to send troops to Haiti to restore President Jean Bertrand Aristide to power after his ouster in a military coup.

African Americans have not had a commanding influence in American foreign policy, but they have had a continuing presence. And on several occasions, that presence has had a decided impact on the outcome of American foreign policy. DeConde writes, "Only in rare instances, as in the case of the Ethiopian War, did the formulators of foreign policy seemingly take into account the wishes of the nation's largest ethno-racial minority."[62] African Americans were successful in changing Nixon administration policy during the Nigerian civil war and in pressuring President Clinton to intervene in the Haitian situation. These are *direct* linkages between the expressed desires of black

Americans and American foreign policy. However, there is a very important, indirect one. King's outspoken stance against the Vietnam War led to a larger, much more powerful and vocal antiwar and peace movement, and it contributed to the eventual withdrawal of Americans from Vietnam.

TRANS AFRICA: AFRICAN AMERICANS AS FOREIGN POLICY MAKERS

Figure 16.1 reveals the rise, fall, and evolution of African American organized interest and pressure group activity up to the founding of Trans Africa. Throughout African Americans' long sojourn in America, they have acted both as individuals and in organizations to impact and influence America's foreign policy. As noted earlier, African Americans as diplomats and foreign service officers developed a presence in the bureaucracy. They were also heard in the streets through protests. And finally, they have spoken through organizations that engage in protests in the streets and lobbying in the halls of Congress. These interest groups have been able on several occasions to convert that presence into foreign policy influence.

Figure 16.1 Sources and Outcomes of African American Foreign Policy-Making Initiatives

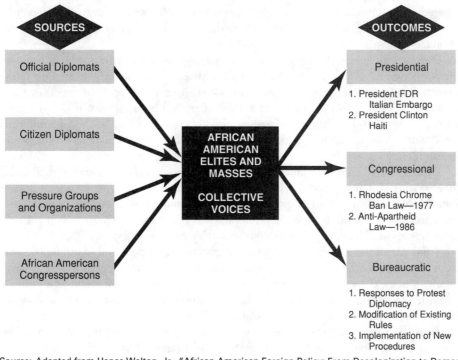

Source: Adapted from Hanes Walton, Jr., "African American Foreign Policy: From Decolonization to Democracy," in Hanes Walton, Jr., *African American Power and Politics: The Political Context Variable* (New York: Columbia University Press, 1997), chapter 18; and Jake Miller, *The Black Presence in American Foreign Affairs* (Washington, DC: University Press of America, 1978).

Trans Africa arose out of the various organizations that preceded it, but it was organized in an event that occurred in 1976 when Congressmen Charles Diggs of Michigan
(chair of the House Foreign Affairs Subcommittee on Africa) and Andrew Young convened thirty black leaders to challenge Ford administration policy toward white-ruled
Rhodesia.[63] Little changed during the Ford administration. The incoming Carter administration, however, was concerned with human rights, and its leaders were willing to
listen to Congressman and later U.N. Ambassador Young. As a result, the political context changed significantly. In May 1978, Young and his colleagues organized Trans
Africa, the first mass-based African American lobby. Here is how it has been described:

> Trans Africa has lobbied on issues of foreign assistance and trade toward Africa and the
> Caribbean; fought to end CIA intervention in Angola through passage of the Clark
> Amendment; worked to sustain America's adherence to sanctions against Rhodesia until
> successful negotiations were completed for the legal independence of Zimbabwe; and
> has, in cooperation with other black leaders and national organizations, launched
> FSAM, the Free South Africa Movement—a movement whose work has led to the pas-
> sage of the Anti-Apartheid Act of 1986 overriding a presidential veto.[64]

To maintain its support, Trans Africa—the "Black American Lobby for Africa and
the Caribbean"—sends out "Issue Briefs" and a newsletter that alerts its membership
and individuals in the Congress to matters on which its leaders want action. It holds
news conferences, public demonstrations, and annual dinners and symposiums to keep
its constituency informed. And to involve as well as mobilize people, Trans Africa has
engaged in boycotts, marches, mass demonstrations, letter writing, and a hunger strike
by its leader, Randall Robinson. Out of these different tactics and strategies, the organization has met with considerable success.

Outstanding among its efforts was its protests against South Africa, which began on
Thanksgiving eve, 1984, as a sit-in at the South African Embassy in Washington. These
protests eventually led to the Comprehensive Anti-Apartheid Act. Introduced by Congressman William Gray of Pennsylvania, this act passed both Houses of Congress but
was vetoed by President Reagan. However, the veto was overridden when Republicans
joined with African American and white Democrats to impose sanctions on the South
African regime.

During the Clinton administration, Trans Africa's executive director, Randall
Robinson, used a hunger strike to force the president to change his policy toward
Haiti.[65] Initially, Clinton had essentially followed the more restricted Bush immigration
policy and had successfully defended that policy in the Supreme Court.[66] Trans Africa,
under Robinson's leadership, helped to reverse that presidential policy.

Trans Africa has also embarked on a program of action designed to influence some
of the African and other third world dictatorships (especially in Nigeria) to pursue, with
America's help, democratic elections and governance.[67] With colonialism as a political
system disappearing from African and third world countries, this new course may yet
help to achieve democracy in the countries of Africa.

Thus, this organizational presence of African Americans, through interest group
lobbying, like its counterparts in other parts of the foreign policy process, has had both
successes and failures in changing America's foreign policies toward Africa and the third
world.

AFRICAN AMERICANS AND CITIZEN DIPLOMACY: HISTORICAL BACKGROUND AND CONTEXT

African American foreign policy leaders have a long history of creating new strategies and tactics to influence and shift the State Department's direction of foreign policy.[68] One of these strategies for articulating the African American position is *citizen diplomacy.*

Professor Karen Stanford has defined citizen diplomacy "as the diplomatic efforts of private citizens in the international arena for the purpose of achieving a specific objective or accomplishing constituency goals."[69] This particular technique for influencing foreign policy arose when George Logan, a white private citizen, decided on his own to intervene when the United States ratified the Jay Treaty with Great Britain in 1798. The French responded negatively and with military force seized U.S. ships on the high seas. Logan went to Paris and asked the French to avoid a military crisis and defuse the situation by releasing the hostages and expressing goodwill. The government responded to Logan's efforts by passing the Logan Act on January 30, 1799, an act that prohibited individual citizens from trying to conduct official diplomatic endeavors.[70] But the government did not prosecute Logan then and it has not ever prosecuted anyone for violating this law. The truth is that throughout America's history, numerous individuals have engaged in citizen diplomacy. In recent times, during the Vietnam War, scores of individual citizens journeyed to Hanoi to participate and engage in citizen diplomacy. Among them were former attorney general Ramsey Clark, movie stars Jane Fonda and Clint Eastwood, and the 1996 Reform party presidential candidate H. Ross Perot.

African American Citizen Diplomats

From the time of slavery, African Americans have consistently engaged in citizen diplomacy:

> By 1833, blacks like the Reverend Nathaniel Paul carried the black plight to England to seek friends and financial support. Blacks from America went as delegates to the World Anti-Slavery Conference held in London in 1840. Here, they tried to attract not only worldwide attention to the black predicament but also to internationalize America's domestic problem. This effort was followed in 1845 with black journalist Frederick Douglass's crossing the Atlantic to seek allies for the black cause in Ireland and England.[71]

As mentioned earlier, in the post-Reconstruction era there were forays by George Washington Williams and Booker T. Washington into the Congo.[72] At the turn of the century, Sylvester Williams and W. E. B. Du Bois launched the Pan-African Congresses. The NAACP sent an observer to Haiti when American occupation began. Black journalist George Schuyler went to Liberia in 1931 for three months to investigate slavery there, and on his return used the data he had amassed on forced labor and slavery to write a novel, *Slaves Today: A Story of Liberia.*[73] In the preface to the novel he stated his objective:

> If this novel can help arouse enlightened world opinion against this brutalizing of the native population in a Negro republic, perhaps the conscience of civilized people will

stop similar atrocities in native lands ruled by proud white nations that boast of their superior culture.[74]

The 1930s were a period of great activity. Colonel Hubert Julian, a fighter pilot, fought for Ethiopia in that conflict and tried to serve as a diplomatic negotiator,[75] while numerous African Americans did the same in the Spanish civil war.[76] African American historian Robin Kelly tells us of these citizen diplomats:

> When the Communist International asked for volunteers to come to Spain in the fall of 1936, African Americans who joined the Abraham Lincoln Brigade regarded the Civil War as an extension of the Italo-Ethiopian conflict. . . . Oscar Hunter . . . explained, "I wanted to go to Ethiopia and fight Mussolini. . . . This ain't Ethiopia, but it'll do." . . . Black volunteers linked the struggles of the Iberian peninsula to racism and poverty in America; for them Spain had become the battle field to revenge the attack of Ethiopia and part of a larger fight for justice and equality that would inevitably take place on U.S. soil.[77]

Beyond these citizen diplomats, there are African Americans who advocated the Soviet point of view about the communist system and its version of world and global peace. Chief among them were W. E. B. Du Bois and the entertainer-scholar Paul Robeson in the 1950s and early 1960s.[78]

Jesse Jackson and a New Model of Citizen Diplomacy

Malcolm X made numerous pilgrimages to Africa and the Middle East, where he met with the heads of state of such nations as Egypt, Ghana, and Tanzania. The purpose of these missions was to universalize the African freedom struggle by developing linkages between the African and African American leadership communities. At the time of his murder, he was attempting to develop support among African and other third world nations for a United Nations resolution condemning the United States for violating the human rights of its African American citizens. Another example of a citizen diplomat was the Reverend Leon Sullivan and his articulation of the Sullivan principles (requiring equality in employment and working conditions) in regard to American corporations doing business in South Africa.

Thus, the Reverend Jesse Jackson was continuing the long history of African American citizen diplomats when he went to Syria on December 31, 1983, to secure the release of Lieutenant Robert O. Goodman, Jr. Lieutenant Goodman was an African American pilot who had been shot down in an air raid over Syria earlier in the month.[79] Out of this history of black citizen diplomats there is a fairly discernible model and pattern.

On the whole, African American citizen diplomats have been (1) well-known domestic leaders, (2) spokespersons for a specific issue, (3) persons wanting to activate world public opinion, and (4) citizens who want to reshape American foreign policy. However, as Professor Stanford demonstrates, the Jackson forays depart significantly from the models of the past.

In Stanford's presentation of Jackson's citizen diplomacy, it differed from past efforts because Jackson was an announced Democratic presidential candidate in the midst

The Reverend Jesse Jackson on one of his many exercises in citizen diplomacy. Here he is with Fidel Castro, the Cuban leader. On this mission, Jackson secured the release of scores of political prisoners.

of the presidential primary season and had a long history of international human rights missions. Jackson also had significant personal relations and friendships with many world leaders. These domestic and global characteristics significantly distance the Jackson model of citizen diplomats from that of his African American predecessors. Jackson's model was unique and different because of his credentials—personal and political.

Moreover, because of the political context of the Democratic presidential primaries, Jackson's citizen diplomat model was ensured of wide media coverage. Hence, successes like attaining the release of Lieutenant Goodman ensured a stepping stone pattern and greater potential for success in other foreign policy initiatives.[80] Such a linkage enriched the Jackson model and further distanced it from the simpler citizen diplomat models of earlier times. None of the previous efforts had attained the success achieved by Jackson.[81]

Two important contributions are embedded in the Jackson model. First, it is clearly another strategy by which African Americans can influence foreign policy. Second, it is clearly a tool with which African Americans have sought to attain universal freedom beyond the boundaries of the nation. Both the *pre-Jackson model* and the *Jackson model* itself have become ways in which the African American community has reached beyond its national confines to assist other members of the African diaspora as well as others to liberate themselves from the oppression of the superpowers and their biased consensus in the Cold War conflict (see Box 16.2).

======================== **BOX 16.2** ========================
Minister Louis Farrakhan's Citizen Diplomacy

Shortly after the Million Man March, the Nation of Islam's Minister Louis Farrakhan embarked on a controversial tour of African and Middle Eastern countries. Among the African countries he visited were Ghana, Zaire, Sudan, Libya, Nigeria, and South Africa. The Middle Eastern countries were Iran and Iraq. In each of these countries Farrakhan was received by the heads of state or government (including South Africa's Nelson Mandela) and Islamic and other religious leaders.

Farrakhan was strongly condemned in the press and by black and white leaders for his trip. The White House press secretary described it as a "thug tour," criticizing especially his visits to Libya, Iraq, and Iran which the U.S. government describes as "rogue," "terrorist" states that American citizens are forbidden to visit. The House Subcommittee on International Operations and Human Rights chaired by Congressman Christopher Smith of New Jersey held hearings on Farrakhan's tour. The hearings, called "Attempts by Rogue Regimes to Influence United States Policy," were criticized by African American members of the committee (Donald Payne and Cynthia McKinney) as biased and a violation of Farrakhan's right to travel and his right of free speech. Farrakhan was also attacked by some African American leaders, especially for his visits to Nigeria and the Sudan. Randall Robinson of Trans Africa was particularly critical, charging that Farrakhan should not have visited Nigeria because the military government there was engaged in widespread human rights violation and was holding the country's elected president in prison. Others criticized the visit to Sudan for the same reasons; also, there is evidence that the Sudanese government tolerates the practice of slavery. Farrakhan's response to these criticisms was that he had raised questions of human rights violation in his meetings with the leaders of both countries and planned to follow up with additional meetings in the future.

Although several members of Congress called for Farrakhan to be indicted under the Logan Act, to have his passport revoked, or to be required to register as a foreign agent, no action was taken against him. Undaunted, he subsequently visited several Caribbean countries, including Cuba, where he was received by President Fidel Castro. Later, he again traveled to Libya where he received a humanitarian award and a pledge of a billion dollars from Colonel Muammar Qaddafi, the Libyan leader. The United States government, however, prohibited Farrakhan from accepting the $250,000 cash prize for the award or the pledge of a billion dollars from Colonel Qaddafi.

THE IMPACT OF AFRICAN AMERICANS ON U.S. FOREIGN POLICY

The thrust of African American foreign policy is to secure universal freedom for African and other third world nations. In the arena of foreign policy making (both advocacy and implementation), one sees African Americans rise out of their parochial domestic interest to address the global issues confronting the descendants of the African diaspora. And these thrusts to free the darker races of the world were designed to have a reciprocal effect. Helping the people of the diaspora might help in elevating African Americans themselves.[82]

The reason is clear. As African American diplomat and scholar Skinner concludes: "African Americans did attempt to ensure that their country understood and sympathized with the plight of their ancestral land. They did so because their very fate was viewed as intimately linked to the position of Africa in the minds of their fellow citizens and the global community."[83] Or as another scholar observes, "Blacks wished to enhance the civil rights struggle at home with the prestige of having behind it the support of African nations . . . [and] . . . that required cultivation through foreign policy."[84] Thus, universal freedom was linked to both a domestic and a global struggle. The two arenas were sources of cross-fertilization. And to achieve this cross-fertilization, African Americans have had to find innovative and creative ways to articulate their concerns for universal freedom in foreign affairs. First, they have spoken from inside the foreign policy bureaucracy, as members of the bureaucratic staff. Second, they have made their concerns known in the street through demonstrations. Third, they have lobbied, most notably through Trans Africa. And fourth, they have used citizen diplomacy.

These strategies, when aggregated, have resulted in significant changes in American foreign policies. There are concrete examples of changes that African Americans have wrought. Usually, studies of African Americans and foreign policy have concluded with the assertions that this group has *tried* to influence the nation's foreign affairs. Such works generally conclude with a broad general statement that this influence in some vague, ambiguous, and indirect manner *may* have had some effect. As we show, the U.S. embargo of Italy in 1930s, the Rhodesian Chrome Ban in 1977, the Comprehensive Anti-Apartheid Act of 1984, and the reversal of the Haiti policy are vivid, visible, and concrete instances of change in which African Americans had a direct impact on U.S. policy that furthered universal freedom. A clear example of this direct policy impact is the Rhodesian Chrome Ban legislation. We conclude with discussion of it, since it is less well known than the anti-apartheid legislation.[85]

Ambassador Andrew Young, while still in the House of Representatives as a congressman from Georgia, introduced on January 1, 1977, a bill that would halt the importation of Rhodesian chromium, a major source of that country's foreign exchange. When Rhodesia issued its unilateral declaration of independence, establishing the white minority rule government, many nations followed the lead of the British and the United Nations and responded with economic sanctions. However, Senator Harry F. Byrd, Jr., of Virginia persuaded Congress to pass in 1971 the "Byrd Amendment." This new law had the effect of permitting Rhodesian ore imports in violation of U.N. sanctions. Congressman Young's legislation repealing this amendment eventually passed and was signed by President Carter on March 18, 1977. With the passage of this law, "the United States was once again in compliance with its international legal obligation under the United Nations Charter."[86]

Table 16.1 reveals the minority-majority coalition that passed the Young bill in the House and the Senate. Sixty-three percent of the House and 72 percent of the Senate voted to repeal the Byrd Amendment. In the House, 80 percent of the Democrats and 29 percent of the Republicans supported the measure. And when the Democratic vote is disaggregated by region and race, 96 percent of the northern Democrats but only 47

―――――――――――――――――――――――――――― **TABLE 16.1** ――――――――――――――――――――――――――――

Party Support Ratios for House Resolution 1746
to Repeal the Byrd Amendment and Sanction Rhodesia

TOTAL PARTY CATEGORIES	PERCENTAGE OF VOTES SUPPORTING	PERCENTAGE OF VOTES OPPOSING	TOTAL NUMBER OF VOTES
HOUSE			
Total Votes	63%	37%	396
Republican Votes	29	71	133
Democratic Votes	80	20	263
Northern Democratic Votes	96	4	182
Southern Democratic Votes	47	53	81
Black Democrats	88[a]	0	16[b]
SENATE			
Total Votes	72	23	92
Republican Votes	51	49	35
Democratic Votes	84	16	57
Northern Democratic Votes	95	5	40
Southern Democratic Votes	59	41	17
Black Democrats	0	0	0

[a]Of the 16 voting African American Democratic members, Congresswoman Collins (D.–IL) did not vote and Congressman William Clay (D.–MO) used a paired vote. A paired vote occurs when a member refrains from voting and asks to be "paired" with an absent member who holds an opposing view.

[b]There were 17 African American members in the 95th Congress, but Congressman Walter Fountroy (D.–DC) was a nonvoting delegate.

Source: Adapted from data in *The Congressional Quarterly Almanac* (Washington, DC: Congressional Quarterly, 1978). For the Senate vote data, see p. 10-S and for the House vote data, see p. 22-H.

percent of the southern Democrats supported the measure. In the Senate, both Republicans and Democrats, in a bipartisan stance, passed the measure. Fifty-one percent of the Republicans and 84 percent of the Democrats made up the enacting coalition. Again, the disaggregation of the Democratic vote reveals that both the northern and southern Democrats supported the measure, with the northern Democrats nearly unanimously behind it with 95 percent.

Overall, Republicans and southern Democrats opposed the measure in the House while in the Senate both groups backed it. With the passage of this bill, the Young legislation became one of the first bills to change America's African foreign policy. Later, Representative William Gray would follow Congressman Young's initiative with his own anti-apartheid legislation.[87]

In fact, African American political scientist Errol Henderson has argued that instead of the Eurocentric nature of American foreign policy, a new and more humanistic, Afrocentric position based on the African American culture should be pursued for a much more meaningful world in America's third century.[88]

SELECTED BIBLIOGRAPHY

Challenor, Herschell. "The Influence of Black America on U.S. Foreign Policy toward Africa." In A. A. Said, ed. *Ethnicity and U.S. Foreign Policy*. New York: Praeger, 1981. A good, brief overview of the subject.

DeConde, Alexander. *Ethnicity, Race and American Foreign Policy: A History*. Boston, MA: Northeastern University Press, 1992. An excellent comparative history, covering all major ethnic groups over the course of American history.

Henderson, Errol. *AfroCentrism and World Politics: Toward a New Paradigm*. Westport, CT: Praeger, 1995. An important new work that suggests and details a new "Afrocentric" approach to U.S. foreign policy.

Kegley Charles, and Eugene Wittkopf. *American Foreign Policy: Pattern and Process*, 3rd ed. New York: St. Martin's Press, 1987. A good introduction to the structures and processes of U.S., foreign policy making.

Krenn, Michael. *Black Diplomacy: African Americans and the State Department, 1945–1969*. Amonk, NY: M. E. Sharpe, 1998. A study of the integration of the State Department after 1945 and the appointment of black ambassadors to Africa and other third world nations.

Miller, Jake. *The Black Presence in American Foreign Affairs*. Washington: Howard University Press, 1978. The standard work on the subject, with an excellent summary and overview from a historical perspective.

Skinner, Elliot. *African Americans and U.S. Policy toward Africa, 1850–1924*. Vol. 1. Washington: Howard University Press, 1992. The definitive work by the African American historian and diplomat, with detailed and comprehensive treatment through 1924. Unsurpassed as a source.

Skinner, Elliot, and Pearl Robinson, eds. *Transformation and Resiliency on Africa*. Washington, DC: Howard University Press, 1983. A good collection of case studies and a wonderful essay on the African American intelligentsia and Africa.

Stanford, Karin. *Beyond the Boundaries: Reverend Jesse Jackson in International Affairs*. Albany: State University of New York Press, 1997. A pioneering exploration of the concept of citizen diplomat, African American citizen diplomats, and Jesse Jackson's role in foreign affairs.

NOTES

1. Hanes Walton, Jr., *Black Women at the United Nations* (California: Borgo Press, 1995): chap. 2.
2. John Hope Franklin and Alfred Moss, Jr., *From Slavery to Freedom*, 7th ed. (New York: McGraw-Hill, 1994): 391.
3. John Stanfield, II, Preface, in Charles Johnson, *Bitter Canaan: The Story of the Negro Republic* (New Brunswick, NJ: Transaction Books, 1987): vii.
4. Michael Marriott, "TransAfrica in the Eye of the Storm: Young Activists on Hill Organize Anti-Apartheid Protest," *Washington Post,* December 12, 1984; Juan Williams, "Black Leaders Find a Hot New Issue: Free South Africa Protests Revive Moribund Movement," *Washington Post,* December 12, 1984, pp. A1, A18.

5. Jake Miller, *The Black Presence in American Foreign Affairs* (Washington, DC: University Press of America, 1978): 1.
6. Ibid.
7. Ibid., pp. 515–25.
8. Elliott P. Skinner, *African Americans and U.S. Policy toward Africa 1850–1924: In Defense of Black Nationality*, vol. 1 (Washington, DC: Howard University Press, 1992): 526.
9. Ibid., pp. 515–25. Black nationality is the idea that American blacks should encourage the United States government to help create, protect, and defend black nation-states in Africa and the Caribbean, as well as oppose European colonialization and conquest of Africa.
10. Ibid., p. 517.
11. Quoted in Skinner, *African Americans and U.S. Policy*, vol. 1, p. 53.
12. Ibid.
13. Alexander DeConde, *Ethnicity, Race and American Foreign Policy: A History* (Boston, MA: Northeastern University Press, 1992): 39.
14. Ibid., p. 40.
15. Ibid.
16. Miller, *The Black Presence in American Foreign Affairs*, p. 18.
17. Ibid., pp. 23–32. See also Norma Brown, ed., *A Black Diplomat in Haiti: The Diplomatic Correspondence of U.S. Minister Frederick Douglass from Haiti, 1889–1891* (Salisbury, NC: Documentary Publications, 1977).
18. Ibid., p. 32.
19. Skinner, *African Americans and U.S. Policy toward Africa*, p. 519.
20. Ibid., p. 517.
21. Ibid., pp. 520–21.
22. Ibid., p. 518.
23. Ibid., p. 516.
24. Miller, *The Black Presence in American Foreign Affairs*, p. 99.
25. Ibid., p. 100.
26. "Franklin and Moss, *From Slavery to Freedom*, p. 98. See also Lamont Thomas, *Rise to Be a People: A Biography of Paul Cuffe* (Urbana: University of Illinois Press, 1986).
27. Skinner, *African Americans and U.S. Policy toward Africa*, p. 52.
28. Booker T. Washington, "Cruelty in the Congo Country," *Outlook*, 78 (October 8, 1904): 375–377.
29. Ibid.
30. Franklin and Moss, *From Slavery to Freedom*, p. 296. See also John Hope Franklin, *George Washington William* (Chicago: University of Chicago Press, 1985).
31. "Frederick Douglass on the Mexican American War," in Herbert Aptheker, ed. *A Documentary History of the Negro People*, vol. 1 (New York: Citadel Press, 1967): 267.
32. DeConde, *Ethnicity, Race and American Foreign Policy*, p. 64.
33. Ibid., p. 63.
34. Ibid., p. 65.

35. Reprinted in Willard Gatewood, *Smoked Yankee and the Struggle for Empire: Letters from Negro Soldiers, 1898–1902* (Urbana: University of Illinois, 1975): 279.
36. Willard Gatewood, *Black Americans and the White Man's Burden 1898–1903* (Urbana: University of Illinois Press, 1975): 279.
37. DeConde, *Ethnicity, Race and American Foreign Policy,* p. 66. See also Willard B. Gatewood, Jr., "Black Americans and the Boer War, 1899–1902," *South Atlanta Quarterly* 75 (Spring, 1976): 234.
38. Ibid.
39. Franklin and Moss, *From Slavery to Freedom*, p. 345.
40. Hanes Walton, Jr., "The Southwest Africa Mandate," *Faculty Research Bulletin* 26 (December, 1972): 94–98.
41. William Monroe Trotter, "How I Managed to Reach the Peace Conference," in Phillip Foner, ed., *The Voice of Black America* (New York: Simon & Schuster, 1972): 740–42.
42. See Stephen Fox, *Guardian of Boston: William Monroe Trotter* (New York: Atheneum, 1971); George Padmore, "Review of the Paris Peace Conference," *Crisis* (November, 1946): 331–33, 347–48; George Padmore, "Trusteeship: The New Imperialism," *Crisis* (October, 1946): 302–09.
43. Franklin and Moss, *From Slavery to Freedom*, p. 433.
44. Ibid.
45. DeConde, *Ethnicity, Race and American Foreign Policy*, p. 107.
46. Miller, *The Black Presence in American Foreign Affairs*, p. 235. See also J. R. Hooker, "The Negro American Press and Africa in the 1930's," *Canadian Journal of African States* (March, 1967): 43–50, and W. E. B. Du Bois, "Interracial Implications of the Ethiopian Crisis," *Foreign Affairs*, 14 (October, 1935): 1982–92.
47. DeConde, *Ethnicity, Race and American Foreign Policy*, p. 107.
48. Ibid.
49. Ibid.
50. Ibid., p. 108.
51. Franklin and Moss, *From Slavery to Freedom*, p. 454.
52. Ibid., p. 453.
53. Ibid., p. 236.
54. Ibid., p. 237. See also Mark Solomon, "Black Critics of Colonialism and the Cold War," in T. Patterson, ed., *Cold War Critics* (Chicago: Quadrangle Books, 1971): 205–39.
55. DeConde, *Ethnicity, Race and American Foreign Policy*, p. 149.
56. Franklin and Moss, *From Slavery to Freedom*, p. 462.
57. Deconde, *Ethnicity, Race and American Foreign Policy*, p. 148.
58. Ibid.
59. For a discussion of King's anti-Vietnam remarks, see Martin Luther King, Jr., *The Trumpet of Conscience* (New York: Harper & Row, 1968). The first African American civil rights group to oppose the Vietnam War was SNCC, which did so in 1966 two years before King.
60. Wallace Terry, *Bloods: An Oral History of the Vietnam War* (New York: Random House, 1984): xvi.

61. Lynne Duke, "Emerging Black Anti-war Movement Rooted in Domestic Issues," *Washington Post*, February 8, 1991.
62. DeConde, *Ethnicity, Race and American Foreign Policy*, p. 143.
63. Ibid., p. 178.
64. Trans Africa, *The Tenth Annual Dinner Program* (Washington, DC: Trans Africa, June 6, 1987): 5.
65. Hanes Walton, Jr., "African American Foreign Policy: From Decolonization to Democracy," in Walton, *African American Power and Politics: The Political Context Variable* (New York: Columbia University Press, 1997): chap. 18.
66. Ibid.
67. Ibid.
68. Miller, *The Black Presence in American Foreign Affairs*, pp. 127–242.
69. Karen Stanford, *Beyond the Boundaries: Reverend Jesse Jackson in International Affairs* (Albany: State University of New York Press, 1997): 9.
70. Ibid., p. 19.
71. Walton, *Invisible Politics*, p. 277.
72. Elliott P. Skinner, "Booker T. Washington: Diplomatic Initiatives," in Elliott P. Skinner, *African Americans and U.S. Policy toward Africa 1850–1924: In Defense of Black Nationality* (Washington, DC: Howard University Press, 1992): 291–348.
73. George Schuyler, *Slaves Today: A Story of Liberia* (Baltimore, MD: McGrath, 1931): 5.
74. Ibid., p. 6.
75. Robin Kelley, "This Ain't Ethiopia but It'll Do: African Americans and the Spanish Civil War," in Robin Kelley, *Race Rebels* (New York: Free Press, 1994): 130.
76. Ibid., pp. 123–60.
77. Ibid., pp. 123–24.
78. See Gerald Horne, *Black and Red: W. E. B. Du Bois and the Afro-American Response to the Cold War* (Albany: State University of New York Press, 1986).
79. For a short account of that rescue mission, see Wyatt Tee Walker, *The Road to Damascus* (New York: Martin Luther King, Jr. Fellows Press, 1985).
80. Stanford, *Beyond the Boundaries*, pp. 1–4.
81. Ibid. In 1997 President Clinton appointed Jackson as a special unpaid envoy to Africa, thus formally recognizing his citizen diplomacy. During the NATO air war on Yugoslavia, Jackson led an interfaith delegation to Belgrade and successfully negotiated the release of three American soldiers held captive. The Clinton administration had discouraged Jackson's mission, but congratulated him on its success. See Richard Boudreaux and Carol Williams, "POWs Freed by Jackson," *West County Times,* May 21, 1999.
82. Ronald Walters, *Pan Africanism in the African Diaspora* (Detroit: Wayne State University Press, 1994).
83. Skinner, *African Americans and U.S. Policy toward Africa 1850–1924*, p. 525.
84. DeConde, *Ethnicity, Race and American Foreign Policy*, p. 181.
85. Herschelle Challenor, "The Influence of Black America on U.S. Foreign Policy toward Africa," in A. A. Said, ed., *Ethnicity and U.S. Foreign Policy* (New York: Praeger, 1981): 139.

86. Summary of Legislation: "Rhodesian Chrome Ban 95th Congress," *Congressional Quarterly Almanac 95 Congress. 1st Session–1977* (Washington, DC: Congressional Quarterly, 1978): 22, 1-C and 10–5.
87. Challenor, "The Influence of Black America on U.S. Foreign Policy toward Africa," p. 139.
88. Errol Henderson, *Afrocentrism and World Politics: Toward a New Paradigm* (Connecticut: Praeger, 1985).

APPENDIX

The Declaration of Independence

In Congress, July 4, 1776

*The Unanimous Declaration of the Thirteen
United States of America*

When in the course of human events it becomes necessary for one people to dissolve the political bands which have connected them with another, and to assume, among the powers of the earth, the separate and equal station to which the Laws of Nature and of Nature's God entitle them, a decent respect to the opinions of mankind requires that they should declare the causes which impel them to the separation.

We hold these truths to be self-evident, that all men are created equal, that they are endowed by their Creator with certain unalienable Rights, that among these are Life, Liberty and the pursuit of Happiness. That to secure these rights, Governments are instituted among Men, deriving their just powers from the consent of the governed. That whenever any Form of Government becomes destructive of these ends, it is the Right of the People to alter or to abolish it, and to institute new Government, laying its foundation on such principles and organizing its powers in such form, as to them shall seem most likely to effect their Safety and Happiness. Prudence, indeed, will dictate that Governments long established should not be changed for light and transient causes; and accordingly all experience hath shewn that mankind are more disposed to suffer, while evils are sufferable, than to right themselves by abolishing the forms to which they are accustomed. But when a long train of abuses and usurpations, pursuing invariably the same Object evinces a design to reduce them under absolute Despotism, it is their right, it is their duty, to throw off such Government, and to provide new Guards for their future security.—Such has been the patient sufferance of these Colonies; and such is now the necessity which constrains them to alter their former Systems of Government. The history of the present King of Great Britain is a history of repeated injuries and usurpations, all having in direct object the establishment of an absolute Tyranny over these States. To prove this, let Facts be submitted to a candid world.

He has refused his Assent to Laws, the most wholesome and necessary for the public good.

He has forbidden his Governors to pass Laws of immediate and pressing importance, unless suspended in their operation till his Assent should be obtained; and when so suspended, he has utterly neglected to attend to them.

He has refused to pass other Laws for the accommodation of large districts of people, unless those people would relinquish the right of Representation in the Legislature, a right inestimable to them and formidable to tyrants only.

He has called together legislative bodies at places unusual, uncomfortable, and distant from the depository of their Public Records, for the sole purpose of fatiguing them into compliance with his measures.

He has dissolved Representative Houses repeatedly, for opposing with manly firmness his invasions on the rights of the people.

He has refused for a long time, after such dissolutions, to cause others to be elected; whereby the Legislative Powers, incapable of Annihilation, have returned to the People at large for their exercise, the State remaining in the mean time exposed to all the dangers of invasion from without, and convulsions within.

He has endeavored to prevent the population of these States; for that purpose obstructing the Laws of Naturalization of Foreigners; refusing to pass others to encourage their migration hither, and raising the conditions of new Appropriations of Lands.

He has obstructed the Administration of Justice, by refusing his Assent to Laws for establishing Judiciary powers.

He has made Judges dependent on his Will alone, for the tenure of their offices, and the amount and payment of their salaries.

He has erected a multitude of New Offices, and sent hither swarms of Officers to harass our people, and eat out their substance.

He has kept among us, in times of peace, Standing Armies without the Consent of our legislatures.

He has affected to render the Military independent of and superior to the Civil power.

He has combined with others to subject us to a jurisdiction foreign to our constitution, and unacknowledged by our laws, giving his Assent to their Acts of pretended Legislation:

For quartering large bodies of armed troops among us:

For protecting them, by a mock Trial, from punishment for any Murders which they should commit on the Inhabitants of these States:

For cutting off our Trade with all parts of the world:

For imposing Taxes on us without our Consent:

For depriving us in many cases, of the benefits of Trial by Jury:

For transporting us beyond Seas to be tried for pretended offences:

For abolishing the free System of English Laws in a neighboring Province, establishing therein an Arbitrary government, and enlarging its Boundaries so as to render it at once an example and fit instrument for introducing the same absolute rule into these Colonies:

For taking away our Charters, abolishing our most valuable Laws, and altering fundamentally the Forms of our Governments:

For suspending our own Legislatures, and declaring themselves invested with power to legislate for us in all cases whatsoever.

He has abdicated Government here, by declaring us our of his Protection and waging War against us.

He has plundered our seas, ravaged our Coasts, burnt out towns, and destroyed the lives of our people.

He is at this time transporting large Armies of foreign Mercenaries to compleat the works of death, desolation and tyranny, already begun with circumstances of Cruelty and perfidy scarcely paralleled in the most barbarous ages, and totally unworthy the Head of a civilized nation.

He has constrained our fellow Citizens taken Captive on the high Seas to bear Arms against their Country, to become the executioners of their friends and Brethren, or to fall themselves by their Hands.

He has excited domestic insurrections amongst us, and has endeavored to bring on the inhabitants of our frontiers, the merciless Indian Savages, whose known rule of warfare, is an undistinguished destruction of all ages, sexes and conditions.

In every stage of these Oppressions We have Petitioned for Redress in the most humble terms: Our repeated Petitions have been answered only by repeated injury: A Prince, whose character is thus marked by every act which may define a Tyrant, is unfit to be the ruler of a free people.

Nor have We been wanting in attention to our British brethren. We have warned them from time to time of attempts by their legislature to extend an unwarrantable jurisdiction over us. We have reminded them of the circumstances of our emigration and settlement here. We have appealed to their native justice and magnanimity; and we have conjured them by the ties of our common kindred to disavow these usurpations, which would inevitably interrupt our connections and correspondence. They too have been deaf to the voice of justice and consanguinity. We must, therefore, acquiesce in the necessity, which denounces our Separation, and hold them, as we hold the rest of mankind, Enemies in War, in Peace Friends.

We, therefore, the Representatives of the United States of America, in General Congress, Assembled, appealing to the Supreme Judge of the world for the rectitude of our intentions, do, in the Name, and by Authority of the good People of these Colonies, solemnly publish and declare, That these United Colonies are, and of Right ought to be Free and Independent States; that they are Absolved from all Allegiance to the British Crown, and that all political connection between them and the State of Great Britain, is and ought to be totally dissolved: and that as Free and Independent States, they have full power to levy War, conclude Peace, contract Alliances, establish Commerce, and to do all other Acts and Things which Independent States may of right do. And for the support of this Declaration, with a firm reliance on the protection of divine Providence, we mutually pledge to each other our Lives, our Fortunes and our sacred Honor.

JOHN HANCOCK

NEW HAMPSHIRE
  Josiah Bartlett,
  Wm. Whipple,
  Matthew Thornton.

MASSACHUSETTS BAY
  Saml. Adams,
  John Adams,
  Robt. Treat Paine,
  Elbridge Gerry.

RHODE ISLAND
  Step. Hopkins,
  William Ellery.

CONNECTICUT
  Roger Sherman,
  Saml. Huntington,
  Wm. Williams,
  Oliver Wolcott.

NEW YORK
  Wm. Floyd,
  Phil. Livingston,
  Frans. Lewis,
  Lewis Morris

NEW JERSEY
  Richd. Stockton,
  Jn. Witherspoon,
  Fras. Hopkinson,
  John Hart,
  Abra. Clark.

PENNSYLVANIA
  Robt. Morris,
  Benjamin Rush,
  Benj. Franklin,
  John Morton,
  Geo. Clymer,
  Jas. Smith,
  Geo. Taylor,
  James Wilson,
  Geo. Ross.

DELAWARE
  Caesar Rodney,
  Geo. Read,
  Tho. M'kean.

MARYLAND
  Samuel Chase,
  Wm. Paca,
  Thos. Stone,
  Charles Caroll of
  Carrollton.

VIRGINIA
  George Wythe,
  Richard Henry Lee,
  Th. Jefferson,
  Benj. Harrison,
  Thos. Nelson, jr.,
  Francis Lightfoot Lee,
  Carter Braxton.

NORTH CAROLINA
  Wm. Hooper,
  Joseph Hewes,
  John Penn.

SOUTH CAROLINA
  Edward Rutledge,
  Thos. Heyward, Junr.,
  Thomas Lynch, Junr.,
  Arthur Middleton.

GEORGIA
  Button Gwinnett,
  Lyman Hall,
  Geo. Walton.

The Constitution of the United States of America

WE THE PEOPLE of the United States, in Order to form a more perfect Union, establish Justice, insure domestic Tranquility, provide for the common defence, promote the general Welfare, and secure the Blessings of Liberty to ourselves and our Posterity, do ordain and establish this Constitution for the United States of America.

ARTICLE I

SECTION 1.   All legislative Powers herein granted shall be vested in a Congress of the United States, which shall consist of a Senate and House of Representatives.

SECTION 2.   The House of Representatives shall be composed of Members chosen every second Year by the People of the several States, and the Electors in each State shall have the Qualifications requisite for Electors of the most numerous Branch of the State Legislature.

No person shall be a Representative who shall not have attained to the Age of twenty five Years, and been seven Years a Citizen of the United States, and who shall not, when elected, be an Inhabitant of that State in which he shall be chosen.

Representatives and direct Taxes shall be apportioned among the several States which may be included within this Union, according to their respective Numbers which shall be determined by adding to the whole Number of free Persons, including those bound to Service for a Term of Years, and excluding Indians not taxed, three fifths of all other Persons. The actual Enumeration shall be made within three Years after the first Meeting of the Congress of the United States, and within every subsequent Term ten Years, in such Manner as they shall by Law direct. The Number of Representatives shall not exceed one for every thirty Thousand, but each State shall have at Least one Representative; and until such enumeration shall be made, the State of New Hampshire shall be entitled to chuse three, Massachusetts eight, Rhode-Island and Providence Plantations one, Connecticut five, New-York six, New Jersey four, Pennsylvania eight, Delaware one, Maryland six, Virginia ten, North Carolina five, South Carolina five, and Georgia three.

When vacancies happen in the Representation from any State, the Executive Authority thereof shall issue Writs of Election to fill such Vacancies.

The House of Representatives shall chuse their speaker and other Officers; and shall have the sole Power of Impeachment.

SECTION 3. The Senate of the United States shall be composed of two Senators from each State chosen by the Legislature thereof, for six Years; and each Senator shall have one Vote.

Immediately after they shall be assembled in Consequence of the first Election, they shall be divided as equally as may be into three Classes. The Seats of the Senators of the first Class shall be vacated at the Expiration of the second year, of the second Class at the Expiration of the fourth Year, and of the third Class at the Expiration of the sixth Year, so that one third may be chosen every second Year and if Vacancies happen by Resignation, or otherwise, during the Recess of the Legislature of any State, the Executive thereof may make temporary Appointments until the next Meeting of the Legislature, which shall then fill such Vacancies.

No Person shall be a Senator who shall not have attained to the Age of thirty Years, and been nine Years a Citizen of the United States, and who shall not, when elected, be an Inhabitant of that State for which he shall be chosen.

The Vice President of the United States shall be President of the Senate, but shall have no Vote, unless they be equally divided.

The Senate shall chuse their other Officers, and also a President pro tempore, in the Absence of the Vice President, or when he shall exercise the Office of President of the United States.

The Senate shall have the sole Power to try all Impeachments. When sitting for that Purpose, they shall be on Oath or Affirmation. When the President of the United States is tried, the Chief Justice shall preside: And no Person shall be convicted without the Concurrence of two thirds of the Members present.

Judgment in Cases of Impeachment shall not extend further than to removal from Office, and disqualification to hold and enjoy any Office of honor, Trust or Profit under the United States; but the Party convicted shall nevertheless be liable and subject to Indictment, Trial, Judgment and Punishment, according to Law.

SECTION 4. The Times, Places and Manner of holding Elections for Senators and Representatives, shall be prescribed in each State by the Legislature thereof; but the Congress may at any time by law make or alter such Regulations, except as to the Places of chusing Senators.

The Congress shall assemble at least once in every Year, and such Meeting shall be on the first Monday in December, unless they shall by Law appoint a different Day.

SECTION 5. Each House shall be the Judge of the Elections, Returns and Qualifications of its own Members, and a Majority of each shall constitute a Quorum to do Business; but a smaller Number may adjourn from day to day, and may be authorized to compel the

Attendance of absent Members, in such Manner, and under such Penalties as each House may provide.

Each House may determine the Rules of its Proceedings, punish its Members for disorderly Behaviour, and with the Concurrence of two thirds, expel a Member.

Each House shall keep a journal of its Proceedings, and from time to time publish the same, excepting such Parts as may in their judgment require Secrecy; and the Yeas and Nays of the Members of either House on any question shall, at the Desire of one fifth of those present, be entered on the Journal.

Neither House, during the Session of Congress, shall, without the Consent of the other, adjourn for more than three days, nor to any other Place than that in which the two Houses shall be sitting.

SECTION 6. The Senators and Representatives shall receive a Compensation for their Services, to be ascertained by Law, and paid out of the Treasury of the United States. They shall in all Cases, except Treason, Felony and Breach of the Peace, be privileged from Arrest during their Attendance at the Session of their respective Houses, and in going to and returning from the same; and for any Speech or Debate in either House, they shall not be questioned in any other Place.

No Senator or Representative shall, during the Time for which he was elected, be appointed to any civil Office under the Authority of the United States, which shall have been created, or the Emoluments whereof shall have been encreased during such time; and no Person holding any Office under the United States, shall be a Member of either House during his Continuance in Office.

SECTION 7. All Bills for raising Revenue shall originate in the House of Representatives; but the Senate may propose or concur with Amendments as on other Bills.

Every Bill which shall have passed the House of Representatives and the Senate, shall, before it become a Law, be presented to the President of the United States; If he approves he shall sign it, but if not he shall return it, with his Objections to that House in which it shall have originated, who shall enter the Objections at large on their journal, and proceed to reconsider it. If after such Reconsideration two thirds of that House shall agree to pass the Bill, it shall be sent, together with the Objections, to the other House, by which it shall likewise be reconsidered, and if approved by two thirds of that House, it shall become a Law. But in all such Cases the Votes of both Houses shall be determined by Yeas and Nays, and the Names of the Persons voting for and against the Bill shall be entered on the Journal of each House respectively. If any Bill shall not be returned by the President within ten Days (Sundays excepted) after it shall have been presented to him, the Same shall be a Law, in like Manner as if he had signed it, unless the Congress by their Adjournment prevent its Return, in which Case it shall not be a Law.

Every Order, Resolution, or Vote to which the Concurrence of the Senate and House of Representatives may be necessary (except on a question of Adjournment) shall be presented to the President of the United States; and before the Same shall take Effect, shall be approved by him, or being disapproved by him, shall be repassed by two thirds of the Senate and House of Representatives, according to the Rules and Limitations prescribed in the Case of a Bill.

SECTION 8. The Congress shall have Power To lay and collect Taxes, Duties, Imposts and Excises, to pay the Debts and provide for the common Defence and general Welfare of the United States; but all Duties, Imposts and Excises shall be uniform throughout the United States;

To borrow Money on the credit of the United States;

To regulate Commerce with foreign Nations, and among the several States, and with the Indian Tribes;

To establish a uniform Rule of Naturalization, and uniform Laws on the subject of Bankruptcies throughout the United States;

To coin Money, regulate the Value thereof, and of foreign Coin, and fix the Standard of Weights and Measures;

To provide for the Punishment of counterfeiting the Securities and current Coin of the United States;

To establish Post Offices and post Roads;

To promote the Progress of Science and useful Arts, by securing for limited Times to Authors and Inventors the exclusive Right to their respective Writings and Discoveries;

To constitute Tribunals inferior to the supreme Court;

To define and punish Piracies and Felonies committed on the high Seas, and Offences against the Law of Nations;

To declare War, grant Letters of Marque and Reprisal, and make Rules concerning Captures on Land and Water;

To raise and support Armies, but no Appropriation of Money to that Use shall be for a longer Term than two Years;

To provide and maintain a Navy;

To make Rules for the Government and Regulation of the land and naval Forces;

To provide for calling forth the Militia to execute the Laws of the Union, suppress Insurrections and repel Invasions;

To provide for organizing, arming, and disciplining, the Militia, and for governing such Part of them as may be employed in the Service of the United States, reserving to the States respectively, the Appointment of the Officers, and the Authority of training the Militia according to the discipline prescribed by Congress;

To exercise exclusive Legislation in all Cases whatsoever, over such District (not exceeding ten Miles square) as may, by Cession of particular States, and the Acceptance of Congress, become the Seat of the Government of the United States, and to exercise like Authority over all Places purchased by the Consent of the Legislature of the State in which the Same shall be for the Erection of Forts, Magazines, Arsenals, dock-Yards, and other needful Buildings;—And

To make all Laws which shall be necessary and proper for carrying into Execution the foregoing Powers, and all other Powers vested by this Constitution in the Government of the United States, or in any Department or Officer thereof.

SECTION 9. **The Migration or Importation of such Persons as any of the States now existing shall think proper to admit, shall not be prohibited by the Congress prior to the Year one thousand eight hundred and eight, but a Tax or duty may be imposed on such Importation, not exceeding ten dollars for each Person.**

The Privilege of the Writ of Habeas Corpus shall not be suspended, unless when in Cases of Rebellion or Invasion the public Safety may require it.

No Bill of Attainder or ex post facto Law shall be passed.

No Capitation, or other direct, Tax shall be laid, unless in Proportion to the Census or Enumeration herein before directed to be taken.

No Tax or Duty shall be laid on Articles exported from any State.

No Preference shall be given by any Regulation of Commerce or Revenue to the Ports of one State over those of another; nor shall Vessels bound to, or from, one State, be obliged to enter, clear, or pay Duties in another.

No Money shall be drawn from the Treasury, but in Consequence of Appropriations made by Law; and a regular Statement and Account of the Receipts and Expenditures of all public Money shall be published from time to time.

No Title of Nobility shall be granted by the United States: And no Person holding any Office of Profit or Trust under them, shall, without the Consent of the Congress, accept of any present, Emolument, Office, or Title, of any kind whatever, from any King, Prince, or foreign State.

SECTION 10. No state shall enter into any Treaty, Alliance, or Confederation; grant Letters of Marque and Reprisal; coin Money; emit Bills of Credit; make any Thing but gold and silver Coin a Tender in Payment of Debts; pass any Bill of Attainder, ex post facto Law, or Law impairing the Obligation of Contracts, or grant any Title of Nobility.

No State shall, without the Consent of the Congress, lay any Imposts or Duties on Imports or Exports, except what may be absolutely necessary for executing its inspection Laws: and the net Produce of all Duties and Imposts, laid by any State on Imports or Exports, shall be for the Use of the Treasury of the United States, and all such Laws shall be subject to the Revision and Control of the Congress.

No State shall, without the Consent of Congress, lay any Duty of Tonnage, keep Troops, or Ships of War in time of Peace, enter into any Agreement or Compact with another State, or with a foreign Power, or engage in War, unless actually invaded, or in such imminent Danger as will not admit of delay.

ARTICLE II

SECTION 1. The executive Power shall be vested in a President of the United States of America. He shall hold his Office during the Term of four Years, and, together with the Vice President, chosen for the same Term, be elected as follows.

Each State shall appoint, in such Manner as the Legislature thereof may direct, a Number of Electors, equal to the whole Number of Senators and Representatives to which the State may be entitled in the Congress; but no Senator or Representative, or Person holding an Office of Trust or Profit under the United States, shall be appointed an Elector.

The Electors shall meet in their respective States, and vote by Ballot for two Persons, of whom one at least shall not be an Inhabitant of the same State with themselves. And they shall make a List of all the Persons voted for, and, of the Number of Votes for each; which List they shall sign and certify, and transmit sealed to the Seat of the Government of the United States, directed to the President of the Senate. The President of the Senate shall, in the Presence of the Senate and House of Representatives, open all the Certificates, and the Votes shall then be counted. The Person having the greatest Number of Votes shall be the President, if such Number be a Majority of the whole Number of Electors appointed; and if there be more than one who have such Majority, and have an equal Number of Votes, then the House of Representatives shall immediately chuse by Ballot one of them for President; and if no Person have a Majority, then from the five highest on the List the said House shall in like Manner chuse the President. But in chusing the President, the Votes shall be taken by States, the Representation from each State having one Vote; A quorum for this Purpose shall consist of a Member or Members from two thirds of the States, and a Majority of all the States shall be necessary to a Choice. In every Case, after the Choice of the President, the Person having the greatest Number of Votes of the Electors shall be the Vice President. But if there should remain two or more who have equal Votes, the Senate shall chuse from them by Ballot the Vice President.

The Congress may determine the Time of chusing the Electors, and the Day on which they shall give their Votes; which Day shall be the same throughout the United States.

No Person except a natural born Citizen, or a Citizen of the United States, at the time of the Adoption of this Constitution, shall be eligible to the Office of President; neither shall any Person be eligible to that Office who shall not have attained to the Age of thirty five Years, and been fourteen Years a Resident within the United States.

In Case of the Removal of the President from Office, or of his Death, Resignation, or Inability to discharge the Powers and Duties of the said Office, the Same shall devolve on the Vice President, and the Congress may by Law provide for the Case of Removal, Death, Resignation or Inability, both of the President and Vice President, declaring what Officer shall then act as President, and such Officer shall act accordingly, until the Disability be removed, or a President shall be elected.

The President shall, at stated Times, receive for his Services, a Compensation, which shall neither be encreased nor diminished during the Period for which he shall have been elected, and he shall not receive within that Period any other Emolument from the United States, or any of them.

Before he enter on the Execution of his Office, he shall take the following Oath or Affirmation—"I do solemnly swear (or affirm) that I will faithfully execute the Office of President of the United States, and will to the best of my Ability, preserve, protect and defend the Constitution of the United States."

SECTION 2. The President shall be Commander in Chief of the Army, and Navy of the United States, and of the Militia of the several States, when called into the actual Service of the United States; he may require the Opinion, in writing, of the principal Officer in each of the executive Departments, upon any Subject relating to the Duties of their respective Offices, and he shall have Power to grant Reprieves and Pardons for Offences against the United States, except in Cases of Impeachment.

He shall have Power, by and with the Advice and Consent of the Senate, to make Treaties, provided two thirds of the Senators present concur; and he shall nominate, and by and with the Advice and Consent of the Senate, shall appoint Ambassadors, other public Ministers and Consuls, Judges of the supreme Court, and all other Officers of the United States, whose Appointments are not herein otherwise provided for, and which shall be established by Law: but the Congress may by Law vest the Appointment of such inferior Officers, as they think proper, in the President alone, in the Courts of Law, or in the Heads of Departments.

The President shall have Power to fill up all Vacancies that may happen during the Recess of the Senate, by granting Commissions which shall expire at the end of their next Session.

SECTION 3.   He shall from time to time give to the Congress Information of the State of the Union, and recommend to their Consideration such Measures as he shall judge necessary and expedient; he may, on extraordinary Occasions, convene both Houses, or either of them, and in Case of Disagreement between them, with Respect to the Time of Adjournment, he may adjourn them to such Time as he shall think proper; he shall receive Ambassadors and other public Ministers; he shall take Care that the Laws be faithfully executed, and shall Commission all the Officers of the United States.

SECTION 4.   The President, Vice President and all civil Officers of the United States, shall be removed from Office on Impeachment for, and Conviction of, Treason, Bribery, or other high Crimes and Misdemeanors.

ARTICLE III

SECTION 1.   The judicial Power of the United States, shall be vested in one supreme Court, and in such inferior Courts as the Congress may from time to time ordain and establish. The Judges, both of the supreme and inferior Courts, shall hold their Offices during good Behaviour, and shall, at stated Times, receive for their Services, a Compensation, which shall not be diminished during their Continuance in Office.

SECTION 2.   The judicial Power shall extend to all Cases, in Law and Equity, arising under this Constitution, the Laws of the United States, and Treaties made, or which shall be made, under their Authority;—to all Cases affecting Ambassadors, other public Ministers and Consuls;—to all Cases of admiralty and maritime Jurisdiction;—to Controversies to which the United States shall be a Party;—to Controversies between two or more States;—between a State and Citizens of another State;—between Citizens of different States;—between Citizens of the same State claiming Lands under Grants of different States,—and between a State, or the Citizens thereof, and foreign States, Citizens or Subjects.

   In all Cases affecting Ambassadors, other public Ministers and Consuls, and those in which a State shall be Party, the supreme Court shall have original Jurisdiction. In all the other Cases before mentioned, the supreme Court shall have appellate Jurisdiction, both as to Law and Fact, with such Exceptions, and under such Regulations as the Congress shall make.

   The Trial of all Crimes, except in Cases of Impeachment, shall be by Jury; and such Trial shall be held in the State where the said Crimes shall have been committed; but when not committed within any State, the Trial shall be at such Place or Places as the Congress may by Law have directed.

SECTION 3.   Treason against the United States, shall consist only in levying War against them, or in adhering to their Enemies, giving them Aid and Comfort. No Person shall be convicted of Treason unless on the Testimony of two Witnesses to the same overt Act, or on Confession in open Court.

   The Congress shall have Power to declare the Punishment of Treason, but no Attainder of Treason shall work Corruption of Blood, or Forfeiture except during the Life of the Person attainted.

ARTICLE IV

SECTION 1. Full Faith and Credit shall be given in each State to the public Acts, Records, and judicial Proceedings of every other State. And the Congress may by general Laws prescribe the Manner in which such Acts, Records and Proceedings shall be proved, and the Effect thereof.

SECTION 2. The Citizens of each State shall be entitled to all Privileges and Immunities of Citizens in the several States.

A Person charged in any State with Treason, Felony, or other Crime, who shall flee from Justice, and be found in another State, shall on Demand of the executive Authority of the State from which he fled, be delivered up, to be removed to the State having Jurisdiction of the Crime.

No Person held to Service or Labour in one State under the Laws thereof, escaping into another, shall, in Consequence of any Law or Regulation therein, be discharged from such Service or Labour, but shall be delivered up on Claim of the Party to whom such Service or Labour may be due.

SECTION 3. New States may be admitted by the Congress into this Union; but no new State shall be formed or erected within the Jurisdiction of any other State; nor any State be formed by the Junction of two or more States, or Parts of States, without the Consent of the Legislatures of the States concerned as well as of the Congress.

The Congress shall have Power to dispose of and make all needful Rules and Regulations respecting the Territory or other Property belonging to the United States; and nothing in this Constitution shall be so construed as to Prejudice any Claims of the United States, or of any particular State.

SECTION 4. The United States shall guarantee to every State in this Union a Republican Form of Government, and shall protect each of them against Invasion, and on Application of the Legislature, or of the Executive (when the Legislature cannot be convened) against domestic Violence.

ARTICLE V

The Congress, whenever two thirds of both Houses shall deem it necessary, shall propose Amendments to this Constitution, or, on the Application of the Legislatures of two thirds of the several States, shall call a Convention for proposing Amendments, which, in either Case, shall be valid to all Intents and Purposes, as Part of this Constitution, when ratified by the Legislatures of three fourths of the several States, or by Conventions in three fourths thereof, as the one or the other Mode of Ratification may be proposed by the Congress; **Provided that no Amendment which may be made prior to the Year One thousand eight hundred and eight shall in any Manner affect the first and fourth Clauses in the Ninth Section of the first Article;** and that no State, without its Consent, shall be deprived of its equal Suffrage in the Senate.

ARTICLE VI

All Debts contracted and Engagements entered into, before the Adoption of this Constitution, shall be as valid against the United States under this Constitution, as under the Confederation.

This Constitution, and the laws of the United States which shall be made in Pursuance thereof; and all Treaties made, or which shall be made, under the Authority of the United States, shall be the supreme Law of the Land; and the Judges in every State shall be bound thereby, any Thing in the Constitution or Laws of any State to the Contrary notwithstanding.

The Senators and Representatives before mentioned, and the Members of the several State Legislatures, and all executive and judicial Officers, both of the United States and of the several States, shall be bound by Oath or Affirmation, to support this Constitution; but no religious Test shall ever be required as a Qualification to any Office or public Trust under the United States.

ARTICLE VII

The Ratification of the Conventions of nine States, shall be sufficient for the Establishment of this Constitution between the States so ratifying the Same.

Done in Convention by the Unanimous Consent of the States present the Seventeenth Day of September in the Year of our Lord one thousand seven hundred and Eighty seven and of the Independence of the United States of America the Twelfth. In witness whereof we have hereunto subscribed our Names,

Go. WASHINGTON
Presid't and deputy from Virginia

Attest
WILLIAM JACKSON
Secretary

Articles in addition to, and amendment of the Constitution of the United States of America, proposed by Congress and ratified by the Legislatures of the several states, pursuant to the Fifth Article of the original Constitution.

(The first ten amendments were passed by Congress on September 25, 1789, and were ratified on December 15, 1791.)

AMENDMENT 1

Congress shall make no law respecting an establishment of religion, or prohibiting the free exercise thereof; or abridging the freedom of speech, or of the press; or the right of the people peaceably to assemble, and to petition the Government for a redress of grievances.

AMENDMENT II

A well regulated Militia, being necessary to the security of a free State, the right of the people to keep and bear Arms, shall not be infringed.

AMENDMENT III

No Soldier shall, in time of peace be quartered in any house, without the consent of the Owner, nor in time of war, but in a manner to be prescribed by law.

Amendment IV

The right of the people to be secure in their persons, houses, papers, and effects, against unreasonable searches and seizures, shall not be violated, and no warrants shall issue, but upon probable cause, supported by Oath or affirmation, and particularly describing the place to be searched, and the persons or things to be seized.

Amendment V

No person shall be held to answer for a capital, or otherwise infamous crime, unless on a presentment or indictment of a Grand Jury, except in cases arising in the land or naval forces, or in the Militia, when in actual service in time of War or public danger; nor shall any person be subject for the same offence to be twice put in jeopardy of life or limb; nor shall be compelled in any criminal case to be a witness against himself, nor be deprived of life, liberty, or property, without due process of law; nor shall private property be taken for public use, without just compensation.

Amendment VI

In all criminal prosecutions, the accused shall enjoy the right to a speedy and public trial, by an impartial jury of the State and district wherein the crime shall have been committed, which district shall have been previously ascertained by law, and to be informed of the nature and cause of the accusation; to be confronted with the witnesses against him; to have compulsory process for obtaining witnesses in his favor, and to have the assistance of counsel for his defence.

Amendment VII

In Suits at common law, where the value in controversy shall exceed twenty dollars, the right of trial by jury shall be preserved, and no fact tried by a jury, shall be otherwise re-examined in any Court of the United States, than according to the rules of the common law.

Amendment VIII

Excessive bail shall not be required, nor excessive fines imposed, nor cruel and unusual punishments inflicted.

Amendment IX

The enumeration in the Constitution, of certain rights, shall not be construed to deny or disparage others retained by the people.

Amendment X

The powers not delegated to the United States by the Constitution, nor prohibited by it to the States, are reserved to the States respectively, or to the people.

Amendment XI

(Ratified on February 7, 1795)

The Judicial power of the United States shall not be construed to extend to any suit in law or equity, commenced or prosecuted against one of the United States by Citizens of another State, or by Citizens or Subjects of any Foreign State.

AMENDMENT XII

(RATIFIED ON JUNE 15, 1804)

The Electors shall meet in their respective states, and vote by ballot for President and Vice-President, one of whom, at least, shall not be an inhabitant of the same state with themselves; they shall name in their ballots the person voted for as President, and in distinct ballots the person voted for as Vice-President, and they shall make distinct lists of all persons voted for as President, and of all persons voted for as Vice-President, and of the number of votes for each, which lists they shall sign and certify, and transmit sealed to the seat of the government of the United States, directed to the President of the Senate;—The President of the Senate shall, in the presence of the Senate and House of Representatives, open all the certificates and the votes shall then be counted;—The person having the greatest number of votes for President, shall be the President, if such number be a majority of the whole number of Electors appointed; and if no person have such majority; then from the persons having the highest numbers not exceeding three on the list of those voted for as President, the House of Representatives shall choose immediately, by ballot, the President. But in choosing the President, the votes shall be taken by states, the representation from each state having one vote; a quorum for this purpose shall consist of a member or members from two-thirds of the states, and a majority of all the states shall be necessary to a choice. And if the House of Representatives shall not choose a President whenever the right of choice shall devolve upon them, before the fourth day of March next following, then the Vice-President shall act as President, as in the case of the death or other constitutional disability of the President.—The person having the greatest number of votes as Vice-President, shall be the Vice-President, if such number be a majority of the whole number of Electors appointed, and if no person have a majority, then from the two highest numbers on the list, the Senate shall choose the Vice-President; a quorum for the purpose shall consist of two-thirds of the whole number of Senators, and a majority of the whole number shall be necessary to a choice. But no person constitutionally ineligible to the office of President shall be eligible to that of Vice-President of the United States.

AMENDMENT XIII

(RATIFIED ON DECEMBER 6, 1865)

SECTION 1.   Neither slavery nor involuntary servitude, except as a punishment for crime whereof the party shall have been duly convicted, shall exist within the United States, or any place subject to their jurisdiction.

SECTION 2.   Congress shall have power to enforce this article by appropriate legislation.

AMENDMENT XIV

(RATIFIED ON JULY 9, 1868)

SECTION 1.   All persons born or naturalized in the United States, and subject to the jurisdiction thereof, are citizens of the United States and of the State wherein they reside. No State shall make or enforce any law which shall abridge the privileges or immunities of citizens of the United States; nor shall any State deprive any person of life, liberty, or property, without due process of law; nor deny to any person within its jurisdiction the equal protection of the laws.

SECTION 2. Representatives shall be apportioned among the several States according to their respective numbers, counting the whole number of persons in each State, excluding Indians not taxed. But when the right to vote at any election for the choice of electors for President and Vice President of the United States, Representatives in Congress, the Executive and Judicial officers of a State, or the members of the Legislature thereof is denied to any of the male inhabitants of such State, being twenty-one years of age, and citizens of the United States or in any way abridged, except for participation in rebellion, or other crime, the basis of representation therein shall be reduced in the proportion which the number of such male citizens shall bear to the whole number of male citizens twenty-one years of age in such State.

SECTION 3. No person shall be a Senator or Representative in Congress, or elector of President and Vice President, or hold any office, civil or military, under the United States, or under any State, who, having previously taken an oath, as a member of Congress, or as an officer of the United States, or as a member of any State legislature, or as an executive or judicial officer of any State, to support the Constitution of the United States, shall have engaged in insurrection or rebellion against the same, or given aid or comfort to the enemies thereof. But Congress may by a vote of two-thirds of each House, remove such disability.

SECTION 4. The validity of the public debt of the United States, authorized by law, including debts incurred for payment of pensions and bounties for services in suppressing insurrection or rebellion, shall not be questioned. But neither the United States nor any State shall assume or pay any debt or obligation incurred in aid of insurrection or rebellion against the United States, or any claim for the loss or emancipation of any slave, but all such debts, obligations and claims shall be held illegal and void.

SECTION 5. The Congress shall have power to enforce, by appropriate legislation, the provisions of this article.

AMENDMENT XV

(RATIFIED ON FEBRUARY 3, 1870)

SECTION 1. The right of citizens of the United States to vote shall not be denied or abridged by the United States or by any State on account of race, color, or previous condition of servitude.

SECTION 2. The Congress shall have power to enforce this article by appropriate legislation.

AMENDMENT XVI

(RATIFIED ON FEBRUARY 3, 1913)

The Congress shall have power to lay and collect taxes on incomes, from whatever source derived, without apportionment among the several States, and without regard to any census or enumeration.

AMENDMENT XVII

(RATIFIED ON APRIL 8, 1913)

The Senate of the United States shall be composed of two Senators from each State, elected by the people thereof, for six years; and each Senator shall have one vote. The electors in each State shall have the qualifications requisite for electors of the most numerous branch of the State legislatures.

When vacancies happen in the representation of any State in the Senate, the executive authority of such State shall issue writs of election to fill such vacancies: Provided, That the legislature of any State may empower the executive thereof to make temporary appointments until the people fill the vacancies by election as the legislature may direct.

This amendment shall not be so construed as to affect the election or term of any Senator chosen before it becomes valid as part of the Constitution.

AMENDMENT XVIII

(RATIFIED ON JANUARY 16, 1919)

SECTION 1. After one year from the ratification of this article the manufacture, sale, or transportation of intoxicating liquors within, the importation thereof into, or the exportation thereof from the United States and all territory subject to the jurisdiction thereof for beverage purposes is hereby prohibited.

SECTION 2. The Congress and the several States shall have concurrent power to enforce this article by appropriate legislation.

SECTION 3. This article shall be inoperative unless it shall have been ratified as an amendment to the Constitution by the legislatures of the several States, as provided in the Constitution, within seven years from the date of the submission hereof to the States by the Congress.

AMENDMENT XIX

(RATIFIED ON AUGUST 18, 1920)

The right of citizens of the United States to vote shall not be denied or abridged by the United States or by any State on account of sex.

Congress shall have power to enforce this article by appropriate legislation.

AMENDMENT XX

(RATIFIED ON FEBRUARY 6, 1933)

SECTION 1. The terms of the President and Vice President shall end at noon on the 20th day of January, and the terms of Senators and Representatives at noon on the 3d day of January, of the years in which such terms would have ended if this article had not been ratified; and the terms of their successors shall then begin.

SECTION 2. The Congress shall assemble at least once in every year, and such meeting shall begin at noon on the 3d day of January, unless they shall by law appoint a different day.

SECTION 3. If, at the time fixed for the beginning of the term of the President, the President elect shall have died, the Vice President elect shall become President. If a President shall not have been chosen before the time fixed for the beginning of his term, or if the President elect shall have failed to qualify, then the Vice President elect shall act as President until a President shall have qualified; and the Congress may by law provide for the case wherein neither a President elect nor a Vice President elect shall have qualified, declaring who shall then act as President, or the manner in which one who is to act shall be selected, and such person shall act accordingly until a President or Vice President shall have qualified.

SECTION 4. The Congress may by law provide for the case of the death of any of the persons from whom the House of Representatives may choose a President whenever the rights of choice shall have devolved upon them, and for the case of the death of any of the persons from whom the Senate may choose a Vice President whenever the right of choice shall have devolved upon them.

SECTION 5. Sections 1 and 2 shall take effect on the 15th day of October following the ratification of this article.

SECTION 6. This article shall be inoperative unless it shall have been ratified as an amendment to the Constitution by the legislatures of three-fourths of the several States within seven years from the date of its submission.

AMENDMENT XXI

(RATIFIED ON DECEMBER 5, 1933)

SECTION 1. The eighteenth article of amendment to the Constitution of the United States is hereby repealed.

SECTION 2. The transportation or importation into any State, Territory, or possession of the United States for delivery or use therein of intoxicating liquors, in violation of the laws thereof, is hereby prohibited.

SECTION 3. This article shall be inoperative unless it shall have been ratified as an amendment to the Constitution by conventions in the several States, as provided in the Constitution, within seven years from the date of the submission hereof to the States by the Congress.

AMENDMENT XXII

(RATIFIED ON FEBRUARY 27, 1951)

No person shall be elected to the office of the President more than twice, and no person who has held the office of President, or acted as President, for more than two years of a term to which some other person was elected President shall be elected to the office of the President more than once. But this Article shall not apply to any person holding the office of President when this Article was proposed by the Congress, and shall not prevent any person who may be holding the office of President, or acting as President, during the term within which this Article becomes operative from holding the office of President or acting as President during the remainder of such term.

AMENDMENT XXIII

(RATIFIED ON MARCH 29, 1961)

SECTION 1.   The District constituting the seat of Government of the United States shall appoint in such manner as the Congress may direct:

A number of electors of President and Vice President equal to the whole number of Senators and Representatives in Congress to which the District would be entitled if it were a State, but in no event more than the least populous State; they shall be in addition to those appointed by the States, but they shall be considered, for the purposes of the election of President and Vice President, to be electors appointed by a State; and they shall meet in the District and perform such duties as provided by the twelfth article of amendment.

SECTION 2.   The Congress shall have power to enforce this article by appropriate legislation.

AMENDMENT XXIV

(RATIFIED ON JANUARY 23, 1964)

SECTION 1.   The right of citizens of the United States to vote in any primary or other election for President or Vice President, for electors for President or Vice President, or for Senator or Representative in Congress, shall not be denied or abridged by the United States or any State by reason of failure to pay any poll tax or other tax.

SECTION 2.   The Congress shall have power to enforce this article by appropriate legislation.

AMENDMENT XXV

(RATIFIED ON FEBRUARY 10, 1967)

SECTION 1.   In case of the removal of the President from office or of his death or resignation, the Vice President shall become President.

SECTION 2.   Whenever there is a vacancy in the office of the Vice President, the President shall nominate a Vice President who shall take office upon confirmation by a majority vote of both Houses of Congress.

SECTION 3.   Whenever the President transmits to the President pro tempore of the Senate and the Speaker of the House of Representatives his written declaration that he is unable to discharge the powers and duties of his office, and until he transmits to them a written declaration to the contrary, such powers and duties shall be discharged by the Vice President as Acting President.

SECTION 4. Whenever the Vice President and a majority of either the principal officers of the executive departments or of such other body as Congress may by law provide, transmit to the President pro tempore of the Senate and the Speaker of the House of Representatives their written declaration that the President is unable to discharge the powers and duties of his office, the Vice President shall immediately assume the powers and duties of the office as Acting President.

Thereafter, when the President transmits to the President pro tempore of the Senate and the Speaker of the House of Representatives his written declaration that no inability exists, he shall resume the powers and duties of his office unless the Vice President and a majority of either the principal officers of the executive department or of such other body as Congress may by law provide, transmit within four days to the President pro tempore of the Senate and the Speaker of the House of Representatives their written declaration that the President is unable to discharge the powers and duties of his office. Thereupon Congress shall decide the issue, assembling within forty-eight hours for that purpose if not in session. If the Congress, within twenty-one days after receipt of the latter written declaration, or, if Congress is not in session, within twenty-one days after Congress is required to assemble, determines by two-thirds vote of both Houses that the President is unable to discharge the powers and duties of his office, the Vice President shall continue to discharge the same as Acting President; otherwise, the President shall resume the powers and duties of his office.

AMENDMENT XXVI

(RATIFIED ON JULY 1, 1971)

SECTION 1. The right of citizens of the United States, who are eighteen years of age or older, to vote shall not be denied or abridged by the United States or by any State on account of age.

SECTION 2. The Congress shall have power to enforce this article by appropriate legislation.

AMENDMENT XXVII

(RATIFIED ON MAY 7, 1992)

No law varying the compensation for the services of Senators and Representatives shall take effect until an election of Representatives shall have intervened.

I Have a Dream

Martin Luther King, Jr.

I am happy to join with you today in what will go down in history as the greatest demonstration for freedom in the history of our nation.

Fivescore years ago, a great American, in whose symbolic shadow we stand today, signed the Emancipation Proclamation. This momentous decree came as a great beacon light of hope to millions of Negro slaves who had been seared in the flames of withering injustice. It came as a joyous daybreak to end the long night of their captivity.

But one hundred years later, the Negro still is not free; one hundred years later, the life of the Negro is still sadly crippled by the manacles of segregation and the chains of discrimination; one hundred years later, the Negro lives on a lonely island of poverty in the midst of a vast ocean of material prosperity; one hundred years later, the Negro is still languished in the corners of American society and finds himself in exile in his own land.

So we've come here today to dramatize a shameful condition. In a sense we've come to our nation's capital to cash a check. When the architects of our republic wrote the magnificent words of the Constitution and the Declaration of Independence, they were signing a promissory note to which every American was to fall heir. This note was the promise that all men, yes, black men as well as white men, would be guaranteed the unalienable rights of life, liberty, and the pursuit of happiness.

It is obvious today that America has defaulted on this promissory note in so far as her citizens of color are concerned. Instead of honoring this sacred obligation, America has given the Negro people a bad check; a check which has come back marked "insufficient funds." We refuse to believe that there are insufficient funds in the great vaults of opportunity of this nation. And so we've come to cash this check, a check that will give us upon demand the riches of freedom and the security of justice.

We have also come to this hallowed spot to remind America of the fierce urgency of now. This is no time to engage in the luxury of cooling off or to take the tranquilizing drug of gradualism. Now is the time to make real the promises of democracy; now is the

325

time to rise from the dark and desolate valley of segregation to the sunlit path of racial justice; now is the time to lift our nation from the quicksands of racial injustice to the solid rock of brotherhood; now is the time to make justice a reality for all God's children. It would be fatal for the nation to overlook the urgency of the moment. This sweltering summer of the Negro's legitimate discontent will not pass until there is an invigorating autumn of freedom and equality.

Nineteen sixty-three is not an end, but a beginning. And those who hope that the Negro needed to blow off steam and will now be content, will have a rude awakening if the nation returns to business as usual.

There will be neither rest nor tranquility in America until the Negro is granted his citizenship rights. The whirlwinds of revolt will continue to shake the foundations of our nation until the bright day of justice emerges.

But there is something that I must say to my people who stand on the warm threshold which leads into the palace of justice. In the process of gaining our rightful place we must not be guilty of wrongful deeds.

Let us not seek to satisfy our thirst for freedom by drinking from the cup of bitterness and hatred. We must forever conduct our struggle on the high plane of dignity and discipline. We must not allow our creative protest to degenerate into physical violence. Again and again we must rise to the majestic heights of meeting physical force with soul force.

The marvelous new militancy which has engulfed the Negro community must not lead us to a distrust of all white people, for many of our white brothers, as evidenced by their presence here today, have come to realize that their destiny is tied up with our destiny and they have come to realize that their freedom is inextricably bound to our freedom. This offense we share mounted to storm the battlements of injustice must be carried forth by a biracial army. We cannot walk alone.

And as we walk, we must make the pledge that we shall always march ahead. We cannot turn back. There are those who are asking the devotees of civil rights, "When will you be satisfied?" We can never be satisfied as long as the Negro is the victim of the unspeakable horrors of police brutality.

We can never be satisfied as long as our bodies, heavy with fatigue of travel, cannot gain lodging in the motels of the highways and the hotels of the cities. We cannot be satisfied as long as the Negro's basic mobility is from a smaller ghetto to a larger one.

We can never be satisfied as long as our children are stripped of their selfhood and robbed of their dignity by signs stating "for whites only." We cannot be satisfied as long as a Negro in Mississippi cannot vote and a Negro in New York believes he has nothing for which to vote. No, we are not satisfied, and we will not be satisfied until justice rolls down like waters and righteousness like a mighty stream.

I am not unmindful that some of you have come here out of excessive trials and tribulation. Some of you have come fresh from narrow jail cells. Some of you have come from areas where your quest for freedom left you battered by the storms of persecution and staggered by the winds of police brutality. You have been the veterans of creative suffering. Continue to work with the faith that unearned suffering is redemptive.

Go back to Mississippi; go back to Alabama; go back to South Carolina; go back to Georgia; go back to Louisiana; go back to the slums and ghettos of the northern cities, knowing that somehow this situation can, and will be changed. Let us not wallow in the valley of despair.

So I say to you, my friends, that even though we must face the difficulties of today and tomorrow, I still have a dream. It is a dream deeply rooted in the American dream that one day this nation will rise up and live out the true meaning of its creed—we hold these truths to be self-evident, that all men are created equal.

I have a dream that one day on the red hills of Georgia, sons of former slaves and sons of former slave-owners will be able to sit down together at the table of brotherhood.

I have a dream that one day, even the state of Mississippi, a state sweltering with the heat of injustice, sweltering with the heat of oppression, will be transformed into an oasis of freedom and justice.

I have a dream my four little children will one day live in a nation where they will not be judged by the color of their skin but by the content of their character. I have a dream today!

I have a dream that one day, down in Alabama, with its vicious racists, with its governor having his lips dripping with the words of interposition and nullification, that one day, right there in Alabama, little black boys and black girls will be able to join hands with little white boys and white girls as sisters and brothers. I have a dream today!

I have a dream that one day every valley shall be exalted, every hill and mountain shall be made low, the rough places shall be made plain, and the crooked places shall be made straight and the glory of the Lord will be revealed and all flesh shall see it together.

This is our hope. This is the faith that I go back to the South with.

With this faith we will be able to hear out of the mountain of despair a stone of hope. With this faith we will be able to transform the jangling discords of our nation into a beautiful symphony of brotherhood.

With this faith we will be able to work together, to pray together, to struggle together, to go to jail together, to stand up for freedom together, knowing that we will be free one day. This will be the day when all of God's children will be able to sing with new meaning—"my country 'tis of thee; sweet land of liberty; of thee I sing; land where my fathers died, land of the pilgrim's pride; from every mountain side, let freedom ring"—and if America is to be a great nation, this must become true.

So let freedom ring from the prodigious hilltops of New Hampshire.

Let freedom ring from the mighty mountains of New York.

Let freedom ring from the heightening Alleghenies of Pennsylvania.

Let freedom ring from the snow-capped Rockies of Colorado.

Let freedom ring from the curvaceous slopes of California.

But not only that.

Let freedom ring from Stone Mountain of Georgia.

Let freedom ring from Lookout Mountain of Tennessee.

Let freedom ring from every hill and molehill of Mississippi, from every mountainside, let freedom ring.

And when we allow freedom to ring, when we let it ring from every village and hamlet, from every state and city, we will be able to speed up that day when all of God's children— black men and white men, Jews and Gentiles, Catholics and Protestants—will be able to join hands and to sing in the words of the old Negro spiritual, "Free at last, free at last; thank God Almighty, we are free at last."

INDEX

Note: References to notes at the end of each chapter appear in the index as, for example, 192n12, which means page 192, note 12.